Praise for *Together in Manzanar*

"Tracy Slater has done her homework and is uniquely positioned to tell the story of Elaine Yoneda, an eyewitness to one of the most explosive parts of the wartime Japanese American experience. **With dramatic flair, Slater captures the untold story of a high-profile mixed-race couple inside an American concentration camp at a pivotal moment in history.**"

—**Frank Abe**, coeditor of *The Literature of Japanese American Incarceration*

"As society evolves and new issues and debates come to the forefront, previously neglected but newly relevant lessons and stories continue to be drawn from the exclusion and incarceration of Japanese Americans during World War II. Drawing on her own experience, Tracy Slater has found such a story, one that promises to expand our knowledge of the general incarceration and that will have specific relevance for many modern American families. . . . Both fastidiously researched and a page-turner, this book will appeal to both those new to the story and those who know it well."

—**Brian Niiya**, director of content for Densho and former curator of the Japanese American National Museum

"A gripping, well-written depiction of one of the most fascinating couples in American history. Not only does Slater recount the biographies of two important labor activists, but she also presents a beautiful story about a family that endured prejudice, separation, and hardship while remaining true to their principles."

—**Jonathan van Harmelen**, historian, University of California, Santa Cruz

TOGETHER in MANZANAR

THE TRUE STORY OF A JAPANESE JEWISH FAMILY IN AN AMERICAN CONCENTRATION CAMP

TRACY SLATER

CHICAGO REVIEW PRESS

Library of Congress Control Number: 2025932357

Yoneda family personal photos, photos in which family members appear, and excerpts from the Manzanar diaries of Karl and Elaine Yoneda are reprinted courtesy of the Yoneda family.

Every effort has been made to contact the copyright holders for the images that appear in this book. The publisher would welcome information concerning any inadvertent errors or omissions.

Typesetting: Nord Compo

Printed in the United States of America
5 4 3 2 1

For Elli, my inspiration

CONTENTS

Part I: The Choice

Part II: The Rupture

Part III: The Reckoning

PART I

THE CHOICE

Karl Yoneda and Elaine Buchman, March 1933. *Courtesy of Karl G. Yoneda Papers, UCLA Library Special Collections*

1 FORCED

March 30, 1942

JUST PAST DAWN ON MARCH 30, 1942, Elaine Buchman Yoneda stood on a Los Angeles sidewalk, unsure where to turn. She looked up at the building before her, solid concrete and stretching half a block: the South Spring Street civil control station, where she'd been ordered to bring her three-year-old son, Tommy, for deportation to a concentration camp.

In the early morning light, a cool wind strafed her cheek and rustled her brown curls. She hesitated for a moment, then straightened in resolve. Reaching under five feet, Elaine was known to stand tall in the face of adversity, rising as if she could launch past such minor constraints as nature, as if she'd tower over anything in her way. She paid no heed to biology's limits; Elaine would stare down anyone who tried to take her son.

Keeping Tommy by her side, she surveyed the crowd of people already waiting, one long line snaking down South Spring Street. Overhead, trolley cables hung in the air, taut black wires against a pale sky. The streetcars would be getting even more use soon, as rubber rations made new tires scarce. Essentials would continue to dwindle now that Japan had bombed Pearl Harbor and the country was at war.

Many in line that morning wore their Sunday best, despite the new deprivations of wartime. They may have been Japanese, but almost all were American too. Some were likely US veterans, Elaine knew, having served their country faithfully. Not even that would matter now.

Before answering the order to appear that morning, men had donned ties and bowler hats, women pressed dresses and starched collars. Girls had forced their straight black hair into neat waves. Most stood quietly as they peered through the early light, some with heads craned forward, as if they might catch a glimpse of their fate. Elaine was the only white person among them.

Looking down, she watched the breeze disturb Tommy's dark ringlets, their hue from her husband, their texture from her. The child breathed in and out, cold air filling his torso, each breath like a gift from the grip of his asthmatic chest. Elaine had spent much of his short life in and out of hospitals with him. Too much dust, too strenuous an exertion could leave him gasping, liable to drown in the liquid of his lungs. But Elaine refused to give in to fear. She would do whatever necessary to protect him.

It was *him* the army wanted, she'd been told over the phone by a priest the night before. *Not you*, the priest had explained. *Not if you're white*, he meant—even though she'd given birth to a half-Japanese child. The clergyman was from the Maryknoll mission, a Roman Catholic order that had long worked with the Japanese American community and was now assisting with their removal from the West Coast. Foreign or citizen, healthy or sick, loyal or lost—all had to go.

But as for Elaine, "Oh, you don't have to go; you don't have to go," he'd said the previous evening, as she'd clutched the handset in her parents' apartment, the darkness shrouding their home in the Jewish enclave of Boyle Heights.

Nor will you be allowed to, he'd suggested.

Elaine had stared, stupefied, into the air. She was trying, with little success, to absorb this frocked man's nonsense. That day, March 29, 1942, Civilian Exclusion Order No. 3 had been issued: two thousand people of Japanese descent living around Elaine were to appear for processing by eight o'clock the next morning at the 707 South Spring Street civil control station, in preparation for transport 220 miles inland to a dusty plain called Manzanar at the foot of the Sierra Nevada. In no more than three days, by April 2 at noon sharp, not a soul among them should be left. Elaine had heard the announcement herself over the radio that evening. It had been addressed to "All persons of Japanese ancestry, both aliens and non-aliens." It conveyed an order, directly from the Western Defense Command and Fourth Army of the United States, with a time and place for those in the vicinity of Los Angeles to report the next day for "registration."

According to the US Army, her son Tommy, like anyone along the West Coast with even "the slightest amount of Japanese blood," was to be rounded up—*evacuated*, they called it—and sent to a camp. Hearing the announcement, Elaine had been frantic. Surely they wouldn't try to take a three-year-old half-Japanese child.

She'd called the nearest army station. She'd called the Maryknoll mission. The only answer she could get was that she needed to appear the next morning, with Tommy, or she'd be in violation of the army's order. According to federal law, she'd be subject to a fine of $5,000, imprisonment, or both.

Now on the sidewalk, with a rising sun throwing shadows across the pavement, Elaine saw a soldier and priest run toward her. "Not here! Not here!" she heard one of them shouting. The men surrounded Elaine and Tommy, then hurried them toward the building, the former Security-First National Bank. Etched columns still flanked the entrance, fluted pillars three stories high, stretching toward the cold expanse of sky.

Elaine knew immediately why these men balked at her presence in a line not meant for whites. Their haste failed to surprise. She had spent years leading labor demonstrations, protesting California's racist and repressive policies, being menaced by Red Squad batons. She'd even been jailed, bruised by brass knuckles. She'd defied the state's antimiscegenation laws by marrying a Japanese American man, a fellow activist. So she would be not be cowed by this priest or soldier before her now.

The men ushered Elaine and Tommy inside, the priest again insisting that it was her son they wanted, not her. As if they were going to roll out the red carpet for her and then expect her to hand over her son. If these men thought she was just going to surrender her child, well then they really knew from nothing.

––––––––––––

Three months and twenty-three days earlier, with Japan's bombing of Pearl Harbor, more than two thousand Americans had been killed. Since then, Elaine, her husband Karl, and their children had mostly stayed inside, avoiding the stares of strangers and barrage of disturbing headlines. JAP BEAST AND HIS PLOT TO RAPE THE WORLD, read a 1942 magazine cover with a white woman pinned beneath a Japanese soldier's rifle. Some newspapers couldn't even bring themselves to print the term "Japanese American." HYPHENATED JAPS FACE THOROUGH INVESTIGATION, reported the January 19 front page of the

Wilmington Daily Press Journal, the local paper on the waterfront where Karl worked as a longshoreman, before he was fired that winter for having Japanese ancestors. On February 2, a *Los Angeles Times* editorial went further: "A viper is nonetheless a viper wherever the egg is hatched. . . . So a Japanese American, born of Japanese parents—grows up to be a Japanese, not an American."

Two weeks later, on February 19, 1942, President Franklin Roosevelt signed Executive Order 9066, officially enabling the forced removal of anyone deemed a threat from the entire West Coast. Newsstands throughout the city placed the *Los Angeles Times* front and center: U.S. Acts to End Jap Peril Here. The implication was clear: even citizens of Japanese descent were now nothing more than "Japs," or danger.

With the inevitability of being banished and with rampant rumors of violence against Japanese across the Western states, Karl had departed Los Angeles on March 23. He'd taken one of the very first transports to the Manzanar concentration camp, officially called Owens Valley Reception Center, in a desiccated plain near Death Valley. He'd volunteered to be among the first to go and build housing for those who would be sent after. Perhaps he could improve conditions somehow or help guarantee the safety and well-being of his community, now that all efforts to halt the forced removal had failed. He was sure that eventually they would all be taken.

The early Manzanar volunteers had been promised union wages, and without a job or source of income, Karl needed the work. To seal the deal, he'd been promised that families of volunteers would be the last imprisoned. He still doubted his wife and son would have to go anyway, because Elaine was white. And who would take a three-year-old half-Japanese child?

So Karl left his family where he thought they would be safe, with Elaine's parents in Boyle Heights. The area held a mix of Eastern European Jews like the Buchmans and Japanese, Armenian, and Mexican immigrants. It was just a short distance from the control station where Elaine and Tommy had been ordered to appear that morning, bordering L.A.'s Little Tokyo, whose streets were lined with Japanese shops. Their signs, once bearing the bold strokes of the traditional kanji characters, were starting to be replaced by English posters: Big Sale, they read; Closing.

While a mixed Jewish Japanese family like Elaine and Karl's would stand out in Boyle Heights, they might not be quite as obvious as they'd been in San Francisco, where the Yonedas lived when they'd married until soon after the bombing of Pearl Harbor. They'd come to Los Angeles to stay with Elaine's parents when Karl went to Manzanar because it still would be close enough to visit him, if visits were to be permitted. In L.A., Elaine could look for war-relief work while her parents watched the children. Though a modest number of Japanese Americans were able to move east right after Pearl Harbor, Elaine and Karl could not; her custody agreement with her first husband—an Irish American machinist with a temper—had stipulated that she stay nearby so he could see Elaine's older child, their daughter Joyce, though he barely bothered to arrange visits.

Elaine's parents, like Karl's, had immigrated to the United States around the turn of the century. The Buchmans had fled the bloody pogroms of Eastern Europe, where reports of the mass murder of Jews were beginning to emerge in March 1942. Yet in Los Angeles, the Buchmans assumed they were safe, because they were American citizens and they were white.

Of course, Karl was a citizen too, born in California. But Karl had gone to Japan as a child when his father fell ill and his parents decided to return to their native village in Hiroshima. Then, as a young man, Karl fled back to California to escape conscription in the emperor's army. Like the US military in 1942, when the Japanese military had looked at Karl in 1926, they saw not an American but an ethnic destiny.

Karl detested Japan's steely imperialism, their thirst to colonize Asia themselves rather than leave it to Western conquerors. He disdained their threats against his widowed mother, who'd stayed in Hiroshima after he'd deserted. Karl and Elaine had together watched in horror as Japan's theory of expansion, its so-called Pan-Asianism, metastasized throughout the 1930s, from slogans to a militarized Manchurian puppet state, to bayonets piercing the flesh of Nanking's Chinese citizens.

Despite the obvious indignity of America's West Coast "evacuation," Karl planned to enlist in the US military and fight the Axis as soon as the Allies would take him. He'd do whatever it took to defeat fascism. Who knew what the Japanese would do to a so-called deserter if they captured US soil? But more than that, Karl needed to protect his family. After all, his beloved Elaine was Jewish, and their son was a Japanese American Jew. Karl had tried to enlist before he'd left for Manzanar, but the Army Recruitment Office had turned him away. Like all Japanese Americans on the West Coast, even war veterans, he had overnight been designated ineligible to serve, considered an "enemy alien" by his own country.

These were among many heavy disappointments Karl had carried with him on the long and lonely trip to Manzanar a week earlier, when he'd departed along with a thousand other able-bodied men of Japanese descent on a cold, gray Los Angeles morning, the chill tempting some to turn up their collars. Karl had been comforted, though, by the thought that at least Elaine, Tommy, and Joyce would be safe in L.A. with the Buchmans. He remembered the promise he'd been given, along with the other husbands who had agreed to be among the first at Manzanar, that their families would be taken last—if, in his case, ever. After all, he assured himself again, who would lock up a three-year-old?

When they finally arrived at the camp, well past sunset, he found little else to lift his mood. He was led by flashlight toward a large, unfinished shed, past wooden skeletons of the barracks he and the others had been told they'd come to Manzanar to build. The shelter for the early arrivals like Karl stood empty, without toilets, water, or even windowpanes. The men were given straw to stuff into sacks for mattresses. Just before midnight, lying in the inky darkness, a bunkmate he knew from Los Angeles called out to him. "Hey, Karl! We weren't supposed to end up in a place like this." Karl made no attempt to answer. Then, exhausted, he slept.

Rising early the next morning in a freeze so deep that water refused to run, Karl and the others found a single spigot rising from the dirt outside one end of their barrack, ice cold and bone dry. Then he got his first full glimpse of camp: a barren, dusty landscape; stacks of construction material; the hospital complex being built up on a hill; barbed wire lacing the front and sides; and soldiers with bayonets and submachine guns guarding the perimeter. In the distance stood the vast snow-capped spread of the Sierras, their beauty so stark against the desert plain, it took Karl's breath.

He ached for Elaine and Tommy, not knowing how or when he'd see them again. Or if. But within three days he'd seen enough of the environment, with its howling sandstorms that stopped the men from working and coated every crevice thick with dust. He knew, even if visits would be permitted, that his wife should not bring their son anywhere near Manzanar. The food alone was a threat, sending the men running repeatedly for the portable toilets. He wrote to Elaine, warning her against visiting even if the opportunity arose. She and Tommy should stay away, at least until Karl and the other early arrivals could improve conditions enough to tamp down the dust, perhaps by planting grass around the barracks and a vegetable garden. With Tommy's allergies and asthma, the camp could kill him.

Manzanar under construction, April 1942. *Photo by Clem Albers, courtesy of the Library of Congress Prints and Photographs Division, Farm Security Administration, Office of War Information Photograph Collection*

At South Spring Street one week later, everything was calm and ordered, at least outwardly. "The physical facilities of each control station should be so arranged as to allow a natural flow of the activities," the US Army's Wartime Civil Control Administration (WCCA) instructed in their Operating Procedures, which would eventually be distributed to administrators staffing 123 control stations up and down the coast. Desks were neatly placed, papers stacked, rifles ready. "Provisions should be made," the procedures noted, "so that only one exit and one entry is available."

Japanese American interpreters had been brought in to translate, particularly for the elders who had emigrated from Japan but had been denied American citizenship because they were neither white nor born on US soil. The interpreters sat behind the long marble counters and wooden desks of the former bank, the smell of packed bodies and coiled nerves in the air around them, their heads bent over reams of paper. Evacuees crowded opposite along the counters, faces grim, bodies pitched forward, as if by looking far enough over the ledge, they might see exactly when and where they would be taken.

The vast majority of these people, unlike Elaine, had no relatives who would be permitted to remain on the West Coast. That morning, they passed through a series of administrators the WCCA had temporarily employed: social workers and consultants from the Federal Reserve Bank and Farm Security Administration, who explained to the future prisoners what *evacuation* really meant and that they had seventy-two hours or less to store, sell, give away, or destroy what they owned. Before leaving for Manzanar, they would be divested of their homes, farms, shops, livelihoods, and even pets, who the army mandated be euthanized if another family—presumably a white one—could not take them.

The WCCA workers then assigned each household a date of departure, no more than three days hence, and a number with two sets of corresponding tags. Family members were directed to attach these to their luggage—no more than they could carry with their own two hands—and then to themselves, before boarding one of the large, dark trains to camp. After they'd done their jobs, the Japanese American interpreters would themselves be shipped off to Manzanar. They would endure the day-long transport knowing they had tried to provide solace and clarity, though unsure if one would forever simply cancel out the other.

As for Elaine that morning at South Spring Street, the priest and army officer were trying to explain a situation she found equally incomprehensible. Though they insisted that Tommy needed to be taken, the priest repeated that she would absolutely not be allowed to go with him.

"It will be too hard for you," he said.

Even in moments of friendly debate, Elaine was known to passionately advance her argument, drawing her small frame upward until she seemed to stand on tiptoe. "Disputatious," an interviewer would one day call her. Now her voice reached full pitch, her body flashing with anger, as if she could launch herself right out of her little heels and loom over these men who simply refused to understand.

"If *he* goes, *I* go!"

Her husband Karl may have already been in Manzanar, but he would soon be leaving camp "*in a khaki uniform!*" to fight for a country that was as much *his* as theirs, she upbraided the pair before her. The government may have taken his job, but they hadn't taken his citizenship, at least not yet. If they took Tommy to Manzanar now, he'd soon be alone there—a three-year-old child. Only half-Japanese. Parentless. In a concentration camp.

Elaine was sure Karl would get to the warfront somehow. She knew he would never betray his ideals, never stop trying to enlist, their shared political passion at the heart of their unbreakable bond. He was a fighter, like her. She was accustomed to carrying on her person a cherished weapon alongside her indominable spirit: a tiny copy of the US Bill of Rights, tucked squarely into a handbag that inevitably matched her pumps. Those words—and those impeccably paired outfits—had seen her through years of demonstrations and court cases. They were with her on the morning she met Karl on a winter day ten years earlier at the Georgia Street prison hospital, less than a mile from where she stood now. She'd gone there representing the International Labor Defense fund, to bail him out. Elaine could still remember how he'd looked, bloodied and disheveled, three days after having been beaten unconscious by the Red Squad at a rally, all for holding a sign about children's hunger. There had been an image of him in the paper just before he'd buckled, uniformed men surrounding him, his sign gone skewed, a tall, trim man about to fall.

But Karl was never one to stay down. He'd proven as loath as she to turn his back on injustice. He'd walked unsteadily out of lockup and into a pale sunshine, toward what had looked like a shimmering star: Elaine, a small, bright firestorm. Together, there was not much that could scare them, other than being denied the chance to fight.

Elaine and Karl had wondered in the days following Pearl Harbor, what would an Axis victory mean for their own Japanese Jewish family? How long would they even survive an Allied defeat? How soon might they be taken along with their children to a place even worse than the camps their own government was planning now?

"The child must go!" the men before Elaine kept insisting. There would be an orphanage there, the priest placated, "a *children's village*," he called it, as if it might boast leafy streets and candy shops, with "well-trained sisters" to look after the little ones.

Elaine saw right through him, though she still had yet to see exactly where Karl had been sent. In her handbag, she carried the first letter he'd mailed from Manzanar. But it remained unopened, having arrived just as Elaine heard the radio announcement the night before, ordering her and her son to the control station the next morning. She hadn't had time to read it, what with her frantic calling from one place to another, looking for a way out of what was surely an insane threat to lock up a three-year-old.

But she knew enough to know not to be fooled by this man who stood pale and impotent before her, this priest whose own god he couldn't see was an illusion. In her mind, she spun through each impossible option. Where could she turn? Who could help her now? For a brief moment, her memory latched onto an earlier horror, one she'd only read about: how the American government, over one hundred years before, had taken whole peoples. The Cherokee. The Choctaw. The Creek. *Dragged them from their homes*, she thought. *At the point of guns. Then decimated them.* She knew her country could, in a flash, do it all again.

As for what the army would do now to her and her child, Elaine wasn't sure. But one thing she knew: they would not take Tommy alone. If she had to, she would claw her way behind barbed wire to protect her son.

Yet what of Joyce, her other child, her white one, fourteen years old and home now with Elaine's parents? The three of them sat in Boyle Heights, alongside an emptying Little Tokyo, waiting and wondering: would Elaine return from Spring Street with Tommy, distraught without him, or not at all? Meanwhile, Elaine stood at the control station and wondered too. Could she leave one child for the other? Would she forsake her first to protect her second?

––––––––––

About 450 miles up the California coast from where Elaine stood, the man who signed the order to send Tommy to Manzanar was busy planning a whole string of camps across the western states. Colonel Karl Robin Bendetsen made a habit of arriving at his desk early and staying late, his collar crisp under his army jacket, pants creased like a blade. Less than three weeks earlier, he'd been named director of the WCCA, established that March specifically to rid the West Coast of its ethnic Japanese population by midsummer.

Before the war, Bendetsen had bent his mind to the legal problems of breaking labor strikes at military-supply plants and interning enemy aliens. He gained a reputation for his clear and decisive position papers, his crystalline strategies for federal seizure of factories and foreigners. With the bombing of

Pearl Harbor in December 1941, Bendetsen pivoted to solving the West Coast "Japanese problem." His solution, proposed in early February 1942, when he was still only thirty-four and a middling major by rank, was to banish not just Japanese aliens but also Japanese American citizens from the western region of the United States.

Before he drafted this plan, the navy's own intelligence agents had researched the loyalty of the Nisei—the children of Japanese immigrants, born in the United States as American citizens. But Bendetsen didn't care to review their findings, even though he was aware of them. Regardless of what they said, he knew his superiors wanted a different tale. He would help the army tell it.

Invigorated by the public thirst for revenge after Pearl Harbor, the chief of Bendetsen's army division, Major General Allen W. Gullion, had been advocating a mass roundup of anyone of Japanese descent on the Pacific Coast since late December. Provost Marshal Gullion displayed little trust of racial and political minorities. This mistrust would not have made him an outlier among the officers of the US military at the time, nor at the army's two most prestigious training institutes, West Point and the Army War College. Gullion had attended both in the prewar period, when American anxieties about immigration ran particularly high. At West Point, the curriculum included readings on the biological basis for intellectual and moral differences among races, with northern Europeans on top. Eastern European Jews were cast as low as—or even lower than—Asians. At the War College, the assigned texts of eugenicist Lothrop Stoddard argued that modern Jews were actually an Asiatic hybrid race with Mongoloid traits and inherited tendencies that would one day would lead them to destroy America's cherished institutions. According to army surgeon Major Charles E. Woodruff, writing the year Gullion graduated from West Point, "The Jew . . . is a typical illustration of a commensal race, welcomed as long as he renders a returning benefit but driven out or killed off as soon as he becomes so numerous that he is a harmful parasite and a national disease. . . . The same law applies to the Jew as applies to a bacillus or any other organism which may be beneficial if few and in place but deadly if numerous and out of place." Soon after Bendetsen began working on the "Japanese problem," the FBI collected evidence of Gullion's central role in a group contemplating a military dictatorship in the United States, hoping to squelch "left-wing influence" on FDR's wife and "put the Jews in their place."

As for Japanese Americans, Gullion believed that citizenship was no excuse for their freedom. The day after Christmas 1941, he called his old friend General John DeWitt, the head of the army's Western Defense Command, to argue for a mass roundup. On February 3, 1942, Gullion announced to Secretary of War Henry Stimson and his assistant secretary, John McCloy, that the Nisei were "probably a more dangerous element . . . than their unnaturalized parents," known as Issei. He had no actual evidence to offer, but he urged the full-scale removal of all ethnic Japanese, alien and US citizen alike. Issei or Nisei made no difference—all should go.

But Stimson and McCloy balked. Locking up US citizens, en masse and without due process, would surely breach the nation's constitution. Later that day, on a call with another general, Gullion reported that "the two Secretaries . . . are pretty much against interfering with citizens unless it can be done legally." This did not prevent Stimson from sharing Gullion's racial antipathy. Banishing Japanese Americans from the West Coast, he wrote in his own diary, would be "trying to put them out on the ground that their racial characteristics are such that we cannot understand or trust even the citizen Japanese." Then, he added, "This latter is the fact, but I'm afraid it will make a tremendous hole in our constitutional system to apply it."

Gullion remained undaunted. On February 6 he wrote to McCloy, urging that "no half-way measures based upon considerations of economic disturbance, humanitarianism, or fear of retaliation will suffice" to safeguard the nation. Then he turned to his trusty assistant, Karl Robin Bendetsen, who trained his focus on executing a plan in lockstep with Gullion's goals. When Gullion dispatched him to the Presidio of San Francisco to convince DeWitt, who was wavering on whether the army really could lock up citizens without a whisp of evidence or guilt, Bendetsen convinced DeWitt he'd found a way. He suggested designating the entire Pacific Coast a military area. He showed Gullion and DeWitt how to craft a legal basis for banishing anyone the government named a threat, asserting the military necessity of removing both foreigners and US citizens of Japanese descent—but not Americans of German or Italian extraction.

"You cannot distinguish or penetrate the Oriental thinking," Bendetsen had written on February 4 in the first planning paper he drafted for Gullion, two days before Gullion had rejected any "half-way measures" to Stimson and McCloy. In the memo, headed "Alien enemies on the West Coast (and other subversive persons)," he argued, "You cannot tell which ones are loyal and which ones are not." The wisest option was to remove them all, he urged, and concentrate them under guard in camps.

By February 13 Bendetsen had swayed DeWitt, helping him write a recommendation that DeWitt submitted to the war secretary, echoing Bendetsen's title while discarding its need for parentheses: "Evacuation of Japanese and other Subversive Persons from the Pacific Coast." The paper warned of impending attacks by the Nisei, arguing that the "Japanese race is an enemy race and while many second and third generation Japanese born on American soil . . . have become 'Americanized,' the racial strains are undiluted." DeWitt then explained the lack of any visible danger signs from Japanese Americans: "The very fact that no sabotage has taken place to date is a disturbing and confirming indication that such action will be taken."

By February 17 Gullion had drafted the wording for Executive Order 9066, which wrote Bendetsen's ideas of "military necessity" into law and was signed and issued by President Roosevelt two days later. By mid-March, Bendetsen had received a double-promotion, becoming the army's youngest colonel.

Along with his new rank and title, he had arranged for his new office, WCCA headquarters, to occupy an entire floor of San Francisco's luxury Hotel Whitcomb. From here, Bendetsen considered, perhaps the military area should be extended across the nation. Then the Japanese could all be rounded up, foreign and citizen alike, from one coast to the next in a clean sweep through the country. He had fretted, though, that word might spread of the free room and board the concentration camps would provide. The government should not advertise, he warned, that it would furnish food and housing for the displaced. In fact, he had initially argued against the military even leading what he called the "resettlement." After all, he pointed out in a February phone call to the assistant chief of the army's Special War Problems Division, their goal was "to kill Japanese, not save Japanese."

Bendetsen had quickly taken to his role heading the WCCA, authoring each step of the "evacuation," as he termed it. As his ideas took shape, they morphed into public proclamations of curfews, restricted areas, and legal punishments, which then became civilian exclusion orders broadcast over radio and posted throughout neighborhoods across the West Coast during the spring and summer of 1942. INSTRUCTIONS TO ALL JAPANESE, began the posters, signed by DeWitt. "All Japanese persons, both alien and non-alien, will be evacuated from this area." Directions would follow to appear for registration within the next few days at one of the control stations spread along the coast. After arriving at these stations, the "evacuees" realized they were about to become prisoners—and that Bendetsen's words would rewrite their entire lives.

———————

Long before that spring, Bendetsen had honed his skills at revision, relying on small tweaks of language to tell a more palatable truth. His father was named Albert M. Bendetson, and he'd passed his surname along to his son. Both Albert and his wife were from families who'd fled the same Eastern European pogroms as Elaine Buchman's parents. But when Karl wanted to join a fraternity at Stanford in 1928 that barred Jews, he claimed a new background and successfully earned his Theta Delta Chi pin. It would not have been much of a stretch, when he wrote his first official planning paper for Allen Gullion on February 4, 1942, to change one small detail and further obscure his identity. Signing his name on that winter day to the bottom of his memo—his tall tale of military necessity and the "Japanese problem" that ushered him into the military elite—Karl substituted an *e* in the last syllable where an *o* had always been. By eviscerating one little loop, he transformed a common semitic ending into a Nordic one. Later that year, Karl R. Bendetsen, né Bendetson, prepared army paperwork making his new identity official.

As a friend from his childhood later explained it, Bendetsen seemed ashamed of being Jewish. He just "wanted to be like everyone else." Now, commanding an entire wartime agency from his floor of the Hotel Whitcomb on a late-March day, Bendetsen just had to keep all his stories spinning. He was optimistic about the future—as long as no one looked too closely, either at his past or his pretense for forcibly removing 120,000 souls to American concentration camps.

———————

As for Elaine on that March morning, Bendetsen's stories and the decrees they prescribed had already fractured her family; she couldn't say when, or even if, her husband would come home. But now at the control station, with the priest and army officer, her anger rising unabated, she knew how to force their hand. She challenged them to uphold the oath to God and government she herself had sworn. She'd uttered a promise when she married, she reminded them, *to honor and cherish*—for even in her distress, she assured the clergyman she would never pledge *to obey*. "I'll be with my child and husband!"

She scanned the days listed for Manzanar's trains. "April 1st and 2nd," read Bendetsen's schedule for taking Tommy and the others from the Spring Street station. She knew just what to choose. She honed her hazel gaze on the men before her. She and her son, *together*, would take the first train out, she announced. She ensured they noted the date she'd chosen from among those on offer: April Fools' Day.

2 | JOINED
1900–1942

THOUGH ELAINE DIDN'T KNOW IT YET, the place where she and Tommy were headed would bring moral quandaries and mortal threats unlike any she had known. Her bravado at the control station that spring morning signaled an implicit faith that she'd find a way to surmount, somehow, the calamity facing her family—the way she had surmounted every other challenge she'd ever confronted. But her faith might have faltered had she foreseen the chaos that would eventually engulf Manzanar. Not that this foresight would have—could have—changed her choice. Elaine was born from struggle, and she'd never let it stop her before.

When Karl thought about Elaine, he thought of a woman who didn't believe in stop signs. Her mother was the same, so perhaps his wife had been this way from the start. She was named Rose Elaine, born at home in a tenement on the Lower East Side of Manhattan. Her parents were Nathan Buchman and Mollie Kvetnay, Jewish emigrants from Mozyr, Russia, near Minsk. They'd met as child laborers at a match factory, where conditions were dirty and dangerous and workers toiled eighteen hours or more each day. As young teenagers, Nathan and Mollie together joined the Bund, the Jewish workers alliance in Russia, to agitate for better conditions.

When Nathan was growing up, his parents were strongly religious, and his father served as the lone Hebrew teacher in their small village. Nathan and his brother joined classes for free, and the other students—all boys—paid to attend. If any of the paying students misbehaved, Nathan's father would call him and his brother up to the front of the class. Ordering them to lower their pants, he would grab a small whip equipped with leather thongs. Then he would strike his sons while the other boys watched. He'd tell the paying students that they'd be punished the same way if they misbehaved again, but they were never the ones who got whipped the next time.

By 1905 Nathan had fled Mozyr. He left during a time of rising labor conflict and bloody anti-Jewish pogroms throughout the Pale of Settlement, the swath of Russian territory where Jews were permitted to settle. In the face of such brutality, the Bund encouraged members to organize for self-defense and strike back if necessary, an ethos with which Nathan and Mollie agreed. But as the century turned, Nathan faced another threat: conscription in the czar's army, whose long history was riddled with antisemitic repression. He fled to New York, and when he'd saved enough, Mollie followed. Elaine was born in 1906 and her brother two years later. Eventually Nathan opened his own barbershop, though he always assured his daughter that his employees deserved—and earned—union wages.

In America, Nathan and Mollie banished religious practice from their home. They settled for a time in Brooklyn, near Nathan's parents, who'd also fled Mozyr. The elder Buchmans continued to practice their Orthodox traditions despite their son and daughter-in-law's secular ways. Nathan and Mollie wove a balance between tolerating the older generation's religiousness, rejecting it themselves, and still holding fast to their cultural identity. They spoke Yiddish at home and socialized mainly with other Jews. Nathan and Mollie flatly refused to celebrate religious holidays, but they marked the workers' holiday, May Day, with a picnic and visit to the annual parade, where Elaine would marvel at the Jewish bakers union in white aprons and hats. The bakers would march with arms raised toward the sky, holding aloft an enormous challah. To young Elaine, it looked like the braided loaf stretched an entire city block.

When Elaine was five, Mollie took the children to visit her parents' farm near Minsk. Unlike Nathan's parents, Ruben and Rachel Kvetnay had stayed behind. That summer, the Jewish Publication Society gathered reports of over a dozen attacks on Jews throughout the Pale of Settlement, little bursts of death and dread across the region. To the east of the Kvetnays' farm, four Jews were killed in a riot. To the south, some Jews were attacked in a park, others in a streetcar, while a small pogrom destroyed a Jewish store. In a different town south of Minsk, one girl was murdered and another injured in an anti-Jewish riot. Throughout July and August of 1912, after each bout of violence was extinguished, another seemed to follow.

As summer morphed into fall, the Kvetnays celebrated the High Holy Days, when Jews across the world welcomed their New Year. Elaine's young cousins were also visiting the farm so they could celebrate the coming year together. On holidays at her grandparents' house, the candles were lit and regular activities ceased, as dictated by religious edict, and the large oven remained unlit.

One day during that New Year's holiday, everything suddenly turned to frenzy. The adults quickly ordered some of the children to hide in the basement and the rest to climb atop the wide, cool oven, covering them with blankets. "Lie still!" they commanded. The children were not to move or make a sound, "not even cough if it choked us," Elaine recalled. She couldn't see what was happening, but she knew it was terrible.

All around them, Jewish farms were burning. Her grandparents' house, surrounded by small plots owned by gentiles, stood some distance from the land being torched. Later, the family assumed this remoteness had saved them. The pogrom ended just before the attackers reached Ruben and Rachel's home. Elaine recalled no fatalities, but she knew Jews in the village were hurt and property was destroyed.

Her grandparents, having narrowly escaped one more calamity, turned their thoughts to God, not action. They prayed and wondered, *Why did He let this happen? How to interpret God's will, when He willed this?* Mollie cut short their trip and returned to New York with the children.

Arriving home, Mollie knew America was where she was supposed to be, to raise her family with Nathan. The long history of violence and antisemitism in Europe was ghastly enough, but her parents' passivity—so different from the fighting promise of the Bund—left her cold. She would not raise *her* children in a household that sat and prayed in the face of injustice. She had no interest in why God had allowed this pogrom—or in any god that would. What sort of pale deity would just stare down from heaven while such plundering and killing occurred? "I was taught that you don't start a fight," Elaine said later, "but you don't run away from one either."

She was also taught that Mollie and Nathan would brook no religious practice in their home. The only time Elaine could remember her father ever striking her occurred after she snuck into synagogue on Passover. She'd wanted to hear the blowing of the shofar, the ram's horn signifying the holiday. Nathan was incensed. "You can be anything you want when you're older," her father told her. "You can even be a nun." But as a child living under his roof, organized religion of any kind would remain forbidden.

Elaine grew up to share her parents' rejection of religious practice, but she remained proud of her Jewish heritage. "It was an identity," recalled a relative, not necessarily a religion. "And she was proud. Because she came from strong people who had strong opinions about things. And they were survivors."

Nathan and Mollie's flight from Eastern Europe in the early 1900s proved lucky. Less than a decade later, another pogrom erupted in Mozyr, leaving dozens of Jews reported murdered and raped. Then, in late August 1941, just a few months before Karl Yoneda found himself under armed guard, the Nazis occupied Mozyr. According to Holocaust historians, they "promptly began to murder groups of Jewish residents. . . . The [remaining] Jews were concentrated in a ghetto. . . . On January 6, 1942, all the ghetto inhabitants were led to the prison and stripped of their belongings. The following day, they were murdered. . . . Most were shot dead; some were drowned."

Karl Yoneda's life was also defined by struggle and escape. Before the turn of the twentieth century, his father, Hideo, migrated from Hiroshima to Hawaii, where he worked the sugar plantations. There, the field supervisors lashed workers with black snake whips if they moved too slowly. Hideo was a stubborn man who returned to Japan to find a wife, where he fell in love with a stubborn woman. Kazue was beautiful, and she hailed from Hideo's own poor village in Hiroshima. As a child she'd badgered the monks, who told her "learning is not for girls," until they allowed her admittance to the temple's private school. Hideo didn't care that she'd already had a child out of wedlock by the time he met her, "didn't care how many bastards she had, she was the woman he wanted to marry," Karl later explained. So Hideo took Kazue with him and went back to America.

When Karl was born, his parents named him Goso: *go* meaning strong, *so* meaning free. They returned to their village in Hiroshima when Karl was seven, leaving the US after their older son died. By that time, Hideo was too sick with tuberculosis and alcoholism for hard labor, "too sick even to yell,"

Karl recalled later, though his father still beat him when he misbehaved. Karl had inherited Hideo and Kazue's stubbornness. "Growing up, I was never physically strong," he said. "But I was stubborn as a mule. I never gave in to illnesses or adversities. . . . I never uttered a word or cried out when my father beat me." Two years after moving his family to Hiroshima, Hideo died, and Kazue told Karl, "Don't be like your father. Don't drink, don't smoke. Be other things."

While Kazue worked long hours as a farmhand and a janitor in a shipyard, Karl and his two sisters spent all day in school, studying and practicing obedience. At night, the entire country was expected to lay down with heads pointed east, "because that's where the emperor was," Karl explained. Karl made top marks academically but failed what was known as "moral education." "How come the emperor is a god?" he would ask the principal. "He's the same as us!" By the time he left school, Kazue had accepted that Karl would never live up to most parents' ideals. But still, Karl said, "She knew I would, someday, be somebody." She told her son, "I don't care what you do. I know you'll do it. I won't stand against it."

When he was still a teenager, Karl became a typesetter and joined Japan's outlawed labor movement, issuing radical publications and participating in strikes. Soon after, he served his first jail term, locked in a tiny, windowless cell with a dozen other men and, he estimated, "a million lice." At night, the vermin crawled so furiously over their bodies that the men couldn't sleep. They were given rice with boiled radishes and tea for meals. "After spending seven days in there," Karl said, "I [walked] out into the sunlight and almost pass[ed] out."

Though Karl was born in California and thus was an American citizen, the Japanese government expected him to serve in the imperial army, whose enforced obedience and harsh punishments dwarfed any he had faced in school. So when news of his conscription arrived, Karl fled, returning in 1926 to the United States. In California he worked as a gardener and a houseboy, joined the Communist Party, and assumed the name Karl Hama: part homage to Karl Marx, part attempt to protect his mother, who was still in Hiroshima. Since Japan's late nineteenth century, a woman's greatest responsibility and honor, *ryōsai kenbo*, was to embody the "good wife, wise mother" ideal, raising and educating children to serve and strengthen the nation. With her only living son's desertion for a life of communist agitation abroad, Kazue was particularly vulnerable to being ostracized.

In America, Karl became what is known as a Kibei, or a Nisei who'd gone to Japan for part or all of his education and then returned to the United States. He was first arrested on American soil in Los Angeles in 1929 for distributing leaflets against Japanese warships docking in California to gather war material, which could be used for the country's military incursions into China. Even from afar, Karl could not accept the rising imperialism of his ancestors' country.

On the day of Karl's first arrest in California, Elaine was likewise in Los Angeles. The Buchmans had moved west when Elaine was fourteen. Nathan eventually bought a small dry-goods store in Los Angeles's Boyle Heights, worked hard, and achieved relative prosperity, at least until the Depression hit.

While Karl was throwing himself into late-1920s West Coast leftist politics, Elaine was avoiding it. She was married by then, having wed an Irish American man named Ed on a winter's day in 1925, at a city hall ceremony her parents acknowledged but did not celebrate. She and Ed had a daughter, Joyce, in summer 1927, and Elaine stayed home to be a housewife. The young family's finances swung up and down, and they periodically moved in with the Buchmans. When the stock market crashed in 1929, Ed was luckily back at work. He was earning a good income as a machinists' foreman in Hollywood film studios, where overtime proved particularly lucrative and where his dark Irish features—sometimes referred to as "Black Irish"—earned him the nickname "Blackie." Though the couple had left-leaning friends, Elaine was little inclined toward politics. She was more interested in fashion, never going out without a matching purse and heels. She called herself "a clothes horse." (Even at home, she wore slippers with heels.) She doubted her friends' frequent accounts of police brutality. Surely, protestors must provoke the trouble they found. Besides, Ed had a good job that neither of them wanted to jeopardize by joining a demonstration.

Despite Elaine's politically insulated life, she could not have helped but sense rising racial violence, antisemitism, and repression following the Great War of her parents' generation, which had worsened in the 1920s as the Depression drew near. US industry leader Henry Ford published his series The International Jew in 1920, warning (falsely, of course) that the Jews had funded the demise of the Russian Empire. They now posed an existential threat to "all that Anglo-Saxons mean by civilization," according to the newspaper he owned and circulated through dealers across the country. Two years later, he published the series as a book of the same name, subtitling it *The World's Foremost Problem* and printing millions of copies.

The year before Elaine and Ed married, Congress passed the Johnson-Reed Act of 1924, eliminating immigration from Asia completely and reducing it radically from Eastern Europe. The act was named for US Representative Albert Johnson, chair of the House Committee on Immigration and Naturalization. A passionate believer in eugenics, Johnson warned of an impending "stream of alien blood," including a deluge of "unassimilable" and "abnormally twisted" (as opposed, presumably, to just normally twisted) Jews, whom he called "filthy, un-American and often dangerous in their habits."

The act was signed into law by President Calvin Coolidge, somewhat less known as the author of a 1921 *Good Housekeeping* article titled "Whose Country Is This?" While the "Nordics propagate themselves successfully," the same could not be said for others, Coolidge wrote. "Biological laws tell us that certain divergent people will not mix or blend," he warned, so "observance of ethnic law is as great a necessity to a nation as immigration law."

In 1927, Albert Johnson repeated this racial philosophy before Congress: "The United States is our land [and] we intend to maintain it so," he said. "The day of indiscriminate acceptance of all races has definitely ended." Then he issued a warning about the Japanese in particular: their imperial ambitions seemed an audacious aping of Western colonialization, suggesting a dangerous belief in the "absolute equality of the Mongolian and Aryan races."

Meanwhile, in a German prison cell, Adolf Hitler was inspired. In America, they "absolutely forbid naturalization of certain defined races," he wrote in *Mein Kampf.*" He'd already hung a portrait of America's Henry Ford in his Munich office, keeping translations of Ford's *The International Jew: The World's Foremost Problem* stacked nearby in his anteroom.

Violent repression of the labor movement was simultaneously becoming more widespread in America. In Los Angeles, this repression was often inflicted by the LAPD Intelligence Division, known as the Red Squad. The division was headed by Captain William Francis Hynes, though most people called him "Red Hynes," a reflection of both the passion and brutality with which he ran his squad. Hynes saved his deepest scorn for American communists, whom he claimed were not even party to the Constitution. "They haven't any rights," he once pronounced. "I'm going to keep right after them." Hynes knew Karl Yoneda from L.A.'s picket lines, and he seemed to nurture a particular antipathy for activists like Karl, lacking both white skin and capitalist impulses. "Get that yellow bastard!" Karl recalled Hynes screaming during a rally, pointing at him from fifty feet away.

—————————

Though Elaine had once shown little interest in politics, by the time Karl entered her life, all that had changed. She'd told him how her world had shaken the first time she saw a woman being beaten and arrested by Hynes's squad: a woman just standing there peacefully, drinking a glass of juice at the edge of a demonstration. Hearing that an organization called International Labor Defense had agreed to defend the woman, Elaine went to their office and offered to serve as a witness. The ILD was established in the United States in 1925 as part of the Communist International's Red Aid network, providing legal guidance, moral support, and financial assistance to political prisoners and labor activists under arrest. Within a month, Elaine had signed up to be an official member; within a year, she was employed by them.

Elaine rose rapidly at the ILD, from office worker to Southern California district secretary, notifying organizers when strikers were arrested so they could arrange bail. She focused on the organization's national campaign for the release of the Scottsboro Nine, a group of young Black teens falsely accused of raping a white woman in the South, tried as adults, and sentenced to death. She also worked on the ILD's efforts to free Tom Mooney, a San Francisco labor activist falsely accused of planting a bomb and sentenced to hang. From her frequent prison visits, Elaine eventually became close to Mooney and his family. She spoke at rallies and marched for workers' causes, and despite wind or rain, she'd march in heels and what she called a "proper hat and gloves." Not even technical difficulties could dim her piercing voice. "When the mike went dead," she said, "they put me on the platform."

In February 1931 she'd just begun working for the ILD when a call came into the office. Red Hynes was on the phone. They had Karl in custody. Come get "that damned Jap," he snapped. "He's going to die anyway."

Karl had been thrown into the Georgia Street jail three days earlier, beaten by police until he lost consciousness. Elaine and another ILD staffer set off to bail him out. They found his head wrapped in dirty bandages, his shirt and undershirt crusted with dried blood. But when Karl recalled whole ordeal, what he remembered most was seeing Elaine that day at the Georgia Street jail, how she'd moved him, how she'd shined in her yellow dress. She was still married to Ed, but he couldn't stop seeing the vision of her, bright as a star coming out of the gloom.

In mid-October 1931 Elaine joined the Communist Party. She'd watched her ILD colleagues, and she admired the ones who belonged to the party. "I saw they were the ones who were the most harassed," she said. They were the ones "the employer class wanted to see decimated. So I decided I would be a Communist."

Ed joined the party too, and sometimes he and Elaine used the last name "Black" when they were confronted by police at protests, a variation of his nickname "Blackie." Likely, he'd be fired if his bosses learned he'd been arrested. But despite their shared political activities, signs of trouble between them had already emerged. He'd been drinking and gambling, and Elaine thought he might be a womanizer, what she called a "chaser," as well. He didn't seem to appreciate Elaine's rapid rise through the ILD ranks either. He may have been politically progressive, but at home, he expected her to be "just a so-called housewife."

And then Elaine was herself assaulted by Red Squad officers. One autumn day in 1931, the ILD organized a day of protests, drawing almost six thousand people and a swarm of Hynes's officers and their proxies. "The mercenaries were out in all their terrible strength, fully accoutered, [and] armed to the teeth," the journal *Open Forum* recounted: "leaden gloves, [sling] shots, night sticks, revolvers, shot guns, rifles, machine guns, tear gas, and gas guns."

When Elaine arrived at the scene, she found tear gas so thick that even tourists in a nearby hotel were evacuating. She saw a group of men set off a gas bomb to shake out a young Black man hiding in a tree; he came skidding down, his body rasping against bark, and Elaine watched men remove his shoes and beat his feet and legs, the whacks reverberating until the man's limbs seemed like pulp. (He was in the movement, and Elaine came to know him. "To this day he walks with canes," she'd later say.) She saw another man being beaten by three officers who had him on his knees, and when she tried to intervene, they clubbed her as well. She had assumed they would not beat a woman, but she was wrong.

In the police car taking her to jail with a clutch of others, the man she'd tried to save turned to the officer who was driving.

"Aren't you ashamed of hitting a lady?"

"She's no lady," the cop replied.

The officer had his gloved hand on the wheel, steering up a hill. He turned to Elaine for a moment. Then he punched her hard in the breast. She hadn't known until then that he wore brass knuckles under his gloves.

When the case went to trial, Elaine and three others defended themselves. It was "my baptism," she'd call it later, the first of many times she would defend herself in court. Around the ILD and Communist Party offices, which shared an address, Karl would hear of Elaine's verve, and he'd quicken at the sight of her—small, passionate, cleverly put together, and always a whirl of motion. She lost that first court case, but after appealing and several more weeks of trial, the whole group won the appeal, and the case was dismissed.

By the time Elaine was offered a promotion in San Francisco a year and a half later, she was falling in love with Karl, too, and facing the first battle she wasn't sure she wanted to fight. She'd separated from Ed in July 1932, and in the spring of 1933 was offered a job as district secretary for the ILD's Northern California territory. Her marriage had ended with an agreement to keep Joyce somewhere accessible to her father, who'd moved to Las Vegas for work. The Buchmans offered to keep Joyce with them if Elaine went to San Francisco, a city too far from Las Vegas for Ed to arrange visits. The girl had already been residing with her grandparents off and on since she'd been born, as her own parents' changing finances had sometimes led them back to the Buchmans' to live.

Despite their progressive political leanings and welcoming home, Elaine's parents—her mother in particular—did not approve of the relationship with Karl. To Mollie, marriages mixing faiths were one thing; those mixing races quite another. Mollie's sentiments were not unusual at the time, and overt public denigration of mixed marriage persisted. The widely syndicated *Los Angeles Times* columnist Fred Hogue wrote, "It is generally accepted that the mixing of white and colored blood" results in "most of the vices of the two and few of the virtues." In sum, "the tendency is to breed down, not up." Franklin Roosevelt agreed, having admitted publicly in 1925 that his support for anti-Japanese immigration was to prevent "mixing the blood of the two peoples," since "the mingling of Asiatic blood with European or American blood produces, in nine cases out of ten, the most unfortunate results." (Roosevelt dismissed any appearance of bias by claiming he had "a great many" Japanese friends, "cultivated, highly educated and delightful" people all, who had assured him they shared his "same repugnance" for miscegenation.)

Elaine eventually accepted the ILD offer in San Francisco. She left L.A. "unsure"—about taking on yet another fight, and about whether fighting for mixed marriage was even the right choice. Karl's family was no more enthusiastic about his relationship with Elaine than hers. His sisters, both married and now in the United States too, called their brother a "Bolshevik trouble-maker," and "a disgrace" for taking up with "that white divorcée." But he could not stop thinking about Elaine. When his siblings' disapproval failed to sway him, they offered him cash and a car to end his attachment. Instead, he moved to San Francisco as well.

Up north, Karl took over editorship of a Communist Party Japanese-language newspaper. On May 26, when Elaine returned to the San Francisco ILD office after a demonstration, Karl was there. She looked at him and knew right then: their bond was worth the fight. They moved in together the next day.

As a mixed couple, Karl and Elaine found it nearly impossible to find long-term housing. But after six months of looking, they finally found someone willing to rent to them. On October 1, 1933, they moved into a fourth-floor walkup at the edge of the Fillmore District. The building was shabby, having survived but not thrived after the great 1906 earthquake and fire, and offered only one shared toilet and bath, on a lower floor. Elaine and Karl were delighted.

As the couple settled in together, news broke of unprecedented violence in both Europe and Japan. That October, the US media revealed what the Nazis were really doing in their new concentration camps, after Hans Beimler, one of the first escapees ever, told his story. The fact that this prisoner was not Jewish, and that Dachau itself was not set up to target Jews specifically, would have been cold comfort to Karl and Elaine. As the labor press reported, Beimler was a former leader of the German Communist Party. Like the many Communists, labor activists, and other political dissidents who were the Nazi's first victims, Beimler testified to weeks in a "torture cell," being beaten "so mercilessly that he nearly died," always under the specter of a rope a Dachau commandant had ordered tied from a beam above his head, where he was encouraged to climb if he could bear the beatings no longer. One day soon, the commandant promised, he'd be hoisted up there if he didn't make the climb himself. Beimler escaped. But, the *Daily Worker* reported, he left behind "50 other revolutionary workers of Bavaria" who were murdered at the camp.

That year also brought news of the killing of one of Japan's most famous dissidents. Takiji Kobayashi, esteemed revolutionary author, had been murdered that February by Tokyo police. In May the *Daily Worker* broke the news in America, reporting that "four hours after his arrest he was found dead, his skull crushed in and his forehead branded with a red-hot iron." In October, less than a week after Elaine and Karl spent their first night in their new home, the *Daily Worker* commemorated Kobayashi as a lasting symbol of widespread oppression: "Last year in Japan, 6,000 revolutionary workers and intellectuals were arrested and tortured by the fascist government," they wrote.

By 1936 Karl wanted a steadier income, and both he and Elaine longed for a permanent place where Joyce could come live, so he took a job as the first Japanese American member of the longshoremen's union on the US mainland. The work was hard and physically draining, but he doubled his income. He and Elaine moved out of their small fourth-floor walkup and rented a furnished four-room flat about three miles west of the Fillmore. Joyce joined them the following summer in time to start the new school year.

By then, Elaine and Karl were legally married. They put less stock in a piece of paper than in their shared realization years earlier—seeing each other through the fray of San Francisco's ILD office and sensing the world go quiet— that they would forevermore fight both for and alongside one another. But Elaine and the ILD were involved in another court battle, and the perception that she was "living in sin" threatened their case. So, in November 1935, she and Karl had snuck away to Washington State to sign a marriage license. Mixed marriage was illegal in California, and the Mann Act made it a federal crime to transport an unmarried woman over state lines with "illicit intent." They were "broke," Elaine said later, but she and Karl borrowed money and a pair of rings from friends, boarded a train separately, and sat apart, meeting up only quickly in the dining car. In Seattle, they signed a marriage license at city hall, and for the first time, Elaine saw Karl Hama write his given name: Goso Yoneda.

By 1938 Elaine and Karl were considering expanding their Jewish Japanese American family, though the world seemed awash in bloodlust. That summer, San Francisco's newsstands told the Yonedas of another atrocity: Japan's Rape of Nanking, with reports of Chinese civilians being "mowed down with machine and tank guns" by the "thousands," or "used for live bayonet practice," or doused with gasoline, "ignited," and "cooked alive." In mid-November, Elaine and Karl learned of Nazi Germany's bloody Kristallnacht pogrom, followed by mass deportations of Jewish men to concentration camps.

Meanwhile, the influence of overseas fascism was deepening at home. When the German American Bund held their rally in San Francisco on May 30, 1938, it drew over eight hundred people to California Hall. The building was a sharply turreted brick affair, built to evoke Heidelberg Castle, rising at the corner of Polk and Turk streets. Scores of men dressed as stormtroopers gathered, wearing silver-gray shirts, blue pants and caps, and military-style Sam Browne belts. The meeting opened with "The Star-Spangled Banner," followed by the *Sieg heil*, and closed with another round of Nazi salutes. Three protestors were arrested but "released on $10 bail, furnished by Elaine Black, who has been prominent in San Francisco Communistic activities. She was acting for the International Labor Defense," reported San Francisco's *Examiner*.

That same summer, almost a thousand men and women in New Jersey formed two long lines and marched in tandem, wearing armbands and flanked by paired American and swastika flags, to mark the opening of a Nazi youth camp. In February 1939, Elaine read of a meeting in Chicago of the so-called Joint Committee of Patriotic Organizations, who threatened to "clean the kikes out of" town and "make Hitler look like a cream puff."

Karl could still remember his wife's immutable pluck in the face of such hatred, particularly when he thought of her final arrest, a few years before he left for Manzanar. On a winter day in 1937, she'd marched in protest against Nazi support of Franco in Spain, defying the swastika swaying above her head in the breeze—"flying day and night," she said. She was detained and charged with rioting, then refused to give the court her home address. She admitted that she had a child, Joyce, in that home, after which the judge permitted Elaine to serve her sentence in short stints. The Depression was on, Elaine explained, and "I used to like the corned beef and cabbage, and I knew Tuesday was the day they had it in the county jail." So come Tuesdays, she'd arrive at the six-story building on the corner of Kearny and Washington Streets. She would walk to the upper floors, where the women's cells were. Later, Elaine would tell Karl how the matron would mark her arrival: "Well girls, it's time for lunch! Here comes Elaine!"

Though 1939 brought the outbreak of war in Europe and Japan's expanding colonial plunder, for Karl and Elaine, it began with great joy. She'd finally gotten pregnant, and in January they prepared for the baby's arrival. Elaine had a hard pregnancy, spending much of it on bed rest. Just before the child was due, California's governor, Culbert Olson, freed Tom Mooney after twenty-two years in prison; Olson pronounced Mooney "wholly innocent," due a "full and unconditional pardon." When they heard the announcement over the radio, Elaine in bed and Joyce by her side, both wept. Elaine's longtime work with the ILD on Mooney's case had come to a triumphant close.

Elaine and Karl's son was born a few days later, on January 10, 1939. They named him Thomas Culbert Yoneda, after both Culbert Olsen and the man he'd freed. Mooney agreed to be the baby boy's godfather ("non-religious of course," Karl said). They had no way of knowing that in three years Mooney would be dead and Olsen would play a pivotal part in another unjust incarceration, this time from the opposite position: encouraging the imprisonment of every man, woman, and child of Japanese descent across the West Coast. By then, Elaine and Karl had stopped using their son's middle name altogether, listing him simply as "Tommy Yoneda."

Throughout the rest of 1939, until the United States entered what would become known as World War II, Karl continued working as a longshoreman on San Francisco's Pier 45 and as the only Japanese American mainland member of the International Longshore and Warehouse Union (ILWU). By this time, many considered him one of the most prominent Japanese American communists in the entire mainland United States. Elaine was now secretary of the San Francisco ILWU's Ladies Auxiliary and Pacific Coast vice president of the ILD. But with Tommy's birth, she cut back on daily ILD tasks. She tried to balance caring for a baby with maintaining attention on Joyce, who was about to turn twelve and entering a turbulent adolescence.

Within five weeks of Tommy's birth, Karl and Elaine began to realize that the child would require more than the usual amount of time and energy. The baby had severe asthma, and as he grew, he developed extreme allergies. Milk, wheat, and potatoes could cause vomiting. Straw would make him wheeze, and dust could suffocate him. They moved into an attic flat on the edge of the Fillmore, near Japantown, and Elaine tried to keep their new home as allergen-free as possible.

Earlier, when Tommy was just a few weeks old, the newly expanded family took a photo all together—one of the few pictures with Joyce that Elaine ever made public. In the snapshot, they pose with Karl on the left, Elaine and Tommy in the middle, and Joyce to the right: all flowing together in one unbroken line. Karl and Elaine are smiling and looking down, utterly absorbed by the baby in her lap. Joyce looks down too, her lips held tight and straight.

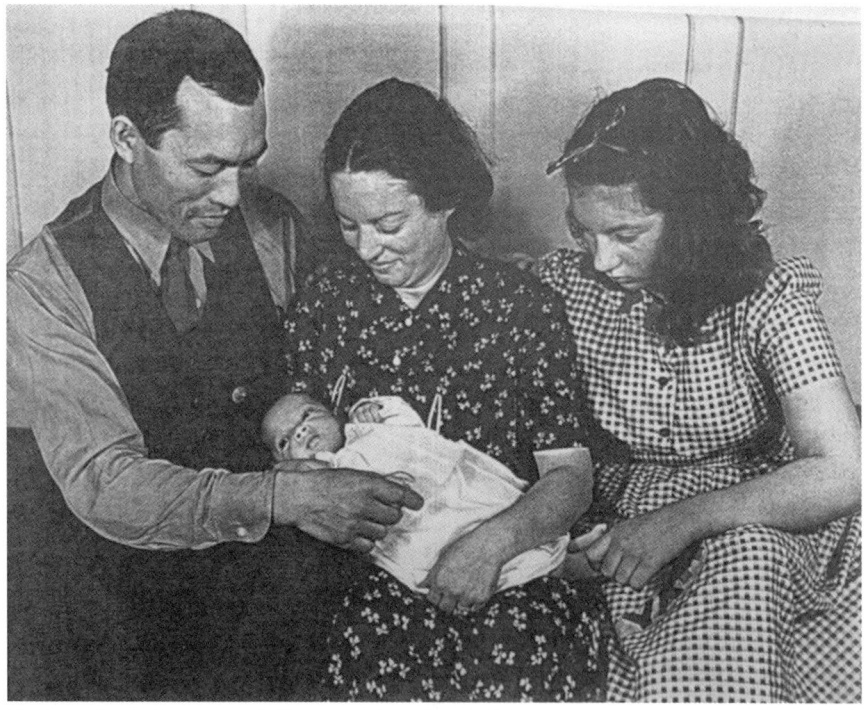

Elaine, Karl, Joyce, and Tommy Yoneda, 1939. *Courtesy of the Yoneda family*

As Tommy grew, Karl became more preoccupied with a widening gap between himself and some in the Japanese American community. The political now became personal in a whole new way for the Yonedas, the leftist parents of the only Jewish Japanese American child on the West Coast (or the only one in records the government would soon gather). Karl noted with fresh alarm the emergence of "Hitler admirers, emperor worshippers, and pro-Japan militarist adherents" around him. In 1937 he'd become the San Francisco editor for the L.A.-based communist paper *Doho*, established to speak out against "the danger of vicious, war-hungry militarists in Japan." By 1939 *Doho* columns were calling out those who purchased Japanese government bonds, arguing that such purchases were funding a militarist regime.

In 1939, three months after Tommy's birth, the Los Angeles chapter of the Japanese American Citizens League (JACL), an organization devoted to supporting education and business success among Nisei, sponsored a lecture by a man named Buddy Uno. Uno was known to wear an Imperial Japanese Army uniform and carry a sword, and Karl heard that his speech praised Japan's aim to "be king of Asia" and "emancipator of all Asian people" through its forays into China. Karl was particularly disgusted to hear Buddy Uno speak of the "brave" Japanese soldiers killing thousands of so-called Chinese "bandits."

Even as Japan's relationship with the United States became more tense throughout 1939 and '40 and the JACL began to distance itself from their forebearers' country, Karl was disturbed by some of their public statements, or more precisely by what these statements omitted. In November 1940 the organization's national president, Saburo Kido, announced over the San Francisco airways, "We Japanese Americans affirm our U.S. loyalty without reservations." But what Karl heard, louder than any declaration of allegiance, was a "failure to denounce Japan's barbarous actions against the Chinese people" or its expanding imperialism—an expansion reiterated in February 1941, when the *Los Angeles Times* reported Japan's determination to spread "Hakko Ichiu," an extension of their military rule and emperor worship "all over the world" in order to "save humanity."

Throughout 1940 and 1941, *Doho*'s editor in chief, Shuji Fujii, repeatedly criticized the West Coast Nisei who he believed were ignoring the crimes of their parents' country of birth—or worse, allowing their "fifth-column" proponents to operate unchecked in America. Karl shared these sentiments: Japan was becoming thick with Nazis and Nazi supporters, both Fujii and Karl wrote. "It is about time that the Nisei made a concerted effort to denounce and stop this nationalistic tide towards Japanistic thinking," Fujii claimed, to begin "routing" these US-based Japanese propagandists so "inimical to not only America, but to the majority of the Japanese people in this country." Karl reprinted these statements in his late December 1941 Special San Francisco Issue to highlight *Doho*'s consistent history of opposing both imperialist support and "fifth-column" activity in the United States.

Karl found respite from such menace in his family and strength in the knowledge that Elaine shared his struggle, always. He was comforted knowing that, despite the turmoil of the world around them and their own incessant determination to fight it, he and Elaine had tried to build a stable home for Joyce and Tommy. For the rest of his days, until he took his last breath, he'd believe—as would Elaine—that this fight derived not from hate or anger but from love: a desire to protect democracy, justice, workers, their own children, and future children everywhere.

Later, looking back from Manzanar, alone and facing indeterminate imprisonment, Karl would have given anything to be back in San Francisco, all together again. If he stared past the dust and dirt of camp, through the rough scrub and barren plain of desert, beyond the mountains scraping sky, he could almost see them all as they'd once been before the war, new and together amid the Fillmore's pulsing energy. He could picture those streets shimmering near as brightly as Elaine, the multicolored Victorians lining the neighborhood on the hill above their flat, a parade of gingerbread trim, turreted towers, and Dutch gables. He could remember the slant of sun as it rose over the district on clear fall mornings, while a few blocks away, the air on Buchanan Street ripened with the tang of garlic pickles and smoked herring. There, the kosher butchers would rise early to stack their cages along the sidewalk, feathers swirling through the rising light amid the screech of birds awaiting slaughter.

3 | COMMITTED
December 7, 1941–March 31, 1942

ON THE MORNING OF MARCH 23, 1942, Elaine's parents had taken her and both children to see Karl off to camp. At the station, they were surrounded not just by those who'd gathered for the transport, including hundreds of other men and a few women; Elaine also saw Maryknoll clergy, a mass of news reporters—their cameras and microphones thrust forward—and "soldiers with guns everywhere," she wrote. Karl was also struck by the milling crowd, the journalists questioning the departing men, and the armed guards surrounding them all. Clutching a card with instructions on where to board, Karl had embraced Elaine and Tommy, climbed some steps up to a dark entryway, and then was gone.

That night, after the train had taken him away, one of the papers ran a picture of Karl's final moments with them. "A Japanese father is shown kissing his son good-bye as he departed for the valley," read its caption. "About 1000 Japs left today."

From the train, Karl had watched Elaine's and Tommy's faces becoming smaller and smaller as the void between them stretched. Seeing them disappear into the distance, feeling the train's inevitable forward force, he felt a lump grow in his throat. On board, no one uttered a word.

Despite the pain of leaving, many of the early volunteers travelling with Karl to Manzanar had signed up, like he had, both in need of employment and with "visions of making it the ideal community," as one incarceree later put it. They hoped to build a place where those unable to fight could "sit out the war," as Karl himself explained. The US government was eager to promote this view. A press release by the War Relocation Authority defined each of Bendetsen's camps as a "pioneer community, with basic housing and protective services provided by the federal Government . . . for the duration of the war." On March 18, just around the time the Maryknoll Brothers were recruiting Karl Yoneda and hundreds of others with the government's promises of construction jobs and fair wages, Bendetsen's WCCA issued its own press release, reporting that complete facilities at Manzanar "for housing and caring for 1000 evacuees" would be ready "by the first of next week"; the entire camp would "house 10,000 Japanese when finished," with facilities "of the 'family unit' type, in order that family units will not have to be split." Moreover, "opportunities for development of small industries"—"commercial fisheries" perhaps, or "pheasant farms"—appeared "excellent," particularly in an environment so "ideally situated, away from the sandy soil near the mountains."

According to Bendetsen's next press release, published on March 20, "General DeWitt has insisted there be no evacuations until these could be conducted with justice and humanity to the affected groups." Bendetsen elaborated,

> The first exodus from Los Angeles by 1000 voluntary evacuees, has been arranged in an orderly manner. These people are eager to leave the area. They will leave by private automobiles, by bus and by trains. They will be given a military escort from Los Angeles to Manzanar—not as an armed guard, but as traffic directors. . . . They go to a well-prepared reception center—not the hardships of a concentration camp.

The next day, he issued yet another statement, claiming that this "exodus" was necessary "to fulfill the Army's mission of minimizing sabotage and espionage in the critical areas of the Pacific Coast."

The West Coast media soon ran with Bendetsen's spin—though they hadn't always been so sanguine about Manzanar's locale. Two weeks previous, on March 5, in one of the first newspaper reports of Manzanar as the end point of a mass forced removal, the *San Francisco News* had run a piece titled "Owens Valley Haunted by Hopes That Failed." The article detailed a troubled past of Native American massacres and governmental water policies that had parched the once-fertile land. It then described government "plans to establish Japanese farm colonies" there, in "California's most widely publicized 'land of solitude.'"

It was an area "blighted," "gloomy, desolated," "weed-choked and barren," across a "succession of 'ghost towns,'" and, lest readers miss the point, "an abode of pathetic, frustrated hopes."

By March 23, when Karl Yoneda departed for Manzanar, the media had changed their tack. The *Los Angeles Evening Herald and Express* ran a series that day with the lyrical headline OVER THE MOUNTAINS THE JAPS MOVE TO A NEW WORLD: "Several of the dormitory-type buildings already stand at the foot of snowy Mt Whitney," and "carpenters are rushing the framework on an eventual 48 city blocks of buildings." NORMAL LIFE IS AIM, pronounced a subhead.

On March 30, the day Elaine had been ordered to hand over Tommy, a *Los Angeles Times* column described Owens Valley as "potentially one of the most fertile in California, and that means all the world." Its new inhabitants were getting a "break"; "couldn't wish for better scenery or a cleaner, more healthful atmosphere"; and "couldn't be censured for hoping, in their own behalf, that the war lasts for years."

The presence of military police at Manzanar, however, played awkwardly in this public narrative. Their commander, Jack Hayes, insisted they were there solely "to protect the evacuees." More to the point, he told the media, "We want the American born Japanese and especially the alien Japanese to realize that our management of Manzanar is the American way."

Life magazine took a more nuanced view when it reported on April 6 of the first groups to reach the place. Though they claimed that the army had "extended a velvet glove to its first voluntary internees," they admitted, "Manzanar, for all its hopes and assets . . . was a concentration camp, designed eventually to detain at least 10,000 potential enemies of the U.S." *Life* noted that four-fifths would be American citizens and the "commanding general of the West Coast area promised the Army would not shrink from using force to complete the evacuation, if other methods failed."

In fact, when Karl Yoneda and the others arrived to barbed wire and guard towers, one of the first observations he heard was, "So this is the American-style concentration camp." They may have volunteered to travel to Manzanar, but there was little doubt that, once there, they had all become prisoners. The towers surrounding them would eventually number eight in total. These were tall wooden structures topped with open platforms. Each had a hand-controlled searchlight that nighttime sentries maneuvered back and forth across the camp in swooping arcs. The guards manning them carried rifles and submachine guns—facing inward, noticed the incarcerees.

In his first days there, Karl thought Manzanar felt "like living in a madhouse." When he'd initially arrived, the land was still being cleared of desert scrub and dead branches, the white construction crew having reached the place only nine days before he had. In late March through early April, Manzanar's general water supply consisted of a few outdoor cold-water pipe-faucets, some portable outhouses, and a ditch for a sewer that flowed alongside the land reserved for Barracks 1–6. Even when housing was completed, it afforded scant shelter. The sidings, floors, and ceilings were still so full of knotholes and gaps that sand blew right through them. Lying down at night, one incarceree said, you could "gaze up at stars through . . . the roof." By day, sandstorms blotted the sun behind walls of dust and cinder, coating the entire camp with grit, from the single naked bulb hanging in each living space to the mess-hall meals to people's undergarments.

On March 24, the first "service" for incarcerees was established: an information office to clarify rules, procedures, and orders mandated by camp administrators, which were posted on a bulletin board. Officials also considered setting a time for a daily morning assembly, during which they thought the white "managers could make statements," or perhaps even "give lectures," in order "to keep the boys informed and in good morale."

Their hopes were quickly dashed. Besides the physical deprivations of Manzanar, the issue of wages caused almost immediate backlash. The Maryknoll priests, relaying information from the WCCA, had promised Karl Yoneda and the others that Manzanar volunteers would earn fifty dollars a month for unskilled help, up to ninety-four for highly skilled work. Camp administrator Clayton Triggs reported the same in the media, though with a few caveats: fifteen dollars would be deducted per person per month to pay for "room and board"; and the government would not turn the money over directly, keeping it "as credit" in an account accessible when the war ended or "the evacuee proceeds to another center"—where presumably they would not be allowed to access their money either.

Eager to start work, Karl and four others began their first full day at camp by walking through the dust to the new information office to ask about the promised construction jobs. "We don't know anything about such promises," an administrator said. "The contractor is doing the work with union members." *Union members*, they knew, meant *white workers*.

The broken wage guarantee was just one piece in the great fake narrative about Manzanar and the other camps that followed. But in the case of Manzanar, this particular false promise also stemmed in part from careless planning and rushed execution. Soon after the camp's inception in early March 1942, Bendetsen's staff turned to the Office of Emergency Management's Central Administrative Services to handle many of Manzanar's practicalities. The WCCA hoped this expediency would help them ramp up quickly enough to turn their attention to their greater goal: ridding the entire West Coast of Japanese by June.

The Central Administrative Services office was in San Francisco, in the new $3 million Western Furniture Exchange and Merchandise Mart—known in the more recent past as the Twitter Building. It stood just two doors down from the luxury Hotel Whitcomb, where Bendentsen's WCCA headquarters occupied a whole floor. Constructed in Mayan deco style, upon its opening five years earlier the Furniture Exchange had earned raves for its sandy-hued terra-cotta detailing, beveled columns, and Mesoamerican friezes. Mayor Angelo Rossi had declared, "The new mart captures the old spirit of the West, and shows that men still have the courage to dream despite obstacles that may arise." What the building didn't offer, however, was reasonable proximity to Manzanar, making administration of the camp particularly ineffective.

For two months, no one detained at Manzanar was sure whether they would ever be paid or at what rate. Three months would pass before they saw any compensation at all—at eight dollars, not fifty, a month for unskilled labor, reaching a maximum of sixteen dollars a month, not ninety four, for the most highly skilled work. In the meantime, internal administrators asked Manzanar's first arrivals to volunteer again: not just their freedom and the forfeiture of their homes, but now their labor too. Otherwise, there'd be little chance to provide even essential operations. When Karl's ad hoc committee of five walked back from the office to their bare barracks and relayed this news to the others, they reacted as expected. Someone said, "The goddamn lying American government!" Someone else—a World War I veteran named Joseph Kurihara—felt a sting inside him begin to burrow deeper, until he tasted blood.

———————————

Joe Kurihara was brought to Manzanar on the same promises and the same train as Karl Yoneda, though they'd soon find themselves on opposite ends of a fatal collision course. Kurihara was forty-seven years old, five foot two, balding, and stout. Born an American citizen in 1895 in Hawaii, he attended Catholic school there, then moved to mainland United States and went to college in San Francisco. When he enlisted during World War I, he "solemnly vouched" to forfeit his life for his country. During his platoon's punishing march to the front, "many boys were dropping off to the side," he said. But not him—he called it a "test," and he had withstood it. Afterward, he joined both the Veterans of Foreign Wars and the American Legion. Kurihara would sometimes wear the Legion's button on his chest, a reminder of the organization's sacred promise "to perpetuate a 100% Americanism."

After Japan's bombing of Pearl Harbor, Kurihara held fast to patriotism, hoping to do his "share as an American." He spent the next six weeks searching for a way. He'd worked as a navigator on a tuna clipper and now thought perhaps he could use his skills to guide bombers to battle. But then he learned that all Japanese Americans, veterans included, had been designated unfit for military service. Next Kurihara considered the merchant marines or working as a shipbuilder. When he went to apply, the guard wouldn't even let him through the gate. He tried to go up to Northern California, where he knew some white professors who could vouch for his loyalty, but at the Los Angeles railway station, the office would not sell a ticket for anyone of Japanese ancestry to leave L.A. By February 1942 his "last ray of hope had vanished." His thoughts turned to Terminal Island, where a Japanese American fishing village lay adjacent to the Los Angeles harbor. Perhaps he could help there.

Terminal Island, across from the Port of Los Angeles, held a village known as Fish Harbor, inhabited by around three thousand Japanese immigrants and their American-born children. Within hours of Pearl Harbor's bombing, Fish Harbor's Issei elders were arrested. In the month following, the FBI rounded up the rest of the community's fishermen. ("Even the bed-ridden," one villager recalled, were "literally dragged from their beds.") Then armed soldiers informed all remaining residents that they had forty-eight hours to leave. Where to go, the soldiers could not say, but by the stroke of midnight two days hence, hundreds of families would have to make themselves disappear, leaving behind their homes and livelihoods forever. Most of the women and children of Fish Harbor faced forced removal alone, without their husbands or fathers, who had already been taken away.

Joseph Kurihara arrived in time to witness the final chaos of a traumatized community. He watched mothers with crying babies, only hours before they'd all be carted away, forced to find somewhere or someone to shelter them off-island, at least until Bendetsen's camps were ready. The prospectors came like vultures, Kurihara recalled, like marauders to the plunder, "offering prices next to robbery." For him too, Terminal Island became a turning point, when "the sting" he could not forget first pierced his soul.

Returning to the city, Kurihara felt confused, not about the inhumanity of the forced removals, but what to do given their inevitability. Once he'd had "absolute confidence in Democracy." Now he'd seen America, "the standard bearer of Democracy," commit what he believed was "the most heinous crime in its history." As for any citizen of Japanese descent who urged cooperation with the government over resistance, they were nothing but "a bunch of spineless Americans." He would "fight them" and "crush them in whatever camp I happened to find them."

Toward the end of March, as news spread that the Maryknoll Brothers were helping recruit volunteers to build Manzanar, Father Lavery from the Catholic mission sought out Joe Kurihara, whom he knew to be a "devout parishioner," and asked him to volunteer. Kurihara cherished the Catholic mandate to help those in need, yet in this circumstance, his reluctance ran deep. Why, he asked, should he help the government construct a camp for people "against whom there were no charges, no trials, no convictions, for either sabotage or espionage?" But Father Lavery pressed his point. He repeated the army's promise: "prevailing wages and special privileges" awaited those who went to camp and built it. Moreover, Kurihara was able-bodied and single, "in an ideal position" to make Manzanar better for the thousands of his brethren who would follow. There would be ten thousand of them, the priest pointed out. They would need help in the desert. Kurihara had already witnessed some of their suffering, up close.

Lacking any other work or way to help, Kurihara arrived at Owens Valley on March 23, 1942, alongside Karl Yoneda. Like the others, he glimpsed the barbed wire and armed sentries, the high, cold mountain barricade against a desert landscape, and he was deeply dismayed. The wind blew with such ferocity, he recalled, that "at times I thought the [barrack] was going to be carried away." Their living quarters were so poor, so dirty and dark, he called them "mushroom barracks," and said the men "slept in the dust, breathed the dust, and ate the dust," without even access to a bath. For weeks, they could wash only under a cold faucet, "right out in the open," for anyone to see. Altogether, he likened Manzanar to being "suddenly forced to live the life of a dog."

When Karl Yoneda and his committee relayed the news that no union wages were forthcoming, nor any paid employment for the foreseeable future, Kurihara's heart broke harder. "The Army made fools out of us volunteers," he said, "and a liar out of a Catholic priest."

He soon renounced his American Legion membership. He no longer wore the button he had once pinned near his heart. In Manzanar, Kurihara had no need for "100% Americanism," for proof that he'd been willing to die for his country. It now seemed to him that all the rights he'd fought to protect in the Great War were "nothing but a hocus-pocus." As for the American Legion pin, that "button [didn't] seem to have any weight," he said.

After learning of the vanishing wages, Karl, Joe Kurihara, and the others spent their first days forming volunteer work groups for yard work and kitchen duty and preparing for an influx of new incarcerees, scheduled to begin on April 1. "There was no direction or organization" Karl recalled, though he did appreciate the "meals three times a day," despite the army's allotment of only about 13 cents per meal, per person. Most in Manzanar found the food unpalatable, but Karl was acquainted with lockup and knew what inmates usually ate. Perhaps in comparison, the camp's meals didn't seem so awful, even if they did tend to send the men running for the outhouse.

The rumors were a different story. In the chaos of the camp's first week, among people with no knowledge of their future or faith in their present, "morale was low," Karl wrote, and people found themselves "picking away at their work half-heartedly." Their days were aimless, the labor repetitive, and they found nothing to occupy their minds amid the dust and dirt and razor-sharp mountains. Rumors began to "spread like wildfire." One incarceree heard that the "Imperial Japanese Army invaded Hawaii Island," landing twenty thousand Japanese soldiers there. Someone else alleged, "the U.S. is so terrified of a possible Japanese landing that they're going to send us to Australia." On March 24 and 25, Karl overheard that the war would be over by September, when Japanese forces would "come to our rescue," and even that "after Japan's victory, it will be a triumphant return to the homeland for us." He noted other comments too, such as "the reason Japanese Americans have been placed into camps is that America is controlled by the Jews."

Manzanar's turmoil pierced Karl, but not in the same way it seemed to rile the rumoring crowd. He'd already spent years fighting the failings of his country as he saw them. With his intimate knowledge of both America's lapses and police brutality, and with thoughts of his own family safely home with white relatives, his disillusionment ran less deep than others'—or at least cut less fresh a wound. He still hoped Manzanar could become, if not a righteous or even comfortable place, at least an organized one, where some could ride out the war and others, like him, could continue trying to enlist.

What Karl Yoneda needed most was to stem the tide of enemy victories, to protect the people he loved from the forces winning overseas. He longed to contribute to the fight against fascism's spread, to continue the struggle that had long defined him, had long fed his soul. To lose *this*—this chance to join the life-or-death battle creeping ever closer—was the loss he could not abide.

Joining with another group of early "volunteers," a few of whom shared his leftist leanings, Karl planned a list of suggestion for administrators "to preserve harmony within the camp," as he explained it later. Perhaps most important, they urged an "an immediate settlement and announcement regarding wages," as well as "creation of employment opportunities for all residents." They also suggested the "establishment of an advisory organ to assess the loyalty of both Issei and Nisei." On the train to Manzanar just a few days earlier, Karl had heard one man's loud protests over being banished to the desert, his loss of faith in his country, his support of Japan's imperialism, and even his hope for Roosevelt's quick demise. Karl had turned toward the voice and seen a man with a long, dark mustache, looking agitated. In that moment, more than disenchantment, Karl perceived danger.

On March 26, he got a letter from Elaine, a brief one saying that everyone at home was fine, though they were concerned about him. He'd written her that morning to warn her from visiting, but he knew she couldn't have received his message yet. He heard no more from his wife for the rest of the week. All he could do was wait and worry.

For Elaine, memories of life in San Francisco were cleaved cleanly into before and after: the morning of December 7, 1941, when Karl went downstairs to wash their new Studebaker under a too-bright sun, then the alarmed announcement on the radio and her calling down to him, and suddenly the dawning realization that the United States had finally catapulted into war. Soon after, Karl left, walking a few blocks west to the center of Japantown to see if he could learn more. Elaine and the children stayed inside.

When Karl returned, he told her that throughout the quarter, people were milling around, looking confused, apprehensive, and horrified. Many Nisei, younger than Karl but with elder relatives in the States, were struggling to imagine what would happen to their parents, who'd been denied citizenship and were now officially "enemy aliens." Would they be deported, their families separated for good?

That night, Karl called a meeting of local *Doho* staff. They telegrammed President Roosevelt: "On behalf of one hundred fifty readers and subscribers in the San Francisco Bay Area of *Doho* Japanese American newspaper, we pledge full cooperation in all endeavors to secure victory for the democracies. We stand ready to join the ranks of the fighting forces under your command to defeat the vicious military fascists of Japan."

Near midnight, the other men prepared to head home. As they left, Karl knew they parted in full agreement: their lives would now be dedicated to overthrowing Japan's imperialists and their fascist partners. He thought about his mother in Hiroshima and wondered if he'd ever have to face her as an enemy. "In case anything should happen to me," he wrote that night, "I've decided to keep a journal to leave behind for my wife and child."

Karl awoke on the morning of December 8, and as he ate breakfast, he heard over the radio about a sweep of arrests: Japanese, Italian, and German nationals suspected of being "fifth columnists," saboteurs. Glancing at that morning's paper, he saw the headline ROUNDUP CONTINUES. He left the flat while it was still early, catching a streetcar eastward, to the docks. By near

7:30, Elaine was up, making breakfast for Tommy and getting Joyce ready for school. On the table, Chinese war relief cards were scattered; Elaine was in the middle of addressing them for Christmas and New Year's greetings, and she hadn't gotten around to putting them away. Just before 8:00 AM, she heard knocking at the door. She opened it to three FBI agents.

Under usual circumstances, she would have demanded a warrant right there and then. She'd had enough run-ins with the law to know her rights. But the country was at war, and the enemy was winning. If she could help answer questions that might lead to a fifth columnist being stopped, she would not hesitate.

She didn't realize her misjudgment until the agents demanded Karl, and suddenly she tensed. He was at work, on the docks, she said. One met her answer with a racial slur, insisting there were no Japanese longshoremen on the West Coast. An officer pointed to the Chinese war relief cards on the table. "A good cover," he scoffed. They ordered Elaine to call the union hiring hall, and the agents learned there was in fact one Japanese American longshoreman employed on the US mainland. Then they left, headed for the waterfront.

Later, Elaine heard that men with submachine guns had stood on the roofs of neighboring houses, watching the front and back doors of the Yonedas' flat. By noon, she learned that Karl had been taken into custody. He'd been escorted off the pier, arrested, and brought to San Francisco's temporary immigration detention center, which stretched along Silver Avenue like a brick fortress. Karl was put in a large holding cell, a converted former gymnasium now lined with rows of triple-decker bunks. When he entered, he saw about fifty other Japanese men, some of whom he recognized, a few he believed to be very "pro-Japan." The air among the bunks was heavy and thick, a mix of smoke and stale.

"Mr. Yoneda!" Karl heard as he entered. "You must have come to the wrong place." Karl looked up and saw an acquaintance, the principal of a Japanese-language school, a man he knew to be both "for Japan" and kind. The man laughed, and so did Karl, the strain breaking for a beat.

"Yes, I think so," Karl replied.

"Well, sit down. Don't worry about the others."

Almost all the men who'd been rounded up were Issei, and among the detainees, Karl counted fewer than a handful that he knew shared his leftist sympathies. Among the Japanese community in America, particularly those who'd emigrated themselves after growing up in a culture intent on conformity, many considered Karl, like all communists, to be at best an outcast, even a degenerate. As the hours stretched, the smell of tension, boredom, and unwashed bodies ripened.

Karl heard "*Inu*," *dog*, called in his direction.

"Spy," someone else added.

"Wait and see. In another couple of days there will be a Japanese navy that will come into the bay and free us!"

"If this wasn't under the control of the US government," another man scoffed, "you would be a machine gun target."

By nightfall, Karl gathered in a corner of the large cell along with the few other left-leaning Nisei. From their spot, they watched and waited, "hoping for strength in numbers," he later told Elaine.

Within thirty-six hours of his arrest, Karl was released. Elaine didn't drive, but a friend from the labor movement took her to pick up Karl, and as they drove home, Elaine told her husband what had happened while he'd been detained. The night of December 8, as Karl sat in the foul air and hoped the pressure in the holding cell wouldn't burst, the regional Communist Party secretary called the Bay Area Nisei Communists to a meeting at the Yonedas' flat. There, surrounded by Karl and Elaine's books and belongings, by years of mementos from their joint fight for the common worker, the secretary announced that the Communist Party of the United States of America, the CPUSA, had come to a decision about its Japanese American members—and their spouses: they were hereby stricken "for the duration of the war." When Elaine heard the words, she was shocked silent. "It was so sudden and unreal," she told Karl as they rode toward the Fillmore, the car skirting the Castro, then Haight-Ashbury, then skimming the edge of Japantown, "that no one uttered a word of protest."

Once home, Karl called a meeting of the Bay Area Japanese American CPUSA members. They discussed their suspension and the nation's young battle, what people were then calling the American-Japanese War. As a group, they decided the growing fight against Imperial Japan would not be served by a complaint against the party, not now at least. They shared the conclusion Karl had reached a few nights earlier with *Doho*'s staff: *every* effort must now focus on defeating fascism. They would continue to meet among themselves, function as though they were still members of the party, and hope that soon the decision would be rescinded.

Looking back later, Karl described the suspension as both irresponsible and wrong, and expressed remorse for not resisting. In staying silent then, Karl and Elaine made their first, though not last, wartime decision that would come to haunt them, despite not seeing any better choice.

In the hours after his release from the immigration detention center, Karl tried to enlist in the US Army. He went to the nearest recruiting station on Fillmore, where great steel arches spanned the street, speckled with electric lights. Fourteen of them had been erected early in the century, designed "to realize Fillmore Street as the 'Great White Way,'" according to one newspaper. By fall of 1943, they'd all be gone, dismantled and melted into scrap iron for the war. Now, as Karl walked below the arcing structures, their latticed metal limbs soaring upward, his chest filled with hopes of joining the fight. When he arrived at the recruiting office and asked for an application, the sergeant on duty replied flatly, "There's no point."

Selective Service officials were now generally classifying Japanese Americans as 4-C or 4-F: "alien" or "rejected for military service; physical, mental, or moral reasons." Karl asked the sergeant, were the same classifications being given to Italian and German American citizens? But he could already guess the answer. *Not a good sign for the future*, he thought.

On December 15 Karl and Elaine read that a stamp of legitimacy had been given to rumors of treachery within. Papers across the country reported that the secretary of the navy, Frank Knox, blamed not his own command or intelligence-gathering for failing to protect Pearl Harbor, but Hawaii-based Japanese spies and traitors. "The most effective fifth column work of the entire war was done in Hawaii," Knox announced, "with the possible exception of Norway."

During the last week of December, a string of murders targeted Japanese residents in California: a thirty-three-year-old Japanese American Army Medical Corps member, who'd been recently discharged—"honorably," but also because of his ethnicity—and then stabbed to death on a Los Angeles sidewalk; a middle-aged garage attendant killed while chatting with a friend; and another gunned down in Sacramento. Meanwhile, as Japan brutalized the Philippines,

Filipino gangs in Stockton smashed windows and beat Japanese American passersby. Over the next month, the attacks on Issei and Nisei in California expanded to include an elderly couple killed in their bed, windows at two homes shattered with over fifty-five shotgun blasts, a young mother murdered, and a nineteen-year-old girl abducted by three Folsom prison guards posing as FBI.

By Christmas Day, Elaine and Karl had seen other minorities wearing buttons for protection: I AM CHINESE or KOREAN AMERICAN. Karl looked down through the window of their second-story flat and watched neighborhood children playing together with their new toys. Then he looked at his own son, about to turn three, playing alone indoors. "We're feeling increasingly hemmed in; it's becoming dangerous just to go outdoors," Karl wrote.

On January 10, 1942, the Yonedas marked their son's third birthday. Of the headlines, Karl wrote in his diary, "There is nothing but bad news." As he watched Tommy celebrate with a few friends, he looked into the children's faces, and he saw innocence and hope. "I've hardened my resolve," he said. "It's for their sake that I'm going to fight." By now, the army had officially classified all Japanese American selective service registrants as 4-C, "enemy aliens." But he would find a way.

———————

In the first few days of January 1942, the Yonedas' fellow citizens had begun publicly agitating for the incarceration of not just Japanese aliens on the West Coast but also Japanese Americans. Elaine and Karl were aghast when Congress quickly picked up the call. On January 20, California representative Leland Ford announced on the House floor that a Japanese American citizen, whom he called "patriotic native-born Japanese" (as opposed to an actual "native-born American") who wanted to contribute to the war effort should "submit himself to a concentration camp" and in doing so "should not object to that small sacrifice." He repeated these claims in the Los Angeles and San Francisco papers over the next two days.

Meanwhile, rumors intensified of a fifth-column threat from inside the US mainland, promoted from on high. In late January, celebrity war correspondent and radio broadcaster Edward R. Murrow—of the now famous farewell "Good night, and good luck"—told a West Coast audience, "I think it's probable that, if Seattle ever does get bombed, you will be able to look up and see some University of Washington sweaters on the boys doing the bombing!" On February 12 the prominent, progressive, and Jewish *Washington Post* columnist Walter Lippmann published an editorial titled THE FIFTH COLUMN PROBLEM that riveted the nation. "The Pacific Coast is in imminent danger of a combined attack from within and from without," Lippmann wrote. He admitted that "since the outbreak of the Japanese war there has been no important sabotage." But his explanation echoed General DeWitt's back in December 1941: "This is not, as some have liked to think, a sign that there is nothing to be feared. It is a sign that the blow is well-organized and that it is held back until it can be struck with maximum effect."

In early February the Yonedas saw the *San Francisco Examiner*'s headline REMOVAL OF ALL JAPS TO THE INTERIOR PLANNED. Less than two weeks later, on the floor of the US House, representative John Rankin announced that the country had embarked on a "race war." "The white man's civilization has come into conflict with Japanese barbarism," he claimed. "One of them must be destroyed." As for Japanese Americans? "You cannot make a silk purse out of a sow's ear."

The rebuttal to Rankin's claim—though none should ever have been needed—already existed in official government files, but it had first been ignored, then hidden away. The Ringle Report had been written and stored almost three weeks before Rankin stood before his colleagues and declared the war another white man's burden. The claim of military necessity was bogus, navy intelligence had found, because Japanese Americans as a group posed no threat at all.

As far back as 1940, Lieutenant Commander K. D. Ringle and his fellow navy intelligence officers had begun spying on the West Coast Japanese community. After months of investigation, they attested that the majority were at very least "passively loyal." The few potential saboteurs could be individually identified and imprisoned; mass incarceration, far from a military necessity, was unwarranted. In the weeks after the United States declared war on Japan, as questions of forced removals began to circulate, Ringle wrote, "The entire 'Japanese Problem' has been magnified out of its true proportion, largely because of the physical characteristics of the people . . . It is no more serious than the problems of the German, Italian, and Communistic portions of the United

States population." Ringle concluded, "It should be handled on the basis of the individual, regardless of citizenship, and not on a racial basis."

When he tried to meet with Karl Bendetsen in February 1942 to explain his findings, Bendetsen declined to see him. The army as a whole simply ignored the navy's findings. The navy, unwilling to rebuke the army, declined to publicize the report. Its contents remained secret to the Japanese American community—including those among them like Karl Yoneda, urging cooperation with the government's claim of "military necessity"; to lawmakers like John Rankin (unlikely to care anyway); and to the American public at large.

J. Edgar Hoover, head of the FBI, was one of the few who had read the Ringle Report, but his advice was similarly discounted. In early February 1942, around the time Bendetsen was ignoring Ringle and Rankin was lecturing to the floor of Congress, Hoover wrote the US Attorney General. "The necessity for mass evacuation is based primarily upon public and political pressure rather than on factual data," he pointed out, to no avail.

Ringle's report remained nothing more than a thin stack of paper, its headline marked CONFIDENTIAL just below its letterhead address: 707 SOUTH SPRING STREET. Ringle had apparently sat in an office at the corner of Spring and Seventh and recorded his findings, in the very same building as the control station where the Maryknoll priest and the army officer would try to take Tommy from Elaine. Four floors above the spot where Elaine had demanded to follow her son and husband to Manzanar, the navy lieutenant commander had written out his report. But when the army received it, its contents were stamped, filed, and buried.

On February 19 Roosevelt signed Executive Order 9066, which would become known as the first official step ensuring the forced removal and imprisonment of all West Coast Japanese Americans. Though the order never mentioned citizens of Japanese ethnicity directly, it ceded control to the army, allowing DeWitt and by extension Bendetsen to remove whomever they deemed necessary. Echoing the Communist Party's exclusion of its Japanese American members, *People's World*, successor to the *Daily Worker*, announced that the government's plans amounted to "a sensible program."

Elaine and Karl immediately understood the order's impact. "We are now as good as bound," Karl wrote. Neighbors offered them space in their garage to store their belongings. "Still," Karl said, "we haven't abandoned our fighting spirit."

A few days later, the Yonedas witnessed the fate of the West Coast Japanese community being sealed before their eyes. About two miles west of their apartment stood a stately, block-long building of pure white stone, where the San Francisco hearings of the Tolan Committee were being held and where the resolution hardened to forcibly remove both Japanese aliens and American citizens. The US Courthouse and Post Office had opened in 1905 and was built to reflect the affluence and growing importance of the United States as a world power. (One magazine immediately named it the "Versailles of the West." Others called it "a post office that's a palace" and "a beautiful poem in marble.") Karl and Elaine attended the Tolan Committee hearings there, listening in from the visitors' gallery in an upper-floor courtroom.

The hearings—officially named the House Select Committee Investigating National Defense Migration but named informally after committee head John Tolan—took place on February 21 and 23, ostensibly to discuss the *possible* removal of enemy aliens from the West Coast. Karl noted that, apart from himself and Elaine and about half a dozen others of Japanese descent, only a few white spectators had bothered to show up. Sitting there, he couldn't help thinking that the sparse attendance reflected a widespread assumption that the matter was already settled—in favor of banishing both alien and citizen Japanese.

Hours of statements passed, confirming the Yonedas' fears. Perhaps the most galling testimony Karl and Elaine encountered that day, as they sat among the gilded splendor of the courthouse and watched their future dim, was from California Attorney General Earl Warren. The most dangerous characters of all, Warren argued, were those American-born, citizen Japanese, who until then had remained silent and seemingly benign. That apparent peacefulness was really just "part of a pattern to lull us into a sense of false security," Warren claimed, in order to "invite another Pearl Harbor," this time in California.

When Karl and Elaine returned on February 23 for the second and final day of the San Francisco hearings, they heard more of the same. They brightened a bit as union leader Louis Goldblatt decried the nation's "wolf pack" mentality conjuring an imaginary "yellow menace," when in fact the Nisei "should not be distinguished from the second generation of any other nationality." But Karl bristled when Mike Masaoka of the JACL give one of the only in-person testimonies from a Japanese American. Masaoka first asserted that the JACL would comply fully in an evacuation of Japanese from the West Coast if such a removal was a military necessity, but if it was the result of "political or other pressure groups" with "motives of self-interest," Masaoka claimed, "we feel that we have every right to protest and to demand equitable judgment on our merits as American citizens."

Karl didn't disagree with this part of the JACL's stance or their demand that they be considered national leaders among the Nisei, since they attracted members from across the country. That was "fine for openers," he felt, but Masaoka followed his preliminary statements by folding under an "onslaught of pitiless, probing questions" from congressmen. "And little wonder, for all that," Karl wrote; since their inception, the JACL had failed in what mattered most to the Yonedas. The organization had never uttered a word of protest against Japan's invasion of China or its members' donations of money and "comfort parcels" for soldiers in the Imperial Japanese Army. "Not one of its members has issued a statement declaring, 'We are bona fide loyal citizens, opposed to the Nazis and warlords,'" Karl wrote in dismay after hearing Masaoka speak.

Karl himself submitted a written statement on behalf of *Doho*, which was entered into the record on the February 23 and listed in the transcript as Exhibit 12. "[On] behalf of the Bay Area *Doho* readers," Karl's statement began, "I wish to state that we are and will cooperate with the United States Government to our fullest extent." *If* evacuation was deemed a military necessity, "we are ready to go," he explained, though orders should be clear, timely, and accurately communicated to prevent "unnecessary hardships."

The bulk of Karl's statement focused on moving the spotlight away from ethnicity and toward ideology. The blanket characterization "painting the entire Japanese race as pro-Japanese fascists is not true and needs some explanation in defense of those who have fought the Japanese militarist clique," he argued. He told the committee that since 1931, "the Japanese fascist-police have imprisoned more than 5,000 workers, farmers, students, and women for antiwar activities and an unknown number have been executed." And perhaps most importantly, this same passionate dedication to fighting fascism "holds true among Japanese in America." Karl closed by vowing, "Our loyalty is first and foremost to the United States and its democratic principles and we are willing to make any sacrifice necessary to safeguard this country."

In a more prominent spot in the hearing transcript than Karl's testimony was Exhibit 2, submitted by the California Department of the American Legion. It was titled "Resolution Urging the Evacuation and Concentration of All Japanese and Their Descendants to a Concentration Camp Under Supervision of the Federal Government."

As the Tolan Committee hearings moved from San Francisco to Seattle and then on to Los Angeles in early March, questions arose about persuading the West Coast Japanese American community to move inland of their own accord. On February 27 in Seattle, Idaho Governor Chase Clark gave an answer: Japanese would be welcome in his state only if they were in "concentration camps under military guard." Committee head John Tolan admitted on March 2 that he had polled fourteen other governors of inland states. "Nine replied, in effect: 'No Japanese wanted—except in concentration camps.'"

But the turning point for Elaine and Karl had already come with the hearings in their city. "We had a sense it was an accomplished fact," Elaine remembered later, and all the testimony and discussion were "just window dressing." Just before the Tolan Committee hearings opened for their next segment in Seattle, the *San Francisco Examiner* ran a front-page headline: OUSTER OF ALL JAPS IN CALIFORNIA NEAR. The communist and leftist press across the entire country continued to remain virtually silent on the topic.

By early March, calls in Congress began for stripping Japanese Americans of citizenship. Mississippi congressman John Rankin read a letter on the House floor from a constituent proposing that after imprisoning Japanese Americans in concentration camps, "we must insist on keeping the sexes separate, or they will use this internment time as an Incubating period."

On March 6 Tom Mooney died, and on March 8, at his funeral, Karl began his own series of goodbyes. Standing with Elaine among the five thousand mourners who'd crowded San Francisco's Civic Auditorium, Karl was proud to be named an honorary pallbearer, along with various national luminaries. He remembered the day a few months earlier when he'd visited the man once known as "the country's most famous prisoner." In November, the Yonedas had taken Tommy to see his namesake at St. Luke's Hospital. Mooney had given Tommy a little trinket, and the boy clutched it with two chubby fists. To Karl and Elaine, he gave advice. Gripping their hands tightly, and with a voice faint but firm, Mooney had told them, "Wherever you go will be the battlefield." He peered at them through thick, round glasses and then left them with an admonishment to fight fascism always. "Until the day of emancipation," he said.

The week after Mooney's death, a large article appeared in *People's World*. KARL YONEDA SAYS FAREWELL, read the headline. NISEI LABOR CHIEF IN PARTING PLEDGE TO BROTHER UNIONISTS. Above the article floated a picture of Karl, Elaine, and Tommy at St. Luke's Hospital. THE YOUNGSTER WAS NAMED TOM MOONEY, read the caption above the photo, his original middle name, Culbert, now replaced.

"With a friendly smile and warm expression of solidarity, Karl Yoneda bids goodbye to the fellows on the San Francisco Waterfront," the article began. "Hit by the blanket evacuation order which will move 90,000 California Japanese to inland settlements, Karl and his wife and children must leave their home and friends for a new and probably harder life."

People's World then quoted Karl on his oft-repeated themes: not all Japanese were the enemy, "a majority stand for honest principles and are as opposed to Japanese imperialism as you are," and the war was one of ideology, not race. But Karl had clearly been swayed by the news reports of fifth columnists, by claims from progressives like Walter Lippmann that saboteurs were everywhere, hunched and waiting to pounce, and by the general leftist attitude that the only fight that mattered now was the one against the Axis. "We know that there are fifth columnists among us," the paper quoted him, "and that this is the only sure way to protect us all from treachery." As for his own "evacuation," Karl admitted, "I won't say I like it, because I don't. But I understand why it is necessary and am doing everything I can to cooperate in the move." As a whole, the article would stand as the first public trace of Karl's tortured effort to mesh loyalty to antifascism and his ideological community, with deep dismay over the mass exile and incarceration of his own ethnic group.

Two days later, on March 14, 1942, the government officially announced the formation of the Wartime Civil Control Administration (WCCA), a joint army-civilian unit to manage the removal of all Japanese aliens and citizens from the entire West Coast, with Karl R. Bendetsen as its leader. On March 16, Elaine's own wartime diary bore its first, terse entry: "Leaving SF. Things stored. Where to?"

That week, Karl Yoneda learned that a new camp being built for Los Angeles's Japanese Americans—Manzanar—would be accepting volunteers before the mass removal began. He and Elaine discussed the news. They agreed the status quo looked grim: there was no foreseeable chance of Karl returning to work on the waterfront anywhere along the coast, nor of being accepted into the army. If he could go to a camp near L.A., and Elaine and the children could stay with the Buchmans, they'd be close enough to visit, if allowed. "I've decided to go to this camp and help convert it into a comfortable living space for the later arrivals," Karl wrote that night. "My wife has agreed," he added, and the "decision made."

In preparation for their departure, the Yonedas attended a farewell party in their honor at a house overlooking the coastal cliffs. Among almost two-dozen comrades and like-minded friends, Elaine and Karl shared a toast to victory and gathering together again sometime, whenever the long and uncertain war concluded. As night fell, Karl stared out at the Pacific and watched the ocean spool, dark and shifting, one relentless current stretching toward Japan.

Two days later, the Yonedas left San Francisco for Los Angeles. Mollie and Nathan agreed that Elaine and the children should move in with them while Karl went to Manzanar. Elaine could find a job supporting the war effort, the Buchmans could watch the children while she was at work, and Joyce would be near enough to Las Vegas to see Ed, as the divorce stipulated. After storing whatever belongings they could with friends, the Yonedas loaded themselves in the Studebaker and headed south. As Japantown and the Fillmore receded in the distance, news broke of yet another tragedy from a location their family had left behind, a place they'd escaped but whose brutality Elaine and Karl feared might someday soon reach them again. That day, the United Press reported that the Nazis had already executed eighty-six thousand Jews in the region of Minsk, near Mozyr. One hundred murdered Jews came from Mozyr proper, where the Germans forced women and children to dig holes in the ice before pushing them under. The Nazis would then liquidate an entire orphanage, burying the children alive, though these details were ones the Yonedas would not hear of until well after Karl had left for Manzanar.

After arriving at the Buchmans' home in Boyle Heights, Karl went to the Maryknoll Japanese Catholic Center on Hewitt Street, a blanched-stone building with a red Spanish-tile roof and likely a statue of a white, weeping Mary somewhere. Later, Karl recalled a priest describing Manzanar as a "reception center" on six thousand acres of federal land, destined for "large-scale co-op plantations." According to the army, all possessions and assets left behind would be safeguarded. Then the father confirmed what most persuaded Karl to go to Manzanar early, particularly since he felt sure they'd all be taken sooner or later: wages for the volunteers "would be on par with local rates" and their families would be the last ones ordered off the coast. If Karl returned in five days for an information session, a Maryknoll priest would provide final instructions for departure.

Before the five days had elapsed, on March 19 congressional delegate Samuel King of Hawaii announced in Washington, DC, "upon consultation with Honolulu's Chief of Police" and "heads of Army and Navy Intelligence," no sabotage had been detected during or after the bombing of Pearl Harbor. Few papers across the country even bothered to report King's announcement, and neither Karl nor Elaine mentioned having heard the news at all.

The night of March 22, Karl wrote of a "simple dinner" with his family, "probably our last meal together for some time." He turned in at midnight, hoping to rest for the long journey ahead.

PART II

THE RUPTURE

Manzanar, June 1942. *Photo by Dorothea Lange, courtesy of the National Archives and Records Administration*

4 DIVIDED
Spring 1942

AT 6:45 AM ON APRIL 1, Elaine and Tommy arrived at the train station near Santa Fe Avenue and Second Street to await their own transport to Manzanar. As on the morning a week earlier when Karl had left, the area was surrounded by soldiers. Approximately one hundred were stationed there, some with leather-holstered guns and black military-police armbands, others with long rifles held tight against their torsos. They stood amid a crowd of about four hundred, many of the women in styled curls and formal coats and the men in hats, as if attired for a very different scene than the one they found that morning. One older woman clutched a bundle wrapped in a soldier's coat, fixed with her son's US Army badge. "A special train" had been prepared, officials told the media, though none of its passengers knew what that might mean. The cars lined the track, eleven in total, the area beside them packed with bodies and stuffed bags, the air with sweat and uncertainty.

Some of the children—the only ones who seemed completely unconcerned—were running with excitement. Tommy too was bouncing in anticipation, repeating, "I'm going to see my daddy again!" He wore a sailor suit with white stripes along the collar, a warmer coat over it, and a tag stamped 00152. Elaine wore her brown paper strip with the same number; each member of every family had been instructed to attach an army-issued matching numbered tag somewhere on their person. These were affixed to the buttons of toddlers in training shoes, pinned to women holding infants, or in the case of one elderly man with dark glasses and a

Leaving Los Angeles for Manzanar on the same transport as Elaine and Tommy, April 1, 1942. *Photo by Clem Albers, courtesy of the Online Archive of California, War Relocation Authority Photographs of Japanese-American Evacuation and Resettlement*

walking stick, hung around his neck, dangling there as he was guided up the train stairs.

When the soldiers lined up by the steps of each car, Elaine knew it was time to board. She tried not to cry or think about how or when she'd see her parents and daughter again, or their friends and home. Eventually, she felt the long, dark row of cars begin moving down the track. Tommy leaned out the window and waved a white handkerchief, still excited about seeing his father. As smoke boiled and rose above the train's back end, the cars picked up speed. Behind Elaine, Los Angeles faded, and along with it, the world she thought she'd known.

Had she stayed in the city with her parents, she would have seen the headlines that day. They were reporting a new congressional statement. According to John E. Rankin of Mississippi, "all Japanese, alien or native born, should be taken into custody immediately and deported to the Orient after the war."

Tommy on the train to Manzanar, waving goodbye. *Courtesy of Karl G. Yoneda Papers, UCLA Library Special Collections*

As Elaine and Tommy traveled north into the desert, their train passed through stretches of pale scrub, black lava, and cracked alkali lake beds, bronze mountains lacing the horizon. While day ticked into evening, Elaine and the other passengers sat in thinly cushioned seats, girded by hard, dark armrests on one side and scratched windowsills on the other. They switched from the train to a caravan of buses at a town called Lone Pine, about ten miles south of their final destination. Elaine and Tommy sat at the back, carrying two small suitcases and a bag of toys. By dusk, they arrived at Manzanar. As the bus rocked over rough terrain, Elaine could see from the window that the camp was still being built. Given a full view of Manzanar's unfinished entryway, she'd have also seen soldiers with long rifles standing near a sign stuck in the dirt, SAFETY ALWAYS written across it in large, cursive loops.

Pulling in, the procession sent up thick clouds of dust. By this time, Elaine had read Karl's message about the poor conditions. "Letter from Karl," she'd written the day before in her diary. "Conditions not so good—but the decree!" Still, she'd been unprepared for what she encountered: tar-paper barracks going up across a desert landscape stretching for miles; barren trees reaching like claws from the dust; tall, thin electric poles spaced evenly throughout the grounds, their upper beams hanging in dark crosses against the sky. Along one stretch of barracks ran a sewer ditch. Up above stood high wooden watchtowers, topped with searchlights and armed men.

As they passed through the guarded entry and alongside the barbed wire, she finally understood. They were all prisoners now.

———————

Karl Yoneda had woken the morning of April 1, 1942, in Manzanar to start a new job as foreman of a fifteen-man team of yard sweepers. Few if any of his crew were enthusiastic about the work, given that a week earlier they'd been asked (tricked, most felt) to "volunteer" their labor. Karl had heard that their eventual wages might match those of the Depression-era Work Progress Administration program, roughly the equivalent of a raw army recruit. At best, this would yield payment well below market levels. "That's pretty pathetic," he wrote in his diary, but since he'd volunteered for enlistment before coming to camp, he supposed he couldn't complain. Most of those around Karl lacked his equanimity, particularly without any guarantee they'd ever be compensated.

But by that morning, the weather had finally cleared, and Karl and his crew worked the ground. While they labored, the men talked—mostly about Japan, Karl complained later. He had no interest in that topic, feeling keenly the lack of a leftist community in camp to share his political concerns.

Sometime before night fell, he wrote to *People's World*. JAPANESE UNIONIST WRITES FRIENDS, the paper's editors titled the missive when they published it later that week. "Finally I arrived at Owens Valley last Monday night with 916 others," Karl explained. "I find the climate very agreeable. Right now we are busy in helping to clean up the grounds, and wages are the same as WPA scales." Neither Karl nor the *People's World* editors made further mention of the conditions of Karl's absence: to prepare for the forced removal of the entire West Coast Japanese American community.

The letter, though brief and straightforward, reveals the devil's bargain Karl had accepted, only to see its terms becoming ever steeper. To prove Karl still valued the Left's struggle against Axis aggression above all, to continue to be heard and included in his ideological community, he'd have to downplay what it cost him personally, while ignoring the injustice thrust upon his ethnic group in the name of fighting fascism. It was an injustice whose real dimensions were becoming ever starker as the truth of their incarceration became clearer. But still, Karl signed off simply: "Yours for victory—Karl Yoneda, Owens Valley, Calif."

———————

Sometime during that day of April 1, the first incarcerees arrived in Manzanar who had not volunteered to go early but been ordered there. They were a group of almost two hundred from Bainbridge Island, Washington, the first community to be transported en masse to a camp. By that evening, Karl heard that other new arrivals were on their way too, five hundred or so of them. No one knew exactly who would arrive, but Karl joined a group of men to assist with luggage. Looking toward the entry gate, he saw a long convoy of buses rumbling forward in a tight row, billowing sand and grit.

The buses pulled inside the barbed-wire boundary, then slowed to a stop. Suddenly, the men realized they knew the faces staring out at them from behind the glass, metal, and grime. They belonged to their families. As shock gave way to chaos, Karl recognized a voice he knew. "Daddy! Daddy!" He looked toward the back of the convoy. Behind one window, he saw his own wife, and next to her, his son—his face small, his expression pure elation.

From inside the bus, Elaine watched Karl as his recognition dawned. As he stared at the long line of vehicles, then locked his eyes on theirs, his cheeks drained of color. Tommy stuck his head out of the window and yelled "Daddy!" again, as if his own excitement were too much to contain sitting down. Karl moved toward them, his face ashen. More ashen than she'd ever in her whole life seen it, Elaine thought.

Then Tommy and Elaine had disembarked, and Karl was there in front of them, and he was yelling. "What are you doing here?" He'd told her not to come, to *stay away.* "Are you bringing our son to be killed?" he bellowed. Tommy had begun jumping up and down, hugging Karl, resuming his refrain: "Daddy! Daddy!"

Later, Karl would remember how he felt, standing there in the dirt, his wife and son finally with him: thankfully, horribly, behind barbed wire and near enough to hold. It seemed like his insides were boiling, seething with a mixture of euphoria and dread.

For her part, Elaine stood before her husband and stayed uncharacteristically silent, at least for a beat or two. Then she took out the copy of their evacuation order and handed it to him. As Karl read the mandate, she explained how she hadn't seen his letter until *after* she'd been ordered to register Tommy for removal to Manzanar, how they'd tried to stop her from coming too—had tried to take their child and keep her from both her husband and her son.

Karl should have known there was no stopping Elaine anyway. He was both surprised and not surprised that she'd browbeaten the army into putting her on the train to Manzanar as well. And anyway, as for his own orders to her to stay away, "I said I'd love and cherish you, but not obey you," Elaine shot back at him. As if he'd had any doubt.

Karl felt despair again when he thought of how baldly his government, whose battle he burned to support somehow, had once again discarded a sacred pledge. They'd promised that the families of Manzanar's first volunteers would be the last forcibly removed. Now here were Elaine and Tommy, fresh off one of the first mandated trains to Manzanar.

But Karl also felt another realization spread through him, tightening his throat: of the bottomless depths of Elaine's love for him and Tommy, in her willingness, her *fight* to come to Manzanar with them. Then he and Elaine both fell silent, and holding each other at last, together they wept.

Later, the Yonedas received their temporary housing assignment in a twenty-by-twenty-five-foot barrack with a pair of strangers and walls punctured by knotholes. They were given three army-style blankets and three mattress "tuckings," which they were directed to fill with straw from a giant pile outside. They pushed their cots into one corner of their room, away from the others, though without any partitions, they still had no privacy. Elaine complained immediately about the straw, given Tommy's allergies, but their only option was to take two extra blankets and double them up for a substitute mattress. Exhausted, she managed only a few words in her dairy before she fell asleep, noting the dark beauty of the desert at night, but seemingly too tired for full sentences: "Valley beautiful full moon majestic Mt Whitney in background."

When they woke early the next morning, the less lovely aspects of Manzanar came sharply into view. The entire camp still lacked hot water, and most barracks had only one cold-water faucet, rising out of the dirt at one end of the building. In the frigid morning air, the water failed to run anyway. Portable toilets—a few for every three hundred or so incarcerees—occupied the other end: small, single-seat privies placed between blocks and hoisted onto sleds, then dragged by a truck back and forth between barracks. Periodically, the sled would be pulled to the sewer ditch for emptying, a gully two feet wide and four feet deep, running alongside five sets of barracks.

Manzanar on April 2, 1942. *Photo by Clem Albers, courtesy of the Library of Congress Prints and Photographs Division, Farm Security Administration, Office of War Information Photograph Collection*

Years later, Taira Fukushima, who'd arrived with Elaine and Tommy, would describe waking on that freezing morning of April 2 to a clear view of the camp's conditions, miles of desert scrub, and the breathtaking rise of mountains beyond. Near his barrack, Fukushima glimpsed a single apple tree in full white bloom, its beauty stark and bright against the dusty plain. "I never saw anything like that," he recalled in an interview. "That was the first time I saw something so beautiful," he said, and then he began to cry.

That afternoon, the Yonedas moved into their more permanent "apartment," a barrack where they were soon joined by overflow from the neighboring family, named Nishimura. Block 4, building 2, apartment 2, occupied the same dimensions as the Yonedas' first barrack. Once again, the space lacked partitions or privacy. It held only five old army cots, one oil heater, and a single bulb hanging from a wire. Bedding consisted of straw mattresses, two army blankets per cot, and no sheets. The two other cots were occupied by their new Nishimura bunkmates: fifteen-year-old George and his seventy-five-year-old grandfather, Chotaro, whom Karl and Elaine described as blind and afflicted with sore-covered legs, which he scratched loudly all night. The Nishimura family was no more pleased. Over eighty years later, Donald Nishimura, who was only eleven when his family was split between the Yonedas' barrack room and the one next door, could still remember how his father disliked Karl. "He's a communist!" he recalled his father, Mokutaru, saying in alarm.

Still, the Yonedas and their neighbors were more fortunate than many. Housing would continue to pose a problem throughout the early months of camp, with some husbands and wives bunked separately and occasionally wives housed alone with unknown men. Others were placed in barracks without doors, windows, or roofs. As these incarcerees settled uncomfortably into their new homes, mourning the forced dispatch of their former ones, others in the Yonedas' old San Francisco neighborhood were preparing to be sent to Santa Anita Assembly Center, where they would be placed in horse stalls, sleeping in the stench of equine urine. ("Only four days had elapsed between the removal of the horses and the arrival of the first Japanese-Americans," one historian noted later. "The only facilities for bathing were the horse showers.")

By afternoon on April 2, the water faucets had thawed and Manzanar's incarcerees could finally rinse their mouths and wash their hands. But a storm had kicked up, sending rough chunks of dirt and sand whipping through the air. By 4:00 PM the atmosphere was "choked," Karl wrote. Elaine couldn't even keep her eyes open when she went outside, and she wondered if this was what it had felt like to be a dust bowler. They began to worry in earnest when Tommy started wheezing. As the wind howled until the sky turned black, Elaine and Karl sat in their new barrack, listening to Tommy's raspy breath and waiting for the storm to pass.

———————

Meanwhile, almost a thousand new prisoners arrived from Los Angeles. They'd first been taken by train to Lone Pine, as Elaine and Tommy had been. There, they found a half-dozen curious townspeople, a handful of local reporters, and a slew of military police, armed as usual with rifles and submachine guns. Buses waited to take the group the remaining ten miles or so to camp; they were marked with destination signboards reading SPECIAL above their windshields. As the convoy headed north to camp, it juddered over the uneven ground. The passengers stared out into gritty darkness, missing what they'd lost and wondering what awaited. As historians four decades later would put it, along with the few personal items they'd been allowed to bring, each traveler carried "a personal burden of rage or resignation or despair to the assembly centers and camps which the government had hastily built to protect 130 million Americans against 60,000 of their fellow citizens and their resident alien parents."

Many arrived at Manzanar terrified. Rumors outside had spread almost as breathlessly as those Karl had been hearing inside. Some showed up for the transport to camp fearing they'd be "concentrated in a narrow valley between two mountains" under an air route, bound to be bombed if Japan attacked. Others had heard that the government was planning to release a reservoir near Owens Valley "and drown us all." Looking back, one woman remembered arriving "convinced they were brought there to be shot," or else to "be worked to death." Another said, "People expected to get killed; I expected to die" there.

On one of the buses that night sat Karl's close friend and leftist comrade, Koji Ariyoshi. Passing through the camp's boundary, Ariyoshi turned around and looked into the darkness behind, and he realized that the world they'd known was now gone. "We cannot go back," said the man sitting next to him. "We are locked up."

Later, Ariyoshi lay on his straw mattress and watched the searchlights from the sentry tower sweeping over camp. He thought they looked like fingers probing into each dark and barren window. In a barrack nearby, Tommy still struggled for air, and Elaine burned with fever from her camp-mandated typhoid vaccine. When the sun rose the next morning, it shone weakly through a scrim of dust. The Yonedas, Ariyoshi, and the two thousand incarcerees now in Manzanar found silt across their beds, blanketing the floor and walls, and sprinkled through their hair. A few unlucky ones who'd slept with lips parted woke to sand-coated teeth. But as the day went on, Karl Yoneda felt relieved. Tommy was still breathing, and upon learning that Koji had arrived with a handful of sailor friends and leftist sympathizers, Karl felt like he had "a hundred new allies" in camp.

The following morning, April 4, Elaine woke tired but somewhat better, and Tommy was improving. His lungs finally clearing, he found himself surrounded by hundreds of other Japanese American children, a marked difference from the months of post–Pearl Harbor isolation. He'd suddenly become part of an immediate community, a new world that could seem, to a three-year-old, strange yet intriguing. "Still feel groggy," Elaine wrote that day in her diary, but "Tommy having a wonderful time."

At some point on the fourth, two sergeants from army intelligence called Karl to the administration building. They questioned him about his communist sympathies and comrades in Manzanar. Karl wrote later that he gave "no names" but assured them that the leftists in camp were actively participating in the struggle against the Axis and wanted to enlist as soon as the army would take them. They would do anything for the war effort, he said. They would "bring the message of democracy" to all those in Manzanar and help build a camp with reasonable living conditions. The majority of the camp's inhabitants were loyal to the United States, Karl insisted. The sergeants thanked and dismissed him. Then Manzanar police arranged an informer to keep close watch over Karl, given his communist sympathies and, in the words of Chief of Police Kenneth Horton, his "Russian" Jewish wife.

By the next morning, Tommy's symptoms had passed, though his reprieve would prove temporary; Elaine had recovered fully from her fever; and Manzanar had grown to approximately three thousand imprisoned people. Still, the Yonedas found moments of joy and even beauty in these early days together. Despite the frigid wind racing in icy drafts down the mountains, Elaine and

Karl noticed a few trees with new blooms along their crooked limbs. When it rained, the Yonedas could see high peaks in the distance, rising through a curtain of mist. The scene appeared like a picture on a scroll, Karl thought, the Sierras draped in clean white snow. On Easter Sunday, the incarcerees were treated to a movie projected outside, though they had to watch from the ground, and they'd organized Manzanar's first baseball match, dividing the teams by the hometowns they'd left behind.

Two days later, a package arrived from Elaine's parents, filled with pots, dishes, and a hotplate; they'd already sent sheets and a wire so the Yonedas could hang a makeshift partition between their own beds and the Nishimuras'. Elaine felt again their unique good fortune at having family who were free and white, who could send them what they needed and provide moral and financial support from the outside. Meanwhile, Karl foraged for lumber and began building shelves, a chest, and a table, using empty nail kegs for chairs. Elaine cooked a modest dinner on the hotplate, and the family of three ate all together, finally alone. "Despite [the] dust," she wrote that week, "we are happy we have come to Manzanar." She made no mention of Joyce, the daughter she had left behind.

———————

Outside Manzanar's barbed wire, headlines continued to worsen. Elaine and Karl had access to much of it. The camp canteen sold a few L.A. papers, mostly from the conservative Hearst company: the *Los Angeles Times*, the *Los Angeles Examiner*, and the *Los Angeles Herald-Express*. Since April 2, Karl had been receiving the Communist daily *People's World*, to which he'd subscribed, along with the *San Francisco Chronicle*. On April 8, the Yonedas learned that state governors across the Midwest had passed anti-Japanese resolutions to bar all "evacuees" from their states. In Inyo County, surrounding Manzanar, the board of supervisors approved a resolution "opposing the release of any incarcerees from the Manzanar detention camp for any reason," which was followed up by a petition, apparently signed by several thousand area residents, that "the Japanese would be kept in the Relocation Area or be buried in the local cemetery." (Though the board of supervisors declined to hold an official vote on the latter, a year later they passed another resolution urging Congress to ensure "that all Japanese, both alien and native born, be forever prohibited from becoming citizens of the United States of America.")

In global news, *People's World*'s pages convulsed with Axis atrocities, culminating in a chilling warning for Jewish families everywhere—even, or especially, a leftist one in a Japanese American concentration camp. The paper reported Nazis throwing children from high windows, bayonetting babies, and dragging young girls to brothels. They described mass executions and the "Far Eastern form of fascism," crowding Japanese "thought prisoners" into cells, including one inmate who spent "two months on his knees in a three-foot-high" concrete box.

On April 16, *People's World* printed a story addressed to Jews the world over, spanning almost a full page. The article described Nazi "special concentration camps," "wholesale slaughter," and a "fresh systematic campaign for the annihilation of the Jews" in occupied countries. It detailed hundreds of thousands of Jews tortured to death and fifty thousand more killed in Kiev, part of the Pale region the Buchmans had once fled—many of whom, children included, were forced to dig their own graves. At bottom came a warning: THE WAR SPREADS, not just through Europe but to other continents, as well. "If there are Jews anywhere who entertain the hope that their wealth or privileged social, political position may save them from the horrors of fascism, they are cruelly mistaken."

As these headlines arrived in Manzanar, its landscape afforded little comfort or distraction. In early spring, the wind slammed through the valley, glacier cold. It moved the sand like a "thick brown wall," in the words of Karl's friend Koji, forcing incarcerees to cover their faces against hurling chunks of dirt and sand. The Yonedas tried tirelessly to keep their barrack clean of dust, but Tommy remained ill off and on. Other mothers would wrap their infants' heads in blankets while they waited in endless lines for the latrines or mess halls. Still, the wind sent a brown scum over the food, the furniture, even the babies' milk.

But if anyone inside Manzanar thought about complaining too loudly—or actually trying to leave—they could look through the rough-hewn windows and up into the guard towers. These were manned night and day by armed military police. Sometimes, incarcerees could see them standing in pairs, one at each front corner of a square wooden frame around the tower's top, leather helmet straps secured under their chins. One photo caught them with their long guns straight up, their heads raised high, rifle butts against the ground. They grasped the gun barrels in both hands, bayonets rising up until the steel points almost pierced the soldiers' helmets. Between the two, pointing out, appeared the thick metal thrust of a floor-mounted machine gun.

Manzanar's military-police battalion was impressively armed—six machine guns, twenty-one submachine guns, and over a hundred other shotguns and rifles—but from the very first days of the camp's existence, the MPs disliked their jobs. According to their lieutenant, they had "been trained and educated to kill Japs, and here they're supposed to protect them." Now, they were stuck in wooden guard towers, and they were bored.

Their orders included shooting anyone who tried to leave the camp without authorization or failed to halt. Later, an interviewer asked a lieutenant what would happen "if a guard ordered a Japanese who was out of bounds to halt and the Jap did not do so." Would the sentry actually fire? The lieutenant said he "only hoped the guard would ask him to halt," because "nothing would suit them better than to have a little excitement, such as shooting a Jap."

All the while, above the guards and guns and towers, the Sierras waited. Afternoons when the weather cleared, they cast their shadow over the valley. Standing in their shade, Koji Ariyoshi looked around camp and sensed depression spreading in the gloom. Sometimes on overcast days, far above the horizon, the clouds would open for a moment and the mountain's sharp peaks would appear as if floating disembodied, looming over camp like a cragged slice of heaven in a broken chunk of sky.

On April 11, Manzanar's newspaper published its first issue. Though named the *Manzanar Free Press* and written by incarcerees, the paper was censored by the administration. As one of its editors would later admit, "There were no personal views. . . . We did not write about what was happening to us, the poor food, the poor medical care, the lack of privacy, having to take showers together." Had they written about such things, "it wouldn't get in the paper." Nonetheless, *Free Press* articles, camp administrators, and even the outside media hailed the paper's democratic symbolism. The first issue addressed General DeWitt and the evacuation plan he and Bendetsen had deployed: "The citizens of Manzanar are sincerely grateful for the government's handling of the situation, and for the kind treatment we have received. Thank you, General!" Upon reading, even Karl Yoneda found it too ingratiating.

Hearing of the *Free Press* launch, *Los Angeles Daily News* amplified this jarring tone. "In spite of its modest size and humble beginning," they wrote, the *Manzanar Free Press* should be hailed as "one of the most important publications in the nation," an "influence for democracy and Americanism among a group of people to whom the two words should by now be synonymous." *Free Press* editors wasted no time reprinting this commentary, though their next issue opened with a headline that began You Can't Leave Camp ("Under army orders, no Japanese may leave this camp, once he has come in from a restricted area.")

This tendency, not just to downplay the poor conditions and deep injustice of the camps but also to uphold them as symbols of decency and democracy, started with Karl Bendetsen and was widely embraced by the American press, particularly leftist papers like the ones the Yonedas received in Manzanar. Four days after Karl left Los Angeles for Manzanar, one of *People's World's* first articles on the removal of Japanese Americans began with the heading Aliens. The piece reported a March 26 order forbidding any person of Japanese descent to leave "Military Area 1," covering much of the West Coast, "except under orderly Army evacuation procedure." *People's World* quoted Karl Bendetsen's claim that the order's purpose was "partly to protect the Japanese." They neglected to mention the other part: keeping the community locked down in preparation for mass imprisonment.

As spring progressed and the Yonedas continued receiving *People's World* in camp, the paper became their one consistent tie to the leftist community outside. April 8's front-page article covered the removal of San Francisco's ethnic Japanese to the horse stalls of Santa Anita's racetrack. Japanese Wave Goodbye to S.F., ran the main headline, appearing under a picture of a little girl in a kimono, sleeves splayed like a butterfly. Kids Take It as a Picnic, said a subhead. The paper described "the evacuation" as efficient and civil, calling the military police "courteous and friendly," despite the "steel helmets and army revolvers gleaming in leather holsters." "The tag around the neck was a tough thing for some of the proud young American-Japanese to take," they conceded. "But no resentment showed itself. None of them liked it, except [one] kindly old man who 'had no sense.'" (No Sense, ran the header above.)

"But they were all glad to cooperate and do their part. They seemed to understand why it was necessary. That is, all except the really old people, who were pained and bewildered."

Amid the media's skewed messaging, Tommy's precarious health, and the war's worsening news, the Yonedas turned to what had always fueled them: activism and agitation. They were undoubtably strengthened by benefits inaccessible to most other incarcerees: family free and on the outside, years of experience being disillusioned and even jailed in their own country, and the privilege of Elaine's whiteness. From their very first days in Owens Valley, neither Yoneda hesitated to challenge administrators about problems within camp.

During April's second week, the portable privies were replaced by more permanent latrines, consisting of two back-to-back rows of five toilet bowls spaced a few inches apart—one set for each block of 350 people or so. The toilets lacked doors or even partitions between them, and the sheds' outer walls of green lumber gaped rudely, baring the latrines to outside view. To one side hung a row of naked shower heads, and to another, a long trough-like sink. When Elaine ventured to her block's facility, she found panicked women and teenaged girls, humiliated at the forced exposure.

Elaine marched herself like a one-woman battalion to the administration building, halfway across camp. There, she found Manzanar's director of service, a man named J. M. Kidwell. She amplified the four feet eleven inches of her body with her bullhorn voice; she assailed him over the latrines' "utter lack of privacy"; she banged her fist on his desk and admonished him over the absent doors, partitions, and shower curtains. There would be widespread "hysteria" among incarcerees, Elaine warned; maybe "even suicides." Later, she reported that Kidwell simply shrugged and said "Army specifications."

Elaine's assertiveness about camp conditions earned her the admiration of some incarcerees and dismay of others. Her loud, emphatic style clashed with traditional Japanese ideals of humility and decorum, particularly for women. Among a population whose heritage lauded harmony, belonging, and submitting the individual to the group, the Yonedas were conspicuous both for their ethnically mixed marriage and their demeanors. Koji Ariyoshi thought Elaine had arrived at Manzanar with a double strike against her: being white and being Jewish among a population who had been exposed to "incessant anti-Semitic propaganda" in both Japan and the United States.

Ariyoshi was impressed with Elaine's ability to win over many of the Issei and Nisei with her agitation for better conditions. But Karl knew that, as a couple, they bred resentment among others, that people questioned why he'd even brought his white wife with him into camp. He'd heard the complaints: Elaine had the right to stay free, so why would she agree to enter Manzanar and then make a fuss? He imagined them thinking of her as a kind of sore thumb, jutting out where she didn't belong.

Elaine was similarly aware of how they stood out. She felt it most strongly in the stares as she and Karl went about their daily lives, particularly when they shared household duties. In a cultural tradition where housework was the exclusive domain of women, Karl made a point of bucking the trend. For laundry days, he'd arrange to have the same day off from work as she did. He'd hoist Tommy on his shoulders and carry both his son and his family's washing across the block. Then, he would bend over the tub holding *Elaine*'s clothes and start scrubbing, as if insisting, in his wife's words, "It doesn't make less of a man out of you if you're helping equally." She sensed a bit of showmanship alongside Karl's heartfelt commitment to gender parity. "Karl was breaking down their custom by going with me," she said, and though she agreed with his politics, sometimes it made her "a little bit uptight."

Like anyone with intimate knowledge of Japanese culture, the Yonedas would have been familiar with the old adage about the hammer and the stake: the one that sticks up gets clubbed down. The proverb hinted at an expectation of conformity that, even in the camp's early days, the Yonedas sensed but did not abide. As historian Arthur Hansen put it, Karl in particular was seen as "a quintessential deviant," "representative of all those characteristics the subculture abhorred." Incarceree Togo Tanaka explained how the Yonedas' outspoken politics would have only made their deviance more apparent. "Among the Japanese community, to be an 'Aka' (Red)"—that is, a Communist—"was a complete and utter brush-off of anyone," he wrote the following winter. "You just didn't belong and that was that." Yet despite Elaine's occasional self-consciousness, neither Yoneda seemed overly concerned with their visibility, at least not during their first weeks at Manzanar.

Three days after Elaine confronted Kidwell, Karl took an even more visible position. He eagerly accepted nomination for block leader in their group of barracks, block 4. As a Kibei-Nisei, his ease with both Japanese and English enabled him to communicate with administrators and those Issei who were not bilingual, and his past labor leadership gave him experience speaking publicly and coordinating a group. Likely, these attributes, combined with his early arrival at camp, contributed to his nomination despite his growing reputation as an outlier.

Elaine either witnessed or participated in the nighttime vote, which Karl noted drew fifty-three people, three of whom were women, and all of whom braved a howling sandstorm to attend. According to Elaine, block 4 was dominated by Issei, who indicated their votes by applause. Elaine thought those who didn't speak Japanese failed to realize why the elders were clapping. Offering a slightly different reading, Karl claimed the nominees were "selected (amidst applause)." Either way, Elaine interpreted it as a "lesson in democratic procedure for many."

Together, the Yonedas submitted two proposals that week to camp administrators: a US flag should be raised at both the post office and administration building, and collection sites should be established for materials useful in war production, such as metal foil. They were heartened two days later, amid what Elaine thought was the worst storm yet that season, when a flag raising ceremony took place. As the stars and stripes were hoisted high, the wind's ferocity seemed momentarily to subside. In the lull, Tommy stood among the older men and boys and saluted like a tiny soldier. "It was good to stand at attention and see Old Glory waving!" wrote Elaine.

After Manzanar's white administrators interviewed all nominees for block leader, they selected Karl as temporary head of block 4, representing its 350 inhabitants. A general election would be held sometime later, when the facility neared capacity and all the barracks had been built and occupied. Karl was also appointed to a five-member constitution and bylaws committee for Manzanar at large. He was told that his role was to "explain the office aims and policies to the residents," and to keep the administration "informed as to how those are received." This was, the officials explained, a movement toward democratic "self-government" for incarcerees; keeping the camp running smoothly was one way to contribute to the war effort, they told Karl. It was exactly what he needed to hear.

By mid-April, life in Manzanar had started to normalize in a surreal sort of way. Though Karl had found the *Free Press*'s initial issue too ingratiating, the paper's editorial staff leaned left, and Elaine took a volunteer position typing—though not writing—articles. Tommy started at a new nursery school that had been set up in the neighboring block, and on April 18, hot water was finally installed for showers and laundry. "Took first hot shower," Elaine wrote on April 19. "How good it felt!" That same day, the whole family attended a wedding in a block 9 barrack, Elaine noting the flowers ("real lilacs and purple irises"), a bouquet for the bride, and a wedding cake and iced tea. In the weeks to come, music and art classes, dances, and church services would also be established by incarcerees.

But the Yonedas were dogged at each turn by Tommy's allergies, asthma, and general vulnerability, and he frequently came down with fevers and vomiting. He'd lasted less than two hours at the new nursery school before being sent home sick, though whether from his recent typhoid shot or a case of the measles that were ripping through Manzanar, neither Elaine nor the incarceree doctors could tell. At block 9's makeshift wedding, Elaine followed her happy description of flowers and cake with worry about Tommy's deteriorating condition. By the next night, he was seriously ill, feverish and vomiting, leading all three of Manzanar's doctors to examine him. Elaine seemed so exhausted by caring for him that Karl felt like weeping when he looked at her. Yet instead of directing resentment toward the government detaining his son in a desert, Karl wondered if his family's misery was yet one more "spin-off" of "the sneak attack on Pearl Harbor."

Elaine's diary from that week suggests that her daughter, Joyce, had been unwell too. On the twenty-first, Elaine received a letter from her mother reporting that Joyce was "a little better." But the diary offers no other information. Whether Joyce had been physically ill or struggling emotionally with her mother's decision to leave her behind, the details have been lost to history. During her first months in Manzanar, Elaine wrote very little about Joyce. Elaine once explained that she'd begun her diary with an eye toward publicizing it later—when and if a reckoning for the mass incarcerations came to pass—so perhaps she hoped to protect her daughter's privacy. Or perhaps she simply wasn't thinking much about Joyce, at least not until months later, when her daughter's troubles became impossible to ignore.

As for her son's failing health that April, the camp's primitive medical facilities could do little. In Manzanar's first weeks, the only hospital comprised a single barrack lacking running water or sterilization tools, barely heated despite the frigid air. "It was so cold that mops had to be thawed in order that the hospital could be mopped," recalled the camp's head doctor, incarceree James Goto. He and his wife, who was also a physician, lived in a barrack room with three other couples who were strangers. Like the Yonedas, they had only sheets for privacy, hung on wires across the room.

On April 13, the hospital moved into larger quarters in a barrack with ten beds and running water, though the water supply across camp was soon found to be contaminated by *E. coli* and mountain runoff. "Immediately," Dr. Goto said, "the total number of patients in the hospital rose to 150. . . . [But] we had only ten urinals and ten bed pans," and when nurses washed their hands between patients, they went outside to an open spigot. In the words of an investigator who visited in June, "the improvised and primitive hospital facilities in the camp were deplorable." (In July 1942, a more permanent hospital facility would open, with 250 beds, rooms for performing operations, a pharmacy, dental and eye clinic, and morgue.)

While Elaine and Karl worried over Tommy, headlines about the war continued to worsen. CRISIS IN FRANCE: GERMANS ESTABLISH PUPPET GOVERNMENT AT VICHY, Karl copied into his diary toward April's end. JAPS ATTACK CALIFORNIA COAST!; AUSTRALIA FACES INVASION RISK. On April 28, President Roosevelt delivered one of his "fireside chats," which the papers headlined WORK, GRIEF, BLOOD: THAT IS THE PRICE WE MUST PAY FOR VICTORY. Karl transcribed part of Roosevelt's treatise in his dairy the next day. FDR fashioned the battle as "a total war," with "one front and one battle where everyone in the United States—every man, woman, and child—is in action, and will be privileged to remain in action throughout this war." The president emphasized that, for loyal Americans, "that front is right here at home, in our daily lives, in our daily tasks. Here at home everyone will have the privilege of making whatever self-denial is necessary," he claimed, and "the price for civilization must be paid in hard work and sorrow and blood."

Manzanar barracks. *Courtesy of the Nagatomi Collection, Manzanar National Historic Site*

Soon after, the Yonedas received a letter from a friend on the outside who'd listened to FDR's fireside chat herself. She wrote to ask, "Did you hear the President's rousing speech last night? He minced no words in his call for the entire nation to pull together in winning the war." She added, "I believe that all of you at Manzanar are making sacrifices towards that same goal."

Late that April, Karl Bendetsen and John DeWitt arrived at Manzanar. The *Free Press* covered the story, calling DeWitt a "most distinguished camp visitor." Along with Bendetsen and four other military men, the general completed a "flying tour" above the property, then made a short stop on ground, viewing the barrack living quarters, a mess hall and latrine, and the rudimentary hospital. Their inspection was followed by a "quick conference with camp officials," after which the army men returned to the nearby airfield, where they took off by 10:30 AM. If they met and spoke with any residents during their brief stay, the paper declined to mention so. Karl Yoneda wrote that they "left promptly after a single tour of the grounds."

Had they inspected the entire camp, DeWitt and Bendetsen would have seen about five hundred wooden barracks placed within one square mile, which had gone up "at the rate of two an hour," according to the *Free Press*. The barracks were grouped into thirty-six blocks—each with its own mess hall, laundry facilities, and latrines. By Bendetsen and DeWitt's visit, the facility held about thirty-three hundred incarcerees, some six hundred of whom were younger than fifteen, including almost one hundred infants ages two and younger—altogether what the *Free Press* termed the "blueprints for a busy, contented community."

The general and colonel might have also seen the living quarters for white administrators and staff: cream-colored barracks with painted interiors and private apartments, each with indoor showers and toilets, stoves, refrigerators, and the occasional air conditioner. Had they stayed for a meal, they might have also noticed that the Caucasian personnel ate in a mess hall with incarcerees, though as one Manzanar documentarian reported, the former were waited upon and ate steak dinners, "while across the aisles, evacuees ate beans."

In later months, the editors of the *Free Press* would tip their hand a bit, revealing the cost of their paper's forced cheerfulness. They admitted the

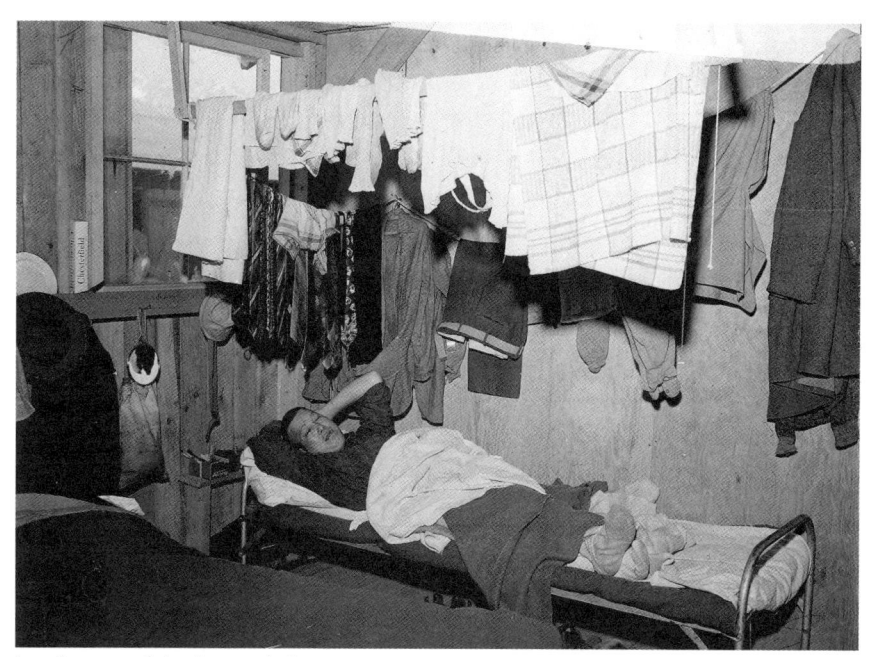

Inside one of the barrack "apartments." *Photo by Clem Albers, courtesy of the National Archives and Records Administration*

"dreaded" task of choosing between columns that provided solace and optimism and those that acknowledged the "cynical bitterness" life in Manzanar could inspire. For now though, while the camp was still taking shape, and with the administration's oversight surely in mind, the *Free Press* stuck faithfully to a near-suffocating exuberance.

The same issue that covered DeWitt and Bendetsen's visit also announced the arrival of three thousand additional incarcerees, or "newcomers," over the following three days, building toward the camp's peak population of ten thousand. These late-April arrivals came after a three week pause in new prisoners, during which workmen installed steps up to the barracks' entryways, windows, and washing facilities, promising a "cozier and cheerier welcome" than the first influx experienced. In a column titled "Howdy! Neighbor," the *Free Press* wrote, "You are stepping into a new venture in your life, accompanied by certain doubts and speculations. . . . You will undoubtably face some inconveniences." But, the paper went on to promise, "these misgivings will vanish as you are assimilated here and as many conveniences are installed. You will discover great adventure in our way of life."

Neither Yoneda recorded their reaction to the column, though on April 28, they both noted one thousand new arrivals, including four new families of mixed ethnicity. "Three Caucasian women married to Japanese men, and a Filipino man whose wife is Japanese," wrote Karl; Elaine mentioned "three more white women with families here."

Reality proved more daunting for the new incarcerees than the *Free Press* had described. That Sunday, Yuri Tateishi and her husband arrived from West Los Angeles with four of their children. She had spent much of the day-long ride to Manzanar weeping; her two-year-old son was taken from the family that morning as they were boarding their transport, as he slept in his mother's arms. A nurse suspected the child had measles, and he was sent all alone to Los Angeles General Hospital—still sleeping—while the family was forced to leave without him. Yuri kept thinking of her toddler waking up all alone, confused and surrounded by strangers, crying inconsolably, his family suddenly gone.

As Yuri's bus neared Manzanar, it approached a bend in the road. Sakae Hirooka, another passenger that day, glimpsed the valley and was momentarily surprised by the beauty of the mountains along the desert skyline. But as the convoy turned, the reality of camp came into view, and she realized her world had turned much darker: the dirty tar-paper shacks for housing, the crowds waiting to be registered and inoculated, and the wind whipping sand.

George Teiichi Akahoshi also saw the lines of people waiting. When he stepped down into the dust and was directed to join them, his anger rose at how they were being herded and counted. Afterward, his family found their barrack, its floor gaping and cracked like the Yonedas'. Sumiko Yamauchi's family covered their heads for protection as they searched for their new barrack, arriving at an unfinished building with wide holes in the floor. The night became so windy and cold—10°F, George estimated—that he felt the makeshift building shake and wondered if they might all freeze to death. From her own thin, straw-stuffed mattress, Sumiko listened to the wind rattling the floorboards and heard the military jeeps going back and forth, sounds to which the Yonedas had by now become accustomed. But as Sumiko watched the searchlights sweeping through the unfinished windows, she wondered if she'd woken in a nightmare.

Three weeks later, Yuri Tateishi's two-year-old son, presumably no longer contagious, was dispatched from Los Angeles General Hospital and sent to Manzanar to become his family's youngest incarceree.

Under such difficult conditions, the camp's population began to splinter. Though Bendetsen, DeWitt, and many US politicians continued to describe Japanese Americans as a purely homogenous group—single-minded, uniformly incapable of loyalty, defined simply as "A Jap is a Jap"—the reality proved much more complicated. Generational, class, ideological, and even ethnic differences resulting from mixed marriages among the Japanese community in America had caused occasional tension before the war. Under the stress and grief of incarceration, these divisions deepened.

The generational categories—Issei, Nisei, and Kibei-Nisei—were generally perceived as the most relevant divisions within all the camps. But in the end, ideological fissures proved even more combustible. Many Kibei-Nisei, though US citizens, had spent their formative years in Japan and felt more at home in its culture; some spoke much better Japanese than English. Many (though not all) Issei felt removed from American culture and unsure what would become of them if the Allies triumphed, because they'd been denied citizenship in America and thus had no country that would claim them besides Japan. According to historian Eileen Tamura, Issei and Kibei-Nisei generally "favored hierarchy, loyalty to the group, and in some cases Japanese victory, believing this would benefit them more than an American victory."

Many Nisei, born in the United States, felt torn between their Issei parents' culture and their own, but as a group they were assumed to hold more diverse and sometimes complex perspectives. According to Tamura, among the Nisei, the JACL leadership in particular were "much more conditioned by American cultural perspectives and norms." But the JACL also inspired much disdain in camp, creating one of the major rifts among incarcerees, particularly after Mike Masaoka's Tolan Hearing testimony and other JACL leaders' insistence that Nisei show their loyalty by cooperating fully and uncomplainingly with the so-called evacuation. They were seen by some Issei "as the people who led them from the freedom of civilian life to the 'prison-like' assembly and relocation centers, while some Nisei were disgruntled that the JACL should presume to 'represent' the community."

Class and geographic differences exacerbated these tensions. Many JACL members were college-educated, urban-bred, and possessed of skills and connections to succeed beyond their own ethnic community. Other Nisei and Issei, particularly those from the farming and working classes, "remained detached from white America."

The small number of leftists in Manzanar—most of them Nisei—formed yet another distinct demographic, fitting uneasily among the others. "*Aka*," or "Red," they were frequently and derisively called in camp (as they'd been in the prewar period too). As one incarceree later wrote, among some in the Japanese American population, to be a "Red" made one a social outcast and even a "sexual pariah," perceived as having "loose morals," dabbling in "unconventional behavior," and transgressing traditional notions of gender, particularly masculinity. The leftist West Coast Japanese also arrived in camp with a reputation for stirring the pot. They had long been particularly critical of JACL leaders like Fred Tayama, who was in Manzanar, too, for his repressive prewar business practices; they abhorred the imperialism of the Issei's official homeland; and they disdained silence in the face of either.

Karl Yoneda found himself in an almost singular category in Manzanar. He was a Kibei, but ideologically, he strayed even further from tradition than many other Nisei. With his outspoken views and his white, Jewish, activist (and loud) wife, he was fast becoming the most vocal and visible *Aka* in Manzanar.

Even FBI Director J. Edgar Hoover understood Karl's unique place within the assumed categories of the Japanese American community. The day before Bendetsen and DeWitt touched down briefly at Manzanar, Hoover officially dismissed a request that had been made back in February to investigate Elaine and "her reported marriage to a Japanese named Carl [*sic*] G Yoneda," with an eye toward determining "if she has rendered any assistance to any Japanese espionage group." On April 23, Hoover deemed such an investigation "fruitless," writing to the assistant attorney general of the US Department of Justice, "Yoneda is one of those rare individuals who is of Japanese descent, but is open and avowed in his Communist sympathies and is anything but in sympathy with the present militaristic regime in Japan."

Though neither Karl nor Elaine would become aware of Hoover's memo until later, they both clearly understood the challenges faced by the different generational and social demographics in Manzanar, as well as their attendant ideological rifts. Elaine in particular sympathized with the bind in which many of the camp's elders found themselves. "You take an Issei who has been removed from his fatherland for twenty or thirty years," she explained once in an interview, and "reads only the Japanese press," and it was no wonder they would come to believe that Japan's imperialism had been a positive force in the world. She knew many Issei had been taught that the militarists were "liberating" in the countries they invaded. "Some [Issei] had strong ties with their homes. They had feelings, that they should rightfully have, for their fatherland," she said. What only strengthened these feelings, she knew, was that the United States, with its racist immigration laws, "didn't permit them to become attached to this country," because they had the wrong kind of skin. When she thought of her own husband's father, she saw a man who had experienced the same disassociation.

Perhaps worst of all for general morale in Manzanar was what Elaine called the "do-nothing" policy of the camp administration: failing to provide proper work, wages, or even an understanding of what the country was fighting for. Camp was just "a big void," she said; of course people were getting stirred up.

Spurred by the administration's inaction, Elaine was determined to counter a lapse she could not abide: the failure, as she saw it, to promote a true understanding of America's role in the war. Just as Karl embraced his position as block leader in the name of inspiring democracy, Elaine found her own activism related to the war cause. Though a modest start, she began sharing news reports as widely and loudly as possible. The minute she saw anything relevant, she'd pass it around, announcing her hope that the United States and its allies would prevail, spreading the message of fascism's deserved demise. Each public proclamation enabled, in some small way, a rewriting of Manzanar's place in her life. The camp no longer had to be an end, or even a pause, to the long narrative of struggle she and Karl had always waged, fighting side by side in the outside world. It became, rather, a new chapter, a fresh context in which to counter forces that threatened to annihilate her ideals and her family—particularly now, as America's enemies continued winning. But in the widening divisions around her, different dangers attended her passionate support of the war, of the fight in whose name the camp had supposedly been built. And as Manzanar's population grew, she could feel the tension grow with it.

5 | SEPARATED
Spring–Summer 1942

"ONE MONTH AT MANZANAR," Elaine wrote in her diary on May 1. She and Karl helped Tommy send a card that day to United China Relief, raising funds for people suffering under Japanese colonization. "I'm sorry it is only a dollar," Tommy wrote with his donation.

That same day, Karl attended his first gathering of a new constitution committee, composed of six block leaders. The main Block Leaders' Council meetings provided scant opportunity for input or leadership; policies were set by the administration, and block leaders discussed how to carry them out.

Karl wanted more. He longed to establish some sort of archetype for all the camps, a blueprint for self-government that the entire Japanese American community could follow in their respective places of imprisonment. He wanted an approximation of the US Constitution and Bill of Rights, complete with bylaws, infused with the spirit of democracy. And he wanted the outside world to notice. "We tried to establish the kind of camp that the rest of America would look up to, a really nice camp," he said. Maybe their entire community could thereby "win the confidence" of the country, as he put it, and one day be welcomed to resettle safely and successfully in the free world. The committee took their first stab at crafting a constitution, then circulated their draft to Issei and Nisei leaders at other incarceration sites.

May 1 also marked International Workers Day. "Our slogan: VICTORY IN 1942!" Karl wrote in his diary. But he felt dismayed by the lack of interest the holiday generated in Manzanar. The most recent headlines from *People's*

World, arriving a few days late in camp, only made things worse. The Yonedas could feel the creep of defeat coming closer, and with it, the seep of fascist brutality. "Nazi atrocities—pillaging, rape, destruction, lynching," Karl transcribed into his diary; "Mandalay Falls; Jap Drive Turns from India to China"; "Seven Thousand U.S. Troops Surrender Corregidor."

Had the Yonedas still been in the Bay Area, they may have seen another headline that day: Japanese Takes Own Life. A local paper attributed the suicide of a twenty-six-year-old Japanese florist to "despondency" over his impending forced removal from home and dispatch to Manzanar. The young man had drunk poison and died alone, his body found in a storm drain.

Though headlines such as these suggest that West Coast citizens were increasingly aware of the suffering in and around Manzanar, Karl and Elaine urged a different focus. When they received several letters that week from free friends worried about how they were faring, they wrote back, "No need to concern yourselves." Instead, they argued, "Let's concentrate our energies on the most pressing immediate objective: Eradicating the Axis!"

Elaine elaborated in another letter. "Whether or not" the forced removal and incarceration of West Coast Japanese Americans was "in violation of the Constitution," she wrote, "is an issue to be addressed after the war. After all, if Hitler and Tojo should win, our limited form of democracy would likely be supplanted by fascism." She concluded with a modest request: that the American public stop using the term "Japs" to refer to their fellow citizens in camps.

In a later interview about the tensions in Manzanar and the violence they were building toward, Elaine made clear that she and Karl thought no ethical middle ground existed. "We have to take [a] side," she said. "We have to line up either profascist or antifascist. We can't be sitting in the middle," no matter what the cost. That June, the *San Francisco News* profiled Karl, illuminating his staunch commitment to nothing above the war effort. Describing his goals in Manzanar (which they named "Miracle Town"), the *News* reported, "Everybody on the waterfront knows [Karl Yoneda], San Francisco's only Japanese member of the Longshoremen's Union. . . . Before he was elected a block leader the other day he gave notice that his only interest is in fighting fascism. They elected him anyhow. Will he ever get back into the labor movement?"

By then, Karl had already begun writing to the media to stress the Yonedas' ideological position publicly. In his first detailed letter to *People's World*, he began, "My family—Elaine and Tommy—joined me at the Owens Valley reception center on April 1st." Building the camp required hard work and the wage issue had yet to be resolved, he admitted. Yet, despite having denigrated the *Manzanar Free Press*'s ingratiating tone a few weeks earlier, he wrote of widespread "appreciation" for camp authorities. He claimed that "the workings of democracy are clearly demonstrated before our eyes" and Manzanar's "American citizens of Japanese ancestry are grateful to our government for the way this grave question of evacuation is being handled."

"What a difference from Fascist controlled countries!" he proclaimed. Karl anticipated that time would vindicate his country, not just because of the war but, he hinted, perhaps also *because* of camps like Manzanar: "This project will take its place in American history—in the fight for the preservation of democracy and defeat of the Axis-Fascists at home and abroad." He again signed off, "Yours for victory, Karl G. Yoneda." Then he added a postscript, plaintive and brief, appearing along the bottom of the page: "PS. Would appreciate hearing from our friends."

Karl sent similar letters to the *San Francisco Chronicle* and the *Los Angeles Times* (the former referring to Karl as a "Patriot Jap-American"). In the *Times* letter, Karl repeated his gratitude to General DeWitt, WCCA general leadership and staff, and camp administrators for "giving us daily guidance to readjust ourselves and show us the way to aid in the war effort to preserve democracy." He again signed off, "Yours for Victory," adding, "P.S. There has been one birth, one wedding and NO deaths to date." He also wrote again to *People's World*, stressing the long prewar history of many Nisei and Kibei-Nisei opposed to imperialist Japan and again insisting that though "many pro-Japan" people existed among them, the "MAJORITY" of Japanese in America were loyal and should not be accused otherwise. "For the public record I want to state that many Japanese Americans as well as alien Japanese reported dangerous elements among us to the proper authorities. . . . I myself reported to the FBI and Navy Intelligence in San Francisco many instances of disloyalty." Though Elaine noted in her diary the publication of her husband's letters, neither Yoneda mentioned whether anyone else in Manzanar had seen them, and if so, how they'd reacted.

They might have found an answer in another part of camp, had they sought out World War I veteran Joe Kurihara. After removing his American Legion button and tucking it away with all faith in his country, Kurihara's resentment had been growing ever more bitter. One day in May, he crossed paths with the former editor of a bilingual paper who'd once published Kurihara's own patriotic writing, back when he still proudly wore his veteran's pin. Now, he was standing in the shadow of a barrack wall. The ex-editor thought Kurihara's eyes looked bloodshot, his body tense; though his face retained some roundness, it showed no memory of joy or laughter. When he spoke, his voice cut like a whip.

Joe condemned the government and its "false imprisonment" of them all, his interlocutor recalled him saying. He expressed biting scorn for Fred Tayama and other JACL members, whom he believed had tried to blackmail wealthy Issei out of their property, threating to report them to the FBI if they refused their lowball offers. He was disgusted by rumors of informers among the Nisei and heard some had purportedly earned twenty-five dollars for every "suspicious" character they turned in.

Kurihara took his grievances outside camp, too, writing to Father Lavery, the Maryknoll priest who had relayed the army's plan to pay union wages to Manzanar's first arrivals. The father had also told him that the families of these early volunteers would eventually be sent to Manzanar to join them—one more broken promise. Because Kurihara was single and without children, his closest family had all been sent elsewhere: two cousins to a camp in Arizona and a brother to the Santa Anita horse stalls with his own family by marriage. Kurihara asked for Father Lavery's help. But the holy man "either couldn't or wouldn't," he later told an interviewer.

When he searched elsewhere for kinship and belonging, another door slammed shut. With the camp's population growing throughout the late spring, other veterans of the Great War arrived, and Kurihara momentarily softened toward the idea of a community brought together under the American Legion banner. Though he'd discarded their pin, he wrote to them now, suggesting they charter a post right there in Owens Valley, joining together the veterans of Manzanar's desert. They wrote back, he recalled later, with a simple "No."

Kurihara directed his greatest scorn elsewhere, though. According to the ex-editor he'd met in May, he directed his "supreme contempt" at those Nisei "who would betray their own people to the arrogant white man" and were still foolish enough to believe "their U.S. citizenship meant anything."

By late spring, Manzanar had reached near its full capacity of ten thousand prisoners, about twenty-three hundred of whom were children. Despite the ample boredom, resentment, and grief around them, the Yonedas continued to find momentary glimpses of happiness throughout the spring and early summer. They picnicked with friends under the shade of a few trees, "some distance beyond the stockade," Karl wrote. Elaine threw Karl a thirty-sixth birthday party, and as nearly forty people packed into their barrack, they toasted to an Allied victory with Coca-Cola. According to a Manzanar documentary reporter, Karl "beamed" and said, "This makes things feel like normal." The party lasted until midnight, the reporter noted, with "storytelling, singing, and hilarity." "Thomas Mooney Yoneda, the couple's four-year-old [sic] son named after the late labor leader, slept through it all." This innocuous scene ran alongside an article on the paper's front page describing a new "iron cage," installed that day at Manzanar's police department headquarters, "completely enclosed and measuring 20 x 20 feet," for those incarcerees who were apparently too recalcitrant for the regular stockade. (Koji Ariyoshi was particularly appalled at this new addition, describing it as "a steel cage . . . with barely room enough for a man to stretch himself in . . . A prisoner put in there became a show thing, and thus it deprived human beings of decency.")

Notwithstanding the jail's new cage, Memorial Day brought an air of festivity to camp, including an outdoor concert. Karl estimated three thousand people attended, partaking in songs, dancing, coffee, and cake. "Everyone was in a good mood," he wrote. "It seemed as if we'd forgotten we're in a concentration camp."

In celebration of the holiday, various marches occurred, memorialized in pictures taken by War Relocation Authority photographers. In one, a small troop of Japanese American Boy Scouts stand at attention, right arms raised in salute to an American flag hung partway up its pole. In another picture snapped from a different angle, the scouts march in a short line, their legs bending in unison, the flag waving before them over sunbaked ground, its shadow a dark ribbon in the dust.

Boy scouts salute the flag while incarcerated at
Manzanar, Memorial Day 1942. *Photo by Francis
Leroy Stewart, courtesy of the National Archives and
Records Administration*

The day also featured a speech by Tokutaro "Tokie" Slocum, which Elaine
found particularly inspiring. Slocum was a World War I veteran who'd been
born in Japan but adopted and raised by a white midwestern family, making
him a rare naturalized Issei citizen. He'd reacted to the repression of the Japanese American community in complete opposite to Joe Kurihara. After Pearl
Harbor, he'd doubled down aggressively on his patriotism, suggesting that
Nisei should turn on their own parents if necessary and publicly announcing
his assistance in the FBI's arrest of various suspicious Issei. As one government official put it, in camp, Slocum had a reputation for being not just an
American through and through, but "115%."

According to Elaine, before the war Karl Yoneda and Tokie Slocum had
been "bitter enemies," due to the latter's "1000% patriotic thinking." Slocum
had always refused to believe his country could ever do wrong, Elaine said,

and that had made him the ideological opposite of Karl, who'd long agitated against America's lapses in labor, civil, and human rights. But "here we find ourselves in the same camp, being allied in a fight to destroy a vicious enemy," she explained. She called it "strange to find ourselves allied."

In his Memorial Day speech from Manzanar, Slocum fashioned camp as the incarcerees' own front line, much as the Yonedas' friend had in a recent letter. "We are fighting a moral battle," Slocum told the crowd, "and by our attitude and conduct we can win a moral victory for America." Elaine was moved by this perspective, writing later in her diary about yet one more rendering of Manzanar as their "battlefield in helping win the war!"

As spring progressed, Elaine worked in the camp library, where she began to attract more resentment, particularly when she was immediately named unit director. "Someone sure mad about it," she wrote briefly in her diary. Karl wrote more overtly about the racial undertones of this resentment, of young women whispering of Elaine's promotion "just because she's white!" though he didn't dispute their assumption. A few days later, as Elaine passed by a group of children, they yelled *keto baba!* ("old foreign hag!"). Karl felt pangs of sorrow and guilt that she'd ended up in Manzanar.

But over Mother's Day weekend, the family welcomed their first guests. Elaine's parents and daughter were allowed into camp, permitted to eat at the mess hall and even stay overnight in the Yonedas' barrack, though this privilege would soon be rescinded. They brought gifts: Joyce a blouse for Elaine, which she immediately put on, and her parents a radio for Karl (though not a shortwave one, which was contraband). The radio thrilled him until he switched it on, searching for news. The first thing he heard was that the Allies had lost yet more ground.

Leftist friends of the Yonedas also visited. One, a reporter for the progressive Jewish daily *Freiheit*, walked the grounds and took furious notes. That month of May 1942 marked the first reports of mass gassings, shootings, and killing centers as part of a Nazi plan to exterminate all the Jews of Europe. These were compiled by the General Jewish Labour Bund in Poland—descendent of the Jewish Bund formerly operating in Russia, to which Elaine's own parents had once belonged—and passed along to the Allied governments. British and American leaders, as well as all major English media sources, either discounted or ignored the news, thinking it too shocking to be true.

Jewish dailies like *Freiheit*, though, followed the story, believing its horrible truth. After touring Manzanar, the Yonedas' reporter friend admitted, "It's not right the way the government has put you people in these camps. But Hitler is the enemy of mankind. We have a duty to see he's overthrown." Their visitor next made clear that the horrors of Nazi Germany would claim his undivided attention—and must do nothing less. "Regrettably, I think there just isn't any surplus energy to devote to your cause." Neither Yoneda seemed bothered by this stark assessment. Nor did Tommy, who according to his father was thrilled to exhaustion by all the excitement; after their friends left, the boy was "was the first to begin snoring."

That night as they slept, Joyce lay atop a makeshift chest, with Elaine and Karl next to Tommy on the floor. Presumably, the Buchmans took the bed. Reflecting on the "carefree" visits, Karl wrote, "it seems the war has temporarily disappeared." Before saying goodbye the next day, Joyce asked if she could spend her summer vacation with them in camp.

In late spring of 1942, the WCCA, which had been run by both the army and civilian administrators, handed control of Manzanar to the War Relocation Authority (WRA), an organization of only civilian appointees. Manzanar was unique among the Japanese American camps in that many of its early incarcerees had come directly from the homes they'd been forced to vacate. Most other incarcerees were housed first in "temporary assembly centers" closer to the coast and later moved to "relocation centers" farther inland. These so-called temporary assembly centers—like the converted race track at Santa Anita—served as a sort of way station until the permanent relocation centers could be readied. Though the conditions at most assembly centers were even more deplorable than Manzanar's, including not just modified horse stalls but also converted pigpens for housing, the WRA explained each as "a convenient gathering point, within the military area, where evacuees live temporarily while awaiting the opportunity" to be moved to a relocation center. (By early fall 1942, all ten relocation centers would be opened and run by the WRA. Until then, the WCCA continued to administer the "convenient gathering points" known as temporary assembly centers.)

Arriving at Owens Valley in late spring, WRA administrators found its residents "disillusioned, confused, and incredulous." But for Elaine, the transfer of Manzanar from WCCA to WRA control coincided with a minor triumph:

a new camouflage net factory opened at the camp. She eagerly sought work there—her chance finally to support the war effort in a direct, hands-on way.

She found the job uncomplicated yet physically challenging. The factory consisted of three tall sheds, eighteen feet high and set atop long concrete slabs, all lacking walls. The facility was hot, smelly, and exposed, and the endless dust storms caused frequent work stoppages. Elaine estimated the sheds reached 120°F in the shade, and the heat required workers to take salt pills every hour or so. They would sit on wooden benches or stand on the hard concrete for long, blistering days, grabbing green and tan burlap strips from wooden stands and reaching up to weave them over the strings of enormous nets. They wore aprons over their clothes and gauze masks to protect against the fumes. Still, Elaine's skin became irritated from the chemical dyes. But both she and Karl radiated with pride over her war work. "Even here in this camp," she wrote to a friend, "we're fighting to overthrow the fascist devils." Karl lauded her efforts. "She is working extremely hard," he wrote, "for me and Tommy, and also for the war effort."

The camouflage net factory, July 1942. *Photo by Dorothea Lange, courtesy of the National Archives and Records Administration*

In general, the net factory bred resentment throughout camp. Positions were only open to US citizens, making Issei ineligible and contributing to complaints about discrimination. Rumors spread about the fumes causing tuberculosis. News of the factory's opening also coincided with an announcement that the wage issue had finally been settled—to widespread disillusionment and disgust. Incarcerees would be paid eight dollars a month for unskilled work, up to twelve dollars monthly for skilled labor and sixteen for professional and technical jobs, less than even the lowest army recruits were earning. Furthermore, they received no indication of when they might actually begin receiving these payments. (Not until mid-July, it turned out.) Soon, Karl overheard comments about the camp being "much too harsh." One Nisei pointed out, "POWs get better treatment than we do, even so far as wages are concerned!"—a correct assessment in terms of wage policy for POWs held in the United States.

Manzanar's incarcerees were still adjusting to the wage-scale news when the camp experienced its first death, a sixty-two-year-old Issei who'd been in ill health. Two days later, Karl joined a small group to select a graveyard site,

Manzanar's first grave, June 1942. Photo by Dorothea Lange, courtesy of the National Archives and Records Administration

settling on one near the camp's back boundary. Then the dead man was buried, lowered into dirt amid the intonations of Buddhist prayer. Sitting in the block leaders' office afterward, Karl welcomed two elders who'd come with a traditional Japanese condolence gift for the family: some money tucked into an envelope. They delivered their gift with a message. "Japan is going to win, you know," Karl recalled them saying. "She's going to create an entirely new world order." He offered no response. "There's no point arguing with old men like these," he wrote later. "I simply listened in silence."

With Manzanar's inaugural grave still freshly dug, another tragedy befell the camp: its first, though not last, shooting.

Hikoji Takeuchi was a young Nisei who'd recently arrived at Manzanar with his mother. More than the loss of their home or the choking dust or having to leave his friends behind, what he minded most was that his mother had nowhere to sit in their empty barrack. There was her bare, hard cot, but nothing else. "That is what I used to grieve," he said later. "I believed that my mom deserved better."

One Saturday in mid-May, Takeuchi determined he would make her a stool, or maybe even a chair where she could rest. The day was clear, and he ventured out in the bright morning sun, looking for wood scraps. He saw a pile of lumber in the distance and a sentry—a military policeman—standing by, but he could see no fence or boundary. So he hailed the MP and asked if he could approach the lumber pile.

The MP assented, and Takeuchi spent a few minutes picking through lumber. He was holding some in his arms when he heard the sentry call him back. The young man turned, a few scraps of wood in his embrace, and began walking toward the guard. Takeuchi recalled later that the man suddenly raised his rifle and leveled it. At first, the young Nisei was confused. *What the devil is he doing?* he thought. Then, *He's leveling off at me.* The MP shot him seven times.

The sentry's story matched Takeuchi's mostly, except for the direction the young man was facing when he was shot. According to WRA investigators, "The guard said that he ordered the Japanese to halt—that the Japanese started to run away from him, so he shot him." But their investigation eventually came to a different conclusion. "The guard's story does not appear to be accurate," they noted, "inasmuch as the Japanese *was* wounded in the front and not in the back" (emphasis in the original).

"Someone shot for not halting," Elaine wrote the day after the incident, apparently having heard the MP's version making its way around Manzanar. Takeuchi survived, but the wounds tore through both him and the entire camp community. A few weeks later, in a confidential memo about rising agitation in Manzanar, Karl Bendetsen addressed the shooting as well as the Yonedas, identifying both as potential trouble spots in camp. He wrote of one "Carl Yoneda [*sic*], a man of a very definite communistic tendency, being the husband of a Russian Jewess, who is of the rabid soap-box type communist." As for the injured young Nisei, Bendetsen stuck with the MP's story but admitted the incident's broad repercussions: "Since the shooting of the evacuee by the Military Police, the evacuees have enclosed their feelings in a shell," he wrote. "They are resigned to the fact that the military authorities are in charge and that they will be punished or shot if they venture across the sentry lines." Bendetsen claimed Takeuchi's fellow prisoners had accepted that "the evacuee who was shot was wrong in being beyond the sentry line, even though given permission by the sentry." But his memo eventually homed in on the most widely damaging part: despite having shot a young, unarmed American citizen, "no punishment [was ever] directed towards the patrolman." Now, the camp's population felt, as Bendetsen put it awkwardly, that "at least [he] should not be allowed the freedom of the county in which to brag about the shooting."

As spring passed into summer, incessant sandstorms and severe heat further depressed morale in Manzanar. Temperatures around the grounds reached past 110°F; inside the barracks, it was worse. Often, the Yonedas found it too hot even to read or write until after 9:00 PM. Listening to their radio brought little relief. One broadcast told them that, with the exception of six patients too infirm to be moved, "San Francisco's streets have been completely cleared of Japanese." A week later, another newscast confirmed the same for the entire Pacific Coast. Though papers began reporting increased Allied bombing strength and an American victory at Midway, Elaine and Karl felt sure the war would drag on and its dangers persist. They were soon proven correct, reading of new Nazi gains against the Soviets. Meanwhile, closer to home, they were dismayed by the claims of Idaho's governor: all the

Japanese in America "breed like rats" and should be "sent packing to Japan, or tossed into the sea."

Along with dismal headlines and scorching temperatures, Tommy's condition worsened again. In addition to his asthma, his allergies caused fever spikes, and Manzanar's doctors suggested an even more restricted diet. When Elaine and Karl tried to purchase special food and have it sent from San Francisco, the heat spoiled the food before it reached them. Sometimes, Karl looked at his son and just wanted to cry. For days, he'd write in his diary of Tommy's poor condition. And then the boy would start to improve, at least temporarily; Karl would watch him playing with the other kids in camp and think about how to protect him. "More than anything," he wrote, "I do not want these children to fall into the hands of the fascists."

On July 4, a violent dust storm brought another spike. When Tommy was still fever-wracked the next morning, he was admitted to Manzanar's makeshift hospital. As Karl and Elaine left the barrack facility, they could hear their son somewhere behind, crying inconsolably for his mother.

While Tommy's condition deteriorated in California's desert, in San Francisco Karl Bendetsen was contemplating the frenetic pace of his seven-day work week. Overseeing the removal of anyone on the West Coast with any "Japanese blood" was in Bendetsen's own words a "most trying" assignment. And yet, he admitted in a letter to his friend Colonel Auer, "the challenge presented made it a problem of such absorbing interest that I would scarcely wish to have traded the experience."

Despite his enthusiasm, Bendetsen had been struggling since early spring with one stray ambiguity. His quandary had arisen on the very day Elaine brought Tommy to the South Spring Street civil control station to register for entrainment to Manzanar. Since then, reports had been coming from control stations up and down the West Coast about a contradiction in Bendetsen's carefully crafted "evacuation" plan. The army had announced that any percentage of Japanese ancestry targeted one for removal and incarceration, but they'd also repeatedly insisted that, as evidence of democratic intentionality and humane policy, their procedures kept families together. In the case of mixed families like the Yonedas, WCCA workers were stumped.

After the priest and army officer failed to stop Elaine from boarding the train with Tommy, the task of categorizing and organizing mixed-family members had fallen mostly to social workers at the control stations, on temporary assignment for the WCCA. They made ad hoc decisions about which families should or could be sent away en masse, who among them could be exempted from removal and incarceration, and what to do about non-Japanese people facing separation from their Japanese (or mixed-Japanese) spouses and children.

For much of the spring, control-station staff relied on a document named the Temporary Exemption Certificate for Mixed-Race Family Group. This form allowed families to apply to WCCA headquarters for permission to remain free and home together. But on May 8, 1942, Bendetsen's boss, General John DeWitt, officially cancelled and retroactively revoked all temporary exemptions for mixed-marriage families. The WCCA announced that instead, "the non-Japanese spouse of a person of Japanese ancestry or the non-Japanese parent of a part Japanese child may elect to accompany his or her Japanese ancestry spouse or child into an assembly or reception center," as Elaine herself had done. But there was a caveat: the non-Japanese mother, father, wife, or husband now had to sign a Request and Waiver of Non-Excluded Persons.

This document, known as WDC Form PM-7, distilled to its essence the double-speak Bendetsen had deployed in his many press releases and speeches as head of the WCCA. "Know All Men by These Presents," the document opened with archaic flourish, "the undersigned does hereby request the privilege of accompanying" their child or spouse to be imprisoned, "in all respects as if he or she were a person of Japanese ancestry." Becoming "as if Japanese" meant that once in camp, the person became a prisoner. A symbolic change in ethnicity thus conferred incarcerability. At bottom appeared a line for the "Signature of Voluntary Evacuee," whereby a spouse or parent was to "expressly represent and agree" that they had "personally solicited the privilege" of joining their loved one behind barbed wire, "without persuasion" or "duress."

During that spring and summer of 1942, another group was deeply impacted by Bendetsen's attempts to neatly define and contain the ambiguous category of "Japanese-ness." Just a few weeks before Tommy's hospitalization, three barracks full of children had arrived in Manzanar, without parents or relatives, to live in its Children's Village, the only orphanage among the US camps. On June 23 forty-one children were removed from the Shonien, a Los Angeles orphanage. The oldest was eighteen, though approximately twenty of the children were younger than seven. The youngest was six months old. A handful were mixed race, like Tommy, though none were on record as being part Jewish.

Eventually, the Children's Village would grow to house over one hundred children, about twenty of whom were of multiethnic lineage. Some had no living parents or relatives, and some had families who, before the war, had been unable to care for them and so placed them in a Japanese orphanage. For mixed-race children who weren't in an orphanage before the war but had neither a living Japanese relative in a camp nor a non-Japanese one willing or able to be incarcerated with them, the army's policy was to take them from their current guardians and send them to Manzanar's orphanage too. As Bendetsen himself had reportedly told one Maryknoll priest, if "they have one drop of Japanese blood in them, they must all go to camp."

One blond-haired boy at the Children's Village had been living in a California orphanage for white children until the bombing of Pearl Harbor, never even knowing he was part Japanese until someone checked his file and alerted the army. He was joined in camp by two teenage girls who'd lived with their white grandmother and also lacked any knowledge of their mixed-Japanese heritage. As for the first forty-one arrivals to the Children's Village in the days before Tommy's hospitalization, their Japanese American caretakers had pled with the army to allow their charges to remain with them at the Shonien for the duration of the war. Instead, Karl Bendetsen issued the order to remove them all.

———————

Four days after Tommy was admitted to the hospital in Manzanar, Elaine and Karl Yoneda tried to visit him, but they were turned away. Their son had been diagnosed with measles and moved to isolation. They left some toys and returned to their barrack. Elaine broke down in tears, and Karl followed. They returned to the hospital the next day, where the nurses told them that their son was "completely covered" in spots. The staff had given Tommy the toys, they told the Yonedas, and he'd looked at the gifts and then the nurses and asked, "But where is Mommy?" The following day, the boy finally began playing with the toys, but he'd periodically stop, ask for Elaine, and start to cry. After two more days, Elaine and Karl were allowed to see him through

Manzanar's temporary hospital barracks, July 1942. *Photo by Dorothea Lange, courtesy of the National Archives and Records Administration*

an observation window. When Tommy spotted them, he began to call out to them, and when they did not leave the glass to come get him, he wept. Looking at his son through the makeshift hospital window, Karl felt utterly depleted. Finally, nine days after being admitted, and in the midst of a severe sandstorm, Tommy was released. He was still too weak to walk, so Karl carried him home through the raging dust, back to their barrack.

Refusing to be stymied by the entwined pressures of their son's worsening condition and their family's indeterminate imprisonment, the Yonedas only increased their efforts to change the world beyond camp. In late spring they'd reached out to their friend and attorney, George Anderson, requesting he serve as their voice in a lawsuit intended to strip Japanese Americans of their citizenship. "When this trial takes place," they wrote, "we'd like you to represent us and testify against [this] proposal." They were dismayed in early summer to read of the former California attorney general's argument at trial, that the US Constitution was drafted entirely "by and for white people."

Turning to matters over which he might have more control, Karl continued to agitate within camp for the democratization of Manzanar. Like Elaine, he also loudly advocated for incarceree participation in the war effort. But as resentment rose from some corners of the increasingly demoralized population, so did threats of violence against anyone who supported either.

At first, the danger remained a mere suggestion. When Karl took the opportunity to sell poppies for the American Legion, he reported hawking 120—but also being threatened. "As for me, I make donations to help Japan's wounded!" a young Kibei-Nisei shouted. "Yoneda is a communist, let's beat him!" overheard Karl's friend Jimmy Oda, a fellow leftist. "At Santa Anita, they beat Shuji Fujii!" Whether or not Karl had already heard of the beating of *Doho*'s former editor, who by now had been forcibly removed to the racetrack stables, he was grateful for Oda's response: "If you want to beat [Karl], you'll have to get past me first!"

But still, Karl was unsettled—not merely or even primarily by the aggression itself but, according to his diary, by the apparent persistence of such ideology within Manzanar, which he categorized as "a major, unsolved question." A few days later, an elder stopped by the block leaders' office to report Japan's attack on Alaska's Dutch Harbor. "It won't be long now before they land in California, too!" Karl recalled him saying. It seemed like there were so many people in camp with this same attitude, Karl thought. He ascribed similar reasons as Elaine had: boredom leading to gossip and rumors. But he also believed it was "a serious problem."

Karl hoped to tip the scale in the opposite direction through his work with the constitution committee. After weeks of work, their near-final document opened with a long preamble echoing the concepts and cadence of its national progenitor:

> We, the people residing in Manzanar Relocation Center, in order to uphold the Constitution of the United States of America, to cooperate to the utmost with the national policy under the present emergency, to uphold the democratic way of life, to insure harmony and tranquility within the community, to promote the general welfare and secure the blessings of liberty to ourselves and our posterity, do ordain and establish this Constitution of Manzanar Relocation Center, Manzanar, California.

Karl seemed to brim with anticipation after meeting with Manzanar's administration to discuss the draft. "It won't be long now before we establish a camp with self-government, based on popular vote by the residents," he wrote.

Eager to see this vision writ large, Karl again contacted *People's World* editors, producing a letter they published under the heading DEMOCRACY AT WORK IN MANZANAR. Karl described the new camouflage net factory, the camp's Memorial Day celebration, and the constitution-in-progress, created to benefit and be ratified by *all* Manzanar's residents, including the noncitizen Issei. "The constitution provides equal suffrage for all over twenty-one— regardless of sex or place of birth," he explained. This democratization would be part and parcel of a campaign that could enjoin incarcerees and free Americans in the same battle: to defeat racist edicts like the one he and Elaine had enlisted George Anderson to fight in their name. "Those of us who are registered voters can exercise our franchise through absentee ballots," Karl wrote, "although attempts are being made . . . to disenfranchise citizens of Japanese ancestry. We expect aid and moral support of all true friends of democracy in defeating this reactionary un-American procedure."

Despite his upbeat letter, Karl and Elaine worried that prospects were actually murkier for a unified front from within and beyond Manzanar. Though Karl hoped the new constitution would instill greater harmony, he admitted that mounting tensions within camp might herald a different result. While the committee drafted their document, three others on the Block Leaders' Council had warned they would resign if the "Americanization program," as Karl described it, went forward. To him, the problem again seemed to be the "pro-Japan faction," becoming stronger and more perilous as time went on.

Within a week of the Kibei threatening Karl, a new danger emerged. A group of young men, some from the recently decimated Terminal Island, began to fashion themselves as a gang of "Black Dragons." The name referenced Japan's ultranationalist Black Dragon Society, or Kokuryūkai, an underground group who revered martial arts; violently opposed Western racism and colonialism, particularly throughout Asia; and supported Japanese imperialism as an antidote. Now, Karl assumed, some of Manzanar's young men had adopted the name in homage to Black Dragon fierceness and pride in being Japanese. Some of them worked on the camp's garbage crew, and they commandeered a truck, flew a skull and bones flag from its fender, and raced from block to block. They wove between barracks with their black banner snapping, yelling insults to block leaders and "slander[ing] America," in Karl's words. "Japan is bombing Alaska," Karl heard the Black Dragons claim; "America's victory at Midway is a lie." They warned incarcerees not to take part in war-related work such as at the net factory. "You'll never be paid the wages you've been promised."

Later, Karl felt sure Joseph Kurihara was one of their leaders, though no firm proof of this remains, and Kurihara himself later denied it. The Yonedas, camp residents, and WRA administrators all noted that the gang, in whatever form it existed, was secretive about its membership, as was the real Kokuryūkai in Japan. According to an WRA memo, incarcerees assumed fewer than twenty people were "actually preforming [sic] the mechanics of [this] 'underground' work" in Manzanar. No consensus exists even today about whether they were actually an organized "pro-Japan" group or just a collection of disenchanted prisoners.

Elaine and Karl thought only a "small handful" were true supporters of Japanese imperialism, but their tactics fomented greater unrest and violence as Manzanar's ideological divisions and general misery deepened, particularly among the camp's Kibei-Nisei. Regardless of larger ideology, Kurihara and his associates—including those Karl and Elaine believed were Black Dragons— showed a clear, unequivocal antipathy toward self-governance in the camp, the camouflage net factory, and anyone colluding with administrators or the incarceration program in general. It did not take long for the Yonedas to end up in their crosshairs.

"Now that management of the camp lies practically within our grasp, as we stand at the very doorstep of self-government, the Black Dragon Kibei gang is spreading propaganda rumors like mad in their attempts to destroy the Block Leaders Council and to upset the daily rhythm of life at Manzanar," Karl wrote in mid-June, sweating under an intense heat topping 100°F. He recorded the Dragon's most recent claims: only traitors worked at the camouflage factory; block leaders were "the FBI's dogs"; almost fifty girls in camp had been impregnated; Japan treated their World War I POWs better than the United States was treating Manzanar's incarcerees; "Roosevelt is a Jew, and Jews hate the Japanese"; and "Yoneda is a Korean dog."

In early summer, Manzanar's prisoners repeatedly woke to ominous leaflets posted on latrine walls or poles throughout camp. The documents were in Japanese, hasty black brushstokes written in the traditional vertical columns. Karl translated the first, titled "A Spy Who Betrays Us," and another with the headline "Wake Up, Manzanar Residents." One began, "White men and Japanese fools trying to put over the camouflage net project. Stop work on the war equipment." It continued, "The spirit of the Japanese soldiers whose blood was shed will weep over you. Think of our post-war period. Names of those who work on the camouflage nets will be published." The second, shorter and terser, repeated the same protest over the net factory, though with the flourish that no "true-blooded Japanese" should work on such "war tools for the U.S.A.," and added a threat about self-government at the camp. They were signed "Patriotic Suicide Corps" and "Manzanar Black Dragon Association."

But when Karl and Elaine went to Manzanar's administration building to protest the Black Dragons' threats, they were dismissed. "You're all Japanese— Try to get along!" Kidwell responded. Manzanar's director, Roy Nash, added nothing more definitive. "They were making us out to be idiots," Karl wrote in his diary of the interaction with Kidwell and Nash. "I was furious."

In July Elaine earned a front-page mention from the *Free Press* in an article titled NET RECORDS BROKEN. The paper reported, "Outstanding single producer for the past week was Mrs. Karl Yoneda, 4-2-2, who, singlehanded, produced four nets per day with an efficiency record of 133 per cent."

Karl, seeing mention in the ILWU labor bulletin of a planned longshoreman battalion, immediately wrote to his union requesting enlistment: "Dear Sir and Brother," he began. "If I am accepted my destination would be entirely up to the U.S. Army—I am willing to be assigned any where [sic]," he vouched. He closed by pointing out that the nation needed every able-bodied man in battle and that he could do much more "by active duty" and "under Army command than in this Japanese evacuee Relocation Center."

Meanwhile, more anti-Japanese news from the outside reached Manzanar. One sidebar in the *Free Press* reprinted a letter from the *San Francisco Examiner* discussing visitors to the camp: "Jap visiting and gift giving to people who are waiting to cut all our throats is disgusting and should be stopped." A *People's World* article transcribed a radio broadcast from San Francisco that included calls demanding the Japanese "be hung, deported," and "deprived of American citizenship" (though presumably not in that order). Karl and Elaine retyped a copy of the transcription and saved it.

As Manzanar's incarcerees were reading a reprint of the *San Francisco Examiner* letter about "Jap" throat-cutting, the camp's new assistant director was settling in. Named Ned Campbell, he'd arrived in mid-June. By early July, he seemed as reluctant as Nash and Kidwell to address rising threats of violence between incarcerees, though he proved highly sensitive to outside anti-Japanese sentiment, if only for the pressure this put on white administrators. In an order passed down by Karl Bendetsen, Campbell and Nash announced severe limits on visitors, starting in the first days of summer. They deployed an "official ban" on general visitation, allowing only permits for those who could prove "legitimate business with camp residents," the *Free Press* reported, though even then, visits would "be limited to short periods" and take place at the camp police station. In a memo to Manzanar administrators, Bendetsen clarified that, though some passes for "ingress and egress" could be issued, they could not be granted to "any persons of Japanese ancestry." Justifying this ban to incarcerees, Campbell urged, "Please bear with us and realize that we people of the Administration are under terrific pressure from the outside."

He applied this ban to the Yonedas during Tommy's hospitalization with measles, refusing a visitor's permit for Elaine's parents with no explanation other than "orders from the head office." Karl was aghast. *How callous a man can he be?* he wondered. But Elaine had felt Campbell's hostility from the moment they met—his denigration of her as a white woman who'd married outside her own race. *A racist from Texas*, she thought.

Campbell did little to disprove this notion among the broader population. At a Manzanar general residents meeting soon after his arrival, as two hundred people crowded into an overheated barrack on an early summer afternoon, Campbell announced, "Whether you're Issei, Nisei, or Kibei, while here in this camp, there is no distinction. You are all Japanese." In a later interview, he admitted he hadn't actually realized when he arrived in camp that he "was dealing with human beings." The incarcerees seemed like "so many bodies," he said. They were "just numbers to me." Manzanar's prisoners could tell. "Every time Ned Campbell speaks," one said later, "he thinks he talks to a slave."

Campbell's boss, Project Director Roy Nash, could also prove bitingly obtuse. "We are in Manzanar for the duration of the war," he wrote in a *Free Press* Independence Day editorial. "At the end, the essential question will be, 'How did we play the game?'" Karl frequently heard rumblings about both Nash and Campbell. "'Roosevelt is a Jew and so is Nash and Campbell,'" he recorded hearing. "It is the opinion of many [here] that this country is run by Jews and that they hate the Japanese," Karl wrote that summer, and though he felt no affinity for Campbell, comments like these sounded to him like "Hitler tactics."

But Nash shared with Elaine and Karl a major concern: distinguishing America's camps from the Nazis' and contrasting its treatment of detainees with that of its enemies. "Our camp is not a prison," Nash reportedly said in a midsummer speech at Manzanar. "It's here to serve as temporary lodging, prior to your stepping into American society." (He failed to correct this misnomer, and the Yonedas did not mention or correct it in their diaries; the incarcerees, after all, had come *from* American society, and were waiting to be readmitted.) After Elaine and Karl went to see Nash to protest the new limits on visitors, she recorded his perspective, apparently agreeing with it: the rule confining visits to Manzanar's police station needed to be changed, because it "smacks" of a "concentration camp."

The director went on to make similar statements publicly. That July, at what the Yonedas heard was a "luncheon party held in the Commonwealth Club in San Francisco," Nash delivered a speech titled "Manzanar from the Inside." Some sympathy for its incarcerees was evident in his address that day, as was his need to whitewash the incarceration site. As an employee of the War Relocation Authority, though, he was careful not to make the place sound too soft, given recent public complaints about "coddling" the Japanese in America's camps. He must have also shared the mounting fears felt by many in the United States, especially the military, about how American POWs were being treated overseas. Perhaps by stressing a lack of overt brutality within US prison camps—citizenship of their detainees notwithstanding—Axis governments would limit atrocities against those they captured. But beyond the many disparate audiences Nash seemed to keep in mind, fundamentally his speech was a mirror made of words: a burnished surface upon which America could gaze and see, shining back, a cleansed reflection of itself.

Nash opened by telling his audience—the almost three hundred members of the club who had come to hear him speak—that "in a recent broadcast from

Manila, three American internees told how well they are being treated." The broadcast announcer then claimed, "What a contrast to the barbarities being inflicted upon the Japanese in California!" The following address would serve to counter such a view, Nash explained, and to "interpret the actuality of a War Relocation Center housing 10,000 evacuees." He noted that Manzanar's inhabitants could even listen to his address on a longwave radio, if they had one. His explanation of the camp was crucial because "our treatment of the Japanese in California" was not just "a token of our good faith" but also "a crucial test of the validity of our war objectives."

Nash's wording was somewhat awkward, but he reported that there were approximately sixty-five hundred American citizens in Manzanar, including twenty-three hundred children. "There is nothing beautiful" about the place, he admitted, and the "barbed shafts of bigotry" had "impinged" upon it—a gesture toward the racism underlying the entire project, which he then qualified by a strangely anthropomorphic description of the camp as "understanding of the military necessity in which it had been sired." Nash also mentioned the barbed wire ("an ordinary three-strand barbed-wire fence") and guard towers with searchlights, though he omitted the submachine guns. He mentioned the many opportunities for entertainment ("Manzanar knows how to

Manzanar, a view from the distance. *Courtesy of Manzanar National Historic Site and the Shinjo Nagatomi Collection*

play," he said), such as the gardens the residents had built, the dances and sports teams and singalongs, the evenings playing classical records over the camp's public address system. He mentioned the military police guarding the perimeter (but not their cache of weapons) and the "interior police force of some seventy evacuees," lead by five "Caucasians," though "no one carries arms within the center." (Presumably he was counting the guard towers as being *above* the center.)

He detailed the attempts at self-government, the publication of the *Free Press*, and the hard work throughout the camouflage factory in support of the war effort, as well as the rampant rumors running through camp (a "luxuriant crop" of them). He also admitted the gnawing uncertainty and humiliation of many elder Japanese, the aliens in the center. One Manzanar resident explained it to him thus, he claimed: "Silently, it would seem, they are apologizing to their children for the misfortune they brought upon their offspring citizens of this country."

Nash did not mention the rising tensions among the incarcerees, whom he never once actually called incarcerees. In closing, he chose a quote from his former boss, the first head of the War Relocation Authority, Milton Eisenhower: "We intend to demonstrate to the world—to our friends and our enemies alike—that this nation, grim in the fight it is waging, can at the same time be tolerant, patient, and considerate in handling this human problem of wartime migration and resettlement."

Nash's lecture aligned perfectly with the times. This distinction between Axis and American camps was a priority of Karl Bendetsen's, and as news began to break more widely of German atrocities against the Jews and other undesirables and Japanese brutality against POWs, the US media and government officials followed Bendetsen's lead. Where once politicians, military officers, newspapers, and even President Roosevelt had been entirely willing to use "concentration camp" to describe the West Coast incarceration sites, the late spring and early summer of 1942 marked a turning point. The term lost its place in the rotation of labels given to the US camps, replaced almost solely by the euphemisms Bendetsen had always preferred: "assembly center," "reception center," "evacuation," "resettlement," or even "internment camp" (though *internment* actually means imprisonment of foreigners). As one California editorial put it, "the Japanese concentration camps" in America are "politely referred to as 'assembly centers' and 'reception centers.'"

Meanwhile in Europe, the Nazis were adopting their own euphemisms, calling their slave-labor, torture, and extermination camps "special concentration camps." For the Yonedas, using "concentration camp" to describe their surroundings became an increasingly ambivalent option that spring and summer, one they sometimes embraced and other times avoided. The problem of defining the Japanese American incarceration would continue to haunt Elaine and Karl, even as Manzanar began to see beatings and fresh shootings, and even as the Yonedas and their son faced threats of grievous harm and death behind the camp's ordinary, three-strand barbed wire.

6 EXPOSED
Summer 1942

ON THE AFTERNOON OF AUGUST 1, Elaine, Karl, and Tommy sat under a stretch of trees at the northern edge of Manzanar. They were joined by the Buchmans, who had finally been permitted through the camp's gates after a month with virtually no visitors allowed. Nathan and Mollie brought food, and the family picnicked near a slope running down to a small stream. Around camp, the spot was known as "Cupid Pit."

Elaine's arms were both swollen, itchy, and painful. Four days earlier, she'd noticed a slight rash near the crook of her elbows, an angry blush she'd tried to ignore. But that early morning of August 1, she'd woken in such pain that Karl rushed to the camp hospital around 2:00 AM, bringing a nurse with medicine back to the barrack. One of Elaine's arms had ballooned. It was hot to the touch, and it hurt badly. By 9:00 AM she was also nauseated, so she dragged herself to the hospital. Most likely an allergy to the dyes at the net factory, the medical staff told her. "Advise: stay away from camouflage," wrote the doctor, Masako Kusayanagi (wife of the camp's head physician, James Goto) on the record of treatment for "Mrs. R Elaine Yoneda, Individual number 906-B." Elaine would need to stop working for at least two weeks.

Later, some colleagues from the net factory visited the Yonedas' barrack, bringing Elaine a watermelon. Then her parents finally arrived, after she'd waited weeks to see them, and though she still felt sick and her arm felt awful, she sat with them in the shade at Cupid Pit. If Joyce had joined them, neither Elaine nor Karl mentioned so in their diaries. The last time they'd seen her had been at the end of June, when their friend Luella "Happy" Brannan had brought Joyce to visit, a final trip before the month-plus ban on visitations. In a photo from that weekend, Elaine, Karl, and Happy stand in one line looking at the camera, a dusty-kneed Tommy in overalls in front, his father's hands clasping his small shoulders as Karl stares straight toward the lens. Joyce stands obscured at back, her face only partly showing, her eyes closed as if fading into a desert she could not see.

Now in August, the Buchmans visited for two days, presumably staying overnight either in Lone Pine or Independence, the towns on either side of Owens Valley. (Though visitors had again been allowed into camp with a pass, overnight stays were now strictly prohibited.) Elaine was still feverish, but as usual she refused to slow down, and they all rode a truck out to the new hospital. The structure stood across the grounds from the old makeshift facility, adjacent to Manzanar's newly occupied Children's Village. Having been intimately familiar with the old setup, the Yonedas marveled at how well-equipped the new one was, and the Buchmans were impressed too. When they left that afternoon, Elaine's parents promised they'd be back. But as the Yonedas watched them go, Karl and Elaine felt worried. From behind the camp's fence, they could imagine Nathan and Mollie driving out the guarded

Elaine, Joyce, Tommy, Karl, and "Happy" Brannan, Manzanar, June 27, 1942.
Courtesy of Karl G. Yoneda Papers, UCLA Library Special Collections

exit, then along the dusty highway toward home, getting farther and farther away. They wondered when they'd see each other again.

In general that summer, Karl had sensed a superficial calm over a deeper uneasiness. "On the surface, life here at Manzanar seems to have been moving in the direction of stability," he wrote. But he detected "an undercurrent of deep dissatisfaction over the undeniable fact that we're in a concentration camp." The dissatisfaction, he believed, was "simply waiting . . . to burst into the open."

Perhaps partly in recognition of this brewing trouble—and according to some historians, partly in an attempt to find incarcerated bodies the United States could exchange for their own POWs held by Japan—the WCCA and WRA had initiated a repatriation-request program that summer. Issei and Nisei with dual citizenship, as well as their family members, could request to be shipped to Japan at some later date, though no guarantees existed. "The acceptance of a formal request for repatriation by the Wartime Civil Control Administration does not bind the government of the United States to grant repatriation," Bendetsen's office explained that summer in a document named WCCA Form R-103, "Notice and General Instructions to Japanese Seeking Repatriation"; "The filing of a repatriation request form does not bind the individual or family concerned to accept repatriation at a later date. . . . However, persons applying for repatriation who are American citizens must understand that by so applying they indicate their willingness to forfeit such citizenship."

Karl had his first premonition of an impending explosion back in early July, when another directive from Washington had been communicated to incarcerees by Ned Campbell: all camp meetings must be conducted in English. When he broadcast the directive during a Manzanar "resident's Open Forum," he told the crowd not only that they should accept the new directive but also that "you're damn fools if you don't. When you hold meetings in Japanese, incidentally, you sound as if you're mad about something." Elaborating more fully, he added, "Persons on the outside demand to know if you're conspiring to blow up [an] aqueduct."

Tension was palpably high at the Block Leaders' Council meeting where Karl Yoneda and the others first debated how to respond. An Issei pointed out, to some modest applause, that since those in his generation had been born in Japan, many could not express themselves easily in English. Another Issei followed, speaking in Japanese, his voice choking with emotion. He recalled how his Nisei son, enlisted in the US Army, was seized by the FBI when he came to Manzanar on furlough to visit his parents; as an ethnic Japanese, he was not allowed to travel in or through the West Coast, not even in active-duty uniform to a concentration camp holding his parents. "We are always discriminated against here," the father said, according to a translated transcript Karl made of the meeting.

Karl's stance was his usual. He told the others that he understood their resentment, but "this is war time and we must sacrifice certain rights." He noted loud clapping when other block leaders protested in response about their rights being trampled anyway. Eventually, the meeting devolved into accusations of Nisei betrayal. The Issei chairman wound down by stating in English, "There are even certain Nisei who boast of having squealed to the FBI, on as many as 175 of the Issei." Karl heard another round of ringing applause.

Much later, Karl would come to regret his stance on enforcing English in meetings. But for now, he doubled down. Tommy was in the camp hospital, ill once again and in a quarantine Karl could not breach. Though powerless to heal his son, Karl could do something about the danger he'd sensed in the block leaders' meeting. In the quiet absence of his child, with the fading echo of Kibei and Issei applause still in his mind, Karl sat down to warn the WRA of the peril he'd heard in the sounds of his own first language. Of course, he'd also heard the sadness in the Issei father's voice, the dejection in the words of other Kibei-Nisei. But to him, Japanese had become, if not fully an enemy's language, an enabler of enemy thought. Perhaps it resonated too loudly with threats behind the barbed wire or with rumors of Japan's great strength. Perhaps the language sounded too much like the imperial thirst of an emperor's tongue, or the voice behind a father's long-ago lashing. But Karl felt sure of one thing: allowing it primacy in camp could only lead to accusation and strife, just as in the block leaders' meeting. This, in turn, would threaten one of the few hopes he had left, and what he believed the country would demand before accepting the freedom of Manzanar's incarcerees: their ability to build a democratic citadel atop the sands of Owens Valley.

That night, he wrote a letter to Nash and Campbell, copying the WRA regional director in San Francisco. He marked the header "Confidential" and enclosed an English transcript of the entire meeting. He urged them to carry through with their directive that all official gatherings be held in English. He warned, "If we allow another meeting such as was held this morning, the block leaders meetings will be turned into germinating nest for undesirable elements and pro-axis adherents." The stakes were high, he urged: "Crystallization of pro-Axis sentiment is getting stronger every day and if we don't guard against it, eventually there will be a clash between pro-axis and pro-America groups in camp."

———————

Ten days later, Karl joined a group of other Nisei men dissatisfied with the Block Leaders' Council to initiate a new vehicle for self-governance in camp. They named themselves the Manzanar Citizens' Federation (MCF). Chaired by Koji Ariyoshi, they formed an unexpected alliance of former JACL leaders and leftists, groups who had frequently clashed politically before the war. But on July 20 they came together. As Karl later described it, the JACL would offer coordination and leadership of the camp community, and the leftist faction would agitate for Japanese Americans' civil rights while also actively supporting the effort to overthrow the Axis. Karl was ambivalent about partnering with men like Tayama, but sometimes circumstances require such action and alliances, he believed. ("Just like the Soviet Union had to make a pact with Hitler," he said later, "sometimes you have to do that.") He always remained starkly self-critical about one aspect, though: their failure to include antifascist women in this first meeting was "a reflection of our male chauvinism," he admitted in hindsight.

The men planned to hold a general forum a week later to introduce the MCF to the broader camp community. They'd each give a brief address on the federation's long-term goals; Karl claimed the topic of incarceree cooperation in the war effort.

The backlash began even before the general forum. The next day, someone dropped by the *Free Press* office, complaining that "Reds like Yoneda ought to be shut away in prison." The threats soon turned darker.

The afternoon of July 23 felt like a furnace in Manzanar. Karl recorded the temperature at 114°F. When Tokie Slocum dropped by the block leaders' office, they ventured outside to talk. For a while, they chatted quietly, skin pricked by a midday heat that was still somehow cooler than inside the barrack. Likely, the men would have heard the low hum of a motor and the growl of rubber over gravel before they actually saw the truck, a behemoth of metal and dirt. It flew a Black Dragons flag from its fender, flapping madly as the tires gathered speed, white skull waving its immortal grin. After the vehicle emerged from out of the hot, dusty air, it headed straight for Karl and Tokie.

Looking up, seeing the truck's fender racing closer, the men leapt up the concrete stairs fronting the office. They heard some sort of impact, and when they looked again, the truck was speeding off, grit and gravel spitting from its wheels. Karl and Tokie stood for a moment, sweaty and shocked. Below them, in the sudden quiet, the bottom steps were smashed.

That afternoon, Karl reported the incident at another block leaders' meeting. Appalled at the attempted hit-and-run, he argued that "appropriate measures" must be taken. His plea was met with widespread silence. After a dead pause, the Issei chairman of the council replied, "Here at Manzanar, JACL informers have been trying to seize control of the camp leadership." Joe Kurihara, who was also at the meeting, added that he'd do nothing for either Yoneda or Slocum.

When Karl told Elaine about the meeting later, then transcribed it for his diary, he noted that the entire episode had concluded with his proposal left "in limbo." But from there on out, according to Kurihara, the rise of the Manzanar Citizens' Federation caused all the following trouble in camp. Joe did not necessarily disagree with the concept of self-government; he even claimed he'd "voiced approval" of it, or at least told an WRA administrator so. Yet really, he blamed the MCF for ruining the small measure of "peace and tranquility" that had settled over Manzanar by summer's start. First the federation had been "quietly organized by those spineless leaders," Kurihara said; then "it brazenly made its appearance." In fact, he believed the MCF was none other than a front for the JACL. He questioned Koji Ariyoshi and Fred Tayama about this, but both denied the federation was just the JACL by another name.

Kurihara remained utterly unconvinced. These men were cowards, he thought as he seethed his way through summer, and he despised them all. He would "blast them to hell." As for "Carl Yoneda [sic]," he was both a "confirmed Communist" and a "minion" of the administration. Yoneda and the MCF gang were the "degenerates of the Nisei," Kurihara explained later in a report titled "Murder in Camp Manzanar."

Between planning the MCF and announcing it broadly in person, Karl and Koji began a petition urging President Roosevelt to open a second front in Europe and tap the manpower within the Japanese American camps. Elaine contributed by typing the petition in the stifling barrack air—still over 110°F inside, she wrote, despite darkness having fallen long ago. The next day, Karl and Koji circulated a copy among incarcerees. All the while, thoughts of new battle losses hounded Karl. "The war is going badly," he wrote later that day. "Everywhere in camp, I keep hearing the comment, 'Japan is strong, I tell you!'"

While many incarcerees supported and signed the petition, others were less enthusiastic, Kurihara among them. Controversy arose over the resolution's actual wording: was it calling for voluntary enlistment from the camps or mandatory drafting? The various versions in Karl's records suggest that Koji and the Yonedas wavered themselves among these choices. On July 23 the initial copy Elaine typed proposed "that the citizen manpower, now residing in evacuation camps, be utilized to the fullest extent . . . by accepting us as draftees and enlistees for front-line duty." But the version Karl dispatched to FDR, dated August 5 and appended to a list of 218 signatures, omitted specific mention of a draft. Instead, it called only for "utilizing the manpower" of citizens in the camps "for front-line duty in the United States Armed Forces."

The MCF's first general forum occurred between these dates and drafts. On July 28 Karl, Koji, and the rest of the federation's organizers presented their goals, including the petition, to the whole Manzanar community. According to Koji and other witnesses, attendees packed the barrack's mess hall well before the meeting was scheduled to begin at 8:30 PM. The temperature still hung around 102°F, and the overflow crowd of six hundred to seven hundred pressed into the building, then piled up in the heat outside, some standing on boxes to get a better view through the windows.

Karl and his MCF compatriots had tried to rectify their initial "chauvinism," as he'd put it, by inviting a woman to present on the topic of camp improvement. She'd dropped out before the meeting could begin though, due to fear of Kibei-Nisei retaliation, Karl heard from Koji. The rest of them prepared to take the floor without her. Just before they launched into their presentations, the entire barrack plunged into darkness.

Kurihara was there somewhere too, his heart pulsing in the blackout conditions, as the *Free Press* later described the scene. His mind was still churning with thoughts of the government's utter betrayal of the Nisei, how their rights had been "pulverized." He imagined all their faith, hopes, and dreams, gathered together and then smashed and strewn "into the field of eternal slavery," like so much dust and waste. *A direct affront to humanity*, he thought. As for drafting

Nisei from the camps where they'd been unjustly imprisoned, *Does America think it can mutilate the soul of its citizens and still claim her right over the bodies?* He'd come to this meeting with a purpose, he admitted later: to fulfill his vow to "crush" collaborators with the government and camp administration, wherever he found them.

By around 9:30 PM, an hour after the event was supposed to begin, Koji and the others decided to start their presentations anyway. Karl was sure the electricity had been cut by a saboteur like Kurihara. The *Free Press* and Manzanar documentary reporter Togo Tanaka both attributed the delay to a "small brush fire" and power-line break. (Tanaka was among a handful of Japanese Americans across all the incarceration centers who had been hired by the WRA as a documentarian to report and preserve, in English, accounts of camp life.) Koji banged his gavel to call the evening to order, and a few minutes later the lights flicked back on. Kurihara felt willing and ready to face whatever happened next. *No matter what danger,* he thought.

As each presenter took the floor and spoke, attendees cheered, according to Kurihara, which made him seethe even more. *They have not as yet learned their lesson,* he thought. But the crowd also peppered the speakers with questions: *What about our civil rights? Why aren't we being paid union wages? What ever happened to democracy?* Karl wrote later that "Chairman Ariyoshi" did his best to answer each query, though not what response Koji actually gave—since one can imagine no good response existed. Karl also noted increasing murmurs throughout the audience.

When Karl got up to speak, he delivered an address titled "Our Role in the War Effort." The *Free Press* quoted his message about the Nisei's double bind. "We have a double duty—to our country and our race," Karl said. "We are Americans of Japanese ancestry and the entire Japanese American population is placed on a testing ground. Whether we like it or not we have to go through this test if we want to survive this war." He held up the example of one of America's first "negro pilots," who despite experiencing harsh discrimination "never lost faith in this country." He told the crowd, "Remember our democracy isn't perfect, but it is the only system that opens the way to perfection." They must all "pitch in and do our share in this great crisis."

The heckling began almost immediately. Though Kurihara later insisted he let Karl finish before responding, Karl remembered hearing Kurihara and another man yelling while he spoke, hurling insults into the hot July night. "You *inu*!" "Spy!" "FBI Informer!" Japan "will win and hang you!" "Traitor!"

All witness testimonies confirmed that after Karl finished speaking and the open forum began, Kurihara took the floor, and it felt like fireworks going off. To Kurihara, it seemed he'd unleashed the explosion he'd long been holding back, a bombardment. He was going to leave the MCF in bits.

"I'm an American citizen," he yelled out to the crowd. "I served under fire in France. Now I'm in this prison. You're all here, too, with me," Kurihara cried. "I've proved my loyalty by fighting over there. Why doesn't the government trust me?" Kurihara could feel the energy rush through the crowd as his speech gained vigor and force. He called it "electric," like a pulse coursing through the room, charged by the live wire of his voice.

Tokie Slocum jumped in. "If you please, Mr. Chairman!" he shouted. "I was a Sergeant-Major in the last war. That was the highest position any Japanese ever attained," he appealed to the crowd. "For this loyalty the Government gave all of us veterans American citizenship."

Kurihara accepted none of it.

"We're here because of military necessity," Slocum insisted.

"Tokie!" yelled Kurihara. "Why are you in here? Isn't it because you couldn't go anyplace [else]?" He heard cheers from the crowd. "Isn't it because you're a Jap?" Now came that electric surge once again. *They're going mad with delight*, Joe thought. "Isn't it because the government doesn't trust you?" More hollers, then stamping and whistling. Later, he'd hear that the noise of the crowd's cheering spread all throughout camp. Now, standing in the overheated barrack mess hall, Kurihara felt he'd done something miraculous: swayed the people before him not just to his own mindset but also to delirium.

When Koji tried to restore order, Tokie Slocum waved him away. "I'll tell you why I'm here!" he yelled. "I'm here because my commander-in-chief, the president, ordered me in here!" But Kurihara knew he'd won, beating down Karl Yoneda, Tokie Slocum, and the rest of the MCF degenerates. "I had turned the table with unquestionable success," he wrote.

It was near midnight when the meeting finally broke up. The outside air was still hot and muggy as the crowd left the mess hall, many lingering out front. Karl, preparing to head back to Tommy and Elaine, heard a shout coming from somewhere out of the dark: "Come on, let's punch out that Yoneda character!"

A small group of Nisei internal police were there, unarmed but with a WRA-issued jeep parked nearby in the dirt. They drove Karl back to his barrack, across the broad, dusty expanses of the south and west firebreaks. Arriving home, Karl found a waiting, worried Elaine. He tried to convince her not to fret, that whatever danger his police escort implied had surely dissipated by now. The Nisei officers urged the Yonedas to alert them if any other trouble arose. Writing later, in the relative hush of his barrack, Karl admitted the police's reassurances could only provide small comfort. "There aren't any phones here and I'm afraid we'd be very much on our own" if danger had followed him back.

But the evening's threats would not stop him from promoting the proposals in which he believed. "I feel sorry for having brought all this upon my wife," he wrote. Still, anyone who knew Elaine could guess her position: she'd neither expect nor want him to turn back either.

One week later, on August 4, Karl and Koji mailed President Roosevelt, attaching their petition dated August 5, 1942, and signed by 218 of Manzanar's citizen incarcerees (including, Karl noted, 47 women). Karl's name appeared at the top, followed further down by Koji Ariyoshi, Tokie Slocum, Jimmy Oda, Fred Tayama, Togo Tanaka, and even Elaine, who'd signed "Mrs. R.E. Yoneda" (Rose Elaine Yoneda), as she was listed in the War Relocation Authority's record of Manzanar incarcerees. The son of their neighbors in block 4, Jimmy Ito, had also signed his name asking to be sent to battle for his country. It would be his last documented appearance on a public list of living camp incarcerees.

On August 11, Karl and Koji sent another copy of the FDR petition to media and union leaders across the country. To Karl, Elaine, and Koji, as well as many of the other signatories, the petition offered bold, unequivocal proof that Japanese Americans were ready and willing to fight for the country and against its enemies, the most powerful rebuttal they could offer to the nation's accusations of danger and disloyalty. Many other Manzanar incarcerees saw it differently. (Those in FDR's administration also took a different view. The president's private secretary reportedly scoffed, "Personally I do not believe the letter should be answered." He indicated that FDR's close advisor, Under Secretary of State Sumner Welles, agreed.)

By the morning of the August 6, Manzanar was buzzing with two controversial pieces of news. One involved the petition itself, which the *Free Press* had announced on their August 3 front page: a "quiet move by a few people" that had suddenly "gained momentum" and attracted "over 200 signatures," calling for both "draftees and enlistees for front-line duty." In the words of an WRA investigator, people were muttering about "giving away other people's sons."

The *Free Press* front page on August 3 also had also run an article about a new WRA directive from Washington, DC, identifying which Japanese Americans might apply for freedom from the West Coast camps. Applicants had to relocate outside the "Vital Defense Area," meaning all of California, Washington, Oregon, Arizona, Nevada, Utah, Idaho, and Montana. Neither Issei nor Kibei-Nisei could apply, only those who had "never lived in Japan or attended school there." Permission could be granted only after an extensive investigation, by which the WRA would somehow ascertain "the loyalty of the applicant." Then the government would provide transportation to the nearest bus or train station from camp, after which the newly freed incarceree would have to make their own way east.

Even many Nisei, non-Kibei incarcerees—citizens who were eligible for relocation—found the new directive unreasonable. As one American citizen put it, he'd already been "ousted from the only part of the U.S." that he knew, losing his business in the process; Why, he asked, "should I take a chance on what little cash I've got left and try to do something on the outside?"

As for Karl and Koji's petition, both block leaders and the majority of Manzanar residents were "violently opposed," according to another WRA researcher. "Their own personal woes were so great and evacuation was so recent" that incarcerees were unable to focus beyond the immediate challenges of their imprisonment. The intrusion of political factors into the personal struggles they were already waging was, the researcher wrote, "bitterly resented." Others feared that sending Japanese Americans to war from Manzanar would further fracture families and leave Issei parents alone behind barbed wire.

Kurihara had been nurturing his own resentment, particularly since the first MCF meeting, and he was determined to prepare for any future gatherings. Through a series of speeches he wrote for this purpose, he planned to unmask "Reds" like Karl and Koji as "informers" and race "betrayers." He considered the whole idea of sending the Nisei to war directly from concentration camps "just as bad if not worse than the Germans' persecution of the Jews."

He planned to publicly dismiss the petition as a "common tactic" of the Left: "They vigorously wave the flag and yell the loudest but with no true intention of sacrificing themselves on the altar of battlefield!"

Kurihara thought of his speeches as little sticks of dynamite, incendiaries he'd use to "bomb the Manzanar Citizens Federation out of existence." Sometimes, he wondered if he'd imagined his incredible success at turning the tables in the first meeting, at making the crowd swoon with his anger. He wondered, too, if he could do it again.

He planned to tell the next assembly that Yoneda and Ariyoshi would be "sitting in a cozy room, comfortably heated and be smoking their pipes of dream [sic], while you are out there suffering from cold and wants, with your very life at stake." Then he'd turn to face the "two-faced hypocrites" themselves: "General DeWitt made a monkey out of [you] spineless leaders," he'd proclaim as he stood before his audience. "If you are not satisfied of being a donkey, I will make jackasses out of you idiots!"

Despite the resentments Karl and Koji could not have helped sensing, the Yonedas remained proud of the petition, clipping and underlining a *San Francisco News* report about it. The article began, "When it comes to willingness to step from a place of complete safety into the front line, you have to hand the ribbon to 218 American citizens who have just petitioned President Roosevelt to open a second front—and send them to it as soldiers." The *News* noted that the "petition has something of a party-line tinge," but "nevertheless, an extra spot of courage was shown by Koji Ariyoshi and Karl G. Yoneda . . . who told the President they were responsible for its composition and circulation—this saying, in effect, that if any rap had to be taken as a result, they'd take it."

The second general Manzanar Citizens' Federation meeting occurred on August 6, nine days after the first. Karl tried to assert that the sacrifices they were making in Manzanar were a product of war, similar to those "the Americans on the outside are doing."

Kurihara retorted: Unlike on the outside, "our civil rights are no better than trash!" Karl rebutted that if their enemies were to continue winning, civil rights everywhere would "truly become worthless."

"I move that the Citizens Federation be renamed the JAPANESE WEL-FARE FEDERATION!" Kurihara jeered to resounding cheers.

Though Kurihara's motion was defeated and the MCF's charter passed, Karl was clearly shaken by the energy of the crowd when Kurihara and his allies spoke. "The pro-Japan faction has been checked for the time being," Karl wrote that night, "but we mustn't let our guard down."

Kurihara recorded his own thoughts about the meeting: another "dismal failure" for the MCF, which along with the crowd's cheers and stamping when he spoke, left him feeling "elated." Togo Tanaka, who also witnessed the meeting, claimed that Kurihara's "statements were repeated with conviction by scores of young men . . . and he was soon regarded as something of a leader and hero among a certain element in the Center."

The next day, the Yonedas received more brutal news. *People's World* had just reported the very first account of mobile gassing units for Jews in Europe, in an August 5 article titled "Thousands Die in Nazi Gas Chamber." Karl transcribed a summary in his diary on August 7, presumably the day the paper reached Manzanar. The article recounted the fates of "thousands of helpless Jews, men, women, and children," who "were herded into trucks . . . then told to disrobe and led into the 'bath.'" Next, the "Nazis began to wield whips and clubs . . . driving them into the automobile execution chamber," which was then "hermetically sealed. The auto would drive into the woods . . . [and] halt about 100 yards from the grave. The chauffeur would turn on the gas apparatus and leave. . . . From the truck would come stifled cries, howls, and poundings on the walls. After a quarter hour however, all was quiet."

"This marks the beginnings of the Nazis' campaign to eradicate the Jewish people," Karl surmised that night. He had no question that if enemy forces reached America, an equally gruesome fate could await his entire family. The article provided the Yonedas with renewed confirmation of their bedrock belief: the struggle against democracy's enemies must be prioritized above everything. They were no doubt still feeling the sting of this confirmation the next evening, when Karl heard calls of "Heil Hitler" ringing through a Manzanar barrack.

Over two hundred people squeezed into a meeting on the night of August 8, run by a group of Kibei-Nisei, to discuss discrimination against Kibei in general. It took place in one of Manzanar's barrack mess halls, a long, narrow room whose tables had been pushed against the walls. In their place, wooden benches had been lined up to face the speakers. Overhead, naked light bulbs hung from the rafters.

The evening's agenda focused on the new WRA directive for relocation, which prevented Kibei-Nisei from even applying to leave camp, despite their status as American citizens. Karl Yoneda was there, but Elaine stayed home as usual; someone had to watch Tommy. The entire event was held in Japanese and broadcast over loudspeakers for the overflow crowd outside, but Karl later translated for Elaine all that happened.

Joe Kurihara was in the crowd. He said that the meeting chairman, a man named Ben Kishi, had asked him to speak; Kurihara declined since he himself was not Kibei-Nisei, just Nisei. He attended rather as a spectator, "to weigh what was transpiring in their minds." Togo Tanaka was also there to observe, and he recorded a translation of Kurihara's comments. "If anyone, any Nisei, thinks he's an American I dare him to try to walk out of this prison," Joe announced. "This is no place for us. . . . It's a white man's country." Cheers from the crowd erupted, Tanaka noted.

When a Kibei-Nisei block leader named Sam Tateishi took the floor, he intimated that Manzanar's administrators might be pocketing canteen profits, and that neither his nor his children's citizenship meant anything anymore. Sam was the husband of Yuri Tateishi, who'd wept all the way to Manzanar in April after their baby son had been taken away on the morning of their forced removal. (After being sent alone to a Los Angeles hospital with a suspected case of measles and then dispatched to Manzanar a few weeks later, he became one of the camp's approximately one hundred incarcerees ages two and younger.) Now, Sam Tateishi's paltry assessment of his children's' citizenship was met with "loud stamping of approval," according to a documentary report. Karl, hearing Tateishi's claims, considered them a betrayal of his responsibility as block leader. *He just poured oil on the fire,* Karl thought angrily.

According to another source, Kurihara then announced, "I was wounded fighting for the United States. I draw compensation for my wounds from the United States government while rotting in a concentration camp." Standing before the mass of shifting bodies under the stark light of the barrack, he ripped open his shirt, exposing scars on his chest. He proclaimed his wounds his "keepsakes" from sacrificing his life for his once-nation. But "it is no longer my country," he cried; "I am now a hundred percent Japanese. I spit on these scars," he said, and then he did.

As Kurihara later documented in his own recollections of the evening, he told the crowd, "We are of the Yamato [Japanese] Race. In your veins and mine flow the Yamato blood, impregnated with the Yamato Damashii [Spirit]." He added, "Look at those Japanese in Japan who are making great sacrifices. Let's follow suit." Karl noted much "foot stomping and wild applause."

When Karl tried to address the gathering, he was met with jeers and insults. One FBI source reported that "the heckling was so loud that it was impossible to hear." Among the heated group, Karl saw Juichi Uyemoto, another Nisei who'd arrived at Manzanar on the same train and whom Karl had overheard calling for FDR's demise. Now, Uyemoto had shaved his mustache in the fashion of one General Araki, a right-wing Japanese military leader, and railed against "Reds." The crowd responded with delighted chants: "Araki! Araki!"

Karl translated other comments too: "The Nisei are a bunch of inform-ers, feeding reports on the camp to the government"; "Nisei like that should be beaten to death!" followed by more loud clapping. At some point, Tokie Slocum, widely considered a traitor and WRA collaborator, was rushed out of the meeting for his protection. Having stayed behind, Karl heard cheers for Adolf Hitler.

When the stomping and noise grew loud enough to alarm a white admin-istrator who'd been standing at the crowd's edge—unable to understand a word—he demanded that the meeting end, *now*. Karl noted that the chairman, Ben Kishi, brought the event to a conclusion with remarks in Japanese: "Our next gathering is going to be a victory celebration . . . because the Japanese army is going to come here and set us free!" With this, Karl wrote, Kishi "brought the house down."

Outside the barrack meeting hall, a Nisei internal policeman offered to drive Karl home. But a large group surrounded the jeep, calling out that Karl was a dog and a spy, threatening to beat him. Jimmy Oda tried to come to his defense until the police convinced the crowd to disperse and put the jeep in gear. When they got to block 4, Elaine was up, waiting once again and deeply concerned. Karl hugged her tightly. He felt his fury rising toward the authori-ties who refused to punish the kind of behavior that had metastasized that night. How could the administration "simply allow these pro-Japan types to go unchecked?" he fumed. After he narrated the events for his wife, she scribbled in her diary, "How long will it be?"

Meanwhile, Karl sat down to try to warn the government once more. He titled his document "Notes and Observations of 'Kibei Meeting.'" He added to the header, "Only Japanese spoken." He did not mark the report confidential, though no indication exists that he meant to publicize it either. After summarizing the events of the evening, he wrote, "It was evident that this gathering was definitely pro-Axis and anti-American. A great many . . . would have done bodily harm to [the] pro-American elements . . . if not for the presence of the Internal Police." Before signing his name, Karl warned that although many Issei and Kibei disagreed with this conduct, many did not, and camp endeavors to support the war effort, such as the camouflage net factory, were in jeopardy.

The next day, Karl and some MCF colleagues met with Manzanar director Roy Nash to discuss the Kibei meeting. The FBI would be alerted, Nash said, and the agitators "given admonitory lectures." Karl wondered if that would make a difference.

According to Joe Kurihara, it did not. A few days after the Kibei-Nisei meeting, he was called into an interview with an agent he described as "the head of the Japanese department" of the Southern California FBI. Kurihara wrote that he happily met with this agent, answered "frankly," and noticed that, like all FBI men, this one seemed simply to ask rote questions someone else had written for him. One was, "Who do you think will win this war?" Kurihara replied that the war had already been won, by Japan. "I know he didn't like it because his face had reddened," Joe wrote later. He felt sorry for having offended the man.

Even before Kurihara was called into the FBI meeting, Karl was unwilling to place his faith in any of Nash's "admonitory lectures," and he mailed a copy of his "Notes and Observations" to multiple senior WRA officers. Along with his report on the Kibei meeting, the mailing included a letter cosigned by Koji Ariyoshi, James Oda, Tokie Slocum, and another leftist, Joe M. Blamey, who was a *Free Press* staffer. They urged the government to investigate pro-Axis activities in Manzanar; embark on a "sincere effort" to protect those loyal to America, regardless of citizenship; provide industry defense work with prevailing wages to all citizens in all the camps; and reinstate the rights of citizenship to incarcerees, including "drafting and enlisting" them (though the letter did not mention freeing anyone).

They also advised separating the in-camp population further. The government should initiate both voluntary expatriation for US citizens wanting to renounce their citizenship *and* open separate facilities for US citizens and aliens. Nisei and Kibei-Nisei who wanted to stay with their Issei parents should be given the choice to enter the latter, and a hearing board should be available for Japanese nationals who wanted to enter the citizens' camp, assuming they were found "loyal to democracy."

Karl, Koji, and James Oda followed up on August 12 with another letter. "We believe in American democracy," they wrote in a cosigned missive to WRA senior officials and various politicians, but "it is the duty of the government . . . to justify fair treatment of American citizens of Japanese descent as well as Japanese nationals" and to "win them over to the cause of democracy." They also urged that *all* incarcerees, including noncitizens, be given the chance to leave camp and relocate east if loyalty could be demonstrated.

That night, Karl wrote his own message to the same recipients, again urging separation of incarcerees into disparate camps. "We recognize the military necessity of evacuation of ALL Japanese from the Pacific Coast," but, he argued, more must be done to protect the loyal, who were becoming targets in camp.

Perhaps unsurprisingly, Manzanar's assistant director Ned Campbell offered his own take on the question of segregating incarcerees. At a camp meeting back in July, when rumors of a proposed separation first began circulating, he mused aloud, "Americanism, to me, is being fair, tolerant, open minded, and rising above small differences. Trying to segregate the citizens from aliens here isn't, to my way of thinking, real Americanism." He followed up with some on-brand advice: "All of you are here; and you haven't got a prayer of a chance to get out of here. So let's be realistic."

By the time Elaine's rash had improved and she could return to the net factory, the workers were on strike. ("Arm is all healed," Dr. Kusayanagi wrote on August 13. "[Patient] feels very much better in general." Then she added approvingly, "lost another pound.") Two days earlier, on August 11, 670 net makers had walked off the job, protesting another new mandate, this one for longer workdays, and the huge wage disparity between in-camp net workers and those doing the same work outside of camp. "Reluctant workers were persuaded [to join the strike] with a length of iron pipe by rowdies," Togo Tanaka wrote in his documentary report. Though the Yonedas felt passionate about supporting the war effort and the net factory, they would not turn on striking laborers. Elaine remained off duty. Karl and Koji brought Nash a list of workers' demands for better payment and shorter hours.

Then two FBI agents came to Manzanar to question Karl, Koji, and some of the strikers. "We stuck to our guns," Karl wrote in his diary, "insisting that the strike [was] legitimate." After a week, the workers returned to the factory, Elaine among them, though Karl noted that Kurihara and his "gang" tried to stop them. "The negotiated agreement stipulates that they're to produce, on average, four garnished nets in an eight hour period," Karl wrote. He made no mention of the enduring wage disparity. The next day, Elaine saw Juichi Uyemoto, "General Araki," hanging around the factory with his mustache, suggesting that he might start working there too. She added a question mark and two exclamation points in her diary. He would be back, she'd learn soon, though not to work.

In the meantime, Karl's writings began to reveal increasing desperation, as if he had started screaming inside. STORM OF DENUNCIATION FROM THE FASCISTS, he noted at the top of a diary page. In another letter to the WRA head, he wrote, "It is a miracle if any pro-American can live in this atmosphere for the duration of war without going thru MENTAL TORTURE." Karl also reported, "There are a few American citizen [sic] of Japanese ancestry who have lost faith in this great democratic country and turned to pro-Axis, such as Joe Kurihara."

Five days earlier, Karl had entered the block leaders' office to find someone had written "Jewish Hall" on the wall near his desk. Then, as a new election for permanent block leaders approached, the Black Dragons began driving from door to door across block 4, waving their flag and warning residents not to vote for Karl: Yoneda petitioned to send all Japanese American soldiers to the front line and "let [the] enemy shoot them first," they were telling people. Also, Yoneda's dangerous and a Red; he's an informer, like Slocum; "he married a white woman and doesn't observe Japanese customs."

Karl, Tommy, and Elaine in front of their barrack apartment. *Courtesy of Karl G. Yoneda Papers, UCLA Library Special Collections*

Two days before the election, Elaine came home from the factory with welts on her limbs and forehead. She told Karl that Uyemoto had shown up again while she was working. She'd been standing alone at one end of the net frame in the open shed. The workers were arranged in an L shape, and Elaine was the lone person on the short side, she explained, exposed all around. She noticed that Uyemoto had shaved down his General Araki mustache, so that now—in what she felt sure was not just an unfortunate coincidence—it looked just like Hitler's. Uyemoto was being trailed by a group of young men with stones in their hands.

After Elaine came home bruised, teary-eyed, and bloodied on the forehead, Karl went straight to the administration building to report the attack. Campbell's response was, once again, "You're all Japanese. . . . I want you to get along."

Two nights later, Karl was defeated for another term on the Block Leaders' Council. Demoted to "Deputy Leader," he wrote in his diary; he'd gotten only thirteen votes. He left the barrack where the voting occurred amid loud whispers of his humiliation. "I expected to lose, but I didn't think it would be such a crushing defeat," he admitted privately. He, Elaine, and their progressive allies could no longer deny, in Karl's own words, that "our campaign to democratize the camp has failed."

Still, they were not ready to surrender their greater goal. "Our days here are not ended yet," he wrote. "We will carry on until the army sees fit to accept our applications for enlistment." But he could sense something ominous coming. Before the week was out, he told Jimmy Oda as much. Something bad was about to happen, he said, some violence about to descend. He wasn't sure exactly what form it would take, but he told Oda to keep a club nearby and not to sleep beneath the window.

———————

Two nights after Karl's election defeat, the Yonedas heard knocking on their door. It was already late, though inside, the barrack apartment still held the daytime heat. Elaine was typing letters when Karl called for the unknown visitor to enter. Over a dozen men walked in.

Ben Kishi, who'd chaired the Kibei meeting, was among them. So was Sam Tateishi, whose comments at that meeting Karl had thought were a betrayal of the man's block leader status. Elaine and Tommy looked up, saw the size of the group, and moved together on Tommy's cot. Karl saw it too and thought, *They're meaning to fix me.* He moved to the wall near the window, so he could get out quickly if he needed to. Both he and Elaine glimpsed more men outside in the dark, "staked all around," as she put it later.

One of Manzanar's most prominent agitators, Harry Ueno, later denied anyone had purposely threatened Karl that night. But a grimmer scene was reported by the Yonedas and Koji Ariyoshi, both in Elaine's unedited diary and in their various edited and published testimonies. Ueno conceded that Karl might have "felt kind of threatened because the way he reacted against a lot of people in the camp." Notwithstanding these claims, Ueno identified the event as "the beginning of the real conflict that started in camp . . . the very beginning."

Everyone who recorded the altercation agreed that the men had come to confront Karl about his written statement to the WRA describing the Kibei meeting on August 8, including the part about Tateishi's accusations against Manzanar administrators. Though Karl had not marked his "Notes and Observations" as confidential, the overall record remains unclear about whether he was surprised by their knowledge of his report; no testimony of the event mentions either way. The men told Karl that he must not be able to understand Japanese correctly, because his translation of the event was all wrong. Their voices began to rise. They had witnesses, someone said, who would swear that his translation was untrue.

Karl asked to see the meeting minutes. Ben Kishi declined. The debate went back and forth, and then three or four began to talk at once, and the noise in the room got louder. "Spy!" someone spat out at him in Japanese. "*Inu!*" Karl watched the men, but he could feel his wife and son's terror without even looking at them. Neither spoke Japanese, but there was no mistaking the mood of the confrontation unfolding before them.

Someone derided Karl for circulating the second-front petition. If Japan won, what did he think would happen to himself and those who'd signed it? Maybe even before that, maybe now, they'd tell the Japanese government all about his mother in Hiroshima. When the Japanese army arrived in California, they told him, he'd be the first one shot.

Elaine was on the bed, trying to still Tommy, who by this point was "cowering" in fear, she said later. Karl thought maybe thirty minutes of argument and threats had passed when he sensed a shift in the air, a new tension in the men's movements. He expected a beating to come next as his wife and son looked on. He thought about what would happen if he was beaten too badly to enlist, too badly to walk, even. He agreed to retract his statement at the next Block Leaders' Council meeting; he'd do so as long as Kishi and Tateishi testified before the same crowd to confronting him in his barrack.

They would have really beaten him to a pulp, Elaine thought as she watched the men leave. *They would have maimed him.* She assumed they'd left without hurting Karl only because she and Tommy had been there too. Still, she knew Tommy had been petrified. When Koji Ariyoshi came by later that night, he saw that Elaine was "still quite shaken up."

Karl stayed awake past midnight. "I don't want to remain here another minute!" he wrote in his diary, though of course he had no choice. Before he slept, he also wrote to his former recruiting station in San Francisco, requesting enlistment once again. A few days later, he took his request even higher. He appealed to the national director of the Selective Service for the US military, asking why they had stopped recruiting Japanese Americans in this time of war. "There are many men—and women—in camp who want to join the fight to defeat the 'Tokio-Rome-Berlin Axis,'" Karl urged. "Your kind and immediate attention will be appreciated." Among the meticulously kept records in his archive today, no response appears.

Meanwhile, at the Block Leaders' Council meeting on August 25, Karl retracted his written report about Tateishi. Three block leaders who'd previously confirmed Karl's version of the Kibei-Nisei meeting had now disavowed their own statements backing him. They had "since been approached by [a] kibei group," Karl wrote later. He also reported that before the council meeting ended, he was not only heckled into denying his version of events but also ordered to "apologize to Tateishi!" He recalled other shouts from the crowd. "Shame on you!" "Are you Japanese or what?"

With Karl facing rising threats and humiliations in Manzanar, Elaine was confronting renewed trouble from outside. On August 14, the Buchmans had written to tell her that Joyce had disappeared. Could Elaine somehow get permission to come help them search for her daughter? Joyce had been gone since she last left her grandparents' apartment on August 9. "Where, how when?" Elaine wrote in shock. As a family, they'd made "a mess," she told her diary, of the whole situation.

Elaine could still remember how Joyce had asked her mother to take her to Manzanar with her, way back in late March. But Elaine had said no. It wasn't any kind of place for her, she'd told her daughter. "You'd better stay with grandma and grandpa." The decision would gnaw at Elaine long past making it. "I didn't know what conditions were going to be like at Manzanar, and I felt I would probably have my hands full taking care of Tommy and his needs because of his health," she said later. "That was perhaps an error," she admitted. "I don't know whether it would have been better for her to go to camp or not."

By August 21 Joyce still had not been found. Elaine, her arms breaking out again in another angry rash, applied for permission to go search for her daughter. She felt torn about leaving when her husband seemed in danger, but now her eldest child might be in danger too. Elaine wrote later that this was the first time she'd asked for any special treatment as an incarceree.

On August 22 Manzanar administrators issued her a form, approved by the WRA office in San Francisco, "regarding Caucasian wives of residents in Manzanar." It was marked TEMPORARY LEAVE. Though Elaine could depart from camp and stay in San Francisco "for three weeks in order to close business in that city," she would have to "return at the end of that time." She also had to abide by a strict curfew: her pass to join the public was only "good between the hours of 6:00 AM until 7:00 PM." Neither Karl nor Tommy would be allowed to leave with her, since she would be traveling through the West Coast, where her husband and son were still barred for reasons of national security.

On the morning of August 25, Elaine stepped beyond the barbed wire and armed guards at Manzanar's entrance, Tommy crying and calling out for her. She was "tearful and despondent" as she left, Karl wrote, driving off with some WRA staff who were headed to L.A. Tommy continued weeping all afternoon.

The *Free Press* that day reported on Elaine's departure: GOES TO DAUGHTER, read the headline. "Mrs. Karl Yoneda has been granted permission to leave Manzanar for three weeks to be with her daughter who is ill in San Francisco," the paper explained. In the wake of her departure, more gossip followed in the mess halls: Karl's "old lady" had "become disgusted with him and run off."

Karl was in their barrack late that night, tired from Tommy's tears and dejected by all the rumormongering, when a friend rushed in with more news. Jimmy Oda had been beaten by a group of fifteen or so Kibei-Nisei. They struck him repeatedly while calling out "Commie scum!" Now Oda was at the camp hospital. The guys who attacked him might be heading to the Yonedas' barracks next, his friend warned. "So watch yourself!"

Near midnight, Karl finished recording the day's tumultuous details. He'd been thinking about all the name-calling and pressure Elaine had confronted in Manzanar, too, and how she'd "endured without a word of protest." He felt his eyes sting with remorse, thinking, *I've brought these hardships upon her.*

Before going to bed, he wrote another memo to Roy Nash, this one clearly marked "Confidential." He described the events of two nights previous: how the large group came to his apartment to threaten him in front of his wife and child, and then the heated council meeting the next day. "I want to state definitely that the Block Leaders' meeting, Monday, August 24, was not democratically controlled self-government, but a demonstration of Manzanar home-style fascism of threat and duress. . . . I will dare say that situation [*sic*] such as this cannot be permitted to continue in this country even tho we are in camp." When Karl was done, he checked the door lock and then tried to sleep, alone next to Tommy.

In Los Angeles that night, Elaine was similarly unmoored. She'd still received no news about her daughter, though she'd been able to see her father briefly when she got to L.A. The next morning, she rose early to take an all-day train to San Francisco, where her mother was making the rounds of their old friends, searching for Joyce. "Went looking—no results," Elaine wrote that night in her diary, and again on August 27: "Looking. No results." She mailed Karl in Manzanar to tell him the bad news.

Her letter would reach him in a camp on edge. "August passed without an explosion," wrote one of Joe Kurihara's interviewers a few years later. "The time bomb that was Manzanar had a little longer to tick."

7 FRACTURED
Summer–Fall 1942

ABOUT 370 MILES SOUTHEAST OF MANZANAR, at a concentration camp in Arizona known as Poston War Relocation Center, another mother of a daughter named Joyce was also trying to bring her child home that summer. This Joyce was only two years old, and like Tommy, she was a mixed-race toddler imprisoned with a Japanese American parent. Like both the Yonedas' children, her family had fractured when the incarcerations began.

Bettine Lawson, the mother of toddler Joyce, was a Nisei married to a white navy petty officer. Milton Lawson was stationed near their home in San Diego—likely one among a handful of reasons he'd remained behind when Bettine and their two-year-old had been taken away in the spring of 1942. Records indicate that only eight Caucasian men on the entire West Coast made, or were able to make, a different choice than Milton, becoming "as if Japanese," in the Western Defense Command's wording, and being imprisoned with a spouse and/or children. In the WRA's database of incarcerees, Elaine Yoneda herself was one of sixty-three white wives or mothers across all the camps.

In Poston, Bettine was longing to take her daughter and leave the desert prison reputed to be even hotter and dryer than Manzanar. She turned to a new ordinance issued by Karl Bendetsen, known variously as the mixed-marriage or mixed-blood policy. The policy served as a sequel of sorts to WDC Form PM-7, the one "allowing" non-Japanese family members the "privilege of accompanying" their relatives to camp.

When the forced removals and incarcerations began in spring 1942, the WCCA had adopted the rule that "the slightest amount of Japanese blood was sufficient to impose liability." By summer 1942 an estimated twenty-one hundred people in mixed-race families had entered one or another of the West Coast concentration camps. Now, Bendetsen was troubled by the ambiguity this unexpected, ethnically heterogenous crew presented. So he devised a plan to measure the Japanese-ness of any particular mixed family who wanted to leave lockup.

In early July, preparing to implement such a plan, Bendetsen sent a letter from his office in San Francisco to a Colonel Ralph Tate in the Washington, DC, office of the assistant secretary of war. "My dear Colonel," the letter began before reporting that all "Center Managers have been directed to report mixed marriages and mixed blood cases." Bendetsen claimed that for families with white or mixed-white members, "their Americanization and their awkward social position" was making "life in the Japanese Centers . . . a trying and often humiliating experience." (As for the trying and often humiliating experiences of the other incarcerees, Bendetsen only noted that the mixed families' "presence in the Assembly Centers was the source of constant irritation to the Japanese, provoked bad feeling and added to the difficulties of administration.")

This proved true for some families but not all. Elaine, for instance, experienced much more direct strife in response to the Yonedas' outspoken ideology than for being white. In any case, according to DeWitt, the policy's underlying objective was really something else: "protecting mixed-blood children from a Japanese environment," or, as one government official put it, isolating them from "infectious Japanese thought."

Bendetsen's first draft of the policy, released in early July 1942, created a complicated matrix of gender and racial categories to clarify the place of mixed-race family members within his overall civil defense plan. Above all else, the policies policing them could not contradict his story of "military necessity," of the supposed threat Japanese Americans posed to the nation because of their biology—not their beliefs or actions. He mapped his matrix onto a set of rules delineating who must remain behind barbed wire, who could be considered eligible for freedom from the camps, and who among these could be allowed to return to home, or alternately must remain exiled from the West Coast, allowed only to resettle east beyond the Western Dense Command Area (i.e., east of Arizona, Idaho, Montana, or Utah).

In his first released draft of the policy, he mandated that a Japanese or Japanese American man and his white wife and "unemancipated" mixed children could be eligible for freedom only if they did not return to the West Coast or anywhere in the WDC area. A white American man could be released and return to the West Coast with his Japanese or Japanese American wife if they had young mixed children with them in camp and if the "environment of the family" could be proven "Caucasian." Otherwise, they would have to resettle outside the restricted area, separate from each other while he returned home alone, or remain imprisoned. "Adult individuals of mixed blood" who were citizens of the United States could be eligible for release and return to the West Coast if they could prove that their home "environment has been Caucasian" before they were put in a camp. Otherwise, they too would have to resettle east of the WDC area or remain imprisoned. Spouses in mixed marriages without unemancipated children had no recourse at all to release under the mixed-marriage policy unless married to someone serving in the US Armed Forces. In this case, the childless woman could be freed only if she agreed not to go home and resettled east.

If an applicant or family met one of these criteria, they would be vetted by the War Relocation Authority, and the next stage of Bendetsen's plan began. Applicants had to pass army intelligence and FBI background checks, provide proof of either a job or other financial support outside camp, and gain approval from the sheriff or local police chief at their intended destination. If an applicant or family was lucky enough to gain freedom, they left camp with an order to report every month to an army station near their intended residence, where they would submit documentation of any family births, deaths, marriages, divorces, changes of address, "or any incident bearing upon community acceptance" of—i.e., objections to—their presence outside camp.

That summer, a week before Elaine's daughter disappeared from her grandparents' home, and while Bettine Lawson was trying to gain freedom for her own daughter named Joyce, the *Manzanar Free Press* noted one of the first incarcerees to be released under Bendetsen's new policy. Raymond Hamamoto was seven years old and incarcerated with his Japanese American father. He was freed and allowed to return to his non-Japanese mother, whom records indicate had never entered camp. "The heretofore impenetrable gates to the outside world swung open this week," the *Free Press* rhapsodized on August 5, 1942, describing only young Raymond's departure. His father presumably had to stay behind in Manzanar.

Nine days previous, on July 27, the paper had reported Manzanar's very first non-Japanese wife to leave lockup with her children, noting the "official release" of "Mrs. Ethel Maruyama, Caucasian wife of a Japanese and two children." Maruyama's husband, like Raymond Hamamoto's father, was not freed with his family.

Though in these two cases, incarcerees seem to have been released shortly after Bendetsen's mixed-marriage policy was announced on July 10, throughout that summer and beyond, his plan for multiethnic families created much confusion. Camp administrators were initially stymied by the policy's sole focus on mixed families of Japanese and European heritage. Unlike the Murayamas, Yonedas, and Lawsons, many mixed families with incarcerated relatives had no members who counted as "white" to the WCCA or WRA. After reading Bendetsen's new policy, administrators at the camps wondered how to handle Chinese, Mexican, Indian, and Filipino husbands—spouses who would not be identified as white but were citizens of "friendly" (or US-colonized) territories. And just what was a "Caucasian environment" anyway?

Within two weeks of the plan's release, confusion among camp staff became impossible to ignore. So Bendetsen and his staff went back to their drawing board of blood and marriage categories—where they would return again and again throughout much of the war—in an effort to resolve the ongoing ambiguities the policy could never seem to settle. The changes they rolled out, beginning in late July 1942, included an expanded category of husbands eligible for release with their Japanese American wives. Once including only "Caucasians," this group grew to encompass the many cases of non-Japanese but also non-white American men, as well as Hispanic Americans and those who were citizens of friendly or Allied-colonized nations such as China, the Philippines, Mexico, and India. These men could now be freed with their spouses as long as they had unemancipated children with them in camp and agreed to resettle east. Eventually, Bendetsen wrote that even a white woman who had "sired" mixed children could be eligible both for release *and* to return home to the West Coast with her young offspring—but only if her Japanese or Japanese American husband were "dead or long since separated" from the family.

By October 1942 Bendetsen seemed to have scrapped the requirement that single, mixed-race adults prove their home environment before the war was "Caucasian," instead settling for a new parameter. As one WCCA social worker explained, any American "whose non-Japanese blood exceeds Japanese blood" could now potentially be eligible to live on the West Coast. A Caucasian home environment made no difference for six-year-old Richard Honda that fall in

Manzanar, however. He'd been adopted by a white family in California, the Spandrios, at the age of four months, after his Japanese biological mother's death. Five years later, the boy was forcibly removed from his family and placed in Manzanar Children's Village. According to a memo about ongoing confusion over WCCA policy concerning mixed families, "The Spandrio family asked to have him returned and claimed that the community would accept the child wholeheartedly." The response arrived on November 13, 1942: "The request for the release of Richard Honda, a person of Japanese ancestry, age six years, to residing [*sic*] in Military Area No. 1 is disapproved."

As for what constituted a "Caucasian environment" in mixed-marriage families with dependent children, Bendetsen usually left that up to WCCA or WRA administrators. He was moved to weigh in himself occasionally, though. He agitated strongly against release for one young mixed white and Japanese woman and her two mixed infants, based on his suspicion that their family culture was insufficiently "Caucasian" in spirit. Theresa Takayoshi, who'd been incarcerated with her Japanese American husband and babies at Minidoka Relocation Center in Idaho, applied for release for herself and her children in order to return to Seattle and live with her white mother. She noted in her application that she did not even speak Japanese. But Bendetsen declared Takayoshi "Japanese pure and simple," as if one side of her heritage had somehow magically evaporated—or perhaps, using Bendetsen's own trope, as if her "blood" had turned all Japanese. The root of this alchemy, in both Bendetsen's view and that of the adjutant general who worked under him, was that the bed was thicker than blood; both Takayoshi and her mother had married men of Japanese descent, evidence that Takayoshi and her children had apparently always "lived in non-American surroundings."

For other applicants under the policy, camp administrators generally tried to define a Caucasian or "American" environment by language spoken, percentage of friends who were Japanese or not, and even the type of food the family ate before the war. But often, they simply deferred to the equally vague category of appearance, as in the case of a woman named Mitsuko Komuro Ramos. She had been forced to leave her home in Santa Barbara and was incarcerated in a camp known as Tulare Assembly Center, approximately 130 miles southwest of Manzanar. Like Bettine Lawson, she had applied for release that summer of 1942. But Ramos had no children, so she knew returning to California would be prohibited. Instead, she applied to leave camp after securing a job offer as a maid in Illinois. She was the wife of a US Army enlistee from the Philippines. Though she was ethnically Japanese and had been born in Japan, her file compiled by WCCA staff noted, in favor of her application, that she did "not appear to be Japanese" at all, having "facial characteristics more nearly typifying persons of Spanish descent," as if she had somehow acquired the ethnic appearance of the Europeans who had once colonized her husband's homeland. According to her file, her husband, stationed in San Luis Obispo with the First Filipino Infantry Battalion of the US Army, agreed that life as a maid in Illinois would be better than in a concentration camp in California, even though they'd be farther apart than ever. Mitsuko would leave behind in Tulare her parents and younger siblings, but she did not live in the same barrack with them in the camp, "nor is the association [with her family] very close, since her marriage to Mr. Ramos, a Filipino."

As for Bettine Lawson, when she applied that summer for release for herself and two-year-old Joyce, the file explaining their eventual success noted, "Neither of them had any contact with Jap. societies" in San Diego. Moreover, Bettine's "appearance" was apparently "Chinese."

The WCCA and WRA showed a similarly obsessive and bizarre streak in efforts to define "unemancipated children." In the case of two pregnant wives that summer, officials balked at the women's release until after they gave birth. Both were expecting their first child, but administrators would not consider a child "unemancipated" before delivery. About 450 miles northwest of Manzanar, at Tule Lake War Relocation Center in Northern California, Ethel Taylor was seven months pregnant that summer of 1942. She was a young Japanese American woman hoping to return home in time for her child's birth, to be with her husband, a white man from whom she'd been forcibly separated that spring when she was removed from their home in Roseville, California. When she appealed to Bendetsen's deputy, Herman Goebel, he declared in an official letter, "This office declines to extend the mixed marriage policy to cover pregnant women." He added for good measure, "Until the child is born, Mrs. Taylor is not eligible for residence in the evacuated area."

At the Portland Assembly Center across the state line in Oregon, a woman in a mixed marriage identified only as a Mrs. Barrinuevo also applied for release, on the grounds of being pregnant with her first child. Portland was an overcrowded, fly-infested camp of cojoined buildings used before the war for housing and showcasing livestock. In the simmering heat of an August summer, on the same day Elaine Yoneda learned of her daughter's disappearance, the manager of Portland expressed his doubts about Barrinuevo's pregnancy. With a meticulousness Bendetsen would undoubtably admire, he ordered her examined by the camp's doctor "for a definite determination in this regards."

In Manzanar, as that summer of 1942 drew to a close, Karl and Tommy Yoneda wondered if Joyce would ever be found while they waited anxiously for Elaine's return. "Today was Elaine's birthday; she's just turned thirty-six," Karl wrote on September 4. It was a painful day for both him and Tommy, and he wished his wife were with them, that he could have given her a party of some kind. Instead, that night at the mess hall, he heard more whispers: "It's true, isn't it?—His old lady has taken off, just like I said." He heard other rumors too: "The guy has come here to hide, because he was expelled from the CIO" (a federation of unions); "He's a roughneck"; "Once the Japanese army gets here, the first one we're going to do in is Yoneda."

A few days later, another sandstorm erupted, and Tommy fell seriously ill once again. "He's having difficulty breathing," Karl wrote in his diary. A scarlet rash had spread over the boy's entire body, a reaction to something he ate, Karl thought, on top of the onslaught of dust. Karl repeatedly took him to the camp hospital, where the doctors ordered a series of injections. But the boy still wheezed and scratched, vomited, and thrashed in his sleep throughout the following days and nights, calling, "Mummy!" over and over in his misery. Karl watched his son writhing and rasping, and he wanted to cry. He also wanted to scream. "Elaine, where ARE you?" he wrote. There'd been no letter from her in her days, and he felt sick about that too.

Still, Karl worked to keep busy. A few days before Tommy's illness, he and the Nishimuras had moved the partition between their adjoining barrack rooms, so the elderly Chotaro and young George Nishimura could live with their relatives, and the Yonedas would finally have privacy. The new setup would make both the Nishimuras and the Yonedas luckier than most, since only about a quarter of all Manzanar's "apartments" held single families by that point; the rest still forced unrelated inhabitants into close quarters. Karl was relieved but chagrined over the Nishimuras' lack of adequate space. "It's unreasonable for nine people to be packed like sardines into a single room," he wrote. "These are inhuman conditions, and I intend to raise the issue at our next Leader's meeting."

Karl also celebrated with his close leftist ally Koji Ariyoshi, who married an incarceree named Taeko Ito on an early September Saturday in one of the camp's barracks, followed by a reception that evening in a mess hall with dozens of friends. Karl was best man. Two WRA administrators served as witnesses and a white priest led the vows in a ceremony the *Free Press* described as "simple." Both the bride and groom wore matching suits of blue. They announced that they planned to "spend their honeymoon working on the camouflage project."

As usual, Karl continued with his own forms of activism. He met with the WRA's western director to discuss again a plan for Nisei enlistment, making Manzanar a camp of Issei and Nisei "who swear allegiance to the United States" as he put it, and segregating out or somehow controlling the "pro-Japaners' unruly behavior." He continued his writing too. The next day, the *Manzanar Free Press* printed a rebuttal he'd written to Socialist Party of America leader Norman Thomas, who'd circulated a pamphlet Karl criticized as "anti-Roosevelt" and whom Karl considered both "anti-Communist" and a secret Hitler supporter. Thomas had written about the curtailment of Japanese American civil rights but failed to "utter a single word about the part that the Japanese-Americans should play to help win this war for democracy," Karl scoffed, "which is more important than arguing about the constitutionality of [the] evacuation order, especially at this time." What was paramount now, Karl argued, was to "conduct ourselves in such a fashion that the United States government will take further steps to recognize our full citizenship status."

Karl noted darker news from outside too: CAUCASIAN DOCTOR ADVOCATES JAPANESE EXTERMINATION. He copied a letter from a white physician printed in the previous week's *San Francisco Chronicle*, who'd insisted that either Japanese men should be sterilized or a decree announced "that every man whose wife has a baby be shot." "Hitlerism, American Style!" Karl wrote in his diary. But both he and Tommy were cheered by more personal news. That same day, they received a letter from Elaine that she'd be back on September 15. "Tommy is ecstatic—'Mummy's coming home!'" Karl wrote.

While Karl had been trying to write his way out of camp, combat the threats around him, and care for an ailing Tommy, Elaine had been in San

Francisco dodging her own series of near misses. She and Mollie had listed Joyce as a missing person and provided her picture to police, but they'd spent days confronting dead ends. Finally, on August 28, Elaine and her mother located her daughter's address, but not Joyce herself. They would be unable to see her until the following week—for reasons Elaine never explained in any extant document. What seems clear is that Joyce had run away—and that she was still reluctant to see her mother, even after Elaine and Mollie tracked where she'd gone.

On August 31 Elaine added one clipped line to her diary: "Saw Joyce." When she wrote to Karl about the reunion, though, she evidently added more emotion. "She sounds extremely happy," Karl wrote after reading her letter, "and it's a great relief for me as well." "When is mummy coming back?" Tommy wanted to know.

Elaine's next diary entries continued to describe only the bare bones. "Saw Joyce," she wrote again on September 5, adding nothing more. Three days later, she'd taken her daughter to "Mt Zion," most likely a reference to the San Francisco hospital Mount Zion, around the corner from their old apartment near the Fillmore. The facility had been built in the late nineteenth century by the city's Jewish community, who described it as a refuge for "the indigent sick without regard to race or creed." An old photograph shows that when Elaine and her daughter sought help there, the building comprised a tidy brick structure with a carved sign above its curved portico. MOUNT ZION HOSPI-TAL, it read, the words a neatly chiseled promise that internal chaos could be righted and swept clean simply by stepping through that arched entry. But what exactly Elaine thought or felt when she and Joyce passed the doorway's threshold remains lost to history. She left no trace publicly, neither about her own nor her daughter's inner turmoil.

Elaine's diary does make clear that over the next few days, she and Mollie discussed the options. One involved placing Joyce in a residential school in Seattle, though by September 10, they were at San Francisco's Juvenile Hall. There, Elaine signed a paper for an evaluation and at least short-term commitment of her daughter, and Mollie agreed to stay nearby while Elaine returned to Manzanar. "Saw Joyce for the last time until relocated," Elaine wrote that day. Whether she was referring to her own relocation from Manzanar or to a future relocation of Joyce, she never specified.

Before returning to camp, Elaine stopped to visit friends at Tanforan Assembly Center, another temporary detention site for Japanese Americans, mainly from the San Francisco Bay Area. Her contacts there, like the incarcerees at Santa Anita, were housed in converted animal stalls. She also spoke to the leftist National Lawyers Guild, whose members asked how she could say the US camps were not so bad. Her biggest criticisms of Manzanar and the so-called centers like it, she told them, were the deprivation and lack of freedom they imposed, and of course that they did not make enough war work available to those held there. She wanted to "finish the war in a hurry and do away with the Axis," she said, and in their current setup, the US detention sites did not support these aims effectively enough. As usual, the specter of fascist brutality loomed largest. Only in consideration of its long, dark shadow—and its potential to sweep America—must one consider the US camps, she urged. America's camps could not be equated to Hitler's, so "we can't condemn them altogether," she argued.

"You preferred certain inconveniences to annihilation?" an interviewer asked her later. "Yes," she answered. As for any kind of public resistance from within Manzanar or similar sites, Elaine, like Karl, foresaw a negative end result. "Our fight for civil rights," she believed, would have to wait until "after the war was over."

When she got back to Manzanar on the late afternoon of September 15, the air still hung heavy at over 100°F. After she passed through the camp gates, Tommy raced toward her, yelling "Mummy! Mummy!" Karl exhaled in relief. That evening, several neighbors came over to their barrack room to welcome her back, and they deluged Elaine with questions about an outside world they'd not seen in six months. Both men and women were flocking in droves to enlistment stations, Elaine told them.

Over the next few weeks, she and Karl listened to records she'd gotten from friends in the Bay Area on a portable Victrola they'd given her as a gift. The Yonedas swooned to Paul Robeson's 1940 album *Ballad for Americans*, feeling grateful to have his powerful voice right there with them in their barrack, singing about slavery and freedom, the nation's history and diversity, and the need to fight injustice. When Elaine sang along, she was known to do so both enthusiastically and off-key, tapping her foot to a beat only she could hear, emitting random tones, and overtaken with the joy of it all.

But she also felt preoccupied with Joyce in the days after her return. "Letter from mama nothing definite yet re: Joyce," she wrote on September 19. Two days later, her entire diary entry comprised one terse line—"Nothing new re: J." She wrote no more for the next three days. Finally on September 26, she received a wire from her mother. Juvenile Hall had released Joyce, and Mollie was taking her granddaughter back to Los Angeles. Elaine felt for the first time in almost two months that the situation had been settled. It would remain so only for a short while.

As the turmoil with Joyce had played out, strife in Manzanar continued to increase over a series of new WRA directives and decisions concerning incarceree self-governance. In essence, the block leaders—almost all Issei—were to be demoted, and a new community council—made up solely of Nisei, the Issei's own children—would have the only chance for input on camp policies and rules. The Caucasian administration alone would still have final say.

Meanwhile, the decline of the Manzanar Citizens' Federation was attracting gleeful attention from certain corners. A few days after Elaine's return, Joe Kurihara published an open challenge to Karl and his MCF colleagues. His "calculation," he wrote privately, "was to smash their prestige." In a letter to the *Manzanar Free Press*, Kurihara observed, "It looks to me that the leaders of the Manzanar Citizen's Federation have holed up. . . . It is an implied admission on their part that they represent the minority instead of the majority of Japanese-American citizens." If they still believed the opposite, "then why not come out and debate the issue out in the public," Kurihara taunted. "No one accepted the challenge," he pointed out later—proof of their inability to "fight it out like a man." His broader strategy had worked: "Having suffered the loss of public prestige," he wrote, "the Manzanar Citizens Federation finally dropped out of existence."

Kurihara made another move around this time that would have more dire consequences for Karl and his ideological allies, though the Yonedas seemed to remain unaware for another few months at least. Neither made mention of it in their writings until December of that year. But according to Kurihara himself, as early as September 1942, he'd drawn up a list of "marked individuals" in camp. It comprised people who'd been active in the JACL and the Manzanar Citizens' Federation. The following January, Togo Tanaka wrote that, at least since mid-September 1942, there had been a "No. 1. public secret" in camp, circulating among the Japanese-speaking population of Issei and Kibei-Nisei. Kurihara called it the "death list." He saved a slot for Karl Yoneda.

———————

In addition to the new rules around self-governance, that late-summer and early fall the WRA announced new procedures for incarcerees—including those not in mixed-race families, those considered 100 percent "full-blooded" Japanese—to apply to leave camp, either temporarily or permanently. In early September, Manzanar incarcerees learned that many American citizens among them could soon be eligible for freedom if they were willing to relocate to the eastern or central United States. EVACUEES ADVISED TO "FORGET CALIFORNIA!" the *Free Press* reported. "The War Relocation Authority's Chief of Employment Thomas W. Holland is advising evacuees to 'look eastward for relocation' . . . Holland has set down a tentative pattern of 'procedure whereby people can get out of the relocation centers,'" but not to the West Coast in general, and certainly not back to California, where the great majority of incarcerees lived before they were imprisoned. The "history of Japanese in that state indicates strong, organized resistance that foreshadows trouble," the WRA insisted. "One of the things which the W.R.A. Employment Division is consciously avoiding in its relocation program is 'anything that tends toward concentration of a large number of Japanese in any one area.'"

By mid-September, Karl Bendetsen was writing to WRA officials to clarify the WCCA's even broader limits on resettlement. "It is the policy of the Wartime Civil Control Administration," he wrote, to release only American citizens, and only for "private employment . . . beyond the limits of the Western Defense Command and not within the States of Colorado and Texas." In addition, Bendetsen indicated that incarcerees might also be eligible for release to attend college, even in the state of Colorado, though "permission to attend colleges located within the area of the Western Defense Command is denied."

By early October, the regulations circumscribing this permanent relocation program for citizens had been approved in Washington, DC. Despite Bendetsen's desired limitations, by the end of that month, the possibility arose for Kibei-Nisei and Issei to apply too. Resettlement east would still only be permitted under certain circumstances, however. "Extensive investigation" and approval by the FBI were required, as well as clear documentation of a guaranteed job offer outside the entire Western Defense Command area, with the possible exception of Utah and Idaho.

Alongside the relocation program, the government announced two other initiatives to begin winnowing the in-camp population. One in particular interested Karl Yoneda; the other shocked even Elaine when she learned of it. In early September, Manzanar's project director had announced a new furlough program based on Idaho's need for sugar-beet toppers, those willing to harvest the fields to increase the nation's wartime food supply by replacing enlisted workers. The call appealed to Karl Yoneda, at least until he could enlist himself one day.

The next month, Elaine added an alarmed entry to her diary corresponding to the other initiative, this one related the possibility of repatriation or expatriation: returning—or, for most incarcerees, going for the first time—to Japan, by relinquishing either American residency or citizenship. The US government had first raised this idea back in July, and by late summer, over four hundred in Manzanar had applied for repatriation or expatriation, though when or if they'd actually be sent to Japan was still unknown. Some had applied because relatives were doing so, and they did not want their families to be separated forever. Others just felt unbearably disillusioned by or unsafe in the United States, even though they were American. "Even if America wins, there'll be small chance for Issei," said one older man. A younger one decided, "If citizenship is going to be taken away from us Nisei, I'm going to Japan."

Now in October, about forty people in Manzanar received unsolicited letters "from 'Col B' about repatriation!!" Elaine wrote. Altogether across the camps that October, Bendetsen sent around 160 of such missives, alerting recipients that they were being considered for repatriation, whether or not they had ever applied for it. In fact, only 9 among the 160 had expressed interest back in July about the future possibility of repatriation. Some recipients of the letter neither were Japanese citizens nor had ever even visited the country.

"Certain Japanese persons are currently being considered for repatriation to Japan," the missive read. "You, and those members of your family listed above, are being so considered." The letter was officially called WCCA E-107, and government records indicate it was created in September 1942 by the WCCA, "especially for persons receiving direct repatriation consideration by the State Department but who had not previously filed a Request for Repatriation."

All 160 of them were signed "Karl R. Bendetsen, Colonel, G.S.C. Assistant Chief of Staff Civil Affairs Division."

With the sudden appearance, unbidden, of the letter at the barracks of forty Manzanar families or individuals, rumors began circulating of Korean spies and other informers in camp. A few weeks later, the *Free Press* printed a short piece clarifying the full stakes of the entire affair: those who signed up for a chance to repatriate to Japan would not be eligible to apply for relocation anywhere in the United States.

Meanwhile, Karl's longing to leave camp reached new urgency. "I've strengthened my determination to get out of this place, the sooner the better," he wrote. He and Koji Ariyoshi promised each other that they would not spend their futures in Manzanar. Instead, they planned to be serving soon in the nation's armed forces.

By the week or so after Elaine's return, the late-September nights had begun to get much colder, despite persistent daytime heat. She and Karl simultaneously planned for winter in camp and for an earlier escape. He lined the walls of their barrack room with plasterboard; the WRA had begun to make some available before the next deep freeze brought fresh misery to the flimsy dwellings. The Yonedas also hoped that, in addition to a bit of warmth, the makeshift insulation would provide a barrier to the dust bearing down on Tommy. Regardless of his efforts to thicken the barrack walls, Karl swore to Elaine that they'd be out before winter. In answer, she wrapped her arms around him.

Karl continued to weigh the furlough option to help save the nation's sugar beets, particularly after Koji left to do so on October 1 and then immediately wired Karl, urging him to follow. Since the previous spring, famers' groups in both Montana and Idaho had been pleading for help harvesting the vital crop. "We Have Exhausted Every Means Available to Us to Get Sugar Beet Field Labor," the North Montana Beet Growers Association had wired their senator in May 1942. "Financial Ruin," they warned for their industry. The association proposed bringing Japanese Americans from the concentration camps to work the fields under armed guard, along with "Assurance These People Will Be Moved from Montana at End of War."

Despite the ungrateful gloss to such an urgent request, Karl still felt pulled to go. (Not even the Idaho governor's own racist remarks—which the Yonedas had noted back in July—could dissuade him: "Japs live like rats, breed like rats and act like rats"; A "good solution to the Jap problem in Idaho—and the nation—would be to send them all back to Japan, then sink the Island.") Rather, Karl's deepest misgivings concerned leaving Elaine and Tommy alone in camp. But together the Yonedas decided he should go to Idaho. It was the only option left for him to actively bolster the country's resources, so necessary for its fight against the enemy.

Before he left, he tried one more time to join the US Army, writing again to the national director of the Selective Service and cc'ing President Roosevelt. He reminded the official that he, Karl, had contacted him back in August, as well as his local draft board, with a request for immediate enlistment or drafting. "To date I have received no reply," he wrote.

On the morning of October 6, Karl hesitated before boarding a bus out of Manzanar. He felt cleaved down the middle when he thought about leaving his family, and for a moment he was unsure he could actually do it. But he climbed up the short steps of the bus and took a seat. He could hear Tommy crying beyond the windows, calling out for Karl to take him too. And then the bus pulled away, past the guarded entry, and Tommy's cries receded in the distance. It would be the last time for six weeks that Karl would see the camp's barbed wire, and it was the first time in six months he'd seen the world beyond Manzanar. The scenery seemed both strange and familiar. Despite the painful departure, Karl thought the world outside looked quite beautiful too.

With her husband gone, Elaine quit the camouflage net factory so she could take care of Tommy on her own. In the days after Karl's departure, two strange events occurred. One involved Joe Kurihara. He and two other men stopped by the Yonedas' barrack. They told Elaine they had a "proposition" for Karl. She wrote to tell Karl about it, and she seemed mystified but not terribly alarmed, for the men left soon after finding her husband unavailable. Kurihara wrote about the encounter as well, in his report "Murder in Camp Manzanar." He said that he'd only wanted to challenge Karl to an open debate. He felt disappointed that neither Karl nor any of the other founders of the Manzanar Citizens' Federation—whom he'd also hoped to challenge publicly—were available or willing to spar with him.

A few days later, the Buchmans arrived for a weekend visit, bringing Joyce. Elaine added little about the reunion in her diary, but she wrote to Karl about it, and he felt relieved reading that it went well after all the recent tension. A different occurrence from that weekend had caught more of Elaine's concern: a public address, called "the Forum," held on Saturday evening after dinner, in the mess hall of one of the barrack blocks. The event featured a pair of speakers. One was manager of the largest low-income federal housing project in California, and the other was a psychiatric social worker. According to the *Free Press*, the first was "an authority on minority problems" who'd come to Manzanar to "discuss the similarity of all American minority groups," while the social worker led "a discussion on mental health problems and their treatment." (How or why the two were connected, the paper did not clarify.)

Elaine arrived too late to hear either man speak, but she joined in time for the post-address conversation. "Some of the questions and discussions!" she exclaimed in her diary. Someone's contribution involved noting that Jews were the "ugliest people on earth."

Elaine attributed this comment to another member of the audience that evening: a white midwestern socialite named Mrs. Nace Satterlee. Satterlee was a fast-talking writer whom Togo Tanaka later described as uncommonly eager to share her thoughts. Though no indication exists that Elaine knew much about her, Satterlee had argued in the 1930s in the *New York Times* against US intervention in the violence in Europe; now, she'd been allowed by the WRA to drop in at Manzanar periodically for a novel she was writing about "the Japanese problem." (According to the *Free Press*, she also "feted guests" with a "chicken spread" in one of the barrack "recreation halls"—which seemed to involve mostly wives of WRA administrators and a few *Free Press* staff.) When Satterlee wasn't doing research or organizing dinner parties at Manzanar, she was "pleasantly holed up," Tanaka reported, in a rented apartment in nearby Lone Pine, pecking away at her typewriter in an effort to finish her fictionalized account of the "evacuation." Elaine wasn't even positive of the woman's name ("Mrs. Satterlee??" she guessed), but the comment hung in her memory of the weekend. She didn't hold the racist banter against the evening's official speakers, though, nor let it dampen her eagerness to address both the world's and the camp's challenges. The next afternoon, she had both men over for an hour of discussion, along with the director of the adult education program at Manzanar and his wife.

Elaine continued to welcome visitors throughout Karl's absence, helping to lighten her loneliness. Their good friend Jimmy Oda—who used to write occasionally for *Doho*, Karl's former newspaper—came to check on her frequently, as did other friends from camp, whom she welcomed to their barrack room with coffee. In late October, Karl sent toys for Tommy ("Will he bring back a football?" the boy wanted to know) and a crate of apples ("Idaho Delicious," Elaine called them) which they passed out to their neighbors. Elaine even had her hair done twice at the camp's new makeshift beauty parlor, where the women sat in a tight line of hardback chairs under a row of conelike dryers or bent their heads over one long, plain table as fellow incarcerees in crisp white dresses combed their hair.

Sometimes, Jimmy Oda came over with his future wife, Mary Sakaguchi—who'd just begun medical school at UCLA when she was incarcerated along with her family—and her younger sister Lily, a college freshman at the top of her class before the war. Koji's new wife, Takeo, and a handful of other friends would join them, too, and they'd all play poker and eat a small meal together.

None of them yet knew that before they were freed from Manzanar, three of Mary and Lily's family members would die within its borders: their oldest brother Obo, who would perish from stomach cancer; twenty-six-year-old sister Chico, who'd been healthy before Manzanar but would die there from sudden, dust-induced asthma; and their father, felled by cancer of the nasal pharynx, which the family would forever believe was made more severe by Owens Valley's sandstorms. Soon after, young Lily would be removed from camp and hospitalized for a nervous breakdown, though she would eventually be sent back to Manzanar, once she was considered well enough.

As the weather grew colder in Karl's absence, Elaine began to sense anew the persistent dangers of the desert for Tommy. The wind made walking a formidable challenge, and dust thickened the air. Even before Karl left for Idaho, their son's condition had begun deteriorating yet again—first wheezing, then relentless vomiting. Alone with Elaine after his father's departure, Tommy cried and struggled to breathe throughout the nights, waking sometimes to sob or gasp or retch. He remained sick off and on during Karl's entire furlough.

On November 7 Elaine received a letter from her parents: Joyce had disappeared again. Her daughter had vanished four nights earlier. For the next few weeks, Elaine only made short, repetitive entries in her diary, each one another hopeless staccato: "Mother in SF left Tues—dad had no news," she wrote. Then, "nothing from folks"; "no word"; "Nothing about Joyce"; "Nothing new."

Of the seventeen Nisei who'd been chosen in September by the WRA for the camp's new constitution committee, each received a series of anonymous letters in November 1942. The missives were written in similar handwriting and signed by the "Blood Brothers," or as another incarceree translated it, "Blood Brothers Who Worry for the Welfare of the People." They argued that since the army had put them all in prison camps and forced them to forfeit their property, the army alone was responsible for running Manzanar; even with the chimera of self-governance, "the Whites"—or "the hairy beasts" according to another translation—would "actually run" things. A series of mixed but memorable metaphors ensued: The government had left the incarcerees exposed like so much "fish laid on the cutting board, about to be sliced. . . . Better lay down and let the government do as it pleases, either cook us or fry us." Complying with WRA hypocrisy would only "tighten the noose around the necks of the people." Those who did not resist should "beware of punishment from Heaven."

Similar messages appeared on posters and leaflets, hung in the dark of night in mess halls and latrines, bearing identical handwriting and signed once again by the "Blood Brothers Corps" or "Black Dragon Society." A few days after these public threats, actual violence erupted: an incarceree member of the internal police force was beaten by a mob in front of his own wife, to the backdrop of her anguished screams. He stood accused of reporting on another inmate who'd smuggled a bottle of whiskey into camp from a work furlough.

Elaine wrote in her diary about the beating, which she heard was administered by a group of young men from Terminal Island. She recorded twenty or so assailants, dressed in full black and lurking in wait around the young policeman's own barrack. When she described the scene to Karl in a letter, he replied with dismay at those who "know of nothing but the use of brute force," and "disturb the peace for Manzanar's majority of residents."

Although still unbeknownst to the Yonedas, another band of incarcerees had Karl in *their* crosshairs that November. According to one of Manzanar's most prominent agitators, Harry Ueno, a group of men had been planning to "attack Karl Yoneda." They were just "waiting [for] him to come back."

8 | PURSUED
Fall 1942

ON NOVEMBER 13, Elaine wired Karl with an urgent message. An army colonel would arrive in Manzanar soon to recruit Japanese speakers for the Military Intelligence Service (MIS). Karl should return quickly. Three days later, he began his trip back from Idaho.

Karl was traveling back to camp with the belief that his furlough in the beet fields had been productive, for himself, the nation, and even the Japanese American community at large. His positive view was shared by many, though not by all. A controversy was emerging in Manzanar about the furloughs and the incarcerees' reception outside camp. "They guarded us like cattle on the trains," one beet-field worker said upon return. "We couldn't even get off at the stations." Others recalled being refused meals at restaurants and permission to sleep anywhere but the local jail. The *Manzanar Free Press* carried a letter, signed only with initials: "The furlough workers were helping to save the nation's most valuable crop but in so doing they were reduced to the level of slaves."

Conversely, Karl thought the people in Idaho had treated him and fellow workers with fairness and appreciation, especially after word spread of their tireless labor. "Dear Editor," Karl himself had written to the *Free Press*, "We are working every day and getting fair earnings, in spite of the fact that there are many improvements to be made in our future contracts because of the hard work." The furloughs in general were undoubtedly a success "when we consider the political and good-will aspects in our future relocation program and post-war situation." He signed off with the official title he'd earned on the job: "Very truly yours, Karl Yoneda, Camp Chairman, FSA Camp, Filer Idaho."

His optimism dimmed slightly on the way back to Manzanar, when his group passed a band of GIs in Reno who threatened to dynamite their bus, yelling, "Let's get those Japs!" But he arrived back to Owens Valley on November 18 with a sense of deep relief. It had been almost fifty days since he'd seen his wife and son. "No matter how often it's called a concentration camp, this is where we live," he confided in his diary. "This is where our wives, our children, our friends are. I feel an undeniable sense of nostalgia and familiarity; in a word, it's good to be back home!" Karl was still determined to use Manzanar as a fulcrum for his own participation in the war. "Here, too, is our place of work, our battlefield," he wrote that same day. "This is the fortress from which we'll defend the peace, security, and democracy of our futures."

Less than a week later, camp administrators announced that the MIS recruiter would arrive on November 27. Karl immediately wired Koji, who was on his way back from Idaho but had received permission to stop in Utah to deliver a talk about agricultural furloughs from the camps. *Come directly back*, Karl urged. Their chance to enlist might finally be here.

By the time Koji returned, Manzanar was more on edge than ever. In late November, the camp inherited its fifth head administrator in its eight-month history. A man named Ralph Merritt was hired as project director, succeeding the strikingly named Solon Toothaker Kimball, who in turn had taken over for Roy Nash. Merritt thought that the "only relationship that Japanese understand is that of father and child," as he reportedly told Kimball. He claimed he had "become the father of Manzanar. The people [were] his children."

Merritt's patronizing aside, Joseph Kurihara assessed the challenge facing the new director as akin to sitting "on [a] volcano." On his second day at camp, Merritt attended a town hall discussion of the latest attempt to create a charter for the incarcerees' so-called self-government. "Look out the window and what do you see?" someone demanded. "There is barbed wire, there is a watch tower, and there is a soldier who guards us by day and night and shoots us if we break the law." Instead of voting on self-government, Merritt's antagonist retorted, "I move that the damned charter be thrown out the window." Undeterred, at the next meeting, Merritt offered that "even the nomad tribes in Africa have a chief and some kind of agreement on how to live together."

Around the same time, the front page of the *Los Angeles Times* reported a riot at Poston War Relocation Center. Karl saw the article, reading of "anti-American, disruptive elements" who attacked an incarceree labeled "pro-administration," chanted military songs from Japan, and waved flags with Japanese messages. He believed that, with recent news of Axis losses and the impending arrival of MIS recruiters at Manzanar, Joe Kurihara and "other anti-American elements among the Kibei" were becoming "highly irritated." They were spreading rumors from block to block, Karl noted in his diary. They were saying, "We're going to start a riot even bigger than the one at Poston"; "Soon we're going to kill all the [Block] Leaders who are pro-American!" They left notes, too: "Those who volunteer for U.S. Army service are traitors."

On November 26, Thanksgiving Day, the *Manzanar Free Press* picked up the story. Media outside camp were publicizing the "defiant group of pro-Axis Japanese evacuees" at Poston, they reported. Though the *Free Press* blamed the "abnormal environment resulting from the evacuation" for fueling the riot, they anticipated that major news sources would completely overlook this underlying cause. "A small minority has again succeeded in turning suspicious eyes on all the Japanese in the relocation centers," they lamented.

Then the *Free Press* weighed the possibility of a similar occurrence at Manzanar. While the camp had so far avoided any major disturbances, its prisoners should not presume this relative tranquility would last. Manzanar too had its own "small minority" of agitators, including the "sulking, ever-active 'blood brothers,'" who'd recently been hanging more posters and making threats throughout camp.

Elaine, Karl, and others noticed the posters that week too, a series of three nailed again to walls throughout camp. Incarceree Hiroshi Fukuwa wrote that some were signed "Manzanar Kokuryukai" (Manzanar Black Dragon Society) and the style matched that of former threats. The messages were similar to past ones too: warnings against working on government projects such as the camouflage nets, doing outside labor to boost the US economy ("Japanese soldiers would be ashamed," Fukuwa transcribed), or cooperating with camp administrators.

In his documentary report, Togo Tanaka offered a bald assessment of the disillusion fueling these threats. In turn, Ralph Merritt drafted a WRA memo citing many of Tanaka's points. Of the agitators themselves, Merritt-via-Tanaka argued, their messages might betray some "fanatic tendencies," but they were "not merely crank notes"; they drew the attention of a broad swath of Manzanar's population, particularly the Japanese-speaking incarcerees. "This does not mean that the majority of this population condones the activity," Merritt restated Tanaka's explanation. "But the atmosphere of suppression and repression accompanying life behind barbed wires and watchtowers, as these people comment, is conducive to such activity. While they may not represent any majority of the Japanese-speaking population, as far as their tactics and nature are concerned, the blood brothers do voice opinion in which the majority share."

In the end, neither Tanaka nor Merritt impugned the government's active role in the unjust incarcerations, blaming instead a more passive oversight or inaction. The fundamental mistake was not the injustice fomenting a spreading agitation, but instead the government's "failure to make a just and necessary separation of evacuees based on attitudes and loyalties in the war."

Karl's focus was also drawn to the danger these threats presented rather than the anger underlying them, sensing an urgent need to remove this menace from the general population. "The authorities are doing nothing whatsoever to keep them in check," he complained to his diary about the Blood Brothers and their ilk. "We must remain on our guard." Elaine felt it too. "I have a feeling that something is going to happen," she told her husband on Thanksgiving. The following day, someone tried to burn down the incarceree-run dry goods store behind one of the barrack blocks. Who or why, no one knew for sure. "Things popping," Elaine wrote in her diary, "but what?"

Over this same period, the *Los Angeles Times* carried news of other turmoil, violence so extreme it shocked the world, even amid the war's unprecedented brutality. The day after their story on the Poston riot, the *Times* reported, HALF OF JEWS IN EUROPE DEAD. For the Yonedas (and likely many other Jews and leftists), it was a not altogether unexpected, but still tragic coda to what they'd read in August of the Nazis' mobile gas units, which Karl had surmised was "the beginnings of the Nazis' campaign to eradicate the Jewish people." Now, the *Los Angeles Times* carried reports of mass shootings ("infants, the elderly, and the infirm are shot immediately"), thousands sealed in freight cars sprinkled with poison gas, immediate murder upon arriving at Hitler's "special camps" for those who had not suffocated to death during transport, and corpses "processed into such war-vital commodities as soap fats and fertilizer."

Meanwhile, within Manzanar, an undercurrent of far more subtle antisemitism continued to simmer. That late-November week, an incarceree member of the education department, Mari Okazaki, feared for the safety of one of the camp's high school's "Semitic" teachers: "There is such a widespread feeling here among the residents that the Jewish moneyed interests were responsible for this evacuation that it sometimes frightens me," wrote Okazaki in a letter to a contact outside camp. "It seems as if another result of this evacuation would be to increase the evil of pitching one racial . . . minority against the other." ("The Japanese definitely consider the Jewish person from a racial as well as economic angle," she clarified.)

Neither Elaine nor Karl mentioned the newest reports of Nazi brutality or the bubbling antisemitism from some corners in camp in their diaries that week. But their frequent news consumption and correspondence with Nathan and Mollie guaranteed they would soon become aware of the former if they weren't yet. As for claims of Jewish responsibility for Japanese American oppression, Karl had been hearing these since he first arrived at Manzanar.

At the moment, though, the Yonedas were immersed in another family crisis. On November 24 Elaine had received a wire from her parents saying that they had found Joyce. This time, the fifteen-year-old had not just run away; she'd gotten married.

Elaine recorded the events in a staccato rush of confusion and near-panic. "Tried to call no answer Dad wire Joyce married no other word folks here Sat," she scribbled in her diary. When she tried to call again the next day, she got no answer. Finally, on the twenty-eighth, her parents arrived in Manzanar with at least a bare outline of the story. "J married someone named Ernest G Barnett age 27 gave age 20," Elaine wrote. Joyce, having lied about her own status as a minor, was now married to a man significantly closer in age to the parents who'd relinquished her than to herself.

By the late afternoon of November 28, Elaine began to confront the very real possibility that she might lose Karl too. That day, with a mixture of pride and apprehension, she watched Karl's induction as a buck private into the US Army, his first step to the Pacific front. Her parents had come to Manzanar in anticipation of his enlistment. Karl, Koji, and their friend Jimmy Oda were among fourteen men, out of close to one hundred Manzanar applicants, who'd passed the language test and been selected to join the Military Intelligence Service. Karl was the oldest among the fresh recruits—the camp's first incarcerees to go to war. None had been deterred by the Black Dragons truck cruising around camp that day, urging Nisei not to enlist.

"At last, the long awaited day has arrived," Karl wrote that night. "We are privates in the U.S. Army; the battlefield is Asia and the Pacific; the enemies are [the] emperor system and the military clique. For the sake of our wives and children, for the future of the Japanese community, for the workers, and lastly for the sake of annihilating fascism and militarism—our lives are now one with the U.S. Army."

The enlistees were scheduled to leave Manzanar within a few days for military training at a place called Camp Savage, in Minnesota. As soon as Karl was inducted and his departure confirmed, the family began the process of applying for Elaine and Tommy's freedom. Though it remains unclear whether the Yonedas were well versed in Bendetsen's mixed-marriage policy (neither mentioned it specifically in their diaries), its confused and overlapping categories would complicate their release from Manzanar to anywhere on the extended West Coast. By the end of 1942, multiple edicts contradicted each other for families like the Yonedas. An October 1942 memo from a WCCA social worker indicated that an "exception" might be made to Bendetsen's policy "if a husband is in the service of the Army, Navy, or Marine Corps"; in that case, "his wife can apply for the privilege" of returning to the West Coast. But a November 1942 letter from Bendetsen himself dictated that a white woman married to a Japanese or Japanese American could apply to take her mixed children back to Military Area 1 only if her husband were "dead or long-separated" from them. Under any iteration of the policy, the US government still classified three-year-old Tommy as a possible menace. Even in the best-case scenario, there would be no possibility of his returning to the Yonedas' former home in San Francisco or the Buchmans' in L.A.—or anywhere from California to the eastern edge of Montana, Idaho, Utah, or Arizona—without being fully vetted and obtaining a special permit. The idea of Elaine returning to freedom without him remained unthinkable. They would apply and hope for the best.

At noon on the day after Karl's induction, the Buchmans returned alone to Los Angeles, hauling a carload of the Yonedas' belongings. Elaine planned to leave the moment Tommy's travel pass arrived. The next day, the boy had his picture taken for his application—as a "potential dangerous enemy!" Elaine wrote—and the Yonedas met with Manzanar assistant director Ned Campbell to discuss the permit process. Campbell was less than encouraging, challenging Elaine's decision to return home rather than follow her husband to army training. "Why don't you go with him?" Campbell wanted to know. "Why are you trying to put stumbling blocks up?"

Elaine was adamant. "My plans do not include following my husband into army camp!" she retorted. "I want to do war work! I want out!" She wanted to provide her son better housing and care, not put him in yet another camp. Her goal was to return to San Francisco or Los Angeles right away and find a job supporting the nation's battle. Campbell wasted no time informing the Yonedas that the WRA's vetting and release procedures generally took a month, at least. The family was shocked and dismayed; Karl would be gone well before then. Still, Elaine remained undeterred. She would get her son to safety and then find some way to contribute herself to the fight against those who wanted to destroy her family and her ideals.

Before any of them might depart, the Yonedas knew they would face fresh challenges. With Manzanar's dissenters agitating ever more forcefully against Nisei enlistment, Karl overheard whispers about preventing the volunteers from leaving for MIS training. Their departure date had been set for December 2. Karl, Koji, and Jimmy needed to keep themselves, and Elaine and Tommy, safe until then.

On the night of November 29, Jimmy and another enlistee came over to the Yonedas' barrack room, a thick wooden club in hand. They sat up with Karl until the early morning of the next day, keeping watch. When they took turns repeating their vigil over the next few evenings, Karl was moved with gratitude.

On the thirtieth, Elaine and Karl noticed a handful of men following them around camp. After night fell over the desert, a dozen or so began lurking around their barrack. Karl looked out and saw them walking circles around the area, and he thought they looked like ghouls. He headed to find the camp police chief, requesting official protection. They offered to do hourly patrols. But would that be enough, the Yonedas wondered? "Ever since we enlisted in the army," Karl wrote, "the Black Dragons have been rumoring they're going to 'cripple that Yoneda character.'"

Alongside her own apprehension, Elaine could feel the anxiety rising in Tommy. She tried not to talk too much about Karl's departure, but the camp's ominous pall lingered around the boy. "Again, gang around the barrack," Elaine wrote on December 1. Late that evening, Koji and Jimmy came over once more. The men spent their last night in Manzanar keeping vigil together over sandwiches and coffee. Throughout the dark, still hours, nothing of note stirred, and in the silence the men thought about going to war and the loved ones they were leaving behind. They knew an uneasy atmosphere had settled over Manzanar, ever more turbulent since their induction. None realized the trouble's full extent.

———————

That November, the JACL had called an emergency meeting in Salt Lake City, Utah, convening delegates from all ten of the WRA's camps. The week-long conference began just before Karl was scheduled to leave Manzanar for Camp Savage. Two incarcerees went as Manzanar's delegates, though the residents never elected them: Fred Tayama from the JACL and now-defunct Manzanar Citizens' Federation and Kiyoshi Higashi, whose family was housed with the Tayamas and who served as chief of Internal Security, the incarceree police force.

Joe Kurihara was among many who followed the JACL meeting through newspapers in camp. He, Harry Ueno, and others were incensed to learn that, after being undemocratically picked as representatives by Manzanar administrators, Tayama and Higashi then took Karl and Koji's petition one step further: they encouraged the entire JACL to publicly pledge full Nisei enlistment from the camps. As Kurihara put it, the pair had gone to Salt Lake City "requesting induction of all Nisei for Combat duty." But he focused most of his anger on Fred Tayama, whom he credited with pushing the draft idea. Kurihara told his fellow incarcerees that Tayama was "committing the lives of thousands of you and your beloved sons on the altar of Destruction." In the words of historians, the JACL committee at large voted "to ask the War Department to reclassify Nisei 'on the same basis as all other Americans,'" though of course the result would be the same as Kurihara's assessment: prisoners drafted and sent to battle from inside American concentration camps. Karl and Koji's petition signed by 218 random incarcerees was one thing; a policy embraced and promoted by the apparent leading organization of Nisei across the country was quite another.

As a result, "the temper of the people," Kurihara wrote, was "getting ugly"; the "air was charged with hatred." In the aftermath of the conference, Togo Tanaka noted that agitation against the JACL was now "everywhere in the center." Kurihara was seen going block to block, telling people that when

Manzanar rioted, it was "going to be a hundred times worse" than Poston's; "We are going to kill all the 'inu'!!"

Kiyoshi Higashi himself had submitted a report at the JACL conference that warned of coming trouble. Though this document was not made public, its contents clarify that Manzanar's own police force foresaw a coming explosion, and they blamed the WRA, at least in part. Though the camps' "pro-Japan element" was modest in size, he wrote, "wholesale experiences of the racial evacuation and living within centers surrounded by barbed wires and watchtowers are in the eyes of many prima facie evidence that a future in this country is hopeless for us." For those who'd become "pro-Japan," these aspects of the camp "are indisputable arguments that Japan's is the righteous cause," Higashi wrote.

But from here, Higashi pivoted away from the injustice of the forced removals and incarcerations, as Tanaka and Merritt had done in their own reports, and toward what he saw as the most immediate problem facing the WRA. As Karl Yoneda had done previously, Higashi urged "segregation of known troublemakers to a separate center . . . in the interests of peace and order." Though Higashi's categorization of the incarcerees was more simplistic than Karl's—the former defined "those who believe in America" as the "wholesome people in the centers"—both men came to a similar conclusion: if the so-called pro-Americans were to "continue to live side by side with those who have lost their faith" in the country, they "must be protected from those who jeer and taunt and threaten."

"WRA administrators must realize the dynamite they are dealing with; they must be realistic," Higashi warned. Ultimately, he foresaw a "bombshell" approaching, of "mob outbreaks, mass demonstrations, gang atrocities and acts of terrorism." In the words of another incarceree policeman, toward the end of November and beginning of December, things in Manzanar were "simmering and boiling to the point where pressure just had to be released."

———

The morning Karl was to leave for Camp Savage, he woke early. He began that day's diary entry with a *Los Angeles Times* headline about Hitler's SHRIEKING ORDERS to FIGHT TO THE LAST MAN! Karl tried to eat breakfast before his 7:55 bus from Manzanar, but when he thought of saying goodbye to Elaine and Tommy, he couldn't swallow.

Before he left, he urged Elaine to "demand and re-demand protection" if trouble arose. Other families of the enlistees were also requesting permission for release or relocation. Karl told Elaine he hoped she and Tommy could get out of Manzanar as soon as possible—much sooner than Campbell had suggested. Tommy worried about his father too. He tucked one of his toy pistols in Karl's knapsack, instructing him how to use it to ward off enemy danger.

In the early morning light, the fourteen men prepared to board their bus, surrounded by the desert cold and Manzanar's police force, who'd come out for extra protection. Neither Manzanar's project director, Ralph Merritt, nor assistant director Ned Campbell bothered to join the send-off of Manzanar's first war volunteers. The families gathered in a crowd, their movements and expressions subdued. "This was not a time for fanfare," Koji Ariyoshi remembered later. "Volunteering was then not a popular thing to do," especially with the small but influential group in camp who considered the enlistees "traitors.'"

Moreover, the bus had parked beyond Manzanar's exit gate, and family members were not allowed to step beyond the barbed wire, not even to see their loved ones off to war. Koji embraced his new bride, Taeko, before stepping through the exit. Karl wondered how the white MPs, fellow soldiers now, could simply stand and watch the new volunteers leave their wives and children, and "deny us a final embrace." He looked back and saw tears of distress and sorrow.

For some, this would be their last goodbye, though of course on that December morning, none of them yet knew who would return and who would not. But the air was heavy with an uncertain mourning anyway, and as the bus pulled away, no one inside it said a word. Koji Ariyoshi looked back one final time and saw the small crowd waving, and his last glimpse of Manzanar was of a "desert city of exiles," as he wrote later, "full of bitterness and charged like dynamite." From behind the barbed wire, Tommy was visibly distraught, and he yelled out for Karl to take him too.

When they got back to their nearly empty barrack room, Elaine couldn't help thinking of when or if they'd see Karl again. *Will we ever be together as a family after this?* she wondered sadly. She was soon distracted by Tommy, whose distress went from constant to severe. He couldn't seem to stop sobbing for Karl; he cried until he began to wheeze, then vomit, and then turn feverish. Finally, by 6:45 PM, Elaine brought him to the camp hospital. His fever spiking, the medical staff warned that he should be admitted overnight. They suspected her son's latest illness was dysentery.

Returning to an even emptier barrack, Elaine sought the company of her friend and neighbor, Yochi Ukita. Yo had kept Elaine's spirits up with cards and coffee during Karl's furlough. Now, the two women talked about Karl, Koji, and the others who'd departed that day, and though Yo stayed all night, Elaine still felt surrounded by loneliness.

The next day, Elaine visited Tommy in the hospital, and she thought he seemed a little better, though the doctors still weren't sure what was sickening him. Elaine sought their help for herself too: her eye had become red and swollen, and they prescribed medicine and a bandage. By December 4 Tommy was still in the hospital, and her eye was still reddened and painful, infected with conjunctivitis and swelling along the lower lid with the beginnings of a stye, the doctor on duty told her.

The hospital released Tommy the next day, though he still had severe diarrhea—an extra burden in Manzanar with one small latrine per block, each serving over three hundred people. As Tommy played quietly or rested in the barrack, he'd call out every so often for his father. While Elaine struggled to care for her son, spiteful new rumors circulated about her husband. Yo's sister told Elaine she'd overheard that "Karl walked out on Elaine and Tommy because he was scared" of other Kibei in camp; people were saying "that's why he went into the army!"

Other rumors were also ripping through the barracks. Just before the MIS contingent had departed for Camp Savage, Harry Ueno, who'd been among the group to threaten Karl in the Yonedas' room in August, accused Ned Campbell and another staff member of stealing thousands of pounds of sugar meant for the incarcerees. Ueno thought the men were planning to sell the valuable wartime commodity on the black market, a charge the administrators denied but that many in camp believed anyway. As a result, Ueno's status began to acquire heroic proportions: an incarceree who'd dared confront WRA malfeasance.

Ueno's accusation added weight to another rumor that had been spreading: that former project director Roy Nash had left Owens Valley for federal penitentiary, having committed graft and other crimes while running Manzanar. Many in camp refused to believe that Nash's real fate—a prestigious, high-paying new position in the nation's capital—had come to pass. As one incarceree put it, "You could show the issei a picture of Mr. Nash sitting under the Washington monument. They still wouldn't believe he wasn't in jail."

On December 4 two other events heightened tensions further in Manzanar. Fred Tayama and Kiyoshi Higashi returned from the JACL conference in Salt

Lake City, which the *Free Press* promptly publicized. That same evening, the FBI detained a popular elder and removed him from camp. With fresh memories of fractured, terrified families after the post–Pearl Harbor federal raids, which removed most Issei leaders from their communities, many incarcerees believed the two events on December 4 were cause and effect. As one WRA historian put it, this was yet one more instance of "stooges, dogs, flagwavers, informers and J.A.C.L. traitors," collaborating with officials "to the undoing of helpless aliens and their children."

Amid so much heightened mistrust and anger, the general feeling in camp remained deeply mixed vis-à-vis the departed MIS enlistees. Even before the *Free Press* could publish a story about Manzanar's first war volunteers, news of their leave-taking spread rapidly. In his role as documentary historian, Togo Tanaka searched out what he called "a cross-section" of reactions, though he seemed to give the most space to ostensibly "pro-Axis" commentary, perhaps to bolster his own argument that Manzanar's agitators were too perilous to ignore.

Regardless of Tanaka's intended implications, his report illuminated an interesting inverse to his and Karl Yoneda's understanding of the ideological divisions in camp and their attendant dangers. Many incarcerees seemed happy to be rid of the military volunteers, considering *them* the actual troublemakers. "I'm glad they're gone. Now we shouldn't have as much trouble," said one. "They're damn fools, and good riddance," said another. "These camps are nothing but concentration camps, and anyone who says he's American should get the hell out and quick. We'[ll] have less trouble then." Another called the volunteers "14 bootlickers," claiming, "Every one was a marked man. . . . They don't have the true blood of the Yamato race; they must be half breeds."

Other opinions spanned pros and cons. One young incarceree responded to the invitation to share his thoughts by asking, repeatedly, his own plaintive question: Did Tanaka think they were all going to be drafted soon? Another said, "I respect those Nisei for joining the American Army," pointing out that they'd never achieve equal status after the war without equal sacrifice. But he stopped short at his own son enlisting, strenuously doubting equal treatment by the American military. Either way, he believed that with the fourteen volunteers gone, the camp's troubles would subside. "They were always waving the American flag around so much, it was too antagonistic," he explained.

"I'm not one to shirk my responsibility," another man said. "I want the United States to win the war. I don't want my country destroyed." But still, he would never volunteer himself, not with his wife and child in camp. "I'd want my wife to be treated as a soldier's wife," and "to have [a] feeling of security for my child," something he expected would be impossible in Manzanar. He felt "terribly sorry for the wives and children of any of them who are left behind in this camp."

Three days after the enlistees' departure from Manzanar, Karl Bendetsen received a medal for putting them there. Standing before his superior officer at the Presidio—bearing erect, smile broad, hair impeccably parted—Bendetsen took his latest accolade. DECORATED, said the caption under a photo of the ceremony in a San Francisco paper; "Lieut. General John L. DeWitt pins Distinguished Service Award on Col. Karl. R. Bendetsen for the latter's handling of west coast Jap evacuations." He was lauded for what the media termed "exceptionally meritorious service to the Government in a duty of great responsibility," as well as for his earlier role breaking up strikes at an airplane manufacturing plant. Then a procession of soldiers marched in Bendetsen's honor alongside the band from the Fifty-Third Infantry, while the young colonel and DeWitt looked on.

Though numerous papers across the country covered the ceremony, none mentioned the words *American* or *citizen* to describe the vast majority of Japanese people "evacuated." To their credit, *Time* magazine did use the term *Nisei*. Then they quoted DeWitt, who praised Bendetsen's West Coast "operation" as having been "completed within the designated time, without mischance, with minimum hardship and almost without incident."

Time also noted that "an unexpected, embarrassing sequel to the Japanese migration" had arisen for Bendetsen and his boss that same week, with a ruling by a Portland federal judge against the legality of the spring 1942 curfew for Japanese Americans. "General DeWitt had no power over citizens," only aliens, the judge established. Now, *Time* reported, "Possible results [include] court action by citizen Japanese who may construe from [the] ruling that they are illegally kept in camps." With this, a new ball began rolling, threatening to unravel DeWitt and Bendetsen's entire "operation," and with it, the latter's gold-medal reputation.

9 | CAUGHT
December 5–7, 1942

AS NIGHT ON DECEMBER 5 swept the Sierras and settled over Manzanar, six masked men entered the barrack room of Fred Tayama. They wore dark-blue peacoats—government-issued, collars raised. Each had a black face covering, and some wore thick goggles, designed for dust storms, to hide their eyes. In their hands, they carried wooden clubs.

When they began beating Tayama, they struck him from above. Working in silence, they brought their clubs up and down, over and over. Tayama remembered later that the small room was so crowded with assailants, they had to avoid side blows to keep from striking each other. His daughter had run, screaming and hysterical, out into the yard around the barrack.

A few hours after a brutalized Tayama had been taken by ambulance to the camp hospital, he named Harry Ueno as one of his assailants. Manzanar police promptly arrested the suspect. Ned Campbell, whom Ueno had recently accused of stealing sugar, drove the police car that carried Ueno out of camp. Manzanar's police chief was in the car, too, and when Ueno asked him to tell his family where they were taking him, Campbell said from the front seat that no one was going to know where he was going, not for a long time. "Too bad," Campbell added, "that your son will be a jailbird's son."

When they arrived at the jailhouse in the nearby town of Independence just before 11:00 PM, the officers removed Ueno's handcuffs and then ordered him to empty his pockets. They gave him a blanket and mattress—the same kind, Ueno noted, that he'd had in Manzanar. With that, he settled in to see what would become of him, taking notes in a small blue spiral notebook that he'd somehow managed to keep with him.

Back at Manzanar, as word spread of the arrest, Ueno's star rose higher. Many incarcerees were convinced that he'd been arrested and taken "outside" not for attacking Tayama but because Campbell wanted to get rid of him. The next morning, a strange silence had descended over camp, and people could feel a pressing tension in the air, as if a ragged breath were being held, just at the edge of exploding.

At first, Elaine remained oblivious. That morning, she finally received a wire from Karl, confirming his arrival in Minnesota. She heard about the attack on Tayama and the arrest of Ueno at lunchtime, but she didn't attribute them much significance. After all, other beatings and reprisals had taken place at Manzanar before. She was more focused on getting her son and herself out of camp. Though the day was cool, the air was clear and crisp, and around 2:00 PM, she and Tommy set out for the administration building to see if any information about his pass had arrived.

As they walked past blocks of barracks and wide, dusty firebreaks, they neared the makeshift post office and the staff mess hall. On the other end of the administration area, near the camp's front gate, stood a long dark barrack with thick wooden doors and a high white sign: POLICE DEPARTMENT. Across a dirt road was a sentry post, rough-hewn boulders stacked into a small, square hut.

Even before she reached the area, Elaine could hear the rumbling of the crowd. Hundreds of people were massed in front of the administration building, and the mob kept growing, getting louder. The building's entrance was completely blocked. Military police were lined along the road by the police station and the jail. At one intersection, a machine gun had been mounted, aimed toward the throng.

Joseph Kurihara stood on the roof of a car, a microphone in his hand. Elaine could see him above the growing mass of people, and to the side a man named Genji Yamaguchi. *Another of the anti-American faction's leaders*, Elaine thought darkly. She saw Ben Kishi, too, who'd been among those to threaten Karl before he left. Kurihara was shouting something in Japanese, and the crowd was cheering back at him. His screams came through a loudspeaker someone had dragged out, rippling through the restless crowd. Witnesses who spoke Japanese understood that he was demanding Harry Ueno's return to

Manzanar. He wasn't afraid to confront those who oppressed them, he claimed; he was willing to die, for the soldiers to shoot him. He threw out his chest and gesticulated wildly, and the people standing in the dust before him shouted back, electrified. Then he yelled that the ones who *really* deserved death were Fred Tayama and all those like him.

Later, Kurihara himself recalled that he demanded of the crowd, "Why permit that sneak to pollute the air we breathe? Let's kill him and feed him to the roving coyotes!" Then he roared, "If the Administration refuses to listen to our demands, let us proceed with him and exterminate all other informers in this camp!" His audience cheered again. At some point, members of the crowd began taunting the line of military police, swearing at them in Japanese and English, jeering as they stood in tense formation.

By now, the gathering had grown well into the thousands. Elaine saw the taunting and the obscene gestures, the grim faces of the police, and she could feel a pressure rising, though she still didn't know exactly what Kurihara was screaming. She could not understand a word of his harangue, until she heard one she recognized, one Kurihara began repeating over and over. *Yoneda!*

In the crowd, she saw one of the columnists from the *Free Press*'s Japanese-language section, and he translated for her. Kurihara was railing against the JACL and Manzanar Citizens' Federation leaders, the man explained. "He says that it's too bad Yoneda and the rest have escaped into the army; that if Yoneda were here we'd kill him!" Then he told her that Kurihara had added an ominous postscript: though Karl was gone, his son was still in camp. They could still get *him*. "Kill them!" "Let's go find them!" the man said people were yelling in reply.

He urged Elaine to leave immediately. He told her to take Tommy home, lock themselves in, and not to go out for any reason. A white administrator who spoke some Japanese also hurried over to warn her. It was dangerous for her to be there, he said. "Get home, quickly!"

In the arid desert afternoon, Elaine stood dead still for a beat, stunned and speechless. She was trying to take in what was happening. That her child had been indicated for death by beating in Karl's place. That a mob was roaring in response to the instigator's goading. She looked across the shifting crowd to Kurihara, high up on a fading car, microphone in his grip, round face reddened, mouth an angry threat. She felt a terror pierce her unlike any she had ever known. She grabbed Tommy's hand and ran.

Elaine fled first to the police station. She remembered Karl's urging before he left, to ask and ask again for protection if anything should happen. But the officers just threw up their hands. With all the commotion, there were no men to spare. Clasping Tommy's hand, she rushed back to their barrack.

As dusk neared on that December afternoon and the light dwindled around the Yonedas' stark apartment, Yo Ukita came over. She promised to try to bring some food and even spend the night if possible, as she'd done earlier that week when Karl left and Tommy had been hospitalized. But she'd been threatened already, she told Elaine; a judo fighter had warned her that if she "continue[d] to keep company with Yoneda's woman," she'd be "beaten." He used an angry slur in Japanese, calling Elaine Karl's *ketobaba-san*, his hairy, barbarian old woman. Another man threatened Yo's parents, saying they'd be in danger if they didn't watch their children carefully.

Then Yo left, and Elaine looked at Tommy and felt both panicked and stuck. *If only Karl were here!* she thought. Outside, she could see a pair of men lurking in the lengthening shadows of a nearby barrack. They were holding wooden clubs. *Something terrible is about to happen*, Elaine thought, silently.

Grabbing Tommy's hand again, she rushed back to the police station. *Ask again and again for protection!* she could imagine Karl urging her once more. Breathless and agitated, she told the officers that she and her son were in danger, that her husband was a soldier in the US Army and now they were alone. The police told her yet again, there were still no men available. In the afternoon, the chaos had started to die down, but it had ratcheted up again since night began to fall. Elaine turned to leave, Tommy in hand, as an officer promised the best they could offer: to try making periodic rounds in their patrol car.

Returning to their barrack, Elaine locked the door and peered out the window. She could see dozens of people dashing back and forth, a confused stream of figures moving through the failing light. She couldn't tell exactly why they were rushing, or what was going on. Soon, a neighbor's daughter appeared briefly at the window sill, the sky now black behind her. She had a message from Yo, she told Elaine, whispering. Her name—Elaine's—had been overheard, multiple times, by men roaming through the area. *Stay inside!* Yo wanted to implore once more. *No matter what.*

Around 9:30 PM, Elaine heard the dinner bell from the mess hall in their block. It rang once and then continued on, tolling through the dark. Elaine could hear yelling from outside too: "Strike! Strike!" Closer by, she heard the Nishimuras from the room next door, a series of low and urgent murmurs coming through the thin wall. She moved closer, trying to listen better. The elders spoke in a staccato rush of Japanese. But then one of their sons began to respond in English, describing another protest that reached riotous pitch, a swell of soldiers brought to put it down, and another brutal beating, this time of Tokie Slocum. Elaine caught only snippets, all of them alarming.

When Yo appeared again, instead of bringing comfort, she brought worse news. Struggling to speak through tears, she told Elaine that the military police had fired into a large crowd; many casualties resulted; more beatings and threats had been meted out. Besides Fred Tayama, a man named John Sonoda had been attacked. He'd applied for enlistment in the Military Intelligence Service like Karl, but he'd apparently not made the cut and had to stay in camp.

Yo still did not know all the details, she told Elaine, but she knew that martial law had been imposed throughout Manzanar, and the incarcerees were planning a total strike at sunup. She also asked for Elaine's forgiveness. She could no longer come to see her. Yo's parents had forbade it after being threatened. But the mob was still outside, still roaming, she warned Elaine. Maybe they would head here next. Then Yo left, and Elaine was suddenly alone again in the flimsy barrack, Tommy trembling beside her.

In the silence left by her friend's departure, Elaine barricaded the door as best she could. She slid the bolt, then tried to move a heavy wooden toy chest, one that Karl had made by hand for Tommy, across the floor. Finding the chest too heavy, she jerked her eyes around the room, searching for anything she could lift. She hauled a bench Karl had made to the door, then piled on top whatever belongings she could grab. Checking the window, she peered outside again. She saw more people lurking in the shadows. She thought they might be pointing right at the barrack apartment where she and her son were hiding, as if explaining, *That's where the Yonedas live.* Tommy was nearly vibrating in an effort to hold back tears, clinging to Elaine and asking for his father to come back.

The agitation Elaine and Tommy had stumbled upon that afternoon at the administration building had actually begun early that morning, when a group of two hundred or so incarcerees met at the block 22 mess hall to strategize bringing Harry Ueno back to Manzanar from jail in Independence. Joseph Kurihara was elected to head a negotiating committee for the effort. Before the morning meeting broke up, the crowd had swelled exponentially, and the committee planned an afternoon gathering to follow.

The afternoon meeting began at block 22 but soon moved to the administration building, where witnesses estimated that by 1:30 PM—around the time Elaine and Tommy arrived at the scene—two thousand people had gathered, though most were onlookers, drawn by curiosity. Kurihara and others made speeches, demanded Ueno's return, and read off names from the "death list," becoming inflamed by reactions from the crowd, as they in turn seemed to ignite spectators' anger even further. Project Director Ralph Merritt, who'd gone out to meet the negotiating committee, later claimed that Kurihara told him that "he didn't care if they starved or shot him—he was willing to die." After a protracted back-and-forth, Kurihara and his committee admitted to Merritt that they were losing control of the mob. The two sides then agreed to a limited set of conditions, including that Ueno would be returned to the jail at Manzanar and the committee would instruct the throng to go home.

Kurihara informed the crowd that they had notched a victory, an agreement had been reached, and they should disperse. Before they did, Kurihara broke out in what one witness described as "a fanatical tirade, disclaimed loyalty to the United States, expressed the hope that Japan would win the war, and threatened death to all informers." Reminded that he and the committee had agreed to terms with Merritt, Kurihara quieted, then announced another meeting that evening at 6:00 PM. By this time, Elaine and Tommy had already fled, seeking refuge in their barrack.

By 3:00 PM camp had become calm, and Ueno was brought back to Manzanar soon after. But when Kurihara and his committee presided over the 6:00 PM meeting, the crowd swelled even larger, reaching four thousand incarcerees by some estimates. Almost all accounts agree that, again, most in the audience were there as spectators. But a more committed group of agitators kept events moving forward, making speeches and airing grievances built up over the past eight miserable months in camp, and the grinding fear and uncertainty that had preceded, beginning precisely, though coincidentally, 364 days earlier, on December 7, 1941.

Since Ueno had been returned to Manzanar, Kurihara and his committee attempted to resign, but their motion was soundly rejected. Some in the crowd demanded that Ueno be given an unconditional release. Others insisted that Tayama and the other "collaborators" be found immediately, beaten, and killed. By this time, night had fallen, and the throng split into groups: some headed to the hospital to find Tayama, others to the jail to free Ueno. "Members of the crowd armed themselves with knives, hatchets, hammers, screw drivers, stones, and any other weapons they could secure," one historian wrote.

At the hospital, the mob searched for Tayama, whom the medical staff, having been forewarned, had hidden under a bed and covered with blankets. Later, Tayama would tell Togo Tanaka that he could hear the screams from his hiding place: "Turn that *inu* over; we're going to kill him! . . . When we kill that *inu*, we're going to cut his head off and put it on a pole and exhibit it all around camp as an example of what happens to *inu*."

Tayama never mentioned whether his wife had also heard the screams, or perhaps he didn't know. She'd been admitted to the hospital that same afternoon, "suffering from anxiety neurosis in a cataleptic state," wrote Manzanar's chief medical officer, a white physician employed by the WRA. "On questioning her friends I found that she had been found in that state in the washroom of her block," in shock and terror at her husband's beating by "a band of ruffians the night before."

Unable to find Tayama and frustrated at their fruitless search, one of the crowd's leaders suggested they now turn their attention to finding and punishing the other "dogs," or *inu*. Tokie Slocum and assorted former JACL leaders were named, as was Togo Tanaka. His incessant questions and note-taking over the preceding months in his role as Manzanar documentarian had given rise to speculation that he was reporting on incarcerees to the WRA, not just documenting general life in camp. But Tanaka, like most of the agitators' targets, had been forewarned and gone into hiding. According to some witnesses, the crowd became increasingly frustrated and began to ransack apartments they found empty.

Meanwhile, the group that had headed for the police station and jail arrived near 7:00 PM and surrounded the facility. Over a hundred military police were summoned. Some people in the throng began to taunt and menace the soldiers. One witness recalled, "Stones, sand, and lighted cigarettes were thrown. . . . Some members of the crowd sang Japanese patriotic songs and spit on the soldiers, while others attempted to disarm several soldiers and reportedly taunted the soldiers 'to shoot.'"

By around 9:00 PM, the crowd would still not disperse, and the military police responded with tear gas, throwing four or five gas grenades. In the smoke and chaos that followed, two MPs fired their weapons: three blasts of a twelve-gauge shotgun and two rounds of a Thompson submachine gun, discharging about fifteen shots. When the panicked crowd cleared, numerous incarcerees lay in the dust. Taken to the camp hospital by ambulance, one, a teenaged boy, arrived dead. "The cause of death was instantaneous death due to bullet wound in the heart," Manzanar's chief medical officer recorded.

Eleven others arrived at the hospital alive but with bullet wounds. As word spread of the shootings, Manzanar remained in chaos. "Mess hall bells tolled continuously," people remembered. "Beatings of alleged informers ensued, and the military police patrolled the camp."

Incarceree Susan Kunitomi Embrey, who'd worked in the controversial camouflage net factory and wrote for the *Free Press*, later recalled how fear spread throughout camp. She lived with her family in block 20, near Manzanar's middle. "A group of men were walking down our block and it was very dark," she remembered. "They were all wearing their navy blue peacoats, and the only sound you heard was the trampling of their feet on the gravel." Hearing the thuds of their footfalls, Embrey's mother urged her daughter to hide. "They might come after you, too," she said. As Togo Tanaka put it, "Mob rule became the law within the center. The death list was being hunted."

That night, after a neighbor warned him that he was in danger, Tanaka tried to hide by blending into the crowd. Wearing his own dark-blue peacoat, he kept his head low and trailed at the back of one of the roving throngs. When they headed to his own barrack apartment, he followed. "I was in the mob, at the rear, taking the situation in, and wondering whether I should live to see the dawn," he admitted later.

When the group arrived at his barrack in block 36, at the northern edge of camp, they found his father, his in-laws, his wife, and their newborn daughter. Tanaka watched from the back as one man entered the room with a wooden club and approached a corner closet, searching for him. Others carried knives.

He heard someone else yell from outside, "If he's not in, let's kill his wife and baby, or his father will do. Kill the father of the 'inu'"!

From inside the room, another man appeared, standing at the doorway. He turned to the crowd piling up near the threshold and brought his hand high. "The wife and baby, the father, the relatives of Togo Tanaka are not [who] we want. It is regrettable that they should have to bear the misfortune of being related to an 'inu.' [But] they are not to be touched. We want only one person, no one else, do you hear?"

Tanaka recalled standing "frozen horror at the rear of the milling mob, not a single friend in sight. I died a half a dozen times wondering what I would do if they attacked my family." He could only hope that the word of the lone man in the doorway would hold.

As midnight neared on the other side of Manzanar, Elaine sat in the Yonedas' barrack in block 4, roiled with fear and uncertainty. Tommy had finally fallen asleep, and though she could hear periodic noises, camp seemed quieter. She still had little idea what was actually happening. She pulled out her diary and began trying to record the day's events. "Things have calmed down outside," she noted; "there is no one in sight." With her hands shaking, she wrote in jagged letters, her *T*'s crossed with long, nervous dashes. She had no notion what would happen next, now that Yo, her only source of information from the outside world, could no longer check on them. "I can't even sleep." Feeling as if she'd suffocate from anxiety and fear, she was overtaken by a sharp, desperate longing for Karl, but then she chided herself. Her husband was away fighting the most important struggle of all. *I'm just going to have to get through this*, she thought. *On my own.*

Near 1:00 AM Elaine heard an ambulance, and then she heard screaming, or maybe it was wailing, coming from the apartment facing theirs, the Itos'. The family had two sons, one serving in the US military since before the war. The other was here in Manzanar, nearing draft age; he had signed Karl and Koji's petition for a second front and battle force from the camps.

Checking the window, Elaine saw people rushing through the night like fleeting shadows in the dark. Unable to contain herself, with Tommy still asleep, she moved aside the lopsided barricade she'd piled before their door. When she reached the apartment across the way, Mrs. Ito was there, weeping as if she'd never stop. Her son James, the one who'd signed Karl's petition, had been the teenager shot and killed by Manzanar's military police.

"Elaine, please leave," the Ito's daughter said. Some around the block were saying it was the Yonedas' fault that James had been killed, that camp tensions had finally boiled over and now twelve people had been shot; it was the flag-wavers and draft-supporters who'd lit Manzanar's fuse.

Elaine looked around the room and saw men fixing her with angry eyes. She wanted to console Mrs. Ito, but she'd never learned Japanese language or customs, and she didn't know the proper way to offer condolences. She was used to seeing this gap as a convenience, even a source of safety: she could never be interrogated or, god forbid, tortured, by the Red Squad about Karl's antimilitarist activities. But suddenly, this ignorance felt like a terrible void. A stab of grief and fury pierced her, and for a brief moment, she wished it had been Kurihara and the others like him—*with their fascist behavior*, she rued—who'd been taken down. Tongue-tied and mortified, she approached James's mother and simply embraced her, and they cried together for a moment.

Rushing back to Tommy, Elaine saw more figures loitering near the barrack. She found her son awake, crying, and calling out for her and Karl. She locked the door. She knew she had to comfort Tommy and then find some way out.

By 5:00 AM she'd formulated the barest outline of a plan. She got Tommy's coat and turned it inside out so the shiny lining showed. She tied a scarf around his head and quickly scanned him up and down. She hoped he looked enough like a little girl that no one would recognize them. Together they stepped out into the cold and wind, the night still dark as dirt. Then they ran.

———————

Soon after dawn broke that morning of December 7, Karl Yoneda was finally issued his official US Army uniform. He put it on immediately, proudly offering his military salute to any officer that passed by. Then he set about finding a newspaper, eager as always to read the war news. He was impressed by a large headline quoting a US admiral's vow to DEMOLISH JAP FORCES. Flipping through the thin, inky pages, his eye caught something about Manzanar, and suddenly everything stopped. There'd been a "Riot" at the camp, the headline said. The article below reported a bare outline: a violent uprising, multiple casualties, and martial law across the entire facility.

A storm surged through Karl's chest: panic, fury, dread, and disgust. He found Koji, and the two men rushed a telegram to Manzanar Project Director Ralph Merritt. *Protect our families*, the soldiers implored. *Let us know what happened and if they are OK.*

Four days—and as many sleepless nights—would pass before Karl would hear anything about Tommy and Elaine. In the meantime, the coverage he read in the Minneapolis papers, like that across much of the country, would frame the events of December 5–7 as an "outbreak of pro-Axis violence on the eve of the anniversary of Pearl Harbor." Ralph Merritt himself had promoted this slant, issuing an official WRA statement on the night of December 6 that read, "On the eve of the first anniversary of Pearl Harbor, a pro-axis group among the Japanese at Manzanar have brought on a crisis which has made necessary . . . the placing of Manzanar under martial laws as protection to the people of Manzanar and the people of Inyo County." Adding to the false implication that the uprising had been purposely timed to coincide with the anniversary of Japan's attack (or purposely timed at all), papers ignored the grievances and heartbreak underlying Manzanar's tensions, which had finally burst open, and glossed over an essential truth: that the greatest number of casualties were wrought by the military police themselves. Within hours of the killing, Karl Bendetsen himself had issued a statement to the press, warning them away from mentioning the shootings at all.

In a frantic bid to glean information and protect Elaine and Tommy, Karl Yoneda wrote to Dillon Myer, national director of the War Relocation Authority. After reading of the riot in the news, he told Myer, he was fearful that "the terrorists responsible are likely to be the same gang that tried to attack me on the nights of 30 November/1 December," just before he left for Camp Savage. "Strongly request that you take the proper action against those pro-axis elements in the Manzanar Center and protect my family from being molested," he pressed. "I am fearful that my wife Elaine, a caucasian [*sic*] and my 3 year old son Tommy might suffer physical attack." He added another plea for immediate issuance of his son's permit to leave camp.

Privately, Karl burned with fury at both the US government and the rioters themselves. "The American government, while allowing me to participate at one of its classified facilities," he seethed, "is still holding back from permitting my son—as if he were a 'security risk'—to leave the pro-Japaner infested concentration camp at Manzanar. This is a completely inhuman attitude on their part, and it makes us out to be fools."

All the men from Manzanar at Camp Savage, Karl noted, wore their worry on their faces. None had received any news other than what they'd read in the papers. Venting their anger loudly to each other, they shared desire for vengeance. One new soldier suggested they arm themselves, "ride into Manzanar," take the "scoundrel" rioters aside one-by-one, "and flog them to death." Karl took a more fatalistic approach: "All we can do is wait," he wrote, sitting alone with his diary. "We're in the army; we aren't at liberty to take matters into our own hands."

Fleeing their barrack in the early hours of November 7, with Tommy wearing his inside-out peacoat and Elaine's scarf on his head, his hand clasped in hers as they raced through the dark and wind, the pair stumbled upon an armed soldier. They'd just gotten past the boundary of block 4 and had reached a dusty firebreak. They stopped short as the MP approached, gun drawn, bayonet tipped forward. He flashed a light on Elaine.

"What are you doing here?" he demanded.

Elaine squinted, the too-bright light bathing her face.

"You belong over there," the soldier said after a moment, pointing beyond the barbed wire. Now he could see Elaine was white. An administrator's wife, he assumed, or a military one who'd wandered into camp looking for her husband—not an incarceree.

"No!" Elaine tried breathlessly to explain. "I'm married to a soldier, but not to anyone stationed here. He's in Minnesota."

Elaine tried to make their situation clear, despite the piercing light and rifle, its steel blade jutting along its barrel. She needed to get to the administration building, she explained. She needed protection for her son. "He's been threatened all day, and there have been men gathering around our barrack. I want protection, and I'm not getting it!" she exhorted. "I want to get the administration building!" she cried again.

"Yes!" Tommy chimed in. "My daddy's a soldier!"

The MP looked them over, recognition finally dawning. He brought the pair along the firebreak to the next block, where another soldier stood watch.

Elaine heard some sort of password, and then the new guard took them forward. They were passed from block to block this way until they glimpsed the administration building ahead in the dark. Drawing closer, Elaine could see military police surrounding the whole facility. Two or three others were clustered around a machine gun, with another machine gun staged nearby.

When they entered the warmth and light of the administration building, Elaine was surprised by the scene. The desks, chairs, and filing cabinets in the main room had all been pushed apart. Two long rows of army cots had been lined up in the center, and dozens of incarcerees were occupying them. Togo Tanaka was there, and so was Fred Tayama, a large bandage on his head. Much of the *Free Press* staff had been brought in, including the man who'd translated Kurihara's threats for Elaine that afternoon. Most of the group whom Elaine would classify as "pro-American" had been brought there to safety along with their families by the Military Police.

When Ned Campbell saw Elaine, standing amid all the others who'd been rescued earlier, he said "Oh." He'd forgotten all about her, he claimed. Despite the draining ordeal of her precarious escape with Tommy, she could feel her fury rising. She didn't believe for a minute he'd really forgotten her, not after all their arguments and clashes. *Deep down inside*, she thought, *he must have hoped the mob would do away with us.*

Elaine looked around at the others on their cots, and though she saw many wives and children, she did not see Taeko Ariyoshi, Koji's new wife. Surely, she thought, if she and Tommy had been in danger, then so would the wife of Karl's closest comrade. Taeko had recently told her she was pregnant too. When Elaine asked and no one knew where the young woman was, she became more anxious. Feeling helpless, Elaine turned briefly to her diary, which she must have tucked into her handbag or overcoat pocket before fleeing their barrack. Her words spilled onto the page, rushed and cramped. At last, she and Tommy tried to sleep, "the building surrounded by troops and guns," she wrote.

10 FINISHED
December 7–17, 1942

AT DAYBREAK IN MANZANAR on Monday, December 7, the group from the administration building was taken by truck to the military police barracks, about three-quarters of a mile south along a dirt road from the main section of camp. Elaine was still in a state of agitation when she and Tommy reached the military encampment. In his last official report as Manzanar documentarian, Togo Tanaka wrote that as they arrived, Elaine told the others, "God, I thought they were coming after me and Tommy; we just got out in time, because I saw a large mob gathering on our block."

She tried to explain what she knew about the aftermath of the shooting: "Jimmy Ito, the boy who was killed last night when the military police opened fire, lived just next door to us. I went to express sincere condolences; the mother was just crying and wept on my shoulders." Reliving the scene in her mind, she said, "I felt so terrible because I knew that the neighbors were all more or less blaming Karl and the others for the whole incident and for Jimmy's death." She paused for a moment, then added, "Jimmy was shot in the back, too—"

A voice abruptly interceded: "Anyone who was in the vicinity had no business [there]," insisted an MP who'd been standing nearby. "And no one was shot in the back."

Fred Tayama was there too, still walking around with his big bandage. He was joined by John Sonoda, who'd been beaten by a crowd after the shooting. He'd arrived for protective custody that morning, bruised and battered, directly from Manzanar's hospital. "Guys still looking for him," Elaine scribbled in her diary. She still saw no sign of Koji's wife.

Eating breakfast at the MP dining hall, Elaine was surprised by the facility, so clean and well-equipped, after months in Manzanar's mess halls. But the rest of the military encampment impressed her less. The group spent all their daylight hours there, the women and children in a small, two-room dispensary. The available space was so limited that the men had to take turns sheltering to stay warm. Tad Uyeno, another incarceree under protective custody, remembered how they loitered in small groups, sometimes squatting on the ground and talking about the riot, piecing together the different parts of the story.

Elaine asked for a wire to be sent to both Karl and her parents, letting them know that she and Tommy were OK. Otherwise, no communication beyond the MP encampment was allowed. The military barracks were close enough to Manzanar proper and situated high enough that they could still see the grounds. Peering through the distance, Uyeno and Tanaka were struck by the utter absence of discernable activity, particularly for a Monday morning. The firebreaks, dirt roads, and areas around the incarceree barracks looked deserted. "People must have been stunned by the turn of events," Tanaka guessed, and were staying inside.

After darkness fell, the whole group moved back to Manzanar's administration building. Soldiers had roped off the entire admin area, and MPs stood guard. In this way, Elaine, Tommy, and the rest were shuttled back and forth over the next few days while WRA administrators tried to decide what to do with them. Once daybreak dawned, they were bustled out of Manzanar, only to return after dark.

Elaine spent most of her time beset with anxiety in the small, cramped dispensary. Outside, the air was frigid and sand stung, and Tommy was still weakened from his recent hospital stay. As for Taeko, Elaine couldn't help fretting: *Where is she? What's happening to her?* Elaine worried about Yo Ukita, as well: Was she facing retaliation for having associated with them?

Crowded with the others, hidden away between the small dispensary and administration building, Elaine began to feel claustrophobic and pinned down, and she desperately missed any sense of privacy. *We can scarcely move!* she despaired. How long would they have to live like this? she wondered. On their third day shuttling between the administration building and the military encampment, the MPs offered her the chance to retrieve clothes and other belongings, under escort, from the Yonedas' former barrack. Riding through camp in a military jeep, Elaine saw a great number of people wearing black armbands. They looked to her like a sign of the Black Dragons; later, she'd learn they'd been passed around camp to signify a united pledge of both mourning and protest after the shootings.

At her barrack apartment, as Elaine rushed to throw together two small suitcases and a bag of toys for Tommy, a black-arm-banded crowd began to gather. "Hurry!" pressed the soldier with her. Elaine grabbed what she could, and as they neared the administration building on return, she guessed— correctly—that she'd never again see the barrack or what she'd left behind.

To Elaine's relief, a Manzanar social worker assured her that Taeko Ariyoshi was safe. Though Taeko had locked herself in her own barrack room the night of uprising, in the aftermath she'd decided she did not need further protection. Manzanar felt to her now "like a camp of the dead. . . . Almost no one saunters out and the streets are practically empty." She indicated in a letter she wrote to Koji that she sensed the danger had passed. "The great majority had not taken part in the riot. They are remorseful and bitter that this has happened." Newly pregnant, she did not want to uproot herself now, particularly without knowing where she'd go.

Elaine was even more relieved when Yo Ukita and her family joined them in protective custody at the administration building and the military barracks, but they stayed only a day or two; the family wanted to return to the main camp. Alys Ukita, Yo's sister-in-law, acknowledged that "since we knew the Yonedas, they said that we were *inus*," and the family was afraid, but they refused to flee completely. "We didn't do anything wrong," she insisted years later. They were not spies, like people were saying about the group in protective custody, and they were not going to hide. "I guess," she remembered, "[after a few days] they decided we weren't spies, so we were able to come back." Elaine longed to have Yo stay with them under protection, but her friend balked at leaving—or perhaps defying—the rest of her family.

Meanwhile, dissension rippled through the WRA and army over where to put the whole protective custody group. Certain WRA administrators wanted to move them to the civilian conservation camp at Cow Creek, an abandoned facility in Death Valley near an area known as Furnace Creek. Though Bendetsen grudgingly allowed that the group comprised "certain persons of Japanese ancestry whose loyalty to the United States is conceded," he still balked at moving or freeing them. Their relocation to the Cow Creek camp "is not approved by this office," he sniffed. But the "foregoing disapproval is that of the undersigned," he admitted, "and does not purport to express an opinion on the above subject on behalf of the War Department." Bendetsen's main concern, as usual, was optics: moving Tayama, Tanaka, Elaine, and the rest out of Manzanar would look like handing victory to the uprising's instigators.

On December 10 Bendetsen's boss, John DeWitt, addressed the events at Manzanar in a phone call with the US assistant secretary of war. Of the potential move to the Cow Creek camp, DeWitt agreed with Bendetsen: it would be "a definite show of weakness." Overall, DeWitt expressed disappointment in the uprising's outcome, particularly since only one incarceree had died. "It wouldn't have been a bad thing if several more had been killed. It would have been a very good thing," he lamented. He'd get his wish the next day, when another young incarceree, twenty-one-year-old Jim Kanagawa, died from bullet wounds.

———————

Despite Bendetsen and DeWitt's objections, on the afternoon of December 10, soldiers moved the entire group to Death Valley. Elaine, Tommy, and the others boarded a convoy of trucks, jeeps, and weapons carriers and were taken under armed guard through the desert. The procession carried sixty-six incarcerees, a mix of those targeted and their families, as well as ten WRA staff—Ned Campbell included—and twelve soldiers. They traveled with a truckful of food, another of furniture, and a third of hay.

The incarcerees, now thinking of themselves variously as "exiles," "refu-gees," or "the so-called 'Pro-America Faction,'" sat in back of the trucks under canopied tarps, open only to the rear. As they pulled out of camp onto the highway and headed south and then east, they could see acres of Manzanar's tarpaper barracks, waning now, converging into one dark mass the farther they rode. With no view in front or even to the side of the moving vehicles, they could only stare at where they'd been, the past unspooling in one unrelenting flow. Eventually, all that remained were the guard towers in the distance, rising above the shadowy blur of camp.

Riding in one of the trucks, Tad Uyeno looked at the unknown soldier riding with them, sitting against the tailgate with a long rifle in his hand. He stared back at Manzanar receding and thought how strange it was that "this was the last time we were to see this concentration camp." He thought about the blame left in their wake, how those remaining in Manzanar believed the exiles were responsible for the sorrow that had descended upon camp, a place now paralyzed by a mass strike, with only the mess halls functioning so the incarcerees could eat. Eventually, he'd remember thinking that "underneath those block roof tops were 10,000 people, more or less dejected, mortified, resentful, conscience[-]tormented and mournful for the death of the youth killed by soldiers."

Hours of rugged landscape later, the sun slid below the mountain line, and the group arrived at Cow Creek. They'd traveled 150 miles east and dipped two hundred feet below sea level, where the days could be even hotter than Manzanar's, the nights even more frigid. The camp, comprising about thirty-five buildings over ten acres, had been abandoned four years earlier, and as Elaine glimpsed it for the first time, she saw a string of rundown structures. The entire place, she thought in dismay, was "unfit for shelter." She and Tommy were given a room with shattered windows and, like all the buildings, no heat.

With limited facilities, the so-called exiles, WRA staff, and soldiers all shared the same latrines, a single shower, and a mess hall. Administrators and military personnel, as well as the incarcerees, began to think of the armed guards and the weapons cache as protection for the "refugees," as some WRA officials began to call them. Neither barbed wire nor guard towers prevented them from leaving the grounds, though there'd be nowhere to go anyway in Death Valley. By now, the WRA was hoping the Cow Creek camp incarcerees would relocate quickly back to civilian communities, though limited by the broad exclusion orders and West Coast prohibitions still imposed on "full-blooded" Japanese Americans. Tad Uyeno saw the veneer of equality further dim after the first few communal meals where everyone sat together. A new rule mandated that administrators and military personnel sit separately from the "refugees," to prevent the appearance of "soldiers fraternalizing with the Japanese!"

Elaine either didn't notice or didn't much care about the shifting boundaries between the incarceree group, the WRA, and the military. She was focused on Tommy's health—declining again, so that she first thought his condition was becoming "critical"—and on an utter absence of communication with Karl. She'd not heard from him in days, and she didn't know if he was OK, if he knew she and Tommy were alive, and if he'd tried to write them but the letter had been lost. Then, passing the camp's makeshift office, she glimpsed Tommy's photo for his exit permit, lying alone on the desk of Ned Campbell's clerk. When she asked Campbell about her son's pass, he told her the application had been dispatched to Washington—even marked "emergency," he claimed. When it arrived back in Death Valley, he said, they would attach the photo to it. Elaine remained unconvinced.

Situated on another dusty plain bordered by high mountain peaks, Cow Creek lacked trees, and when dusk fell early on the December nights, the decrepit buildings took on an eerie cast, "as if we had come to a ghost town," Tad Uyeno said. Elaine, looking out on the colorless sand dunes, felt bereft. The first delivery of food from Manzanar brought fresh reminders of the resentments and divisions they'd recently left behind. When the corrugated cartons packed with canned goods arrived on December 11, some had been marked in both English and Japanese with insults: "dog food," one box was labeled; "flea powder," said another.

For Karl, however, December 11 brought great relief. Late that afternoon he received a wire via the War Department, sent that morning from Ralph Merritt at Manzanar: "WIFE AND CHILD SAFE," he read, as his world came rushing back. "WE ARE ASSEMBLING INFORMATION ABOUT AGITATORS CAN YOU ASSIST US PARTICULARLY AS TO THOSE WHO ASSAULTED YOU BEFORE YOU LEFT HERE."

Elaine, still unsure whether Karl knew how or where they were, sat down to write him. She'd been unable to do so yet, she wrote, because she felt incapable of sitting calmly enough to compose either herself or a letter. "We've gone through so much distress, hardship, and general commotion," she attested—a rare admission on her part that she was overwhelmed by forces facing her, that "at times I wasn't certain what was going to become of us." The riot seemed to her like a nightmare. Unable to still herself or her thoughts, she felt the nightmare persist. She thought about where they were, and though sometimes the mountain vista beyond the dunes looked beautiful to her, Death Valley felt like a name that fit.

Attempting a coherent letter to her husband, she let her mind creep back to the afternoon and night of December 6. She remembered an incident she'd not written about yet in her diary, allowing it to spill onto the page only as she began to tell Karl the whole story. She recalled how, as the crowd had grown in front of the administration building on the afternoon of the uprising and the agitators had begun taunting the line of soldiers, she'd spotted a young MP whom she knew to be Jewish. To Elaine, it seemed the mob began cursing right at him, focusing on him as they yelled and chanted. *"Pearl Harbor! Banzai!"* they screamed to his face. She did not need to remind Karl that it had been just two weeks since the L.A. papers had brought Manzanar the latest news of Jewish fate in Axis territory: half the population in Nazi-occupied Europe gone, mass gassings and murder at Hitler's "special camps," corpses processed into "soap fats and fertilizer." Before she could linger in dismay at the young Jew taunted by war slogans, she'd heard Kurihara over the loudspeaker and turned toward him. She told Karl how she understood only one thing amid his angry stream of Japanese—the name "Yoneda!" yelled repeatedly—and how a closer, more intimate horror then swept over her.

Elaine tried her best to narrate the rest, explaining how she and Tommy had finally made their middle-of-the-night escape. When she finished her long letter, Tommy placed his hand palm-down on a sheet of paper, and Elaine traced its outline. He'd wanted to send Karl an actual kiss, but this would have to do, she told them both. She closed, "Your loving wife, Elaine."

Even after she'd written to her husband, the events of December 6–7 continued to strafe her mind, and she felt fury again as she thought about Kurihara and his collaborators. She counted only twenty or so in all of Manzanar whom she really blamed as truly, ideologically "pro-Japan." The rest in the crowd were simply following, she believed, just caught up in the moment and the resentments of incarceration. But as for Kurihara and Kishi, they were "just like Hitler," she thought, not caring who they hurt or targeted in pursuit of their goals, not hesitating to draw up lists of enemies and plans to destroy them. They seemed lunatic to her, and she wanted them charged and convicted not just as instigators of a riot but also as "wartime insurrectionists." They'd tried to kill her son. She'd spare no mercy for them now.

Elaine and the others, finding themselves in a new and broken-down camp, spent their first days trying to clean up the grounds, repair the broken windows, and make the place habitable. She tried to patch the windows of the room where she and Tommy slept, stuffing newspapers and blankets into jagged holes. Fred Tayama, still bandaged, joined his brother to manage cooking duties. With their prewar restaurant experience, they prepared meals far better than those the Yonedas had eaten in block 4's mess hall.

But Elaine spent most of her time waiting and worrying about Tommy, his absent pass, and Karl's missing letters. The days felt lonely and flat, and the landscape only confirmed her sense: when she stared out at the barren plain and colorless dunes, they seemed to go on forever. Elaine wondered if they'd ever get out. Tommy asked over and over for his father, questioning why he hadn't written them. But still no mail arrived, and the boy developed another high fever—perhaps from his endless weeping for Karl, Elaine thought, compounded by the environment and his recent stay in Manzanar's hospital. Her sadness, which she'd seemed to keep at bay throughout their almost nine months at Manzanar, now descended so fast and thick she found it hard to speak. She noticed another strange silence as well. "Absolutely nobody has been speaking about the riot," she wrote to Karl.

A few days past their arrival at Cow Creek, Tommy's fever lowered, and the child began to seem freer, lighter. He played with the other children on the wide, flat plain, "with no stockade" in sight, Elaine noted. Sometimes, the children would give each other rides in a pair of old, dilapidated wheelbarrows. One day, Death Valley park rangers showed a slide show and gave a tour of the surrounding area. Elaine found some of the landscape beautiful, but afterward, she thought about the place and its history, how a group of pioneers, in search of gold, passed through the valley but got stuck. First their food and water ran out, and then five starved to death. The rest were rescued, but even so, they returned to the world like mere shadows, "in a half-dead condition," she wrote.

While Elaine waited and worried, others from Manzanar were on various journeys of their own, though to places as bad or even worse. One was Dr. James Goto, the camp's head physician and most senior Japanese American on the medical staff. He'd been on duty the night the eleven incarcerees had been admitted with gunshot wounds from MP bullets, James Ito already dead ("brought into the hospital cold and stiff," another doctor recalled), Jim Kanagawa soon to follow. An infantry major in the military police battalion filed a report about the shootings, attesting that the "crowd started to break up and run, immediately that [*sic*] the gas bombs were discharged. . . . Some M.P.s, number and identity unknown, fired without orders into that portion of the crowd which came charging toward them." But at the hospital, Dr. Goto found different evidence, recorded in the official medical report. As one analyst summarized it, the hospital transcript revealed "that virtually every wound inflicted on the Japanese" indicated "fleeing" from the gas rather than charging toward the line of soldiers.

Soon after, Goto and his family were moved to the Topaz concentration camp in Utah. (There, in just a matter of months, another prisoner would be shot dead by a soldier: a sixty-three-year-old man killed while walking his dog inside the barbed wire fence.) Years later, Manzanar incarceree Mary Sakaguchi, who married Karl and Elaine's close friend Jimmy Oda, recalled that one day, Dr. Goto was just gone. "A white doctor took his place," she said. A month after the Goto family's move from Manzanar, a military hearing absolved the two soldiers in the December 6 shooting, ruling they'd killed James Ito and Jim Kanagawa and shot the nine others in self-defense. (Over in Topaz, the sentry who'd killed the sixty-three-year-old dog walker would eventually be absolved too, for an incident alternately named "an accident" and a "justifiable military action.")

That December, Kurihara and his fellow agitators were facing their own bleak fate. The negotiating committee from the afternoon of the uprising, along with Ueno and a few others considered leaders, were removed at 4:30 AM on December 7 and taken fifty miles north to the county jail in Bishop. Handcuffed and guarded by men with machine guns, they rode through the early morning freeze in an exposed truck, on a wet floor chunked with snow, Kurihara recalled later. Three nights later, they were handcuffed and moved again, driven past Manzanar to the Lone Pine jail, where they were celled with others who'd been removed from camp. For a few days, officials wondered what to do with them, then settled on preparing a new isolation camp for their longer-term incarceration.

In the Lone Pine jail, they lived sixteen packed into one cell. According to Kurihara, their imprisonment began with only one allotment of food a day and no heat. For the entire time in Lone Pine, the men had one small basin in their cell with which to wash all their clothes, bodies, and dishes for meals. All were American citizens, and though they were accused of being "leaders of the Manzanar Incident" and making "threats of death to informers," in the words of federal officials, none were ever officially charged or prosecuted. They would stay in Lone Pine lockup until they were moved to a series of isolation camps where they faced constant monitoring and at times deplorable conditions. The director of one called the whole operation "Gestapo methods," by which the men had been taken from their families—indefinitely, for all they knew—and locked up with "no warrants, no trials, no sentence." The wife of Sam Tateishi, who'd had her two-year-old son taken away to Los Angeles General Hospital during the family's transport to Manzanar, now watched her husband being taken along with Kurihara, Ueno, and the others. She recalled later, "It occurred to me that I might not ever see him again."

On the evening of December 16, Ned Campbell traveled from Manzanar back to Death Valley with a stack of mail and official papers. He handed Elaine eighteen letters from Karl and told her to pack. Tommy's permit had been approved. They would leave for Los Angeles the next morning.

Tommy's pass consisted of a card not much larger than the tag he'd worn on the train to Manzanar. It was issued by the Western Defense Command and Fourth United States Army from DeWitt's office at the Presidio. One side bore his picture: a small, dark-haired boy in a wrinkled sweater doing his best to stand straight, his arms behind his back, the rough wooden wall in the background occupying significantly more space than the child. The other side gave notice from the military: To ALL PERSONS CONCERNED. "The bearer of this permit is Thomas Yoneda, a person of Japanese ancestry," the card announced. The rest explained that for Tommy, "the provisions and proclamations, exclusions orders, and Civilian Restrictive" orders for the West Coast that had been mandated by the military were "hereby suspended." His permit would be "good until revoked."

Her son's pass to freedom in hand and in a state near euphoria, Elaine read all of Karl's letters out loud for Tommy. The boy listened closely, riveted to hear news of his father. She looked up and saw his eyes, wide and round as if he might swallow every word.

Before the night was over, Elaine had one last confrontation with Ned Campbell. A letter from Ralph Merritt at Manzanar had accompanied Tommy's permit, adding additional instructions. "Immediately upon your arrival in LA," the missive ordered, she must contact army officials confirming that she had "taken Thomas" to Military Area 1 and submitting the address where they would be staying. Campbell spelled out other WRA guidelines. He added that Elaine would have to file a report once a month, attesting that her son had not been involved in any conflicts due to his ancestry nor taken any actions to endanger national security; she would alert the army to any change of address; and she would ensure that Tommy be accompanied at all times by his mother "or another Caucasian escort."

But what about their nonwhite friends, Elaine asked, their Black or Chinese American or Filipino ones, for instance? As part of an ethnically diverse labor community, her social circle included many people who were not "Caucasian," but these were friends who might help watch Tommy for an afternoon, if she were working or needed to go out. Would they allow that?

Campbell, exasperated, had no clear response—nor did he think one necessary. Instead, he chastised her: Why was she always asking "unnecessary questions," he demanded, always "raising obstacles?"

Later, Elaine remembered protesting, "I'm not raising obstacles. I don't want to get entrapped. I don't want to have Tommy taken away from me. You know I am going to work. I may not find a place to put him," she insisted, other than with friends who happened not to be white.

Campbell shot back in irritation that she should just forget it. She should just assume the obvious, as he saw it: that anybody permitted in Military Area 1 would be acceptable. Elaine retorted that she hoped he was right. If he wasn't, if she got into trouble or someone tried to take Tommy away again, and god forbid back to camp, she'd "subpoena him as a witness," she promised. Once again, the thought raced through her head that Ned Campbell, deep down in his heart, was a loathsome man.

The next morning, at 10:20 AM, Elaine and Tommy boarded an army truck headed out of Death Valley. Tommy had been nearly levitating in excitement as they said their goodbyes around Cow Creek. Their plan was to ride past Manzanar to Lone Pine, where they would catch an afternoon bus to Los Angeles, scheduled to arrive in L.A. near midnight.

A small group of women came out to see them off. Elaine could feel tears in her eyes, then rolling down her cheeks, and she could see the others gathered dabbing their faces. She thought again of Yo and wished she were there to say goodbye, in a safer place than Manzanar.

"What's the matter, Mommy?" Tommy asked. She took out a small hand mirror and handkerchief to blot her tears. She saw, to her surprise, an old woman staring back. Her hair, brunette when her husband had left Manzanar a few weeks earlier, was now "stark white." *What's Karl going to say when he sees it?* she thought.

But Elaine would not dwell on that now. She and Tommy were headed home, "out of the entrapment," she wrote in her diary, "and into 'free' America."

PART III

THE RECKONING

Remains of a Manzanar tower. *Courtesy of the Nagatomi Collection, Manzanar National Historic Site*

11 | BURNED
1943–1945

BY THE TIME ELAINE AND TOMMY had resettled in San Francisco, 1943 had dawned, and Elaine's nerves had finally begun to calm. She and Tommy had stopped for a while between Death Valley and the Bay Area to stay with the Buchmans in Los Angeles, where Elaine had vacillated between feeling euphoric and shaken. Then they'd moved north again.

Elaine found it easier to secure employment in San Francisco than L.A. But the country was still hostile to mixed-race families, and finding housing proved a challenge. Even famed humanitarian Eleanor Roosevelt, in her widely syndicated My Day column, told the nation, "I would like to make it clear that I would never advocate [mixed marriage]." Her warning: "Over the centuries a strong racial strain will probably obliterate a weaker one." As for mixed Japanese American families resettling west, national sentiment was even less welcoming. When the Western Defense Command issued a press release later in 1943, explaining that "certain Japanese Americans in mixed marriage status" had been freed and allowed to return home with their mixed children, a congressman from Seattle telegrammed in protest: "Vast majority [of] coast residents," are "violently opposed to this procedure and feel that all Japanese for security reasons should be barred from West Coast areas for the duration" of the war.

Eventually Elaine and Tommy found accommodations in San Francisco in a large, old house owned by a longshoreman friend, near enough to their former home that the area felt familiar. They had one room to themselves with access to a kitchen shared among a handful of tenants.

Elaine had hoped to find work in a war-related industry, but childcare constraints limited her. She first took a job at the Hills Bros. coffee plant on the Embarcadero, alongside the waterfront. She worked on what she called the "belt line," jarring coffee, a rationed good now packaged in glass bottles to save tin for war materials. After a few months, she finally found employment directly related to the war effort, as an office manager for the United Electrical, Radio and Machine Workers of America. Located in Oakland, the position required a longer commute, but she was able to place Tommy in a daycare for mothers working in the war industry. Her days were long, tiring, and nonstop: she'd typically rise at 6:30 AM, get Tommy to the childcare center and then herself to work before 9:00 AM, return home again just after 5:00 PM, pick up her son, make dinner, and get him to bed around 8:30 PM. Sometimes she'd bring extra work home to complete after Tommy fell asleep so she could earn overtime wages.

If the unrelenting pace overwhelmed her, though, she left no trace of it. What mattered was that she was working in a union job again, supporting the industries fueling the battle to defeat fascist forces. When Karl wrote to her about his own food rations improving, she described the shortages and long lines at the butcher and market, adding, "That's how it should be—our soldiers need and deserve the best."

Eventually, Elaine resumed her work against repressions closer to home. She led the Coleman Defense Committee to free yet another young Black man falsely convicted of robbery and rape and joined the effort to establish a new World Federation of Trade Unions. She also immersed herself again in the International Labor Defense fund, which soon changed its focus to civil rights more broadly, protecting Black veterans who'd returned from battle only to be brutalized at home, and advocating for equal treatment for minorities.

Besides working and caring for Tommy, Elaine's most constant activity after their return to San Francisco was writing to Karl. She composed a letter almost every day, sometimes adding a lipstick kiss, frequently enclosing a drawing from Tommy, and often signing their private term of affection, "your wiffle." Through Karl's letters, she could trace the progression of his war service with as much detail as he could divulge: his graduation from MIS school, his refusal of the offer to teach there (he wanted to serve overseas, at the front), and his departure from the United States on a ship bound for Calcutta. From there, Karl was moved around the China-Burma-India Theater as part of the

Office of War Information's psychological warfare team, writing propaganda leaflets to air-drop behind enemy lines and battlefield radio announcements in Japanese. These broadcast the Allied take on war news as well as information to encourage surrender, promising medical care for the wounded and fair treatment for captured soldiers.

Through it all, Elaine wrote constantly. Memories of being close to Karl would sustain her, she told him, and "keep me warm until we can be together again." Until then, she urged, "Be well dearest, take care of yourself." Sometimes, Elaine would try to amuse him. "Taken a short haircut look like a skinned rabbit!" she dashed off. She also regaled him with stories of their son. When Tommy asked why they'd been sent to Manzanar, Elaine told Karl she'd explained that it was "because he was considered of J[apanese] ancestry," and "since daddy was a nisei[,] that made him a sansei." Tommy was "just thrilled by that word," she wrote. "And when people ask him what he is—he says sansei, because daddy is nisei who is fighting the nips!" When Karl sent pictures home, Tommy would kiss each and every one, Elaine assured her husband. Most of all, she wrote, "I will always love you." She would wait and love and think of him, she promised, until one day they could "raise our darling son together in a democratic world."

Despite the amusing anecdotes, in truth Tommy was struggling mightily in the aftermath of Manzanar. Trying to emphasize the positive for a husband at war, Elaine told Karl in February 1943 that Tommy had finally stopped weeping or seeming terrified at the mere mention of Manzanar, though he had mentally melded the war's many dangers into one: "He used to tell me not to talk [about it] . . . that he did not like Manzanar because there were Nazis there," she wrote. The drawings Tommy made for Karl, to be enclosed with his mother's letters, featured bombs raining down on Japan, swastikas in flight, or the Japanese flag in flames. She explained that he'd sometimes color these pictures as if in a "spell," during which he'd "keep on drawing endlessly, almost always the same theme—a Japanese plane or Nazi plane on fire—a tank, etc."

But Elaine was wary of telling Karl too much, and in fact, their son's nightmares continued unabated. Tommy would frequently wake in a state of terror, calling out for his father, inconsolable with the fear that Karl would be hurt. The boy told Elaine that he hoped Karl would be sent to fight Hitler, not the Japanese, who were so dangerous, they might even be like "the mean ones" he'd seen threaten his father in Manzanar.

Elaine also avoided mentioning Axis atrocities directly in her letters to Karl, but she continued to write of their shared goal for fascism's demise. She admitted to a longing for herself and others to be free from "fear of having to destroy or be destroyed." She knew Karl's overarching aim in life mirrored hers: "to preserve a happy future for our son and all other children."

Their shared commitment to this fight would have been repeatedly reinvigorated during Karl's deployment, and not just by the general direction of the war and his military service. By the time of Elaine and Tommy's arrival in San Francisco, new details had emerged about the Nazi project to completely annihilate the Jews—as well as communists, antifascists, and other undesirables—in occupied territory. What also emerged was confirmation from the US State Department of the irrefutable truth of this project's progression. The suggestion even surfaced that Hitler had already achieved his goal, at least for European Jewry.

When Elaine reached Los Angeles and San Francisco, becoming reimmersed in her Jewish family and leftist community, she had unfettered access to such news and to people who would notice and discuss it. In early December the *Los Angeles Times* had noted that a day of fasting, prayer, and mourning was planned by Jewish organizations around the world for the fate of Jews "in the regions controlled by Hitler, who face literal extermination," based on "well authenticated . . . documents in possession of the American State Department." They also reported that "a complete campaign of extermination" had been "decreed by Hitler," to be completed by December 1, 1942. Though Allied governments had delayed making the news public until late November and major media remained slow to broadcast it, throughout December papers began revealing that as far back as summer 1942, sources had documented the annihilation of "2,000,000 European Jews," while "an estimated 5,000,000 more" faced the same fate by years' end. Nazi methods involved "machine-gunning, asphyxiation, deliberate starvation, torture and subjection to disease." FDR himself reportedly suffered "shock" at the news.

On December 21, 1942, journalist Varian Fry in the *New Republic* broke the news of gas chambers and crematoria. "There are the extermination centers, where Jews are destroyed by poison gas or electricity," he reported. "There is burning alive, in crematoria, or buildings deliberately set on fire. There is the method of injecting air-bubbles into the blood stream: it is cheap, clean and efficient, producing clots, embolisms and death within a few hours."

A variation of this news had already been widely broadcast to American audiences the week before. On December 13, 1942, on his famed CBS Radio broadcast, Edward R. Murrow had admitted to being "almost stunned into silence" by the details, which would have surely been discussed for weeks at Jewish dinner tables around the nation, including one at which Elaine and Tommy would have sat five days later, when they finally reached the Buchman home from Death Valley. Murrow had opened with a simple explanation: "What is happening is this. Millions of human beings, most of them Jews, are being gathered up with ruthless efficiency and murdered." Before he had finished his report, he told the American public, "The phrase 'concentration camps' is obsolete, as out of date as economic sanctions or non-recognition. It is now possible only to speak of extermination camps."

If Elaine—or Karl—had any inclination of protesting the American concentration camps now that they'd both escaped one, reports like these undoubtably contributed to their reticence then, and throughout the entire war. They were both clearly scarred by these latest details of Nazi atrocities, as they'd long been by Japanese imperialist ones. They "were sure there would be ovens in Manzanar and other camps" if the Allies lost, they said later; they also thought that "all of us, including all non-white and white antifascists[,] would end up in those ovens."

Elaine and her husband remained both ambivalent about and committed to their choice: even though the American camps "violated our Constitutional and basic human rights," Karl said, "we had no choice but to accept the racist U.S. dictum . . . over Hitler's ovens and Japan's military rapists of Nanking." The time to "thrash out the question of our rights" would only come if and when the war ended in Allied victory. As for the men they believed to be pro-Japan sympathizers in Manzanar, they held little ambivalence: they'd have made "good 'oven-tenders.'"

Two weeks after Murrow's report, while Karl was still undergoing MIS training at Camp Savage, he was interviewed by an army major about the "trouble makers and leaders of the disloyal element" in Manzanar, as the Navy Intelligence Office termed them. ("Though Carl [*sic*] Yoneda is a well-known Japanese communist and for that reason, a <u>blue-card suspect</u>," the reporting officer noted with emphasis, his "statement concerning conditions at Manzanar may be <u>considered reliable</u>.") When asked if he thought Joe Kurihara, Harry

Ueno, Ben Kishi, and Sam Tateishi, were "dangerous, pro-Japanese leaders," Karl responded, "Definitely so."

"Would you be willing to testify in case of investigation?"

"I am willing to testify in closed doors or in public."

Karl told the major about the group who'd come to his barrack in August to threaten him—the "mean ones" of Tommy's nightmares, though Karl did not know how they still haunted his son. He also told his superior how, at the Kibei-Nisei meeting in August where he'd been forced to retract his statements about Sam Tateishi, he had "learned the names of almost all of them and turn[ed] this list of names in to the FBI."

Back in Owens Valley, Manzanar spent the winter of 1942–1943 in mourning. The two young men who'd been killed during the uprising were buried in the last days of December 1942. A photo commemorating the event shows a mother in black, a dark veil barely obscuring her grief as she bends toward her child's coffin. Behind her, rows of mourners in formal wear look down toward parched grass, while a lone monk in long robes, there to perform last rites, stares directly toward the camera.

Manzanar's project director, Ralph Merritt, also attended the funeral. He commemorated the event by writing to his aunt. "Last Monday we buried our dead," he wrote. "The only soldier present stood at the head of one of the coffins—the brother of the dead boy. This soldier of Japanese ancestry was on active duty at a distant point, but the Army granted my request to bring him home to his family." Merritt found particular meaning in the monk's last rites: "The Buddhist Priest prayed that the lives of these young men would be a sacrifice for the sins of all the camp."

Soon after, Kentucky senator A. B. "Happy" Chandler and his wife arrived at Manzanar. They were there as part of a congressional effort to investigate agitation at the Japanese American camps, ascertain whether the incarcerees were being "coddled" by the civilian-run War Relocation Authority, and judge whether the military should wrest control. As Ralph Merritt wrote in an internal report that newspapers publicized widely, Senator Chandler declared almost two-thirds of the incarceree population—citizens included—disloyal to the United States, ready and willing to "commit 'almost any act for their Emperor.'" Mrs. Chandler, wrote Merritt, "took the opportunity to express her very vigorous opinion about all Japanese, which was summarized by the expression that they should be put on shipboard and dumped in the ocean when Tokyo was bombed."

As for Kurihara and the others accused of fomenting the Manzanar uprising, after a few weeks in the Lone Pine and Independence jails, they were moved to an isolation camp in Moab, Utah. Later in 1943 Kurihara and his fellow citizen dissidents were moved again to an isolation camp called Leupp. (The few Issei among them at Moab were taken to a detention camp for aliens.) Still, not one of them had actually been charged, tried, or convicted of any crime. The director of the War Relocation Authority, cognizant of the unconstitutionality of detaining citizens in an isolation camp without due process, knew Leupp was not a viable long-term solution, and by early December 1943 he moved Kurihara and the other Nisei and Kibei-Nisei to the Tule Lake War Relocation Center, in Newell, California. Long before reaching Tule Lake, though, Kurihara had decided to leave the United States and abandon his citizenship. He'd begun studying Japanese reading and writing in Moab, preparing to expatriate to a country he'd never even seen.

Kurihara's plan to leave the United States had been adopted by a surprising number of other incarcerees, particularly from Manzanar. For many, the root of their decision could be traced to a seminal event across all the camps that began in the first month of 1943, in the pall of Manzanar's uprising: registration for Nisei combat duty and a questionnaire about loyalty to America. Both concepts—enlistment and determination of loyalty—were ones Karl Yoneda had urged. But the practice, as the US government conceived it, proved far more damning than the theory. The results caused much greater damage than either Yoneda expected.

The "loyalty questionnaire" was an expansion of a January 1943 government plan to recruit an all-Nisei fighting battalion. A form was delivered to all incarcerees, not just men of draft age. Two of its questions in particular proved confounding and deeply problematic. Question 27 asked Japanese American men if they were willing to serve in combat wherever ordered. Question 28 asked if signers "would swear unqualified allegiance to the United States and forswear any form of allegiance to the Emperor of Japan."

Nisei men were confused whether answering yes to the first meant they were volunteering, there and then, for immediate combat duty; some with family members in Japan feared that if they agreed to go wherever sent, they'd be forced to face relatives on the battlefield. All citizen incarcerees resented being asked to foreswear loyalty to an emperor who was not and had never been their own, and some worried the question was a trap: if they foreswore loyalty to Japan's emperor, would they be charged with having once harbored such loyalty? Many also resented the request to fight as citizens when their rights as citizens had been so thoroughly breeched by being herded into concentration camps.

Issei, who'd been denied citizenship in the United States and therefore forced to retain their Japanese citizenship, feared answering yes to Question 28 would leave them without legal status anywhere. And families with Issei parents and Nisei children—numbering a significant portion of incarcerees—worried that providing different answers among them would lead to permanent forced separation, the elders exiled to Japan.

Even Elaine and Karl, when they learned about the questionnaire and the debacle in its wake, derided the plan as both unfair and ineffective. Three unexpected outcomes occurred, all of which in hindsight might have seemed inevitable. Almost a quarter of incarcerees across all the camps answered no to Question 28; at Manzanar, a full half did so. Just over 5 percent of draft-age Nisei were moved to answer yes to Question 27, about volunteering without limitation. This ultimately yielded fewer than a thousand who passed physical examinations and were inducted as a result of the questionnaire into the all-Nisei battalion—a paltry percentage of the draftable incarcerated population. Most damning, a skyrocketing number of applications followed for repatriation or expatriation. By the end of 1943 almost ten thousand people had applied to leave the United States, and the majority of new applicants were citizens. In 1944 the number climbed by almost twice: approximately 16 percent of all incarcerees.

At Tule Lake, where Kurihara had finally been sent, three thousand people refused to answer the questions at all or answered equivocally (e.g., they'd volunteer for military service, but only if their families were freed and allowed to return home, and their full citizenship rights restored). Many claimed—irrefutably, from the standpoint of logic—that they were acting in the true spirit of Americanism in refusing to accept such a breach of civil rights.

All were categorized "disloyal," along with anyone who'd answered no to one or more questions. The War Department's original plan had been to segregate those who'd answered unsatisfactorily in the small isolation camp at Moab. Now, that plan seemed pitifully inadequate. Instead, Tule Lake, with its already large population of so-called disloyals, became the nation's new segregation camp within a concentration camp: more barbed wire for an eight-foot double fence deemed "man-proof," twenty-eight guard towers, a thousand military police, and a fleet of armored cars and tanks.

WRA officials and social scientists who'd studied the camp populations from within had emphasized repeatedly that resistance to the questionnaire did not necessarily signal disloyalty but rather disenchantment and a desire to avoid further family separations. Politicians such as Happy Chandler considered the results proof of the opposite. They touted the whole debacle as just one more justification for stripping Nisei of citizenship.

By midyear, Congress had passed the Renunciation Act of 1944, the nation's first law allowing renunciation of citizenship. By October of that year, administrators across all the camps received instructions for facilitating renunciation and expatriation. Almost 20,000 people had joined Kurihara in his plan to leave America, more than 10,000 of them citizens. By war's end, a little over 5,000 people followed through. The other 5,409 Nisei changed their minds, seeking a legal path to restoring citizenship and staying in the United States. But not Kurihara. He remained at Tule Lake, studying and reading the Bible in Japanese, until he was released to await transfer aboard a navy ship to the far side of the world.

The legacy of the loyalty questionnaire stretched even wider and longer. As historians would note four decades later, "During three years of rising humiliation, 20,000 people chose this means to express their pain, outrage, and alienation," in one of the few "nonviolent ways to protest" their illegal incarceration. As a result, the entire West Coast Japanese American population became divided, slotted into categories of disloyal versus loyal. "Debates continue to rage today about how to shake the stigma and misunderstandings that resulted from the registration crisis and subsequent segregation of the incarcerated population."

"Full blooded" ethnic Japanese people, except women married to and raising the children of non-Japanese men, were prohibited from returning to the West Coast until January 1945, a month after the US Supreme Court finally acknowledged that a loyal American citizen could not be held in a WRA incarceration camp. Before that, between early 1943 and January 1945, the WRA encouraged those who "passed" the loyalty questionnaire to relocate out of camp, with diminishing but still considerable restrictions on where and how they could resettle. For most of these citizens, freedom required building new lives far from the former West Coast homes they'd already been forced to forfeit, in a nation still rife with anti-Japanese sentiment.

Many Americans wanted to prohibit any person of Japanese descent from being freed—ever. A few months after Elaine's return to San Francisco, she was chilled by a letter displayed on the front page of a Denver paper, proclaiming rabidly racist sentiments against anyone of Japanese ethnicity. She did not record the exact headline, but the media was packed with similar commentary as the camps began slowly to release more people. Across the so-called excluded areas, anti-Japanese groups sprung forth, dedicated to barring their fellow citizens' return: in Sacramento, the Home Front Commandos; in Los Angeles, the Pacific Coast Japanese Problem League; in San Diego, No Japs Incorporated.

Just as Elaine and Tommy were settling back into "'free' America," as she'd wryly put it on her way out of Death Valley, the state of Arkansas made it illegal for anyone of Japanese descent, including American citizens, to own land there. By early June 1943 a civic group in Oregon was agitating for the wholesale deportation of all Nisei to Japan. Then a group of over a hundred thousand people from across five western states petitioned the federal government to keep anyone with Japanese ancestry—again including Americans—from returning to the West Coast, indefinitely. A writer to the *Los Angeles Times* offered three words that spring for allowing all those wrongfully incarcerated to come home: STUPID AND DANGEROUS. "As a race, the Japanese have made for themselves a record for conscienceless treachery unsurpassed in history. Whatever small theoretical advantages there may be in releasing those under restraint in this country would be enormously outweighed by the risks."

Ultimately, many Americans considered the Pacific struggle "a holy war," in the words of one 1943 bestselling US book. A *New York Times* front page in January 1943 featured an Allied general explaining, "Fighting Japs is not like fighting normal human beings. . . . The Jap is a little barbarian." Confirming that he was making a biological or racial, not cultural, argument, he elaborated, "We are not dealing with humans as we know them. We are dealing with something primitive. Our troops have the right view of Japs. They view them as vermin."

America was in a battle of "Oriental Races Against Occidental Races for the Domination of the World," the *Los Angeles Examiner* trumpeted. Conversely, the battle against the Nazis was pitched as "a family affair" among people of "common racial . . . roots." As famed American journalist Ernie Pyle put it after being embedded with troops in both Europe and Asia, "In Europe we felt that our enemies, horrible and deadly as they were, were still people." But "the Japanese were looked upon as something subhuman and repulsive; the way some people feel about cockroaches or mice."

As Allied victory seemed more likely and the US government began allowing Japanese Americans in nonmixed families to return west, they were frequently met with violence, intimidation, and humiliation. Signs reading No Japs Allowed or No Japs Welcome dotted storefronts and windows. One barbershop owner ejected a disabled private who was wounded in battle, awarded a Purple Heart, and wearing his army uniform; the store's sign read, Japs Keep Out, You Rat.

Dozens of shootings and torchings flared across the West Coast: a family eating dinner, only to have six shotgun blasts burst through their window; others sleeping in a house sprayed with gasoline and lit on fire; people escaping an arson attempt, only to be shot as they fled into the open. One family had two sons who'd served in the war—one killed in battle, the other decorated for bravery—when they returned from camp to find their home and possessions burned. Meanwhile, three men, charged with placing a bomb on a returnee's farm, were acquitted after their attorney's defense claimed, "This is a white man's country. Let's keep it so."

Before this slew of arson and shootings, when only Elaine and Tommy and various other mixed-race family members were allowed to breathe the West Coast air, Karl Bendetsen had been busy documenting the scope and success of the policy that had ostensibly freed them. In late 1942 or early 1943 his staff was tasked with compiling a final report on the "West Coast evacuation" for General John DeWitt, to be delivered to the secretary of war and then the government at large. Retrospection seems to have prompted some uncertainty on Bendetsen's part, at least at first. Looking back on the forced removal and incarceration of every man, woman, and child of Japanese descent on the West Coast, Bendetsen showed rare ambivalence (at least among what remains in extant records). "Of course [the difficulty of determining loyalty] is probably true of white people, isn't it?" he asked a colleague that January, while discussing the justifications included in his report. "You know that old proverb about 'not being able to look into the heart of another'? And 'not even daring to look into your own'. . . . well maybe there's something in that."

To another, he mused, "Maybe our ideas on the Oriental have been all cock-eyed. . . . Maybe he isn't inscrutable." In the end, though, what worried Bendetsen the most remained the surface image of it all. "I'm scared to death principally because of the public relations part of it," he admitted. "That's it, to put it in a nutshell."

By the time he got to reporting the results of the mixed-marriage policy, Bendetsen left no trace of his ambivalence. First, he offered statistics: 465 "persons of Japanese ancestry" had been released from one or another concentration camp and allowed to return home between the latter half of 1942 and the first half of 1943. This group comprised 290 mixed-race children under eighteen years of age, 34 mixed adults with children, 68 childless mixed adults (though none possessing 51 percent or more "Japanese blood"), and 72 Japanese American mothers of mixed children whose family environment had been deemed sufficiently Caucasian. No Japanese American fathers had been freed and allowed back, nor their non-Japanese wives, unless the husbands were "dead or long since separated," or, like Karl Yoneda, off at war. (One sole exemption had been granted, the final report noted: a single "full-blooded Japanese male, a citizen of the United States, was authorized to reside in the evacuated area" with his non-Japanese wife; in this one case, "a special exception was made . . . because of long and honorable service in the United States Navy.") Ultimately, the document explained, the program for mixed families could be considered a success, since mixed children were now "being reared in an American environment," while mixed adults "predominantly American in appearance and thought have been restored to their families, to their communities, and to their jobs."

Despite the blatant racism and sexism of the mixed-marriage policy to contemporary eyes, no one in the US government in 1943 seemed to blink at its depiction of success. But problems did arise, related to the very issues that had been troubling Bendetsen during the drafting of the document. When he passed the whole report for review in April 1943 to the assistant secretary of war, John McCloy balked, reportedly "livid" at two claims in particular: first, that loyalty of ethnic Japanese was impossible to determine because of their "ethnic strain," and this impossibility—not an urgency born of time— accounted for the plan's "military necessity," and second, that no person of Japanese descent should be permitted back on the West Coast until the end of the war, "regardless of the improved military situation." McCloy's main concern was that such claims would doom the federal government in a series of cases before the Supreme Court challenging, as DeWitt later admitted, "the constitutionality of the entire program."

So Bendetsen simply rewrote the offending sentences, leaving out the part about "military necessity" derived from "ethnic strains." Then he swapped in a new cover page, gave the report a new date, and submitted the revised package to the secretary of war, pretending it contained the true and original justifications for the entire West Coast "evacuation." Finally, he ordered a subordinate to destroy all nine copies he'd had printed of the original report, along with its original cover page.

On June 29, 1943, as Elaine was in San Francisco—likely penning one more letter to her husband, her son beside her drawing another Japanese flag in flames—a young army warrant officer just a few miles away at the Presidio typed up a secret memo: "I certify that this date I witnessed the destruction by burning of the galley proofs, galley pages, drafts and memorandums of the original report of the Japanese Evacuation." The Justice Department, in preparing for a case about the constitutionality of the whole episode, was never apprised of the destroyed copies or the redated submission. Only a handful of people would ever know that proof had once existed of the patently racist reasoning behind the West Coast evacuation—until a young, Japanese American researcher uncovered a missed tenth copy four decades later.

After trumpeting the successful incarceration of anyone on the West Coast with any Japanese ancestry and then erasing the evidence of its worst justification, Karl Bendetsen saw his war career dwindle. Eventually, he served in London and elsewhere in Europe, and then as the war wound down, as a congressional liaison staff member in Washington, DC. He never rose higher than a colonel heading the Wartime Civil Control Administration. In December 1945 he resigned from the army altogether. Seemingly though, he successfully kept his own ethnic strain a secret throughout the war. A 1943 National Jewish Welfare Board card from the Bureau of War Records lists a Karl R. Bendetsen, Colonel, as among the American Jewish personnel serving in the army, his next of kin listed as "Albert M. Bendetsen." NO PUBLICITY, the card says, stamped in huge letters across its entire surface.

Karl Yoneda had never seen a battlefield so strewn with death and blood, with the charred and broken bodies of both Japanese and American soldiers. In Burma's battle of Myitkyina during the spring of 1944, he witnessed the worst violence and misery of his war experience. He crouched in trenches with combat soldiers, swatted away a thick stream of insects, found leeches buried in his skin. Soon, he burned with fever from malaria.

White GIs always escorted Japanese American MIS soldiers to prevent them being mistaken for the enemy. In a battle's lull in Myitkyina, one of Karl Yoneda's GI escorts dragged a loudspeaker into the brush and positioned it toward a bamboo grove shrouding the opposing battalion. Someone from the US side played Japanese music, calling enemy attention, hoping to stir longings for home, or comfort, or any place far from battle. Then Karl and his MIS comrades broadcast messages enticing surrender, to accompany the propaganda leaflets they'd written for airdrop over enemy lines.

The maudlin plan rarely worked. Few Japanese soldiers emerged from the grove waving white flags in the loudspeaker's blare. But some who did surrender eventually—sometimes after being wounded or taken by surprise— remembered the music. "The programs were a breath of fresh air to all listeners," Karl said some of the captured men admitted. And the flyers, they assured him, "were very useful for toilet needs."

After particular battles, Karl and his unit took responsibility for culling so-called intelligence material—papers, notes, battle orders, letters, diaries—from abandoned enemy posts and dead Japanese soldiers. On one Myitkyina corpse, Karl found a packet of postcards, sixteen of them dated over two short months. They bore drawings by the young daughter of the dead soldier, kindergarten-like sketches: a girl, a boy, a cucumber, a clock. She'd even written her name in careful letters. She'd told her father she hoped he'd come home safely.

Karl felt a pull when he saw Keiko's little pictures, read her wish that would never now come true. He thought of Tommy, likely the same age as this now-fatherless girl. He knew, somewhere in the war-torn reaches of Japan, she deserved to have the postcards returned to her somehow, now that her father never would—to know he'd had carried them with him always, even in his last moments. Instead of turning the postcards over to the MIS translation center, Karl pocketed them. He would send them to Keiko someday, once this brutal war was over.

Thinking about Tommy, he felt a different kind of worry. Though Elaine had kept the severity of his health issues from Karl, her letters had begun to include fewer and fewer of their son's scribbles and sketches. Karl could tell something was wrong.

By late summer of 1944 Tommy had become too ill even to write or draw. His psychological trauma seemed to have morphed into his most severe physical debility yet. He was even sicker than he'd been in Manzanar, though Elaine would forever believe the depth of his decline resulted from his time in camp. He'd been away from proper medical care for so long there, the conditions had been so poor and the circumstances so stressful, she couldn't help but assume Manzanar had made his illness that much worse.

Tommy spent a month under observation at San Francisco's French Hospital, a sprawling arrangement of brick buildings about two miles west of Japantown, where Elaine was only permitted to see him through an observation window. In October he was diagnosed with asthma, extreme allergies, and a suspected case of rheumatic fever and was admitted to an isolation ward at Stanford Home for Convalescent Children, about thirty miles south in Palo Alto. The hospital occupied a blanched stone mansion, seemingly scrubbed of all dirt and decay, where both the nurses and patients were clad in pure white. Stanford's doctors espoused a strong belief in the healing properties of fresh air, and in fine weather they would line their young charges' beds against an outside wall. Then the children could grasp the white iron bars of their cots and hoist themselves up until they were standing both in bed and in the bright, warm sun. Elaine was allowed to visit Tommy only on weekends, and no close physical contact was permitted at all. He stayed for eight months.

Just as Tommy was entering the convalescent hospital, Elaine received a letter from the US Army. As of the end of that month, October 1944, she would no longer be required to file a monthly report for one "Thomas Culbert Yoneda"—unless for some reason he changed his name. If he should die, the letter noted with brisk dispatch, his permit "should be returned for cancellation." It closed, "Very truly yours."

But Tommy did not die, and he remained at Stanford until June 1945. When he began to heal enough to resume sketches for Karl, Elaine sent them in her missives to the Pacific front. "Tommy was proud as a peacock that you liked his drawing," she assured her husband. As summer neared and Tommy's discharge from Stanford drew close, Elaine was relieved to learn that he'd been eating so well, he'd gained ten pounds. He told Elaine he was excited to go home, to be able to touch and hug her; he was going to be "promoted soon," he explained with all the gravity and pride due one's official hospital release.

Elaine wrote little about Joyce in her letters to Karl, or at least in the letters they made public. One can read between the omissions in the Yonedas' archives, however, to guess that she remained both concerned for Joyce and eager to protect her daughter's privacy throughout the very public lives Elaine and Karl had chosen to live. In an event never mentioned by either Karl or Elaine in any of their many published interviews and writings, nor in the private letters they bequeathed to various libraries, in March 1943 a tiny classified appeared at the bottom of a *San Francisco Examiner*'s back page: "Not responsible for any debts contracted by my wife, Joyce E. Barnett, after March 2, 1943." The notice was signed by the man Joyce had married just four months earlier: Ernest Barnett, from "1338 Steiner" Street in San Francisco, right near where Elaine and Tommy were living. Though Joyce had lied about her age the previous fall when she married the twenty-seven-year-old, claiming she was five years older than her fifteen years, she was clearly now a young teenager headed for her first divorce.

What Elaine did divulge, in the letters she eventually made public, was that she saw little of Joyce between Manzanar and war's end and that her daughter remained elusive. In the spring of 1945 she wrote Karl that Joyce had returned, seemingly out of the blue, to live with the Buchmans again in Los Angeles. "Says she's going to stay put this time! Let us hope so," Elaine reported somewhat cryptically. In the next few months, her daughter returned to San Francisco. Joyce stopped by a few times, either at Elaine's work or rented room, but would not tell her mother where she was living. A

September 1945 letter from Elaine to Karl divulged Joyce's claim that she was working as a hat trimmer in a millinery; Elaine thought her daughter looked "good [yet] rather fat," then reassured Karl, "but her face is real pretty and healthy looking."

Joyce also wrote occasionally to Karl herself. Elaine included one letter in the papers she left behind, allowing a fleeting glimpse of an adolescent who seemed sweet, adrift, and longing to be part of an unbroken family. "Dear Soldier Dad Karle," Joyce typed the late-June day Tommy was released from the Stanford Home for Convalescent Children. "Well, it sure has been a long time since I've written you." She thanked him for some presents he'd sent and reported Tommy's return home. "He sure is big and fat to," she told Karl, with traces of a teenager whose schooling had been interrupted by family upheaval—and perhaps who was unused to typing. "Some day soon Iwillhave my picture taken and I will send you soom.... With all my LOVE, Your LOVING daughter."

By the time Karl received Joyce's letter, he was stationed in China. He was still there on August 6, 1945, when celebration erupted throughout his unit. Between victorious cheers and euphoric hollers, Karl learned that Hiroshima had been flattened. The United States had dropped something called an "A-bomb." No one actually knew what kind of bomb that was, but the utter destruction of the coastal city meant Japan's surrender was near, and all around Karl, men wearing his same uniform rejoiced.

Amid the widening, delirious mayhem, Karl's own world shrank a measure. He thought in shock about his mother. He was deeply relieved the war's end seemed near. But why, he asked the air, did it have to be Hiroshima, where his dear mother lived?

As news broke over the United States of the nuclear obliteration of Nagasaki on August 9, followed by V-J Day on August 15, Elaine walked back from work in San Francisco amid the "bedlam" of celebration, as she put it, the streets in Chinatown so packed with revelers that it took hours to get home. She felt all the pent-up emotion of the war and now of its conclusion roiling inside her, but her heart would not release it. She wrote to Karl that she wanted to cry, but her body simply refused. Four days later, she felt the same. "I think it would be better if the tears would come," she told him. But still, every "passing minute is a diamond to me," she wrote, "because every move of the clock's hand brings me closer to you."

With the demobilization of millions of troops causing long delays in the return home, Karl left Asia on October 13, on board a ship from Karachi to the United States. He arrived in New Jersey three weeks later and from there flew to California. On November 11, 1945, Armistice Day, Karl walked out of the gates of Camp Beale, just north of Sacramento. Then he saw them: his "two most shining stars," Elaine and Tommy. They ran toward each other in a rush, embraced, and cried. A friend who'd driven Elaine and Tommy to Camp Beale loaded Karl's duffel into the trunk and drove the Yonedas south toward San Francisco. It felt to Karl like a long, long road they'd taken to where they finally were: a family together, headed home.

Two weeks later, on a gray, rain-soaked day, Joseph Kurihara and fifteen hundred other former incarcerees of America's concentration camps boarded the USS *Randall,* a former navy warship. All were either repatriating or expatriating—the latter having given up their US citizenship, becoming known as "renunciants." Most were single men; many were Kibei-Nisei, some Issei. Kurihara was the only adult Nisei among them who was not also a Kibei.

After the vessel departed from the coast of Seattle, it headed across waters Karl Yoneda had recently traversed, though in the opposite direction. On December 8, 1945, four years and a day from the bombing of Pearl Harbor, the ship arrived in Tokyo Bay. If the former prisoners of the US government—Issei and Nisei alike—looked past the deck toward land, they'd glimpse a country none of them had ever actually known at all: one now "devastated," as the historian Eileen Tamura put it, "by poverty, starvation, homelessness, and death."

12 RETURNED
1945–1985

AT 11:00 AM ON NOVEMBER 21, 1945, ten days after Karl arrived home from war, the last two incarcerees left Manzanar. With the departure of a mother and her four-year-old son, the camp officially closed. Although the West Coast exclusion of Japanese Americans formally ended on January 2, 1945, in the months following, many former prisoners had been unable—in some cases unwilling—to leave, because they could find nowhere to go. By June 1945, Manzanar's project director, Ralph Merritt, noted that about three thousand of the four thousand who remained in camp hoped to return to Los Angeles, but a great many lacked housing; some had even left Owens Valley only to come back, unable to find a place to live. By November, 180 families remained, approximately 75 of them without secured housing. All were told they'd need to vacate Manzanar by the twenty-first of the month. If they left camp the way most former incarcerees did, they'd be given twenty-five dollars and a one-way bus ticket to rebuild the former lives that had been taken from them.

In San Francisco, with Karl home and the Yonedas finally all together, Tommy stuck constantly to his father's side. Elaine had told Karl the full extent of their son's physical and emotional struggles since they'd left Manzanar. With his father back though, the boy was thrilled.

Almost immediately, Karl resumed his public role, vouching in the media for Nisei loyalty and advocating for a new Japan. On the day he walked through the gates of Camp Beale, honorable discharge in hand, an article about him appeared in the *San Francisco Chronicle* titled A LOYAL AMERICAN. The piece described Karl's past labor and antifascist activism, the Yonedas' time in Manzanar, and his wartime service, including two unit citations and two battle stars. Now, Karl told *Chronicle* readers, Japan's future should be democratic, shaped by a "coalition of the Social Mass, Labor, and Communist parties."

Inserting a cliffhanger highlighting the war's stakes for Karl and soldiers like him, the paper added, "His mother was last heard from by letter from Hiroshima only a few months before the bombing." By the time the article was published, though, Karl had already learned of Kazue's miraculous survival, having received a Red Cross telegram to this effect a few weeks previous. Perhaps the interview for the *Chronicle* had been conducted before he learned her fate. Either way, one could imagine Karl—always on alert for a rousing detail—approving the cliffhanger, which in any case remained technically true: he had not yet heard *from* her, regardless of whether he'd heard *about* her.

Years would pass before Karl and Elaine heard the entire story of Kazue's survival. The morning of August 6, 1945, his mother had been employed at a shipyard miles from her home in the city, on the far outskirts of Hiroshima. She'd left near sunrise to reach work on time. The day dawned clear and bright, and at the shipyard that Monday morning, Kazue looked up at a quarter past eight and saw "a strong light [that] flashed through the sky." A fierce wind followed, carrying debris and what Kazue would learn were human remains. Then "a dark cloud covered the sky and black rain started to fall," she recalled later. The shipyard buildings, far enough from Ground Zero, were undamaged, though their windows shattered from the force and their walls became dusted with Hiroshima's incinerated citizens.

It took days before Kazue could reach the city center. There, she found no trace of her home or belongings. "Hundreds of half-naked people, some with horrible burns on their bodies, walked around the yards, like a parade of ghosts, all pleading for water," she said. "It was hell created on earth." Unsure what to do, she headed toward her brother's farm in a poor village far outside the city, where she'd been born and where her family still worked the land.

One day, laboring in a field, one of her cousins looked up and saw a ghost himself, walking toward him in slow procession up the road. When the apparition neared, he realized it was Kazue, back from the city where her family had assumed she'd been turned to ash. Karl's mother stayed with them for a year, then returned to Hiroshima, where she would wait nearly fifteen more years to see her only living son.

In late 1945 Karl would dress in his US Army uniform when he and Elaine went looking for a new apartment. Still, they could find no one willing to rent to them. Karl tried placing an advertisement: "Wanted: two-bedroom house or apartment [to be rented] by Japanese American veteran, Caucasian wife, and six-year-old son." He did not receive a single response. He tried knocking on doors of places listed in the classifieds, carefully attired in his stars and stripes. When prospective landlords saw him, they would shake their heads and close the door. Sometimes, Karl would see them through a closed window, where they'd simply turn away without opening the door at all. To compound the Yonedas' troubles, the Waterfront Employers Association refused to hire Karl back as a San Francisco longshoreman.

The Yonedas' situation started to look more hopeful when Karl's union backed him in arbitration and he won back his waterfront position. Karl was further cheered when he was greeted with what he called "warmth and sincere regret" at the headquarters of the California district of the Communist Party. Friends there thanked him for his heroism, congratulated him on his safe return, and admitted they "deeply regretted" two things in particular: "the party's serious wartime errors in suspending comrades of Japanese ancestry" and "not speaking out against the 'evacuation order.'"

So many Japanese Americans, returning either from US camps or Allied battlefields, had trouble securing housing and employment that military leaders began issuing statements about the Nisei role in America's victory. "From an intelligence point of view," one major general told the press, "the greatest single contribution to the Pacific war" was made by Nisei officers like Karl. They had actually "shortened the war," he explained. "Language detachments (of Nisei) were placed with every division, corps, and army in the Pacific . . . [joining them] in action," and "their loyalty was never questioned. Had they been captured, they ran an even greater risk than the rank and file of other American troops."

When Karl did finally secure reemployment on the docks, he was able to work for only a few short weeks. Then he collapsed. At a navy hospital in

Oakland, he was diagnosed with kidney damage, wrought by malaria and other remnants of war. Eventually, he had a kidney removed. Even before that, he understood he could never again work as a longshoreman.

With no prospects for an income, the Yonedas realized they would have to leave their beloved San Francisco once more. Their thoughts turned to Penngrove, near Petaluma, about an hour north. In the early 1940s a community of Jewish socialists and communists had begun gathering there, many building chicken farms to earn a living. The Yonedas had visited the area before the war. Nathan and Mollie Buchman had friends there and relatives nearby who owned a summer cabin on the adjacent Russian River. Perhaps, Karl and Elaine thought, the clean air and rural pace might be good for Tommy.

They pooled a GI loan with funds from the Buchmans, and in April 1946, the Yonedas bought a small Penngrove chicken ranch. Nathan and Mollie came north to help, since their daughter admitted, with her Old-World intonation, that she and Karl "knew from nothing" about chickens. Although Tommy seemed to thrive, the clean air and rural pace did less for Elaine and Karl. They hated the work: a mix of grueling physical labor and intellectually unsatisfying chores. But they were able to earn a modest income, and they stayed for thirteen years, keeping Tommy in school and a stable environment. The Yonedas maintained their Communist Party memberships, but they were too busy with the ranch and Tommy's schooling to sustain much activism.

In 1948 the US government passed the Japanese American Evacuation Claims Act. As a result, Karl, along with other Japanese American former incarcerees, collected a modest sum from the government for property lost during their incarceration. The Yonedas received only a few hundred dollars—less than half of the losses they could document. They were notified in 1952 that Elaine was "deemed ineligible," as were all spouses or family members without Japanese ancestry. Many had entered the camps in exchange for "agreeing" to be "as if a person of Japanese ancestry" for the duration of their incarceration, in the words of the Western Defense Command form for non-Japanese relatives requesting "the privilege" of accompanying their imprisoned children or spouses to camp. Congress declined to reimburse any of them. In the eyes of the US military, once released, they had once again magically transformed, reverting to their former ethnic identities, erasing their past embodiment of another one.

The 1950s also brought the era of McCarthyism to the nation. In Penngrove, Tommy, perhaps more than any of the Yonedas, absorbed the tension of the political moment. He was eleven—only a handful of years from the trauma of Manzanar and then months of isolation in Stanford Hospital—when the Wisconsin senator launched national fury at American communists. McCarthy threatened, "When a great democracy is destroyed, it will not be because of enemies from without, but rather because of enemies from within." Elaine was pierced when Tommy came running home from civics class to ask, "Will I have to go to a concentration camp again, because my other grandparents came from Russia?"

For Elaine and Karl, Penngrove coincided with minimal government harassment. Their lack of time for political activism had left them strangely buffered. Though the Yonedas felt sure they—and their friends—were being watched and their phones tapped, they wrote about only one actual visit from the FBI. Karl was vaccinating some baby chickens when two agents appeared, claiming some pretext about a reference for a Nisei who wanted to reenlist. Karl was unsurprised when his suited interlocutors moved on to questions about labor and Communist Party figures. Karl refused to answer, though he did respond. "If you want to know why I am sticking this chicken in the ass, I'll tell you. Otherwise I'll meet you in my attorney's office."

Penngrove also kept the Yonedas near to Joyce, who'd stayed behind in San Francisco, and they visited her regularly. Still, after Manzanar, the four of them never lived together again. According to one of Elaine and Karl's descendants, Joyce "bounced around between affairs and marriages and her grandparents" in Los Angeles. Between Elaine and her daughter, "it was tumultuous." The family would gather and share meals, but the strain never dissipated. "I don't know if Joyce resented not having [her mother] all to herself, or not getting what she needed, but Joyce turned to alcohol," the Yonedas' granddaughter recalled many years later. "She became an alcoholic, quite severe."

Elaine herself admitted sometime in the 1970s that Joyce, on the cusp of adolescence when Tommy had been born, had once been jealous. But she always insisted that her daughter remained a faithful sister, telling an interviewer, "To this day, if anybody says anything about Tommy, regardless of whether he has done right or wrong, she will battle for him." She paused for a moment, then added, "There was a very close affinity there in that respect."

Their granddaughter offered a slightly different take fifty years later: "Tommy still loved his sister," but other times it seemed like Joyce "kind of despised" her younger brother. Or maybe it was just that Joyce "was a difficult character. No doubt about it. It just seemed like there was wounding from her childhood that she never got past."

———————————

The Yonedas left Penngrove in 1960 after selling the ranch and seeing Tommy off to Stanford University. He'd graduated from the local public high school in 1957, class president and football team captain, with awards for academic, athletic, and leadership excellence from both the Japanese American Citizens League and B'nai B'rith. After the B'nai B'rith award, he "walked off with just about every other honor at Petaluma High School," reported one local paper that had been following Tommy's achievements since he swept the second-grade sack race at the annual school picnic. When he left for Stanford, Tommy did so with an academic scholarship in hand.

The summer they sold the ranch, all three Yonedas made their first joint trip to Japan. Each in their own way, they played roles in the sixth World Conference Against Atomic and Hydrogen Bombs: Elaine representing the women's auxiliaries of the West Coast International Longshore and Warehouse Union (ILWU), Karl attending as a representative of the ILWU Local 10, and Tommy attending as a member of the general US delegation. Then they visited Karl's mother in Hiroshima. Neither Elaine nor Tommy had ever met Kazue, and thirty-two years had passed since Karl had seen her last.

After Hiroshima, Elaine and Karl traveled to a city north of Tokyo known as Ashikaga. They carried the address of someone they had never met, and an old, war-torn packet of postcards. When a young woman about Tommy's age answered the door, Karl asked for Keiko Akiba. "I am Keiko," she replied. Karl handed her the postcards he'd taken from the dead Japanese soldier on the battlefield in Burma sixteen years before. "I thought you might like to have these," he said simply, forging a lifelong bond between the Yonedas and the once-little girl whose father Karl had only met in death. Elaine became her American mother, Keiko claimed later, Karl her "adopted American father."

After their trip to Japan, Elaine and Karl resettled in San Francisco. There, they joined the Japanese American Citizens League, two decades after they'd vacillated between an uneasy alliance and outright dismay with various JACL leaders in Manzanar. The Yonedas' Bay Area JACL chapter was known as "a 'renegade' group," agitating for issues usually ignored by the more conservative national leadership—farmworkers' struggles, the Black Power movement, and eventually the Vietnam War. Elaine and Karl also refocused on causes supported by the ILWU and America's communists, particularly the latter's struggle against the country's latest imperial incursions.

Though they were aging, when Karl looked at Elaine, he still beheld a bright constellation, burning with some unstoppable force of light, joy, and obstinance. She continued to picket, marching tirelessly, tapping the pavement in pumps, her head held high, her voice like a bulldozer, her hat barely grazing five-feet. "There wasn't a petition demanding that the U.S. get out of Vietnam that she didn't circulate," one of Elaine's contemporaries wrote. When they sought solace as a family in nature, Tommy would watch, amused, as she'd "hurry off in her high heels," heading right through some "wavering field of green grass."

Elaine was still active enough that the FBI kept watch, too, sending information about her to the CIA, the military, the Department of Justice, and the Department of Immigration and Naturalization Services. Always "the life of the party," one document said, she "usually does more talking than anyone else." Elaine was less impressed with another report. After she received copies of her own FBI files, she swore she'd never forgive the agency for calling her "chunky." She appreciated that they'd added six inches to her estimated height, though.

By his young adulthood, Tommy seemed to have built a more private life than his parents, working with his hands more often than his voice. Still, Elaine and Karl proudly clipped newspaper stories about his own quiet activism. One noted his year as an exchange student at Keio University in Tokyo, from where he traveled to Vladivostok, Russia, to protest resumption of nuclear-weapons tests. After college, he became a carpenter, and in 1965, following the 1964 bombing of eleven Black churches in the South, he traveled by pickup truck to Mississippi from San Francisco, where he was living with his wife and two-year-old daughter. FORMER PETALUMAN HELPS, announced his old hometown paper, writing of his work rebuilding the bombed-out houses of worship.

Tom, as he came to be known, would sometimes join Karl and Elaine on their annual pilgrimages to Manzanar. Their first occurred in 1953, when the three returned together to what was not much more than a windswept landscape full of memories. Every year after, whether their son could join or not, Karl and Elaine made the journey back.

In the winter of 1969, a national struggle emerged over repeal of a detention act known informally as the "Concentration Camp Law," authorizing the capture and detainment of "any person suspected as a threat to internal security" in times of national emergency. That December, in honor of this movement for repeal, various Japanese American coalitions organized the first mass pilgrimage to Manzanar. About 150 people gathered, joining Elaine, Karl, and a group of reporters at a site that was no longer marked on any current maps. Most drove up to camp from Los Angeles in a series of buses and a caravan of cars, following a path seared into the minds of the oldest passengers. As they approached from the highway, across the flat desert landscape, the only visible remnant of Manzanar was a decaying white stone obelisk rising up from tufts of sagebrush.

Elaine and Karl, coming from San Francisco, drove up in a Volkswagen Squareback. Karl was at the wheel in a dark-blue cap, his dark hair wisping at the nape—looking according to one participant like "a famous Asian actor . . . handsome with his sharp and alert facial features." The desert was bitterly cold, with a biting, penetrating wind, and as the day went on, it got darker and colder. Elaine wore black gloves and a knitted black hat, with a white scarf and dark, tiger-print coat, her blue skirt swaying below the hem as her nose reddened in the cold. The former incarcerees stood among sand and saltbush, rusted car parts and shards of broken army-issue plates, and they reminisced about being exiled by their country.

Then they got to work. They cleaned the grounds, planted trees, and cleared dried shrub from the camp's old graveyard. They placed flowers and wreaths on the single chipped tombstone that remained—an infant's. They did the same to a clutch of makeshift graves they erected that day for a handful of other people, some of the nearly two hundred who had died in camp and whose burial places had been marked only with small stones. They brushed, cleaned, and painted the monument rising up from the graveyard grounds, restoring the background to its original bright white and placing orange fruits and yellow flowers along its pedestal. They repainted the black Japanese characters that ran vertically down its obelisk, translating to "Soul Consoling Tower." As one reporter noted, these characters remained illegible to most of the crowd, almost uniformly born in the United States; many of their parents had stressed safety in assimilation, not in their Japanese heritage. Still, Karl felt that they all shared a common bond that day, vowing that "it must never happen again to anyone. The 'evacuation' story must become common knowledge."

Elaine being interviewed at the 1969 Manzanar Pilgrimage. *Courtesy of the Evan Johnson Collection, Manzanar National Historic Site*

In a closing speech, former incarceree Jim Matsuoka told the crowd, "When people ask me, 'How many people are buried in this cemetery?' I say, 'A whole generation is buried here.'" Interviewed by reporters, Karl had a "fierce" expression and terse response when queried about his own arrival at Manzanar. "March 23, 1942, he snap[ped]." Explaining her presence to an inquisitive writer, Elaine recalled Tommy's incarceration at three years old. "They thought he might be the enemy," she said. Before the day was out, the Yonedas stood together behind a lone strand of barbed wire to have their picture taken: Karl's fist held high; Elaine's black-gloved hand rising up in a peace sign.

Three years later, at the 1972 pilgrimage, eight hundred people gathered to mark the thirtieth anniversary of Manzanar's establishment and its designation as a California historic site. Occurring in late March, the day was hot and windy, the air filled with blowing tumbleweeds and sand, the mountain peaks still snowy in the distance. Karl and Elaine, both now in their seventh decade, arrived wearing a matching set of buttons for the Wendy Yoshimura Fair Trial Committee, supporting the Manzanar-born fugitive in the Patty Hearst case. Karl, in a crochet cap belying his seventy-one years, gave a speech: "Manzanar is everywhere, whenever injustice raises its ugly head," he told the crowd.

Elaine looked on, a sheer scarf over her white hair, cat-eye glasses blocking the glare and dust. "It is the Indian reservations with close to one million Native Americans still contained in them; it is the ghettoes where thousands upon thousands of racial minorities are shunted," Karl intoned. "It is the prisons where thousands are confined because most of them are poor and of a different color and race."

Although Manzanar had by now been designated a California historic site (and would become a National Historic Site in 1992), controversy arose throughout the 1970s and beyond over how to articulate its past. In 1972, the California Department of Parks and Recreation agreed to post a memorial plaque but delayed installation due to disagreements about what words to use. In particular, they objected to *racism* and *concentration camp*.

Elaine and Karl worked as part of the newly formed Manzanar Committee to insist both terms be used. Although they struggled during their incarceration with calling Manzanar a concentration camp, by the 1970s, Elaine's

Karl and Elaine at the 1972 Manzanar Pilgrimage. *Courtesy of the Manzanar Committee / Embrey family*

ambivalence had faded, though perhaps had not disappeared. "I am appalled at some of the campaigns that are going on, to remove words like 'concentration camps' and 'racism,' because what was it?" she told an interviewer. "The official documents of the government and the statements of the government at that time, even in the newspapers, called them concentration camps. Why shouldn't we call them concentration camps?" But Elaine, still preoccupied with interpreting Manzanar alongside the antifascist struggle and Nazi mass extermination, immediately followed up with an addendum: "They were not the same, of course, as the camps that Hitler maintained."

Manzanar's historic designation in 1972 coincided with a deep, emerging concern among Nisei, Sansei, and Yonsei (successive generations of Japanese Americans) over memorializing America's concentration camps, redress for former incarcerees, and ensuring the country never repeated this past. Karl and Elaine joined the national campaign for redress and reparations for all former incarcerees, focusing their efforts on securing union support. Both also testified in 1981 for the San Francisco hearings of the Commission on Wartime Relocation and Internment of Civilians (CWRIC). Two years later, they hailed the CWRIC's findings that the incarceration of Japanese Americans was due to "racial prejudice, war hysteria, and a failure of political leadership," rather than any military or security necessity, cracking the door to future reparations.

Alongside this quest for redress and reparation, the Yonedas joined many former incarcerees in a more intimate kind of reckoning. The 1970s and '80s gave rise to much debate over how to understand what had actually happened in the camps among those imprisoned there, including during the Manzanar uprising; what each person suffered behind barbed wire; what they'd done to survive such suffering—and finally, how to commemorate all of it.

Like many, Karl Yoneda never forgot his anger. Neither did he relinquish his commitment to calling out the presence of pro-Axis sentiments in camp and the danger of those who threatened his wife and son. As his granddaughter said almost eighty years after Manzanar closed, "Karl was [incensed] to the end of his days" about what happened in camp in December 1942 and during the events leading up to it. After all, "Elaine was in terror for her life. And in terror for [her son]." Karl would neither forgive nor forget: not the threats, nor the cultural tendency embraced by many incarcerees (as he saw it) to avoid complaining or "ratting out" another, even if someone was being threatened. "So he made it his mission to educate everybody about the Black Dragons and what they did."

As the mission grew among the Japanese American community to honor all the incarcerees had achieved by surviving the camps and rebuilding their lives, Karl in particular worried about a new kind of forgetting. He argued against misremembering support in the 1930s and early '40s for Japan's imperial "war chest" provided by Issei and US-based "Japanese nationalistic organizations." He'd counted eight thousand members in eighty-two chapters across the nation, he asserted. "These are some of the true facts of our past history that have been ignored," he wrote in one letter to a newspaper, "but should be publicized for the benefit of those of Japanese ancestry and others."

As for the war years, "the activities of the pro-Japan Axis groups in the various camps" must not be whitewashed, he argued. "In Manzanar it was the Black Dragons, made up mainly of Kibei." These groups deployed "terroristic actions resulting in beatings and even death." Their existence "cannot and must not be buried, whether it did us good or not, if we want to relate our history as it really was and is."

As Karl urged space in the collective memory for controversial issues like the Black Dragons, others in the Japanese American community began promoting the martyrdom of Joe Kurihara and Harry Ueno. One public-facing figure called Kurihara a "hero for the '70s," a "dissident" whose refusal to accept his incarceration challenged all Americans to honor the nation's own ideals.

By 1980 another prominent Japanese American activist pointed out, "We were wrong when we ask, 'Why was there no resistance?' There was. We have failed to make it a part, a proud part, of our history." His point proved empowering and healing for many, including some who felt immense guilt and shame over having been incarcerated at all. Historians began to advocate for a renewed terminology about what Karl and Elaine called the Manzanar Riot, terming the event a "revolt"; a legitimate though "intense expression of a continuing resistance movement"; and "of a piece with the Japanese American community's continuous struggle to preserve its cultural heritage and determine its identity."

Neither of the Yonedas were swayed. They clipped almost every article promoting what they called this "distortion of history," and wrote in protest of each one. Calling Kurihara and Ueno heroic was "misinformed" and "a great disservice to those who lived through the turmoil and chaotic Manzanar camp." Elaine wrote a forceful letter to the media about whether Kurihara was a hero or patriot: "To me, he never was either," she stated emphatically. "He was an embittered manipulator who helped turn some camp residents' frustrations into a pro-Japan cause, with a small number foolishly becoming '100 percent Japs' (his words) shouting for 'Victory for Japan,' which to me meant and still means plaudits for the rapists of Nanking and Hitler's butchers." Together, Karl and Elaine wrote an editorial castigating all of Manzanar's leading agitators: "Were they then truly 'genuine protesters' against evacuation or 'kamikaze-type supporters of fascist militarism?' We believe most of that group belong in the latter classification." The damage endured, Elaine wanted people to know; "the nightmares of the ensuing riot . . . remain even to this day."

But both Yonedas ascribed fault for Manzanar's internal violence to a narrow cohort. "Certainly, the Manzanar riot was the culmination" of the deprivations and humiliations of incarceration, they wrote in a joint letter to a major Japanese American newspaper. This helped explain the large crowds that had roved through camp. But the origin of the riot could be traced only to "a small group of ruthless, misguided men" and the "administration's lack of action."

Writing to two prominent historians advocating for the terms "Manzanar Revolt" or "Uprising," the Yonedas conceded sympathy for Issei who espoused "pro-Japan" views, "since they were denied U.S. citizenship [and] thus their ties remained close to their homeland." But, they insisted, "We did not hear the words 'resist'/'resistance movement' against the evacuation, used either in English or Japanese, in private nor at meetings, during the time at Manzanar—it was always 'stop the pro-American war efforts, because that will be working against Japan, etc.'" (emphasis theirs). Moreover, they demanded, "why did committee member Kurihara, speaking in Hawaiian Japanese, publicly call for an attack upon our almost 4 year old son? . . . Wasn't this [just] plain cold-blooded hooliganism?'" The missive closed with Karl's full name in bold black pen at bottom, and below that, Elaine's signature, fainter but no less present.

In the reckoning over Manzanar and the other camps, some former incarcerees, descendants, and historians labelled Karl "an informer." Many pointed out that his denouncement of Kurihara and fellow agitators contributed to their harrowing fates. One scholar and survivor of the camps, Peter Suzuki, referenced Karl's 1942 interview at Camp Savage by a navy intelligence officer. Suzuki had been a teenager when he was incarcerated with his family first in Puyallup Assembly Center ("Camp Harmony") and then at a camp known as Minidoka. In 1986, he wrote to the *Pacific Citizen* newspaper, reporting that Karl, along with James Oda and Koji Ariyoshi, had all "denounced" the leaders of the Manzanar uprising during "formal interrogation sessions." All three were "informers," he announced. Other historians since have also referenced Karl's repeated letters to camp administrators, WRA officers, and other government officials.

But Karl consistently proved unapologetic about the information he passed along, and when he compiled his public archive, he included most—though not all—of the reports he submitted about Kurihara and his allies. "I, too, advocated segregating those fascist and fanatic leaders," he announced in his own public letter to a newspaper in 1981. "They inflicted injuries on many, including my wife Elaine who received a bloody forehead and leg bruises from rocks thrown at her. . . . Their threats—through Japanese leaflets . . . cruising around in a trash truck . . . and the physical encounters—constantly created fearful unrest among the 'relocated evacuees.'"

Karl remained singularly insistent that Kurihara and his fellow agitators represented, first and foremost, a threat to the entire war effort: "Elaine and I reported their terroristic activities, which tried to undermine the Allied war efforts against the fascist Axis," he admitted in the same letter. "If that makes us 'informants' in the eyes of some misguided or indignant 'Johnny-come-lately-crusaders,' they have lost sight or do not realize what WWII was all about." He closed once again with the fear he and Elaine had shared above all else during the war: "What if Hitler's hordes and Imperial Japan rapists of Nanking had won the war, where would we be today?" Suzuki's response to points like these: just more "stock phrases, terms, labels and shibboleths . . . in defense of [Karl Yoneda's] role as apologist and agitator (the present euphemism is 'activist') for the second front while at Manzanar."

Still, both Elaine and Karl did admit to various regrets. "We personally made many mistakes," they wrote to one editor in a note accompanying their rebuttal to an editorial. In 1974 Elaine told an interviewer that she harbored some ambivalence over "our acquiescence" to the incarceration. "Yes, we had to go, but we should have been a little more vocal in our protest," she said. She wished, back in 1942, that she'd said something like, "'We know you're denying our civil rights, but we're *going* to do this because of this and that.' We should have an understanding, right then and there, of why we were doing it."

Her ambivalence seemed even deeper on an afternoon in 1977, when an interviewer asked her to name her life's greatest struggle or disappointment. She briefly mentioned her first, failed marriage, then quietly moved on—with no trace of her usual bravado—to her time in Manzanar. "The fact that I finally acquiesced to the evacuation although I knew it was a violation of basic human rights. I didn't speak out against it, although I would not have fought it physically," she qualified. Then she continued, "But the fact that I didn't raise my voice in protest . . ." she said, trailing off.

On the day of this interview, over thirty years had passed since the liberation of Nazi camps like Buchenwald and Auschwitz, when the world finally learned the full extent of what had been trickling out in horrifying hints during the Yonedas' incarceration. Since that time, the words *concentration camp* had stuck to descriptions of the Nazis' extermination machine, and for most in the American public—including many survivors of the Holocaust—the term would forever mean mass torture and murder on a most depraved scale. The euphemism embraced by Hitler, to obscure the truth of *his* camps, had by now transmuted in the public consciousness. It had become a synecdoche of sorts, a single term encompassing the greatest, grisliest crime in history—a crime in which the US government, following the narrative of World War II in America's collective memory, had come to a heroic rescue. As a result, the true, actual name for camps like Manzanar—widely called both "concentration camps" and the more euphemistic "relocation centers" during the war—receded further. Such a recession, perhaps inadvertently, robbed former Japanese American incarcerees, their families, and their descendants—as well as all Americans—of a crucial term for our shared past. That afternoon in 1977, it only increased Elaine's ambivalence over her own detainment in Manzanar. In the taped recording of her interview that day, her voice dipped to its quietest, most tentative pitch as she added one last comment: "In fact, I really thought for a period that they weren't really concentration camps. Of course, to me concentrations camps meant the oven." Whether this answer qualified as a regret or struggle, Elaine never clarified.

Karl revealed his own regrets throughout the 1970s and '80s. Standing amid the sun and sand as he gave his speech at the 1972 pilgrimage, with Elaine looking on, he echoed her concession that they "did not speak out loudly against the evacuation orders." The next year, he admitted that he'd been mistaken to back the WRA's stance on prohibiting the use of Japanese at official incarceree meetings. But other regrets involving Manzanar must be gleaned—and only guessed—between the lines of what he said. More frequently, one finds hints of ambivalence in what he excluded from, rather than included in, his public writings.

In one 1974 interview, he sharply criticized the US government not just for how they handled the loyalty questionnaire but for drafting incarcerees in the first place. "Those who resisted being drafted in 1943, 1944, for this I certainly condemn the actions of the government. They have no business drafting those that were kept in camps," he said, calling this "really one of the greatest mistakes that the government made." He remained cagier about whether he himself had ever considered advocating a draft directly from the camps. In the August 1942 petition for a second front that he and Koji Ariyoshi sent to FDR, they urged the president to "utilize the manpower of Americans of Japanese ancestry, now in evacuation camps, for front line duty in the United States Armed Forces." In yet another version of the petition, reproduced in his letter to an editor in 1981, Karl recalled that he and Koji had urged that "the citizen manpower, now residing in evacuation camps, be utilized to the fullest extent . . . by accepting us as draftees and enlistees for frontline duty in the U.S. Armed forces'"—phrasing drawn from an early draft of the petition, a draft they never sent, instead revising it before dispatching it to FDR. Defending this earlier, prerevision wording, he went on to argue, "What was wrong with the petition in that horrendous year of 1942? Does one sit and wait for a mainland invasion by the Imperial Japan forces with well documented mass raping and killing during their 1937 Nanking attack and Hitler's furnaces of a [*sic*] Camp Buchenwald?"

But in his Manzanar diary, which he edited for publication in the 1980s and '90s, arranging for both Japanese and English editions, he used less direct phrasing. As his English translator, Ian Forsyth, put it, the petition to FDR involved a "request that you accept the applications of those citizens now interned at relocation centers, who wish to aid the war effort by volunteering for active service on the front lines." An even more interesting change in terminology occurred between the Japanese and English editions of this Manzanar diary. In the Japanese version, published in 1988, Karl consistently used *kyosei shuyojo*, or "concentration camp" to refer to Manzanar, adding in English on the title page, under the name in Japanese, "Manzanar Concentration Camp Diary." By 1997, he'd had a change of heart. He sent Forsyth a letter that year after reviewing the translated manuscript in English, asking him to replace every last instance of *concentration camp* in the text with *internment camp*. It was thus published in English with the title *Manzanar Internment Camp Diary*.

But both the Yonedas remained clear and forthright about what actions they never regretted during their incarceration. Ultimately, they said, "we feel we followed a path which helped the evacuees and the fight against the fascist Axis." Karl told the crowd gathered at the 1972 pilgrimage, "My strongest desire at that time in history was to join the US Armed Forces to fight the fascist Axis, and I do not regret my active duty with the US psychological warfare team . . . against the Japanese Imperial Army." Together, they wrote, "Although we were guilty in not speaking out against the Evacuation Order and acquiesced fully, we have NO GUILT OR SHAME regarding our efforts to defeat [the] Axis. We were sure that there would be ovens in Manzanar and other camps if the Mein Kampers [*sic*] won the war and that all of us . . . would end up in those ovens."

For Elaine, the legacy of Manzanar required relentlessly highlighting its existence and the forces from which it sprang. "The story of Evacuation—concentration camps—must be told, and retold, not only to our children but to the white and non-white world," she argued. Doing so would "help wipe out racism from our society."

A final legacy involves a more personal narrative. Elaine remained committed to interpreting Manzanar as one link among the many in her history as a fighter, a woman who refused to back down before injustice. Testifying about her experience as a Manzanar incarceree, she said, "I literally forced my way into camp April 1, 1942." And she did.

But by highlighting her brave choice, Elaine inadvertently mimicked the same devastating half-truths the Western Defense Command deployed when they forced non-Japanese mixed-family members to "agree" to the "privilege" of accompanying their relatives—their children or spouses—to detainment. On one hand, they were all given a choice, in the baldest sense of the word. On another, what parent or protector would ever really choose, given any other choice in the world, to relinquish their child to an American concentration camp?

———————————

A last regret, which neither Yoneda ever mentioned publicly, involved their children. Their granddaughter came to believe that neither Elaine nor Karl could heal Joyce's lack of connection, to themselves and especially to Tommy. She surmised this rift derived from both the separation during Manzanar and their constant activism. "That was another part of the family dynamic," their granddaughter recalled. "'I can handle saving the world, but I don't know what to do with this, because family is just supposed to get along,'" she imagined Elaine and Karl saying to themselves. "'So, let's go save the world. [Even though] I don't know what's going on with dinner.'"

Both Yonedas carried a lot of guilt, their granddaughter said. "Because times were so hard for their kids." For Elaine particularly, there were "some hard choices. . . . But [Joyce] was another casualty of a parent not being there. . . . Elaine didn't talk about it much, but I know that it hurt her heart," and she "always had a feeling of sadness, for how things were with her and Joyce and for how much her daughter struggled." Still, Elaine never stopped loving Joyce, her granddaughter insisted. Eventually, "Elaine was pretty much resigned to the fact that she was just going to love [Joyce] the way that she was."

Tommy's lifelong trauma became another near lacuna in the Yonedas' public story. Although Elaine and Karl occasionally referred to his lasting nightmares and distress, they said little publicly that would suggest any deep psychological instability. But a dark edge skirted Tommy's many achievements, and he struggled with mental illness throughout his entire adult life: periods of intense activity, dogged by spans of deep, deep lows. "The trauma really fractured his mind," his middle daughter surmised. "Dark stuff, the really tough stuff, would just blow through his system." With Manzanar and the war and being sick afterward, she said, it all "really haunted him."

Inarguably, the Yonedas' son built an admirable life. When a labor historian interviewed Tom just before his death at age 82, she asked him if the Yonedas had been a happy family. "Yes," he said. When she asked about Joyce, whom she noted was "so absent from the record," Tom said she had been "very much part of the family, and that Elaine felt very close to her."

Tom eventually had three children of his own, and they all clearly adored him, feeling proud of their multicultural heritage. In a poem his daughter Yvonne wrote for him in 1985, she said of her father: "You work so hard . . . I would not blame you / If you wondered why you work so hard." She surmised:

> Perhaps it's the Japanese peasant in you
> That gives you unreal endurance
> Perhaps it's the Jewish parent in you
> That gives you such a gift
> For selfless giving

"Whatever it is," she concluded, her love for him unqualified, "You are my father."

Tom himself told the historian that he counted himself both "Jewish and Buddhist." He explained, "Though neither of my parents believed in religion at all and would not step foot into a house of worship, I have found meaning and comfort in my later years in both religions. I like to alternate weekends," he said, "going to the neighborhood synagogue one Saturday and to the local Buddhist temple the next week." He also admitted that he still had flashbacks from Manzanar: the barbed wire fences, angled to prevent escape; the armed guards, their rifles topped with bayonets. "We hold these dramatic moments within our being," Tom told her, "and they contribute to our very makeup."

Although Tom offered no other information to this historian about his lasting trauma, according to his daughter Yvonne, such dramatic moments could pierce right through her father, skewering his very hold on reality. Sometimes, he had such intense emotion coursing through him that his daughter described it as "almost levitating." Other times, she said literally, "he thought he was Jesus."

As for Tom's children, the shadow of Manzanar extends. Standing in the dusty cemetery at the 1985 pilgrimage when she was nineteen years old, Yvonne wrote, "My skin grows hot / Inside I burn."

13 | SETTLED
1945–2021

JOSEPH KURIHARA SPENT HIS POSTWAR YEARS moving around Japan. Soon after the American occupation began, he was hired by the US military, joining many of the renunciants from the Japanese American concentration camps working as translators or interpreters. Joe moved to Kyushu, Japan's southern island, for the job, but he quit after a year. He went to Tokyo, where he lived until he died, never returning to the United States. According to historian Eileen Tamura, "Despite having renounced his U.S. citizenship and declaring himself Japanese," Kurihara "was never fully comfortable in his adopted land."

Joe suffered a fatal stroke in November 1965, at the age of seventy. His elder brother and sister had traveled to his bedside and were with him when he died. "Among the personal possessions he left behind," Tamura noted, was a newspaper story from years earlier "announcing the restoration of citizenship to Nisei renunciants." Unlike Joe, these former incarcerees had changed their minds in time about expatriating and never left their homeland of America.

Karl Robin Bendetsen spent his postwar years rewriting his wartime service. In 1949, he submitted a biography to the Department of Defense for public distribution. He listed his position during the war as simply "Assistant Chief of Staff G—5 of the Fourth Army, with headquarters in San Francisco." He made no mention of overseeing the forced removal and incarceration of the West Coast Japanese American community, omitting completely his appointment as Director of the Wartime Civil Control Administration, through which he authored the entire project of the camps. In a memo that same year, he claimed, "I took no part in the decision to evacuate these people"; the job was "distasteful and trying"; "no assignment could have been more unattractive to me." The following year, as the journalist Ken Ringle reported, Bendetsen had a new job at the Pentagon, and when his office distributed his biography, it included his wartime promotions and medals, with "no mention of his successful efforts to have American citizens transported by racial decree."

Ringle was the son of the navy official who'd written the Ringle Report, buried by the military in 1942 after proving that the Nisei represented no mass threat at all. Forty years later, the younger Ringle followed Bendetsen's increasingly bald public revisions during the hearings for the Commission for Wartime Relocation and Internment of Civilians. The year after both Bendetsen and the Yonedas testified at these hearings, the former colonel granted an interview to Ringle, echoing much of his CWRIC testimony: the great majority of Japanese Americans were never imprisoned at all; "any resident of a relocation center was free to go any time"; the camps had amounted mainly to "free board and room"; and the only barbed wire at Manzanar "was stretched between stumps because there were cattle in the area."

After the commission recommended to Congress that the country pay reparations to the former incarcerees, Bendetsen traded letters with John McCloy, former assistant secretary of war, naming the entire affair the "Great Japanese 'rip off.'" As for his own role, Bendetsen claimed, he "certainly didn't want this task, but having been ordered to do it . . . [as] an officer of the Army," he'd committed to carrying his orders "into effect with great care and devotion to mercy and justice."

Meanwhile, Bendetsen had been busy rewriting his own ethnic story. In 1972, he submitted an entry to the *National Cyclopaedia of American Biography*, listing himself as "Bendetsen, Karl Robin . . . son of Albert Moses and Anna (Bensen) Bendetsen, grandson of Benedict and Dora Robbins Bendetsen, and great-grandson of Bendedict Benediktssen, who came to this country from Denmark about 1815." In 1983 he added a few centuries to his Anglo-Saxon immigrant background, claiming that his "Danish ancestor came over here in 1670." (Records trace all of Karl Bendetsen's ancestors as having emigrated from the same place as Elaine Yoneda's: the Pale of Settlement, the only location where Jews were allowed to live across the Russian Empire. All are listed as arriving in the United States during the late 1800s.)

Despite these revisions, Karl Bendetsen's legacy also included a seemingly strong and loving bond with his own son, whom he'd had christened at the Presidio Chapel in the summer of 1943 after legally changing his own name, bequeathing his child a birth certificate without the final, semitic-sounding *o*. Brookes Bendetsen clearly loved and respected his father, and in an interview with a local historian nearly sixty years after the war ended, he said, "I don't think he had a malicious bone in his body. I know he was not a racist in any way, shape or form." As for his father's wartime actions, Brookes had certain faith that "whatever he did at that point in time, I think he believed it was an absolute necessity." He added, "I think governments . . . should always err on the side of national security. I think that was his absolute approach."

When this historian pointed out that old newspapers offered various versions of Karl's surname, Brookes seemed unsurprised but also unaware of any significance. "You know, he changed the spelling of the name. As far as I know. At some point, to make it easier, seemingly. Make it easier to . . . spell." But here, his interviewer stopped, neglecting to push any further: "I did not ask what he knew about his father's ancestry."

Tucked into the files of a lawyer gathering testimony for the CWRIC hearings, one finds another clue about Bendetsen's many conflicting stories of his World War II service. Angus Macbeth was special counsel to the CWRIC, and he interviewed both Bendetsen and McCloy in the early 1980s. Macbeth admitted that his discussions with both men were of limited use, because what they said often contradicted the historical record. Macbeth attributed these factual lapses not to "an intention to deceive but to the ravages of time"—and also "to the fact that neither saw the internment as a momentous element of his life."

Karl Bendetsen died of a heart attack in Washington, DC, on June 28, 1989, at age eighty-one. He was buried at Arlington National Cemetery. His obituary appeared two days later in the *Washington Post*, opening with the role for which he would be most remembered, despite what he remembered most. It began by identifying the dead as "Karl R. Bendetsen, 81, one of the chief architects of the U.S. government's internment of Japanese Americans in World War II," the fact with which his public legacy would hereafter start and end.

———————

For Elaine and Karl Yoneda, their bond endured a lifetime, unshakable. Their granddaughter Yvonne described Elaine as Karl's eternal "muse." Her frenetic energy also endured—almost up to the very last minute. Family said that even in the Yonedas' later years, something "always had to be moving." Every night, they'd hunker down and play Scrabble, the TV going in the background, Elaine wearing only one earbud so she could follow the news and still talk while they played. She beat Karl almost every time.

Elaine "never wanted to miss a thing, *ever*," their granddaughter said. They both still gave interviews, and when Karl was questioned in Japanese, Elaine would join right in—though she still spoke none of his native language. She would nod her head in emphatic agreement and occasionally throw in some English commentary, as if perhaps she knew her husband so well, she could follow along by osmosis if not by letter.

Friends, colleagues, and comrades noticed the same inseparable bond. "It is so reassuring to see such a great love," said one on the occasion of Elaine's seventy-third birthday; not only Elaine's identity as a woman and activist but also her marriage to Karl remained truly "inspirational." One historian admitted, "I find it difficult to write about Elaine apart from Karl." Later, a family friend went even further, writing that it was "impossible to think of Elaine without Karl."

In the days before her death, her husband could sense what was coming. She'd started to quiet somewhat over the previous weeks, and the day before their fifty-fifth anniversary, in May 1988, he noticed Elaine was having trouble walking, and she couldn't keep down her food. Karl promised to go shopping for a wheelchair, to take her anywhere she wanted to go: the movies, an opera, the shops, a demonstration, "or even a heaven if there was one," he told her.

"Never mind the wheelchair," she said. "I want to go to the longshoremen's parking lot." Jessie Jackson was scheduled to appear and help load food and supplies bound for Nicaragua. "I want to give them moral support," she told Karl. "I don't want to miss anything."

The morning of their anniversary, Elaine woke early to prepare for a trip to Lake Tahoe. They planned to celebrate their fifty-five years by gambling. "Grandma liked to play the nickel machine," Yvonne said, "because you get more for your dollar." Karl watched her laying out her clothes, and in his heart, he knew they would never make it there. He thought about how, one time, they had joked that they might die together, holding tightly to each other's hand. Elaine laid out an evening dress, adding jewelry, a handbag, matching shoes.

Elaine and Karl in San Francisco, 1986. *Courtesy Labor Archives and Research Center, San Francisco State University*

Then she crumpled in Karl's arms. He heard her tell him softly that she loved him, and then she kissed him one last time. Karl called 911, but they could not revive her. Next, he called his granddaughter. "She's gone," he said, and then he just cried. "I didn't know death comes so quietly," he wrote later, "as if someone had stolen the life from her."

The *New York Times* ran her obituary, as did various other papers around the nation, all noting her prominence in the labor and civil rights movements. One activist wrote from Australia, saying she was sure "Elaine is unionizing Heaven." In all the national coverage of her death, Elaine's time in Manzanar was only passingly mentioned.

Within two weeks of losing her, Karl published a poem for his wife in the Communist Party newspaper *People's World.* "Oh, my beloved comrade Elaine," he wrote to her, though she would no longer be able to read it. "Oh my beloved companion . . . my beloved revolutionist . . . my beloved fighter." To him, she would be "forever" the "beautiful . . . dynamo."

To their family, Karl promised he'd take care of Joyce. He knew Elaine would have wanted him to ensure her daughter's rent was paid, bills covered, and basic needs met. Tom's own daughter was pregnant when Elaine died, and he too was broken by the loss of his mother. He seemed unable to fully grasp her passing, though. Despite his daughter pointing out the obvious impossibility, he told her he was sure her unborn baby was the literal reincarnation of Elaine.

Joyce passed away in 1998. Karl died in 2007 and Tommy in 2021.

In 1969 two brief scenes occurred that best capture the legacy of the Yonedas' bond and of Elaine as a woman both of and beyond her time. One appears in video footage from the first official Manzanar Pilgrimage. It shows Elaine and Karl standing behind a lone strand of barbed wire, a lopsided green tent behind them, a photographer in front. Karl's dark hair under his navy cap swept the curve of his neck, tendrils flying in the wind, his fist held high; Elaine's nose was pink from the icy air, her black hat incapable of containing the white whisps blowing beneath it. A videographer was also there, filming the Yonedas during their first time back in Manzanar amid a whole community who'd been incarcerated there too, or been born to families of survivors.

Elaine and Karl appear against the old film's grainy background, the sound lost to history, but the sight of them unmistakable, together between the old barbed wire and the newer sheltering tent, two figures vivid and bright. Next to Karl, Elaine raises her black-gloved hand in peace, or perhaps a victory sign, then waves it back and forth, her smile broad—as if triumphant in her assurance that in the end, peace will always, eventually, win out. Someone from the crowd to the side seems to yell out suddenly in jest, and Elaine turns, shouting back a slogan or a joke—the silent soundtrack unable to reveal which—as Karl begins to chuckle. Elaine, her spirit high as her peace sign, her head tipped in laughter, continues remonstrating and gesturing toward her audience on the side, waving one hand in a "V," the other in passionate explication. Karl's face, watching her radiant energy, seems to break open then in mirth, as if even here, his joy in her surmounts every last thing around them.

The second scene leaves no visual trace at all, except as words on a page. The story it tells can only be summoned in the mind, and it begins, perhaps paradoxically, at the place Karl Bendetsen was buried. If one could stand at his grave today and reverse time, rewind it like an old film reel until a November night in 1969, one would see Elaine standing close as she'd ever come to where Bendetsen would one day lie silent in a box. It was the March Against Death in Washington, DC, and as dusk fell over Arlington National Cemetery, protestors lit candles, then called out the names of American soldiers or Vietnamese citizens lost in the nation's latest battle across the sea. "My name is Thomas Rosenur of Wisconsin," Karl Yoneda yelled, standing as always right at his wife's side. "My name is Jay Dee Richter," came another voice amid a sea of votives blinking in the breeze. "Vinh Linh, North Viet Nam," someone else intoned. When her turn arrived, Elaine cried, "My name is Fred DeLa Cruz of Guam."

Of course, Elaine had never met Corporal DeLa Cruz, never looked into his eyes before he fell in battle in central Vietnam's Quang Nam province, just two months earlier at age twenty-two. She never even knew the date or location of his death, this fellow American from another land their country claimed, soil somehow of the same nation yet halfway across the world from hers. But with her one candle sparking through the night, Elaine illuminated the most striking vision of herself, of the promise and privilege of her story: one woman, standing straight and singular against the dark, who not just embraced but embodied a whole range of identities, even conflicting ones, without erasing, denying, or relinquishing any of them.

ACKNOWLEDGMENTS

SOMETIMES, IF WE'RE VERY LUCKY, we embark on a project that both captivates us and coincides with incredible generosity from all sorts of unexpected sources. That was my experience with this book.

Foremost thanks go to the Yoneda family, in particular Yvonne Yoneda Donaldson, carrier of her grandparents' bright spark. I was moved time and again by her willingness to share memories, mementoes, private documents, laughter, painful truths, and even one of her grandmother's earrings so I could carry Elaine's sparkle with me while I wrote. I will always treasure her kindness, and the kindness and generosity of her sisters in allowing me full breadth and autonomy to tell this story.

I remain deeply grateful to Amy Bishop-Wycisk for picking my query out of a slush pile and giving me a chance on a second book with little similarity to my first. Her honesty and wise counsel helped make this project stronger in ways it could never have been without her, providing me the confidence to go forward. Jerome Pohlen's editorial support at Chicago Review Press proved amazingly detail oriented and amazingly kind, and it has been a treat to work together. I remain in awe of the substantial and substantive copyediting, fact-checking, and other editorial insight from Devon Freeny and Benjamin Krapohl (who even found multiple errors to fix in this paragraph). The citations alone were a herculean task, and they went well above and beyond those. My gratitude also extends to Preston Pisellini for a cover design that perfectly captures the spirit of this history, and to Melanie Roth, Lauren Chartuk, and Bianca Maldonado, for all manner of assistance shepherding this book into the world and helping it find its audience. Additional thanks go to Leslie Meredith for support with logistics and for going with the flow!

Scholars, writers, and historians who gave immeasurable assistance during the writing of this book include Brian Niiya from the amazing organization

Densho, whose online encyclopedia and documentation enabled me to flesh out so many aspects of this history. Both Brian Niiya and Frank Abe were also unspeakably generous in their willingness to read and comment on parts of the proposal (and in Brian's case, on the final manuscript too, providing insight of a breadth and meticulousness I could never have found elsewhere). Like the aforementioned historians, Professor Jennifer Ho touched me with her kindness when I brazenly reached out and asked her if I could send my project description for her to consider supporting with a grant-application recommendation. Ian Forsyth's translation of Karl Yoneda's diary sat by my elbow almost every moment I was writing; he proved an incredible source, a wonderful sounding board, and a friend who boosted my morale when my energy flagged. I am also indebted to the work and generosity of Professor Rachel Schreiber, whose biography of Elaine helped me contextualize some of the most essential resources in the Yonedas' archives, who generously sent me material from her own files during COIVD's lockdowns, and who agreed multiple times to discuss over Zoom various aspects of the Yonedas' lives. Dr. Natasha Varner formed the entirety of my mini writing group while I wrote this book, providing much-needed camaraderie and hugely helpful commentary.

Much of this book was written amid Toronto's long lockdown and closures due to COVID, and time and again I was amazed by the support and generosity I received from archivists at libraries that remained physically inaccessible. Maxwell Zupke from UCLA Special Collections sent me a wealth of documents; Catherine Powell and Alexandria Marie Post of the Labor Archives and Research Center at San Francisco State University helped me arrange a postpandemic visit and sent me much needed information when I was remote. I also thank Frances Kaplan of the California Historical Society, the staff at the University of Toronto's Robarts Library (without whose External Researcher permissions I could have never written a book of US history while based in Toronto), and the staff at the wonderful Toronto Public Library.

Other scholars, writers, and historians who helped with advice, research and information, recommendations for finding sources, answers to random questions (frequently asked out of the blue), or commiseration about upcoming deadlines include: Connie Walker, Sarah Bone of the National Parks Service, Tamiko Nimura, Bruce Embrey, Tad Miyo-Ukita, Andrew Way Leong, Dr. Steph Hinnershitz, Akemi Johnson, Ryoko Hirose, Diane Mehta, Ann Tashi

Slater, Yoosun Park, Paul Spickard, Arthur Hansen, and Kimiko Marr of the Japanese American Memorial Pilgrimages. For additional advice, support, and answers, I remain indebted to: Amy Stanley, Naomi Hirahara, Ben Railton, Alysia Abbott, Janice Nimura (whose suggestion about the importance of archivists proved spot-on), Brandon Shimoda, Kimiko Guthrie, Aileen Lane, Eric Muller, Selena Moon, and Emily Hall.

The writer and historian Marty Levine and fellow students in his Historical Narratives online class helped me find community and direction when I first started working on a sample chapter for my proposal. I credit their support with helping me find and sign with Amy, my agent. Early interest in the book from Hanna-Lee Sakakibara and Midori Takahashi was so helpful and encouraging. Thanks also to the narrative nonfiction podcasts and their hosts who kept me inspired from proposal to final manuscript: Brendan O'Meara of the *Creative Nonfiction Podcast* and Kate Carpenter of *Drafting the Past.*

I count the following friends among the true gifts in life. Marc Kaufman, Megan Sullivan, Colleen Sheils, and Trish Shinkoda Smith all read early (and not-so-early) drafts and gave me invaluable advice and feedback, in addition to their incredible friendship. Tim Huggins and Jessica Goodfellow unfailingly showed up at the other end of the phone line to give support and insight. Gretchen Clark and Lisa Theisen helped keep me laughing, as well as connected to my life in Japan. For camaraderie, support, and playdates in Toronto that freed me up to write more, my gratitude also goes to the entire Shinkoda-Smith family, the Konomi-Gerards, the Ebrahimi and Hosseini family, the Kheirollahis, the Wongs, and the Coleman duo.

Thanks also to the staff and teachers at Hollywood Public School—especially Alisa Feldbloom, Penni Rosen, Joanna Gribilas, Lisa Tyl, Erica Cho, Shoshana Solomon, Scott Notman, and Bill Waldman—for keeping our kiddo safe and engaged, and for helping us through those long COVID school closures. (Alisa and Joanna, I'm still in awe of your patience and online mastery!) For postpandemic writing, I'm indebted to both the coffee and staff at Toronto's Charmaine Sweets and Contra Café—I couldn't have finished this book without the caffeine, the carbs, or the warm, bright table space I found at both places.

Thanks too to my family in the United States for your continued love—to my parents, for nurturing my education and connection to my Jewish identity, and to my siblings Robin, Lauren, Scott, Alison, and Randy for your interest in my writing and for being there through thick and thin (and Robin—for your honest and helpful feedback on the original first chapters too!). Additional thanks to our family in Japan: to Rei Hiroki and Miyako Hanatani for keeping us rooted there while we lived temporarily in Toronto.

Finally, the greatest thanks of all to Toru and Elli, for being my everything.

NOTES

1. Forced: March 30, 1942

"Oh, you don't have to go": Elaine Black Yoneda, interview by Arthur Hansen, March 3–4, 1974, San Francisco, CA, transcript in oral history 1377.2, 17, Japanese American Oral History Project, Center for Oral and Public History, California State University, Fullerton.

"All persons of Japanese ancestry": J. L. DeWitt, "Western Defense Command Civilian Exclusion Order No. 3 Pertaining to the Internment of Those with Japanese Ancestry at Manzanar," March 30, 1942, Pacific Northwest Historical Documents, University of Washington Libraries, Special Collections, https://digitalcollections .lib.washington.edu/digital/collection/pioneerlife/id/15392/.

"the slightest amount of Japanese blood": John M. Hall to E. J. Ennis, November 27, 1942, Japanese American Veterans Association Research Archive, Digitized Documents Project, http://www.javadc.org/java/docs/1942-05-28%20Mixed%20Marriage %20Cases-Ltrs,%20Memos%20dated%201942-05-28%20thru%201943-07-15 %20Pgs23_ck.pdf, 10.

"Not here!": Elaine Black Yoneda, interview by Hansen, 18.

Jᴀᴘ Bᴇᴀsᴛ ᴀɴᴅ Hɪs Pʟᴏᴛ: *Jap Beast and His Plot to Rape the World: Uncensored Photos* (Country Press, 1942), via Bancroft Library, University Archives, Bancroft pamphlet folio pf DS777.53 .J32 1942.

Hʏᴘʜᴇɴᴀᴛᴇᴅ Jᴀᴘs: "Hyphenated Japs Face Thorough Investigation," *Wilmington (CA) Daily Press Journal*, January 29, 1942.

"A viper is nonetheless a viper": W. H. Anderson, "The Question of Japanese Americans," *Los Angeles Times*, February 2, 1942.

U.S. Aᴄᴛs ᴛᴏ Eɴᴅ Jᴀᴘ Pᴇʀɪʟ: Kyle Palmer, "U.S. Acts to End Jap Peril Here," *Los Angeles Times*, February 19, 1942.

the inevitability of being banished: Karl had assumed that "the inevitable has finally arrived" since at least February 4, when AG Biddle announced that, "effective as of 24 February," "Japanese, Italian, and German enemy aliens" were prohibited from traveling "in excess of five miles from their homes," in preparation for being rounded up and removed from the Pacific Coast. Karl Yoneda, *Manzanar Internment Camp Diary (English Translation), 12/7/41–12/17/42*, trans. Ian R. Forsyth (Ian R. Forsyth, 2021), 63. By that time, only Japanese Americans, however, were considered "enemy aliens," a designation they'd been given on January 5. The label for Italians and Germans applied only to noncitizens.

BIG SALE: Herald Examiner Collection, image 00068543, March 21, 1942, via "There and Back: Los Angeles Japanese and Executive Order 9066" by Eleanor Boba, Los Angeles Public Library, April 10, 2017, http://photofriends.org/there-and-back-los-angeles-japanese-and-executive-order-9066/; Clem Albers, "A shop just before Japanese were evacuated from 'Little Tokyo'" (photograph), April 1942, via Library of Congress Prints and Photographs Division, http://loc.gov/pictures/resource/ppmsc.09964/.

considered an "enemy alien": Karl Yoneda, *Ganbatte: Sixty-Year Struggle of a Kibei Worker* (Asian American Studies Center at UCLA, 1983), 116.

tempting some to turn up their collars: For a description of the departure that included Karl Yoneda, see Hiroshi Fukuwa, "Manzanar Diary," 1942–1943, via CSU Dominguez Hills Collection, https://ddr.densho.org/ddr-csujad-34-2/: "Monday, March 23, 1942: Today, it will be an unforgettable day in my life. Goodbye, Los Angeles! Although it was not cloudy or a wind did not blow too hard, it was cold. I waited outside for 2 hours, turning up the collars of my overcoat."

"Hey, Karl!": Karl Yoneda, *Camp Diary*, 82.

barbed wire lacing the front and sides: Karl Yoneda, *Camp Diary*, 82–83; Karl Yoneda, *Ganbatte*, 126–127. Many incarcerees noted the barbed wire upon their arrival, particularly at the camp entrance, although sources do not fully document when the entire boundary of the camp was finally enclosed on all four sides by barbed wire. WRA documentation suggests that the front and sides were guarded by barbed fencing early on, and sometime toward the end of 1942, the entire perimeter was closed off. See "Fencing" in Harlan D. Unrau, *The Evacuation and Relocation of Persons of Japanese Ancestry During World War II: A Historical Study of the Manzanar War Relocation Center* (National Park Service, 1996), https://www.nps.gov/parkhistory/online_books/manz/hrs8a.htm.

warning her against visiting: Karl Yoneda, *Camp Diary*, 86.

"The physical facilities of each control station": Cited in Yoosun Park, *Facilitating Injustice: The Complicity of Social Workers in the Forced Removal and Incarceration of Japanese Americans, 1941–1946* (Oxford University Press, 2019), 64.

"Provisions should be made": Colonel Hass, "Operating Plans for Civil Control Stations," April 7, 1942, cited in Richard Neustadt to Wartime Civil Control Administration, April 7, 1942, via John M. Flaherty Collection of Japanese Internment Records,

California State University Japanese American Digitization Project, San Jose State University Department of Special Collections and Archives, https://cdm16855 .contentdm.oclc.org/digital/collection/p16855coll4/id/12136.

what evacuation really meant: Park, *Facilitating Injustice*, 73n3.

"It will be too hard for you": Vivian McGuckin Raineri, *The Red Angel: The Life and Times of Elaine Black Yoneda, 1906–1988* (International Publishers, 1991), 208.

"Disputatious": Arthur A. Hansen, "A Riot of Voices: Racial and Ethnic Variables in Interactive Oral History Interviewing," in *Barbed Voices: Oral History, Resistance, and the World War II Japanese American Social Disaster* (University of Colorado Press, 2018), 131.

"If he goes, I go!": Raineri, *Red Angel*, 208.

"in a khaki uniform!": Raineri, 208.

tall, trim man about to fall: "Police Have Dampening Influence on Red Demonstration on Main Street," *Los Angeles Times*, February 11, 1931.

"The child must go!": Raineri, *Red Angel*, 208.

collar crisp under his army jacket: "Karl Bendetsen (left) pointing out a feature on the map of the Pacific Coast areas with Stanford grad, Hugh Fullerton (right), at right, served on Bendetsen's staff" (photograph), c. July 1942, via *Densho Encyclopedia*, accessed May 5, 2022, https://encyclopedia.densho.org/sources/en-denshopd -i212-00001-1/.

Before he drafted this plan: For more about the navy's intelligence office reports on the loyalty of the Japanese American community, see Brian Niiya, "Kenneth Ringle," *Densho Encyclopedia*, accessed May 5, 2022, https://encyclopedia .densho.org/Kenneth%20Ringle; and Brian Niiya, "Munson Report *Densho Encyclopedia*, accessed May 5, 2022, https://encyclopedia.densho.org/Munson %20Report. For Bendetsen's knowledge of these reports, among others indicating the overall loyalty of the Nisei, see Alice Yang Murray, *Historical Memories of the Japanese American Interment and the Struggle for Redress* (Stanford University Press, 2008), 19. For Bendetsen and Gullion's primary responsibility for the decisions and policies leading to the forced removal and incarceration of the West Coast Japanese American community, see Roger Daniels, *Concentration Camps, North America* (Krieger Publishing Company, 1993), 71–72. As Daniels writes, "Stetson Conn, then a civilian historian for the Department of the Army and later the Army's Chief of Military History . . . found in the contemporary evidence 'little support for the argument that military necessity required mass evacuation' and pointed, accurately, to the machinations of Gullion and Bendetsen and their success in bending the civilian heads of the War Department to their will."

"The Jew . . . is a typical illustration": Charles E. Woodruff, "The Complexion of the Jews," *American Journal of Insanity* 62 (1905–1906): 327–333, cited in Joseph W. Bendersky, "Racial Sentinels: Biological Anti-Semitism in the US Army Officer Corps, 1890–1950," *Militaergeschichtliche Zeitschrift* 62 (2003): 335.

"left-wing influence": This information comes from a report on army captain Melvin Purvis from the Federal Bureau of Investigation's website, released through the Freedom of Information Act. The file notes, "A memorandum dated 3/11/42 stated that Captain Melvin Purvis was a member of a group centered around Major General Allen W. Gullion, Provost Martial General of the US Army. This group contemplated a military dictatorship in the US whose objective was 'to put the Jews in their place' and to remove the 'left-wing friends of Mrs. Franklin D. Roosevelt from public affairs.'" Melvin H. Purvis, file number 67-7489, FBI, accessed May 5, 2022, https://vault.fbi.gov/Melvin%20Purvis/Melvin%20Purvis%20Part%201%20of%202.

"probably a more dangerous element": Cited in Peter Irons, *Justice at War: The Story of the Japanese American Internment Cases* (Oxford University Press, 1983), 45.

"the two Secretaries": Cited in Klancy Clark de Nevers, *The Colonel and the Pacifist: Karl Bendetsen, Perry Saito, and the Incarceration of Japanese Americans During World War II* (University of Utah Press, 2004), 102.

"trying to put them out": Cited in De Nevers, 113; see also Kai Bird, *The Chairman: John J McCloy & The Making of the American Establishment* (Simon & Schuster, 1992), 151–152.

"no half-way measures": Cited in Daniels, *Concentration Camps*, 63.

"You cannot tell which ones are loyal": Karl Bendetsen, memo to Allen W. Gullion, February 4, 1942, PMG 014.311 Gen. A/E, RG 389, National Archives, cited in Michi Nishiura Weglyn, *Years of Infamy* (University of Washington Press, 1996), 95.

"Japanese race is an enemy race": Cited in De Nevers, *The Colonel*, 118.

By February 17, Gullion had drafted: By this time, Secretary of War Stimson had come on board with the plan for mass removal of both aliens and citizens of Japanese descent, particularly after FDR had agreed to defer to the War Department. As John Hersey explains the timeline, "On the day Biddle transmitted his final protest to Roosevelt [February 17, 1942], Stimson convened a meeting with War Department aides to plan a Presidential order enabling a mass evacuation under Army supervision. Gullion was sent off to draft it." John Hersey, "Behind Barbed Wire," *New York Times Magazine*, September 11, 1988.

"resettlement" and *"to kill Japanese, not save Japanese"*: Telephone conversation, Bendetsen and Gufler, February 21, 1942, State Department Records (CWRIC 2806-07),

cited in Commission on Wartime Relocation, "Exclusion and Evacuation," chap. 3 of *Personal Justice Denied: Report of the Commission on Wartime Relocation and Internment of Civilians* (US Government Printing Office, 1983), 101, https://www.archives.gov/files/research/japanese-americans/justice-denied/chapter-3.pdf.

Instructions To All Japanese: J. L DeWitt, "Civilian Exclusion Order No. 1," Headquarters Western Defense Command and Fourth Army Presidio of San Francisco, California, March 24, 1942, via Berkeley Library, University of California, https://digitalassets.lib.berkeley.edu/jarda/ucb/text/cubanc6714_b016b01_0001_1.pdf.

"wanted to be like everyone else": De Nevers, *The Colonel*, 53.

"I'll be with my child": Raineri, *Red Angel*, 7.

"April 1st and 2nd": Karl R Bendetsen, memo to Commanding General, WDC & Fourth Army, All Sector Commanders, Staff and Branch Heads of CAD, Division Heads and Units of WCCA, March 29, 1942, in "Memos: Transfer of Evacuees, etc.," US War Relocation Authority, 14, via Online Archive of California, https://oac.cdlib.org/ark:/13030/k6gt5vjf/.

2. Joined: 1900–1942

"Lie still!" and "not even cough": Elaine Black Yoneda, transcript of oral history by Lucille Kendall, 1976–1977, 83, 108, Women in California Collection, California Historical Society, San Francisco, CA; Raineri, *Red Angel*, 4.

"I was taught that you don't start a fight": Elaine Black Yoneda, transcript of oral history by Kendall, 35.

"You can be anything you want": Raineri, *Red Angel*, 4.

"It was an identity": Yvonne Yoneda Donaldson, interview by the author, February 27, 2021.

"promptly began to murder": "Mozyr," Yad Vashem, accessed November 4, 2024, https://collections.yadvashem.org/en/untold-stories/community/14621716-Mozyr. The Buchman-Yoneda family records and recollections indicate that Mollie's parents, Rachel and Ruben Kvetnay, had died by the time the Nazis took over Mozyr. Rachel's death is recorded in Elaine's archive as occurring in late 1928 or '29, and though Ruben's DOD is listed as "unknown," Elaine's granddaughter indicates that there remains no evidence or hint that her great-grandparents either perished in or survived the Nazi Holocaust—a factor that surely Elaine and Karl would have mentioned in their diaries or public statements about the intimate threat the German fascists posed. Elaine Black Yoneda, transcript of oral history by Kendall; Donaldson, interview by the author, April 21, 2023.

"learning is not for girls" and *"didn't care how many bastards"*: Karl Yoneda, interview by Betty E. Mitson, March 2, 1974, San Francisco, CA, transcript in oral history 1376.1, 2, Japanese American Oral History Project.

"too sick even to yell" and *"Growing up"*: Yoneda, 7.

"Don't be like your father": Yoneda, 2.

"because that's where the emperor was" through *"I won't stand against it"*: Yoneda, 3.

"a million lice" and *"After spending"*: Yoneda, 15.

ryōsai kenbo: For a fuller explanation of this term, see Shizuko Koyama, *Ryosai Kenbo: The Educational Ideal of 'Good Wife, Wise Mother' in Modern Japan*, trans. Stephen Filler (Brill, 2013).

called herself "a clothes horse": As cited in Ranieri, *Red Angel*, 11.

"all that Anglo-Saxons mean by civilization": Daniel Schulman, *The Money Kings: The Epic Story of the Jewish Immigrants Who Transformed Wall Street and Shaped Modern America* (Knopf, 2023), 439.

"stream of alien blood": Cited in Roger Daniels, *Guarding the Golden Door* (Hill and Wang, 2004), 47–48, 55.

"Nordics propagate themselves successfully": Calvin Coolidge, "Whose Country Is This?," *Good Housekeeping*, February 1921, 13–14, 109; Daniels, *Guarding the Golden Door*, 54.

"The United States is our land": Cited in Daniels, 55.

"absolute equality of the Mongolian and Aryan": Cited in Adam Hoschschild, *American Midnight* (Mariner, 2022), 50.

"absolutely forbid naturalization": Cited in Hoschschild, 351.

nearby in his anteroom: Schulman, *Money Kings*, 439.

"They haven't any rights": Cited in Frank Donner, *Protectors of Privilege: Red Squads and Police Repression in Urban America* (University of California Press, 1992), 61.

"Get that yellow bastard!": Karl Yoneda, *Ganbatte*, 40.

"proper hat" through *"they put me on the platform"*: Joyce Maupin, "Remembering Elaine," box 4, folder 10 ("Clippings, etc."), Elaine Black Yoneda Collection, Labor Archives and Research Center, San Francisco State University.

"that damned Jap": Elaine Black Yoneda, interview by Mitson, 8.

"I saw they were the ones": Raineri, *Red Angel*, 36.

what she called a "chaser" and *"just a so-called housewife"*: Raineri, 22; Elaine Black Yoneda, transcript of oral history by Kendall, 12; Elaine Black Yoneda, interview by Hansen, 16.

"The mercenaries were out": George H. Shoaf, "The Iron Heels Descends," *Open Forum* 8, no. 45 (November 1931): 2, https://digitallibrary.californiahistoricalsociety.org/object/32427.

"To this day he walks with canes": Raineri, *Red Angel*, 39.

"Aren't you ashamed": Elaine Black Yoneda, transcript of oral history by Kendall, 20.

"my baptism": Yoneda, 21.

"It is generally accepted that the mixing": Fred Hogue, "Social Eugenics," *Los Angeles Times*, May 26, 1940.

"mixing the blood of the two peoples": Franklin D. Roosevelt, "The Average American and the Average Japanese Have Very Cloudy and Often Erroneous Points of View About Relations Between the Two Countries," *Macon Daily Telegraph*, April 25, 1925, reprinted in Franklin D. Roosevelt, *F.D.R., Columnist*, ed. Donald Scott Carmichael (Pellegrini & Cudahy, 1947), 58.

"unsure" through *"that white divorcée"*: Karl Yoneda, *Ganbatte*, 60.

"torture cell" through *"50 other revolutionary workers"*: "A Nazi Concentration Camp from the Inside," *Daily Worker* (Chicago, IL), October 19, 1933.

"four hours after his arrest": "Mass Memorial for Japanese Communist," *Daily Worker*, May 20, 1933.

"Last year in Japan, 6,000 revolutionary workers": Michael Gold, "What a World: A Wreath for Our Murdered Comrade Takiji Kobayashi," *Daily Worker*, October 7, 1933.

They were *"broke"*: Elaine Black Yoneda, interview by Mitson, 26.

"mowed down with machine and tank guns": George A. Fitch, "The Rape of Nanking," *San Francisco Chronicle*, June 12, 1938.

"released on $10 bail": "Das Deutsche Haus, Polk & Turk Sts., San Francisco," German House Association (San Francisco, CA), 1908, Open Collections Program, Widener Library, Harvard University, Cambridge, MA, https://curiosity.lib.harvard .edu/immigration-to-the-united-states-1789-1930/catalog/39-990098701100203941; "Jeering Demonstration Meets German Bund," *San Francisco Examiner*, May 30, 1938.

"clean the kikes out": Cited in Raineri, *Red Angel*, 159.

"flying day and night": Elaine Black Yoneda, transcript of oral history by Kendall, 221.

"I used to like the corned beef and cabbage": Yoneda, 63.

"Well girls, it's time for lunch!": Raineri, *Red Angel*, 146–147; "County Jail No. 1—1915 to 1961," Eras in SFSD History, SFSD History Project, accessed June 1, 2023, https:// www.sfsdhistory.com/eras/county-jail-no.-1-1915-to-1961.

"wholly innocent": Cited in Raineri, *Red Angel*, 154.

"non-religious of course": Karl Yoneda, *Ganbatte*, 104.

"Hitler admirers, emperor worshippers": Yoneda, 106.

"the danger of vicious, war-hungry militarists": In the immediate aftermath of Japan's 1937 invasion of China, *Doho* also strove to counterbalance other Japanese papers

in the United States. These, Karl and his colleagues believed, were all beholden to Dōmei, the Japanese government–censored news agency that mainly reprinted militarist propaganda. See in particular San Francisco Supplement, *Doho*, December 13, 1941, 1, for an overview of the paper's founding and central purpose.

"be king of Asia": Karl Yoneda, interview by Ronald C. Larson and Arthur A. Hansen, March 3, 1974, San Francisco, CA, transcript in oral history 1353.2, 8, Japanese American Oral History Project.

"brave" and "bandits": Karl Yoneda, *Ganbatte*, 106.

"We Japanese Americans affirm" and "failure to denounce": Yoneda, 10.

"all over the world": A. T. Steele, "Fatalism of Japanese Most Baffling Factor," *Los Angeles Times*, February 7, 1941.

"It is about time that the Nisei": Shuji Fujii, *Doho*, June 1, 1941, and October 5, 1941.

3. Committed: December 7, 1941–March 31, 1942

"soldiers with guns everywhere": Elaine Black Yoneda, "Manzanar Diary," March 23, 1942, box 37, folder 6, Karl G. Yoneda Papers, Library Special Collections, Charles E. Young Research Library, UCLA.

"A Japanese father is shown kissing his son": The actual caption had included a typo: "A Japanese father is shown kissing his son good-by [*sic*] as he departed for the valley. About 1000 Japs left today," which has been corrected in the narrative for easier reading. *Los Angeles Evening Herald Express*, March 23, 1942, box 10, folder 2, Karl G. Yoneda Papers. Other details from this scene can be found in Elaine Black Yoneda, statement to the Commission on Wartime Relocation and Internment of Civilians, Los Angeles, CA, 1981, cited in Lawson Fusao Inada, ed., *Only What We Could Carry: The Japanese American Internment Experience* (Heyday Books, and California Historical Society, 2000), 157.

"visions of making it": Brian Niiya, "A Mattress Factory, Female Administrators, and Other Unusual Things About Manzanar," *Densho Catalyst*, April 20, 2021, https://densho.org/catalyst/10-unusual-things-about-manzanar/.

"sit out the war": Karl Yoneda, *Ganbatte*, 125.

"pioneer community": "Questions and Answers for Evacuees: Information Regarding the Relocation Program," War Relocation Authority Regional Office, c. 1942, box 1, Kaoru Ichihara Papers, Special Collections, University of Washington Libraries, Seattle, WA.

"for housing and caring" through *"ideally situated"*: Cited in Unrau, *Evacuation and Relocation*, https://www.nps.gov/parkhistory/online_books/manz/hrs7a.htm.

"General DeWitt has insisted": Cited in "Close Affairs, Get Ready to Start Moving, Japanese Told," *Pasadena Post*, March 20, 1942.

"to fulfill the Army's mission": Press release, Wartime Civil Control Administration, Western Defense Command and Fourth Army, March 21, 1942, RG 210, entry 7, Headquarters Records, Basic Documentation and Informational Files, box 6, file "Federal Government—Headquarters, Western Defense Command, War Department," cited in Unrau, *Evacuation and Relocation*, https://www.nps.gov/parkhistory /online_books/manz/hrs7a.htm.

"plans to establish Japanese farm colonies": "Owens Valley Haunted by Hopes That Failed," *San Francisco News*, March 5, 1942.

"Several of the dormitory-type buildings": "Camp Is New City for Japs," *Los Angeles Evening Herald and Express*, March 23, 1942.

"potentially one of the most fertile in California": Tom Cameron, "Japanese Get 'Break' in Owens Valley Move," *Los Angeles Times*, March 30, 1942.

"to protect the evacuees": "Camp Is New City," *Evening Herald*.

"extended a velvet glove": "Coast Japs Are Interned in Mountain Camp," *Life*, April 6, 1942, 15.

"So this is the American-style concentration camp": Karl Yoneda, *Ganbatte*, 127.

"like living in a madhouse": Yoneda, 128.

"gaze up at stars through . . . the roof": Togo Tanaka, "Summary Report on Center Requested by Dr. Carter," July 24, 1942, 199, via Berkeley Library, University of California, https://digitalassets.lib.berkeley.edu/jarda/ucb/text/reduced /cubanc6714_b210o10_0006_2.pdf.

"managers could make statements": Cited in Unrau, *Evacuation and Relocation*, http:// www.npshistory.com/publications/manz/hrs/chap7.htm.

"room and board" through *"the evacuee proceeds"*: "Camp Is New City," *Evening Herald*.

"We don't know anything": Karl Yoneda, *Ganbatte*, 127.

"The new mart captures the old spirit": Cited in Jay C. Barmann, "How the Internet Reshaped Market Street's Art Deco Monolith," *Curbed San Francisco*, April 6, 2020, https://sf.curbed.com/2019/1/22/18184279/twitter-building-bio-history -origins-architect-furniture-exchange.

"The goddamn lying American government!": Karl Yoneda, *Ganbatte*, 127.

"solemnly vouched" through *"test"*: Joe Kurihara, "Autobiography" (unpublished typescript, 1945), 5–6, Japanese American Evacuation and Resettlement Records, Bancroft Library, University of California, Berkeley.

"to perpetuate a 100% Americanism": "The American Legion Preamble," American Legion, accessed June 5, 2023, https://www.legion.org/documents/pdf/pre ambleinterpretation.pdf; Eileen H Tamura, *In Defense of Justice: Joseph Kurihara and the Japanese American Struggle for Equality* (University of Illinois Press, 2013), 32.

"*share as an American*" and "*last ray of hope*": Kurihara, "Autobiography," 37.

"*Even the bed-ridden*": Morris E. Opler, "The Case of a Terminal Islander (from a Nisei)," December 15, 1942, file 61.318, no. 6, box 347, entry 16, RG 210, Manzanar Relocation Center Community Analysis Section, as cited in Unrau, *Evacuation and Relocation*, https://www.nps.gov/parkhistory/online_books/manz/hrs9d .htm.

"*offering prices next to robbery*": Kurihara, "Autobiography," 37.

"*the sting*": Kurihara, 37.

"*absolute confidence*" through "*the most heinous crimes*": Kurihara, 37.

"*a bunch of spineless Americans*": Kurihara, 38.

"*devout parishioner*" though "*in an ideal position*": Tamura, *In Defense of Justice*, 52; Emily Brown, "Story of Joe Kurihara," n.d., 14, via Online Archive of California, https://oac.cdlib.org/ark:/13030/k6dn4d1m/.

"*at times I thought*" through "*suddenly forced to live*": Joseph Y. Kurihara, "Niseis and the Government of the United States," in "Autobiography," 13; Dorothy Swaine Thomas and Richard S. Nishimoto, appendix of *The Spoilage: Japanese American Evacuation and Resettlement* (University of California Press, 1974), 368.

"*The Army made fools out of us*": Tamura, *In Defense of Justice*, 52; Brown, "Story of Joe Kurihara," 15.

"*nothing but a hocus-pocus*": Thomas and Nishimoto, appendix of *The Spoilage*, 368; Tamura, *In Defense of Justice*, 33; Kurihara, "Niseis and the Government," 4.

"*There was no direction*": Karl Yoneda, *Ganbatte*, 128.

"*morale was low*" through "*spread like wildfire*": Karl Yoneda, *Camp Diary*, 85; Karl Yoneda, *Ganbatte*, 128.

"*Imperial Japanese Army invaded Hawaii Island*": Fukuwa, "Manzanar Diary," https:// ddr.densho.org/ddr-csujad-34-2/.

"*the U.S. is so terrified*" through "*the reason Japanese Americans*": Karl Yoneda, *Camp Diary*, 84–85.

"*to preserve harmony*" through "*establishment of an advisory organ*": Yoneda, 87, 90.

"*On behalf of one hundred fifty readers*": As cited in Yoneda, 36.

"*In case anything should happen*": Yoneda, 37.

Roundup Continues: Yoneda, 37.

"*A good cover*": Elaine Black Yoneda, interview by Hansen, 3.

"*pro-Japan*" through "*hoping for strength in numbers*": Details and quotes from this scene come from Karl Yoneda, *Ganbatte*, 115; Karl Yoneda, interview by Larson and Hansen, 18–19; and Brian Niiya, "San Francisco (Detention Facility)," *Densho Encyclopedia*, accessed June 28, 2023, https://encyclopedia.densho.org/San %20Francisco%20(detention%20facility).

"for the duration of the war" through *"that no one uttered a word"*: Karl Yoneda, *Ganbatte*, 115; Karl Yoneda, *Camp Diary*, 41.

"to realize Fillmore Street": "Fillmore Street Will Soon Be Known as the 'Great White Way,'" *San Francisco Recorder*, September 16, 1907.

"There's no point": Karl Yoneda, *Camp Diary*, 43.

"alien" or "rejected for military service": In the weeks after Pearl Harbor, an official designation had not yet been decided upon by the US military, so Selective Service agents were making ad-hoc decisions, usually choosing 4-C or 4-F for Japanese Americans, but not always. By January 1942, the official designation for Japanese Americans hoping to enlist became 4-C, alien.

"The most effective fifth column": United Press, "'Navy Not on Alert in Hawaii'—Knox; 3385 Casualties," *Times-Advocate* (Escondido, CA), December 15, 1941.

"We're feeling increasingly hemmed in": Karl Yoneda, *Camp Diary*, 53.

"There is nothing but bad news": Yoneda, 58, 59.

4-C, "enemy aliens": "Timeline: Japanese Americans During World War II," National Park Service, September 16, 2021, https://www.nps.gov/tule/planyourvisit/timeline-japanese-americans-during-world-war-ii.htm.

"patriotic native-born Japanese": 88 Cong. Rec. 502 (1942).

"I think it's probable": Cited in Roger Daniels, *Prisoners Without Trial: Japanese Americans in World War II* (Hill & Wang, 1993), 38.

"The Pacific Coast is in imminent danger": Walter Lippmann, "Today and Tomorrow: The Fifth Column on the Coast," *Washington Post*, February 12, 1942.

REMOVAL OF ALL JAPS: "Removal of All Japs to the Interior Planned," *San Francisco Examiner*, February 5, 1942; also cited in Karl Yoneda, *Camp Diary*, 63.

"race war" through *"You cannot make a silk purse"*: 88 Cong. Rec. 1419 (1942).

"passively loyal" through *"It should be handled"*: Lieutenant Commander K. D. Ringle, USN, memo to the chief of naval operations, "Japanese Question, Report On," January 29, 1942, Los Angeles, CA, reprinted as "Ringle Report on Japanese Internment," Naval History and Heritage Command, https://www.history.navy.mil/research/library/online-reading-room/title-list-alphabetically/r/ringle-report-on-japanese-internment.html.

"The necessity for mass evacuation": Commission on Wartime Relocation, *Personal Justice Denied*, 73, cited in Brian Niiya. "J. Edgar Hoover," *Densho Encyclopedia*, accessed July 5, 2023, https://encyclopedia.densho.org/J.%20Edgar%20Hoover.

"a sensible program": *People's World*, February 20, 1942, cited in Irons, *Justice at War*, 81.

"We are now as good as bound": Karl Yoneda, *Camp Diary*, 67.

"Versailles of the West": "James R. Browning US Court of Appeals Building, San Francisco, CA," US General Services Administration, accessed June 24, 2023, https://

www.gsa.gov/real-estate/historic-preservation/explore-historic-buildings/find-a
-building/all-historic-buildings/james-r-browning-us-court-of-appeals-building
-san-francisco-ca.

"a post office that's a palace": "Thousands Cheer at Opening of Magnificent New Post Office," *San Francisco Call*, August 30, 1905.

"part of a pattern to lull": Karl Yoneda, *Camp Diary*, 67; *San Francisco Chronicle*, February 22, 1942, cited in Karl Yoneda, *Camp Diary*, 301n8.

"wolf pack": *Hearings Before the Select Committee Investigating National Defense Migration*, pt. 29 (US Government Printing Office, 1942), 11181.

"political or other pressure groups": Cited in Morton Grodzins, *Americans Betrayed: Politics and the Japanese Evacuation* (University of Chicago Press, 1974), 195.

"fine for openers" through *"Not one of its members"*: Karl Yoneda, *Camp Diary*, 69.

"[On] behalf of the Bay Area": Karl G. Yoneda, report, February 23, 1942, in *Hearings Before the Select Committee*, pt. 11 (US Government Printing Office, 1942), 11266.

"painting the entire Japanese race": Yoneda, 11266.

"Resolution Urging the Evacuation": *Hearings Before the Select Committee*, 11237.

"concentration camps" and *"Nine replied"*: "New Order on Aliens Awaited," *San Francisco News*, March 2, 1942.

"We had a sense": Elaine Black Yoneda, interview by Hansen, 11.

OUSTER OF ALL JAPS: "Ouster of All Japs in California Near," *San Francisco Examiner*, February 27, 1942.

"we must insist on keeping the sexes separate": 88 Cong. Rec. A931 (1942).

"the country's most famous prisoner": "Interview with Mooney Offers Strange Contrasts," *San Francisco Examiner*, November 29, 1931.

"Wherever you go": Raineri, *Red Angel*, 178; Karl Yoneda, *Camp Diary*, 71.

"With a friendly smile" through *"I won't say I like it"*: "Karl Yoneda Says Farewell: Nisei Labor Chief in Parting Pledge to Brother Unionists," *People's World*, March 12, 1942.

"Leaving SF": Elaine Black Yoneda, "Manzanar Diary," March 16, 1942.

"I've decided to go": Karl Yoneda, *Camp Diary*, 76. Elaine's "Manzanar Diary" offers a slightly different date for this news (March 17, 1942), though the discrepancy does nothing to alter the general timeline of the Yonedas' departure for Los Angeles and of Karl's decision to go to Owens Valley ahead of the forced removal.

eighty-six thousand Jews: United Press, "Mass Murder of Jews Told," *Pittsburg Press*, March 16, 1942.

Germans forced women and children: "Murder Story of Mozyr Jews in the Pripyat River Near Mozyr," Yad Vashem, accessed December 22, 2024, https://collections .yadvashem.org/en/untold-stories/killing-site/14626468.

liquidate an entire orphanage: Marilyn Harran et al., "1942: The 'Final Solution,'" in *The Holocaust Chronicle* (Publications International, 2000), 306.

"reception center" through *"would be on par"*: The physical buildings of the Maryknoll Seminary can still be seen at "The History of St Francis Xavier Chapel—Japanese Center," St Francis Xavier Chapel, accessed July 7, 2023, https://sfxcjcc.org/history-1. For other details from this scene, see Karl Yoneda, *Camp Diary*, 77; and Karl Yoneda, *Ganbatte*, 125.

"upon consultation with Honolulu's Chief": "Refute Charges on Hawaii," *Nichi Bei*, March 19, 1942, as cited in Tamotsu Shibutani, *The Initial Impact of War on the Japanese Communities of the San Francisco Bay Region: A Preliminary Report* (University of California, Berkeley, 1942), 70, via Online Archive of California, https://oac.cdlib.org/ark:/28722/bk0014b1h0t/.

"simple dinner": Karl Yoneda, *Camp Diary*, 79.

4. Divided: Spring 1942

"A special train": "Women Will Leave Today," *Los Angeles Times*, April 1, 1942.

"I'm going to see my daddy": Box 11, folder 1, Karl G. Yoneda Papers.

"all Japanese, alien or native": Associated Press, "'We Must Get Rid of Japs,' Mississippian Says," *Los Angeles Times*, April 2, 1942.

SAFETY ALWAYS: Clem Albers, photograph of Manzanar entryway, April 2, 1942, via *Densho Encyclopedia*, https://encyclopedia.densho.org/sources/en-owensvalley-1/.

"Letter from Karl": Elaine Black Yoneda, "Manzanar Diary," March 31, 1942.

"That's pretty pathetic": Karl Yoneda, *Camp Diary*, 89.

"Finally I arrived" through *"Yours for victory"*: Karl Yoneda, "Japanese Unionist Writes Friends," *People's World*, April 6, 1942.

"What are you doing here?": Elaine Black Yoneda, interview by Hansen, 22.

"I said I'd love and cherish": Hokubei Mainichi, "Elaine Black Yoneda, 1906–1988," May 28, 1988, box 4, folder 9, Elaine Black Yoneda Collection.

"Valley beautiful full moon majestic": Elaine Black Yoneda, "Manzanar Diary," April 1, 1942.

"I never saw anything like that": Taira Fukushima, interview by Kirk Peterson, August 9, 2011, Las Vegas, NV, Manzanar National Historic Site Collection, via Densho Digital Repository, https://ddr.densho.org/media/ddr-manz-1/ddr-manz-1-124-transcript-9303091919.htm.

"He's a communist!": Karl Yoneda, *Camp Diary*, 92–93; Elaine Black Yoneda, interview by Hansen, 23. In both of these sources, the Yonedas described their bunkmates as uncle and nephew, but according to Aileen Hitomi Lane, who is the niece of George and great-granddaughter of Chotaro Nishimura, the two were grandfather

and grandson. The quote about Karl being a communist was passed on to the author by Aileen Hitomi Lane, in an email interview on November 16, 2023.

"Only four days had elapsed": John Dower, *War Without Mercy* (Pantheon, 2012), 82.

atmosphere was "choked": Karl Yoneda, *Camp Diary*, 92.

"a personal burden of rage": Commission on Wartime Relocation, *Personal Justice Denied*, 94–95.

"concentrated in a narrow" through *"People expected to get killed"*: Unrau, *Evacuation and Relocation*, http://www.npshistory.com/publications/manz/hrs/chap7.htm; Bruce Embrey, quoted in "'A Place Like This': The Memory of Incarceration," season 8, episode 2 of *The Berkeley Remix*, November 13, 2023, https://update .lib.berkeley.edu/2023/11/13/the-berkeley-remix-season-8-episode-2a-place-like -this-the-memory-of-incarceration/.

"We cannot go back": Koji Ariyoshi, *From Kona to Yenan: The Political Memoir of Koji Ariyoshi* (University of Hawaii Press, 2000), 52.

"a hundred new allies": Karl Yoneda, *Camp Diary*, 92.

"Still feel groggy": Elaine Black Yoneda, "Manzanar Diary," April 4, 1942. For an interesting explanation of how and why some people, particularly children, remembered positive times in the US camps—and why this still does not negate the overall tragedy of the West Coast forced removal and incarcerations—see Brian Niiya, "Ask a Historian: Why Do Some Survivors Say Camp Was 'Fun'?," *Densho Catalyst*, May 10, 2023, https://densho.org/catalyst/why-do-some-survivors-say-camp-was-fun/.

"no names" and *"bring the message"*: Karl Yoneda, *Ganbatte*, 30.

"Despite [the] dust": Elaine Black Yoneda, "Manzanar Diary," April 13, 1942.

"opposing the release": Cited in Roy Nash, "Public Relations in Owens Valley," n.d., 13, in "The Manzanar Riot," US War Relocation Authority, 1942–1943, via Online Archive of California, https://oac.cdlib.org/ark:/28722/bk0013c9780/.

"that all Japanese, both alien and native": "Resolution No. 43-6, in the Matter of Amending the Alien land Law and the Passage of Legislation to Prohibit Japanese Language Schools in the State of California," reprinted in agenda packet, County of Inyo Board of Supervisors, Independence, CA, April 20, 2021, https://www .inyocounty.us/sites/default/files/2021-04/20210420AgendaPacket_1.pdf.

"Far Eastern form of fascism": "Japan from the Inside Is a Picture of Poverty and Fear," *People's World*, April 8, 1942.

"special concentration camps" through *"If there are Jews"*: "Soviet Jews Issue Appeal to Brethren Throughout World," *People's World*, April 16, 1942, 6. Though neither Karl nor Elaine mentioned this particular article in their diaries, Karl's notes throughout the spring show a deep preoccupation with news of Axis war gains and fascist brutality and with the necessity of subsuming all else in the fight against

both. He cites directly from a similar article from the April 29 edition of *People's World*, which reached him in Manzanar on May 1: "According to the 29 April issue of PW, the Soviet Union has lodged a third diplomatic protest over Nazi atrocities—pillaging, rape, destruction, lynching." Karl Yoneda, *Camp Diary*, 105.

"thick brown wall": Ariyoshi, *Kona to Yenan*, 55.

"been trained and educated" and *"if a guard ordered"*: Cited in Unrau, *Evacuation and Relocation*, https://www.nps.gov/parkhistory/online_books/manz/hrs13b.htm.

"There were no personal views": Diana Meyers Bahr, *The Unquiet Nisei: An Oral History of the Life of Sue Kunitomi Embrey* (Palgrave MacMillian, 2007), 68, cited in Patricia Wakida, "Manzanar Free Press (Newspaper)," *Densho Encyclopedia*, accessed September 21, 2023, https://encyclopedia.densho.org/Manzanar%20Free%20Press%20(newspaper).

"The citizens of Manzanar": Karl Yoneda, *Camp Diary*, 96. Historians Arthur A. Hansen and David A. Hacker would later discover that Manzanar's white public relations representative, Robert Brown, wrote the statement, attempting to head off DeWitt's likely objection to a camp newspaper. Cited in Karl Yoneda, *Camp Diary*, 310n4.

"In spite of its modest size": "World Hears of Free Press," *Manzanar Free Press*, April 15, 1942.

"Under army orders": "You Can't Leave Camp for Jobs, Says Army," *Manzanar Free Press*, April 18, 1942.

"Military Area 1": "Aliens: Army to Conduct Evacuation," *People's World*, March 27, 1942.

described *"the evacuation" as efficient*: Mike Quin, "Japanese Wave Goodbye to S.F.," *People's World*, April 8, 1942.

"utter lack of privacy": Raineri, *Red Angel*, 211.

"incessant anti-Semitic propaganda": Ariyoshi, *Kona to Yenan*, 55. For a fascinating look at Nazi influence in Japan in the interwar period, spanning a widespread embrace to passive acceptance of antisemitism among the Japanese press, cultural pamphlets, and even dictionaries, see Ricky W. Law, *Transnational Nazism: Ideology and Culture in German-Japanese Relations, 1919–1936* (German Historical Institute and Cambridge University Press, 2019).

"It doesn't make less of a man": Elaine Black Yoneda, interview by Hansen, 38.

"a quintessential deviant": Cited in Rachel Schreiber, *Elaine Black Yoneda: Jewish Immigration, Labor Activism, and Japanese American Exclusion and Incarceration* (Temple University Press, 2022), 139.

"Among the Japanese": Togo Tanaka, "A Report on the Manzanar Riot of Sunday December 6, 1942," 4, via Berkeley Library, University of California, https://digitalassets.lib.berkeley.edu/jarda/ucb/text/cubanc6714_b211o10_0012_1.pdf.

"*selected (amidst applause)*": Karl Yoneda, *Camp Diary*, 96.

"*lesson in democratic procedure*": Elaine Black Yoneda, "Manzanar Diary," April 13, 1942.

"*It was good to stand at attention*": Yoneda, April 17, 1942.

"*explain the office aims*": Karl Yoneda, *Camp Diary*, 100.

"*Took first hot shower*": Elaine Black Yoneda, "Manzanar Diary," April 19, 1942.

"*spin-off*": Karl Yoneda, *Camp Diary*, 99.

"*a little better*": Elaine Black Yoneda, "Manzanar Diary," April 21, 1942.

"*It was so cold that mops*": Cited in Togo Tanaka, "Over Half of Manzanar's Population Employed in Regular Project Jobs; Schools Open, Idleness Drops," September 12, 1942, in Manzanar documentary reports 60–91, US War Relocation Authority, 303, via Online Archive of California, https://oac.cdlib.org/ark:/28722/bk0013c987z/.

"*Immediately*" and "*the improvised and primitive hospital*": Cited in Unrau, *Evacuation and Relocation*, https://www.nps.gov/parkhistory/online_books/manz/hrs10.htm.

CRISIS IN FRANCE through AUSTRALIA FACES INVASION: Karl Yoneda, *Camp Diary*, 97, 99.

WORK, GRIEF, BLOOD: Yoneda, 103.

"*a total war*": Franklin D Roosevelt, "Fireside Chat 21: On Sacrifice," April 28, 1942, https://millercenter.org/the-presidency/presidential-speeches/april-28-1942 -fireside-chat-21-sacrifice. Tokyo had been promoting a similar ideal since late 1941, when Prime Minister Tojo announced to the public, "Our daily life is war, and we are all warriors, even without guns." Kemper, *Our Man in Tokyo*, 347.

"*Did you hear the President's*": Karl Yoneda, *Camp Diary*, 108.

"*most distinguished camp visitor*": "General DeWitt Visits Camp," *Manzanar Free Press*, April 25, 1942. The article also notes that, in addition to a barrack and the hospital, Bendetsen and DeWitt also visited Manzanar's small guayule shrub "farm," where incarcerees were trying to grow guayule plants as a rubber substitute.

"*left promptly*": Karl Yoneda, *Camp Diary*, 101.

"*at the rate of two an hour*" and "*blueprints for a busy*": "Contractors Near Completion," "Women in Minority, Says Census," and "Model Community Being Planned," *Manzanar Free Press*, April 25, 1942.

"*while across the aisles*": Commission on Wartime Relocation, *Personal Justice Denied*, 158, citing Elizabeth Nishikawa, testimony, August 4, 1981, Akiko Herzig-Yoshinaga, interview, July 20, 1982. The historical record remains unclear about when the staff barracks were completed and when they stopped eating steak across the aisle from incarcerees, so it is possible DeWitt and Bendetsen arrived either too early or too late for such spectacles. Either way, both would have been aware of the policies mandating much different treatment in terms of housing for the so-called evacuees than for white administrators.

"dreaded": See for instance the editorial "Thanksgiving, 1941," *Manzanar Free Press,* November 16, 1942. The editors write, "We have long dreaded this editorial as well as the one we wrote for the Fourth of July, and the one we must write on December 7. It is easy enough to sit back smugly and scribble a few pretty platitudes. But whatever we say, be it an expression of solace in the many things for which we can still be thankful, or cynical bitterness in the mockery of the word 'thanksgiving,' will not assuage the poignant desolation that assails the heart as all file into the mess hall for the slab of Thanksgiving turkey. Lest the public think us "ungrateful," let us remind them that it is not the overladen table we miss, but the warm security and coziness of home. . . ."

"newcomers": "Howdy! Neighbor," *Manzanar Free Press,* April 25, 1942.

"Three Caucasian women": Karl Yoneda, *Camp Diary,* 103; Elaine Black Yoneda, "Manzanar Diary," April 28, 1942.

"favored hierarchy": Tamura, *In Defense of Justice,* 59.

"much more conditioned": Tamura, *In Defense of Justice,* 60.

"as the people who led them": Unrau, *Evacuation and Relocation,* https://www.nps.gov/parkhistory/online_books/manz/hrs9c.htm.

"remained detached": Arthur A. Hansen, *Manzanar Mosaic: Essays and Oral Histories on America's First World War II Japanese American Concentration Camp* (University Press of Colorado, 2023), 24. See the chapter "Camp," in *Japanese American Celebration and Conflict* by Lon Kurashige (University of California Press, 2002), for more about class conflict among incarcerees, as well as "Part 1: Essays," in Hansen's *Manzanar Mosaic,* 20–25, for a helpful general overview of analyses concerning the demographic divides in camp.

"sexual pariah": Lon Kurashige, "Resistance, Collaboration, and Manzanar Protest," *Pacific Historical Review* 70, no. 3 (August 2001): 415–416, https://www.jstor.org/stable/10.1525/phr.2001.70.3.387.

"her reported marriage": John Edgar Hoover, memo to Assistant Attorney General Wendell Berge, "Re: Elaine Black," April 23, 1942, box 5, folder 1 ("FBI Files"), Elaine Black Yoneda Collection.

"You take an Issei": Elaine Black Yoneda, interview by Hansen, 66.

"Some [Issei] had strong ties": Yoneda, 93.

"do-nothing": Yoneda, 73.

5. Separated: Spring–Summer 1942

"One month at Manzanar": Elaine Black Yoneda, "Manzanar Diary," May 1, 1942.

"I'm sorry it is only a dollar": Tommy Yoneda to United China Relief, May 1, 1942, folder 2, box 8, Karl G. Yoneda Papers, cited in Allison Varzally, "Romantic

Crossings: Making Love, Family, and Non-Whiteness in California, 1925–1950, *Journal of American Ethnic History* 23, no. 1 (Fall 2003): 1, https://www.jstor.org /stable/27501377.

"We tried to establish": Karl Yoneda, interview by Larson and Hansen, 27.

"Our slogan: VICTORY": Karl Yoneda, *Camp Diary*, 105–107.

"despondency": "Japanese Takes Own Life," *Pasadena Post*, May 2, 1942.

"No need to concern yourselves": Cited in Karl Yoneda, *Camp Diary*, 105.

"Whether or not": Cited in Yoneda, 106.

"We have to take [a] side": Elaine Black Yoneda, interview by Hansen, 45.

"Everybody on the waterfront": "Manzanar, Miracle Town", *San Francisco News*, June 4, 1932, cited in Karl Yoneda, *Camp Diary*, 322n14.

"My family—Elaine and Tommy": "A Letter from Manzanar, Japanese Evacuation Center," *People's World*, April 21, 1942.

"Patriot Jap-American": *San Francisco Chronicle*, July 24, 1942, reprinted in "The Washington Merry-Go-Round," box 10, folder 5, Karl G. Yoneda Papers.

"giving us daily guidance": Karl G. Yoneda, letter to the editor, *Los Angeles Times*, May 7, 1942.

"many pro-Japan": Karl Yoneda, "Japanese Americans' Loyalty on Record" (letter to the editor), *People's World*, April 29, 1942; "Majority of Japanese Are Loyal to the U.S." (letter to the editor), *People's World*, June 8, 1942, both from box 10, folder 5, Karl G. Yoneda Papers.

"false imprisonment" through *"supreme contempt"*: Brown, "Story of Joe Kurihara," 15–19.

"some distance beyond the stockade": Karl Yoneda, *Camp Diary*, 105–106.

"beamed": Togo Tanaka, "Block Residents Fete Leader at Birthday Party," July 16, 1942, in Manzanar documentary reports 21–33, US War Relocation Authority, 166–167, via Online Archive of California, https://oac.cdlib.org/ark:/28722/bk0013c985v/.

"iron cage": Togo Tanaka, "Police Department Acquires Jail Cell, Will Move to New Quarters Sometime 'Next Week,'" July 16, 1942, in Manzanar documentary reports 21–33, US War Relocation Authority, 162.

"a steel cage": Ariyoshi, *Kona to Yenan*, 75.

"Everyone was in a good mood": Karl Yoneda, *Camp Diary*, 121.

"115%": Brown, "Story of Joe Kurihara," 24.

"bitter enemies": Elaine Black Yoneda, interview by Hansen, 88.

"We are fighting a moral battle": "'Ours Is a Moral Battle,' Says Vet," *Manzanar Free Press*, June 2, 1942.

"battlefield in helping win": Elaine Black Yoneda, "Manzanar Diary," May 30, 1942.

"Someone sure mad": Elaine Black Yoneda, "Manzanar Diary," May 12, 1942.

"just because she's white!": Karl Yoneda, *Camp Diary*, 111–112.

"It's not right the way": Yoneda, 109. For an important overview of how the majority of the American Jewish press and US Jewish organizations reacted—or rather didn't react—to the race-based incarceration of the West Coast Japanese American community, see Ellen Eisenberg's *The First to Cry Down Injustice? Western Jews and Japanese Removal During WWII* (Lexington, 2008).

"was the first to begin snoring": Karl Yoneda, *Camp Diary*, 109.

"carefree": Yoneda, 110.

"a convenient gathering point": "The War Relocation Work Corps: A Circular of Information for Enlistees and Their Families," US War Relocation Authority, 1942, UCLA Library Digital Collections, https://digital.library.ucla.edu/catalog/ark:/21198/z1j695cb. For information on Portland Assembly Center, where incarcerees lived in a converted space once used for expositions of livestock as pigs, sheep, and cows, see Brian Niiya, "Portland (Detention Facility)," *Densho Encyclopedia*, accessed March 1 2024, https://encyclopedia.densho.org/Portland%20(detention%20facility).

"disillusioned, confused, and incredulous": Unrau, *Evacuation and Relocation*, https://www.nps.gov/parkhistory/online_books/manz/hrs10.htm.

"Even here in this camp": Cited in Karl Yoneda, *Camp Diary*, 113.

"She is working extremely hard": Yoneda, 119.

"much too harsh": Yoneda, 114; POWs held in the US received "80 cents a day per prisoner employed, roughly based on the $21 a month paid the American private in 1941," according to the US Army. In addition, each POW was to receive 10 cents daily, regardless of their labor, to purchase necessities. George G. Lewis and John Mehwa, *History of Prisoner of War Utilization by the United States Army, 1776–1945* (Center of Military History, US Army, 1982), 77–78.

"Japan is going to win": Karl Yoneda, *Camp Diary*, 115–116.

"That is what I used to grieve": Hikoji Takeuchi, interview by John Allen, November 7, 2002, Manzanar National Historic Site Collection, via Densho Digital Repository, https://ddr.densho.org/media/ddr-manz-1/ddr-manz-1-10-transcript-0a1cbf1dc7.htm.

What the devil is he doing?: Takeuchi, interview by Allen.

"The guard said that he ordered": Philip J. Webster, report on investigation of Manzanar Relocation Area, August 31–September 2, 1942, US War Relocation Authority, quoted in Unrau, *Evacuation and Relocation*, https://www.nps.gov/parkhistory/online_books/manz/hrs13c.htm.

"Someone shot for not halting": Elaine Black Yoneda, "Manzanar Diary," May 17, 1942.

"Carl Yoneda [sic], a man": Karl R. Bendetsen, memo to director of the War Relocation Authority, "Situation at Manzanar Regarding Military Police," June 5, 1942,

Manzanar National Historic Site Collection, via Densho Digital Repository, https://ddr.densho.org/ddr-densho-122-856-mezzanine-156abd6d49/.

"San Francisco's streets": Karl Yoneda, *Camp Diary*, 117.

"breed like rats": Cited in Yoneda, 144–145.

"More than anything": Yoneda, 130.

a *"most trying" assignment*: Karl R. Bendetsen to Colonel Auer, June 3, 1942, box 349, Karl R. Bendetsen Papers, Hoover Institution Library & Archives, cited in De Nevers, *The Colonel*, 138.

"the non-Japanese spouse": W. K. Shaughnessy, "Memorandum on Mixed Marriage Exemptions to Evacuation," May 12, 1942, via John M. Flaherty Collection, https://cdm16855.contentdm.oclc.org/digital/collection/p16855coll4/id/6887.

"Know All Men by These Presents": Dorothy Hart Nakamura, "Request and Waiver of Non-excluded Person," July 11, 1942, Japanese American Archival Collection, Department of Special Collections and University Archives, California State University, Sacramento, https://cdm16855.contentdm.oclc.org/digital/collection/p16855coll4/id/12429. No such form seems ever to have existed for Elaine Buchman Yoneda, or Rose Elaine Yoneda, as she was officially listed by the War Relocation Authority. One has never been found in any of the Yoneda family archives or personal papers known to their descendants, or in WCCA documents at the National Archives in College Park, MD, suggesting that, since Elaine went to Manzanar on the very first day of involuntary transports, her case at least in part helped give rise to this form.

"they have one drop": Cited in Weglyn, *Years of Infamy*, 76–77; Anne Neuberger, "Setting Japanese American Captives Free," *Maryknoll*, December 1, 2021, https://www.maryknollmagazine.org/2021/12/setting-japanese-american-captives-free/.

"completely covered": Elaine Black Yoneda, "Manzanar Diary," July 9, 1942.

strip *Japanese Americans of their citizenship*: Greg Robinson, "Regan v. King," *Densho Encyclopedia*, accessed December 22, 2024, https://encyclopedia.densho.org/Regan%20v.%20King.

"When this trial takes place": Karl Yoneda, *Camp Diary*, 117–120.

"by and for white people": Yoneda, 133; Natasha Varner, "Japanese Americans Incarcerated During WWII Could Still Vote, Kind Of," *Densho Catalyst*, October 13, 2016, https://densho.org/catalyst/luxury-voting-world-war-ii-concentration-camps-today/.

"As for me" through *"If you want to beat [Karl]"*: Karl Yoneda, *Camp Diary*, 119.

"a major, unsolved question": Karl Yoneda, *Camp Diary*, 119.

"It won't be long now": Yoneda, 123. Later in this entry, Karl admitted the elder Issei's statement wasn't entirely rumor based: "However, I was listening to the radio

after dinner: 'The Japs have made an air raid on Dutch Harbor . . . [and] . . . Alaska is in danger.' So now I realize what Shida told me wasn't just a rumor, after all." This realization did little to dampen his worry over the pro-Japan sentiment he feared was spreading through Manzanar and the danger he believed this sentiment posed.

"We, the people residing in Manzanar": "Democracy at Work in Manzanar: Evacuees Honor War Dead; Draft Laws, Initiate War Production," *People's World*, June 4, 1942, as cited in translator's notation, Karl Yoneda, *Camp Diary*, 316n12.

"It won't be long now": Yoneda, 121.

"The constitution provides equal suffrage": "Democracy at Work in Manzanar," as cited in translator's notation, Karl Yoneda, *Camp Diary*, 316n12.

"Americanization program" and *"pro-Japan faction"*: Karl Yoneda, *Camp Diary*, 120.

"slander[ing] America": Yoneda, 124; Elaine Yoneda, letter to the editor, *Hokubei Mainichi*, May 10, 1983, box 3, folder 3, Elaine Black Yoneda Collection.

"Japan is bombing Alaska": Karl Yoneda, *Camp Diary*, 126.

"actually preforming [sic] the mechanics": Ralph P. Merritt, memo to E. R. Fryer, December 1, 1942, 2, in "The Manzanar Riot," US War Relocation Authority, https://oac.cdlib.org/ark:/28722/bk0013c9780/.

only a "small handful": Elaine Black Yoneda, interview by Hansen, 60.

"Now that management of the camp": Karl Yoneda, *Camp Diary*, 128.

"White men and Japanese fools": Leaflet titled "A Spy Who Betrays Us" posted in every washroom in Manzanar, June 24, 1942, property of Karl G. Yoneda, Yoneda family personal papers, sent by Yvonne Yoneda Donaldson to the author, March 26, 2021.

"true-blooded Japanese": Leaflet titled "Wake Up, Manzanar Residents" posted in every washroom on June 26, 1942, property of Karl G. Yoneda, Yoneda family personal papers, sent by Yvonne Yoneda Donaldson to the author, March 26, 2021.

"Patriotic Suicide Corps": For more information about these leaflets and some alternate translations into English—though none that change the tenor or meaning in any significant way—see Karl Yoneda, *Camp Diary*, 131, 133; Karl and Elaine Yoneda, "Manzanar: Another View," *Rafu Shimpo Supplement*, December 19, 1973, box 11, folder 7, Karl G. Yoneda Papers; and Karl Yoneda, *Ganbatte*, 133. A useful overview of some of the differences in literal translation among the Japanese version Karl had saved in his personal files (Yoneda family personal papers, sent by Yvonne Yoneda Donaldson to the author, March 26, 2021) and the English versions offered in the prementioned sources, can be found in the translator's notation, Karl Yoneda, *Camp Diary*, 321–322n13.

"You're all Japanese": Yoneda, 124.

"Outstanding single producer": "Net Records Broken," *Manzanar Free Press*, July 27, 1942, Manzanar National Historic Site Collection, via Densho Digital Repository, https://ddr.densho.org/ddr-densho-125/.

"Dear Sir and Brother": Karl Yoneda to Germaine Buleke, Vice President, ILWU 1-10, box 10, folder 5, Karl G. Yoneda Papers.

"Jap visiting and gift giving": "What the World Is Saying," *Manzanar Free Press*, July 27, 1942; *People's World*, July 14, 1942, cited in "Broadcasting Americanism—Unionists Nip Race-War Talkers," box 10, folder 5, Karl G. Yoneda Papers.

"official ban": "Concerning Visitor's Permit," *Manzanar Free Press*, July 7, 1942, Manzanar National Historic Site Collection, via Densho Digital Repository, https://ddr.densho.org/ddr-densho-125/.

"ingress and egress": "Authority to Issue Passes," *Project Director's Bulletin* 11 (July 16, 1942), box 10, folder 5, Karl G. Yoneda Papers.

"Please bear with us": Togo Tanaka, "Residents Exchange Opinions, Questions with Assistant Project Director at Open Forum," July 12, 1942, in Manzanar documentary reports 21–33, US War Relocation Authority, 144, via Online Archive of California, https://oac.cdlib.org/ark:/28722/bk0013c985v/.

"orders from the head office": Karl Yoneda, *Camp Diary*, 138.

"Whether you're Issei, Nisei, or Kibei": Yoneda, 134.

"was dealing with human beings": Ned Campbell, interview by Arthur A. Hansen, August 15, 1974, Carmel, CA, transcript in oral history 1329, Japanese American Oral History Project, cited in A. A. Hansen and D. A. Hacker, "The Manzanar Riot: An Ethnic Perspective," *Amerasia Journal* 2, no. 2 (1974): 144n15, https://doi.org/10.17953/amer.2.2.1kl24477mkk70q51.

"Every time Ned Campbell speaks": Board of Review, *Harry Yoshino Ueno*, December 1942–January 1943, WRAA, coll. 122, box 16, as cited in Arthur A. Hansen and David A. Hacker, "The Manzanar Riot: An Ethnic Perspective," *Amerasia Journal* 2, no. 2 (Fall 1974): 112–157 & 144n15, https://doi.org/10.17953/amer.2.2.1kl24477mkk70q51.

"We are in Manzanar for the duration": Roy Nash, "A Message," *Manzanar Free Press*, July 4, 1942, Manzanar National Historic Site Collection, via Densho Digital Repository, https://ddr.densho.org/ddr-densho-125/.

"Roosevelt is a Jew and so is Nash": Karl G. Yoneda, memo to Dillon Myer, National Director, War Relocation Authority, "Notes and Observations," August 19, 1942, Manzanar, CA, box 10, folder 6, Karl G. Yoneda Papers.

"Our camp is not a prison": Karl Yoneda, *Camp Diary*, 139; Elaine Black Yoneda, "Manzanar Diary," May 20, 1942.

"luncheon party": As cited in Commission on Wartime Relocation, "The Relocation Centers," chap. 6 of *Personal Justice Denied*, 177.

"in a recent broadcast from Manila": Transactions of the Commonwealth Club of California 37–38: 340; Roy Nash, "Manzanar from the Inside," text of an address delivered July 31, 1942, San Francisco, CA, Inyo County Free Library Collection, via Densho Digital Repository, https://ddr.densho.org/ddr-densho-342-3/.

"What a contrast to the barbarities" through *"no one carries arms"*: Nash, "Manzanar from the Inside."

"luxuriant crop": Nash, "Manzanar from the Inside."

"Silently, it would seem": Nash, "Manzanar from the Inside."

"We intend to demonstrate": Nash, "Manzanar from the Inside." See also Karl Yoneda, *Camp Diary*, 154–155, for more about Karl's reaction to Nash's speech.

"the Japanese concentration camps": "Use It" (editorial), *San Gabriel Sun*, June 11, 1942, cited in Togo Tanaka, Manzanar documentary reports 1–20, US War Relocation Authority, 20, via Online Archive of California, https://oac.cdlib.org/ark:/28722/bk0013c9849/.

"special concentration camps": In this way, the Nazis were tweaking a term that had heretofore meant a place where political prisoners or minority groups were concentrated without trial for reasons of state security, usually following an executive decree or military order.

6. Exposed: Summer 1942

"Cupid Pit": "Form for Picnic Permits," US War Relocation Authority, Manzanar Relocation Area, box 10, folder 6, Karl G. Yoneda Papers; Jeffrey F. Burton, "Bairs Creek Picnic Area (Picnic Ground No. 1)," in *Garden Management Plan: Gardens and Gardeners at Manzanar* (National Park Service, December 2015), 63, https://irma.nps.gov/DataStore/DownloadFile/580978.

"Advise: stay away from camouflage": Case file for Rose Elaine Yoneda, 8, 11, evacuee case files, 1942–1946, Records of the War Relocation Authority, National Archives, College Park, MD.

"On the surface": Karl Yoneda, *Camp Diary*, 139. Note that in the translated version of his diary, cited throughout here, the translator, Ian Forsyth, used "internment camp," not "concentration camp," due to Karl's ongoing ambivalence about the latter term. During the translation process in the 1990s, Karl requested that Forsyth replace the latter with the former in his published English translation. But as confirmed to me by Forsyth in an email, in the original Japanese version, this entry and all others that use the term "internment camp" originally used *kyouseishuuyoujo*, most often translated as "concentration camp" (email with the author, October 20, 2023). See also p. 227 in this book for more about Karl's eventual ambivalence over naming Manzanar a "concentration camp."

"The acceptance of a formal request": "Notice and General Instructions to Japanese Seeking Repatriation," Western Defense Command and Fourth Army, in "Selection of Important Record and Registration Forms Utilized by the Civil Affairs Division Western Defense Command," United States War Relocation Authority, via Online Archive of California, https://oac.cdlib.org/ark:/13030/k6kk9k6p/.

"resident's Open Forum": Togo Tanaka, Manzanar documentary report 23, July 12, 1942, Manzanar documentary reports 21–33, US War Relocation Authority, 139, via Online Archive of California, https://oac.cdlib.org/ark:/28722/bk0013c985v/.4.

"We are always discriminated against here": Karl Yoneda, memo to Roy Nash and Ned Campbell, July 10, 1942, Manzanar, CA, box 10, folder 5, Karl G. Yoneda Papers.

"this is war time": Karl Yoneda, *Camp Diary*, 141.

another round of ringing applause: Karl Yoneda, memo to Nash and Campbell.

"If we allow another meeting": Karl Yoneda to Nash and Campbell.

"Just like the Soviet Union": Karl Yoneda, interview by Larson and Hansen, 38.

"a reflection of our male chauvinism": Karl Yoneda, *Ganbatte*, 135.

"Reds like Yoneda": Karl Yoneda, *Camp Diary*, 147.

"appropriate measures": Yoneda, 148.

"in limbo": Yoneda, 148.

"voiced approval": Kurihara, "Autobiography," 39.

utterly unconvinced: Kurihara, 39.

"blast them to hell": Brown, "Story of Joe Kurihara," 22.

"confirmed Communist": Joseph Kurihara, "Murder in Camp Manzanar," April 16, 1943, 25, Commission on Wartime Relocation and Internment of Civilians Collection, Densho Digital Repository, https://ddr.densho.org/ddr-densho-67-18/.

"The war is going badly": Karl Yoneda, *Camp Diary*, 149.

"that the citizen manpower": "Petition to Honorable Franklin D. Roosevelt, President of the United States" (unsent draft), July 23, 1942, box 10, folder 5, Karl G. Yoneda Papers.

"utilizing the manpower": "Petition to Honorable Franklin D. Roosevelt, President of the United States," August 5, 1942, box 10, folder 6, Karl G. Yoneda Papers.

blackout conditions: "Blackout!," *Manzanar Free Press*, July 31, 1942.

"pulverized": Joe Kurihara, "Speech #1," in appendix to "Autobiography," 5.

"small brush fire" : "Blackout!," *Manzanar Free Press*; Togo Tanaka, Manzanar documentary report 36, July 29, 1942, in Manzanar documentary reports 34–59, US War Relocation Authority, 233, via Online Archive of California, https://oac.cdlib.org/ark:/28722/bk0013c986d/.

No matter what danger and *They have not as yet learned* : Brown, "Story of Joe Kurihara," 24.

"*Chairman Ariyoshi*" *did his best*: Karl Yoneda, *Camp Diary*, 151–152

"*We have a double duty*": "Federation of Citizens Holds Meet," *Manzanar Free Press*, July 31, 1942.

"*We are Americans of Japanese ancestry*" through "*pitch in and do*": Karl Yoneda, "Our Role in the War Effort," text of a speech delivered July 28, 1942, Manzanar, CA, box 10, folder 5, Karl G. Yoneda Papers.

"*You inu!*": Karl Yoneda, *Camp Diary*, 152.

"*I'm an American citizen*": Cited in Tanaka, Manzanar documentary report 36, 233–234.

He called it "electric": Brown, "Story of Joe Kurihara," 23–24; Kurihara, "Autobiography," 40.

"*If you please, Mr. Chairman!*" through "*We're here*": Cited in Tanaka, Manzanar documentary report 36, 234.

"*Tokie!*" *yelled Kurihara*: Brown, "Story of Joe Kurihara," 24.

"*I'll tell you why*": Cited in Tanaka, Manzanar documentary report 36, 234.

"*I had turned the table*": Kurihara, "Autobiography," 40.

"*Come on, let's punch*": Karl Yoneda, *Camp Diary*, 152.

"*There aren't any phones here*": Yoneda, 152.

"*I feel sorry for having brought*": Yoneda, 152.

"*Mrs. R.E. Yoneda*": "Petition to Honorable Franklin D. Roosevelt," August 5, 1942.

"*Personally I do not believe*": Translator's notation, Karl Yoneda, *Camp Diary*, 328n5.

"*quiet move by a few people*": "Two Hundred Sign Petition," *Manzanar Free Press*, August 3, 1942.

"*giving away other people's*": Philip Webster, report on investigation of Manzanar Relocation Area, August 31–September 2, 1942, US War Relocation Authority, 11, via Online Archive of California, https://oac.cdlib.org/ark:/13030/k6pg1zw2/.

"*ousted from the only part*": "Work Must Be Out of Vital Defense Area," *Manzanar Free Press*, August 3, 1942.

"*violently opposed*": Morris Edward Opler, "A History of Internal Government at Manzanar," Manzanar Relocation Center, March 1942–December 6, 1942, 21, box 12, Manzanar War Relocation Center Records, Library Special Collections, Charles E. Young Research Library, UCLA.

"*informers*": Kurihara, "Speech #1," 6.

"*just as bad if not worse than the Germans*'": Joe Kurihara, "Speech #2," in appendix to "Autobiography," 10.

"*common tactic*" and "*They vigorously wave the flag*": Kurihara, "Speech #1," 5.

"*bomb the Manzanar Citizens Federation*" through "*sitting in a cozy room*": Kurihara, "Speech #2," 10–11.

"two-faced hypocrites": Kurihara, "Speech #1," 4.

"When it comes to willingness": Arthur Caylor, "Small Salute: Behind the News," *San Francisco News*, August 17, 1942, box 10, folder 6, Karl G. Yoneda Papers.

"the Americans on the outside" through *"elated"*: Kurihara, "Autobiography," 41–42; Karl Yoneda, *Camp Diary*, 157.

"statements were repeated with conviction": Tanaka, "Report on the Manzanar Riot," 31.

"Thousands of helpless Jews" through *"This marks the beginnings"*: "Thousands Die in Nazi Gas Chamber," *People's World*, August 5, 1942, cited in translator's notation, Karl Yoneda, *Camp Diary*, 329–330n10; Karl Yoneda, *Camp Diary*, 158.

"to weigh what was transpiring": Kurihara, "Autobiography," 42.

"If anyone, any Nisei": Cited in Togo Tanaka, Manzanar documentary report 47, August 12, 1942, in Manzanar documentary reports 34–59, US War Relocation Authority, 257–260, via Online Archive of California, https://oac.cdlib.org/ark:/28722/bk0013c986d/.

"loud stamping of approval": Tanaka, 257–260.

"I was wounded fighting": Cited in Morton Grodzins, *The Loyal and the Disloyal; Social Boundaries of Patriotism and Treason* (University of Chicago Press, 1956), 105. Though Grodzins never identified the speaker of these words as Kurihara, all other documentation of the meeting points to Kurihara as the only meeting attendee who could claim them, particularly since both the sentiments at the theatrics align with Kurihara's own recollections of his actions. I was pointed to this quote by the historians Audrie Girdner and Anne Loftis, who attribute it to Kurihara despite Grodzins's omission, in their seminal work *The Great Betrayal: The Evacuation of the Japanese-Americans During World War II* (Macmillan, 1969), 259, 496n55.

"We are of the Yamato": Kurihara, "Autobiography," 42; Karl Yoneda, *Camp Diary*, 160.

"the heckling was so loud": "Social Disorganization: Divergent Orientations: Kibei Meeting," n.d., in "Miscellaneous Notes," US War Relocation Authority, 2, via Online Archive of California, https://oac.cdlib.org/ark:/13030/k6d224sj/.

"Araki! Araki!" through *"Nisei like that should be beaten"*: Karl G. Yoneda, "Notes and Observations of 'Kibel Meeting' held August 8th, 1942 at Kitchen 15" and "From the Minutes of the Block Leaders Council of August 14, 1942," box 10, folder 6, Karl G. Yoneda Papers; Karl Yoneda, *Camp Diary*, 160; translator's notation, Yoneda, 330n11. Curiously, Karl left the Hitler cheer out of his diary's description of the evening, adding it only to the transcript of the meeting he wrote in English for the WRA. Other witnesses or participants recalled events that mirrored Karl's recollections in other ways, but no one else mentioned the use of Hitler's name during the August 8 meeting in Manzanar, although Koji Ariyoshi did write about

the general antisemitism of incarcerees who'd been exposed to much anti-Jewish sentiment in both the United States and Japan. Ariyoshi, *Kona to Yenan*, 55.

"Our next gathering" through *"simply allow these pro-Japan"*: Karl Yoneda, *Camp Diary*, 160.

"How long will it be?": Elaine Black Yoneda, "Manzanar Diary," August 8, 1942.

"Notes and Observations": His full title, abbreviated in the text for reading convenience, was "Notes and Observations of 'Kibei Meeting' held August 8th, 1942 at Kitchen 15."

"Only Japanese spoken": Karl Yoneda, "Notes and Observations of a Kibei Meeting," August 8, 1942, box 10, folder 6, Karl G. Yoneda Papers

"given admonitory lectures": Karl Yoneda, *Camp Diary*, 160.

"the head of the Japanese department": Kurihara, "Autobiography," 42–43.

"sincere effort" through *"loyal to democracy"*: Karl G. Yoneda, James Oda, J. M. Blamy, Koji Ariyoshi, and Tokutaro Slocum to Dillon Meyer, National Director, War Relocation Authority, August 10, 1942, Manzanar, CA, box 10, folder 6, Karl G. Yoneda Papers. Togo Tanaka and the *Free Press* added additional warnings through other venues. The newspaper ran an article titled "Let's Watch Our Step": "Heat lightning has charged the valley atmosphere with danger," the piece began, "but the rumbling . . . is not all thunder." Rather, the "pro-America and pro-Japan" groups, who now stood "glaring" at one another, were on the verge of outright combustion. In his semiweekly documentary report to the WRA, Tanaka warned that the "pro-Japan" faction was growing. The majority of Manzanar's population could be characterized as "fence-sitters" not looking for added turmoil, Tanaka explained, but two factors were drawing them closer to the pro-Japan group: outside news of politicians threatening to strip Japanese Americans of their citizenship and the WRA's failure to clarify the ultimate fate of the incarcerees, or even its own "aims, purposes, and ultimate goals" in administering the camps. "Let's Watch our Step," *Manzanar Free Press*, August 12, 1942; Tanaka, documentary report 47, 261–263.

"We believe in American democracy": James Oda, Karl G. Yoneda, and Koji Ariyoshi to Dillon Meyer, National Director, War Relocation Authority, August 13, 1942, Manzanar, CA, box 10, folder 6, Karl G. Yoneda Papers.

"We recognize the military necessity": Karl G. Yoneda to Dillon Meyer, National Director, War Relocation Authority, August 13, 1942, Manzanar, CA, box 10, folder 6, Karl G. Yoneda Papers. Togo Tanaka was also urging the same solution in his documentary report that he wrote on August 12, a solution he called a "drastic surgery," admitting the "cruelty" that may result by separating families. But Tanaka envisioned an idealized outcome that would squash accusations of American concentration camps for its citizens: "Creation of [a] Pro-America Center can

be the object of pride and serve as the prize exhibit of the goal of the W.R.A. program. . . . In time when the hysteria and hatreds of war will have passed by and the calm of peace once again pervades this land these truly relocation centers, not concentration camps, will serve as monuments to Democracy and the enlightened agencies of the American people." Tanaka, documentary report 47, 261–263.

"Americanism, to me": Cited in Togo Tanaka, Manzanar documentary report 16, July 1, 1942, in Manzanar documentary reports 1–20, US War Relocation Authority, via Online Archive of California, https://oac.cdlib.org/ark:/28722/bk0013c9849/.

"Arm is all healed": Case file for Rose Elaine Yoneda, 10.

"Reluctant workers were persuaded": Tanaka, documentary report 47, 256.

"We stuck to our guns": Karl Yoneda, *Camp Diary*, 161.

"The negotiated agreement stipulates" through *She added a question mark*: Yoneda, 164; Elaine Black Yoneda, "Manzanar Diary," August 17, 1942.

STORM OF DENUNCIATION: Karl Yoneda, *Camp Diary*, 165.

"It is a miracle if any pro-American": Karl G. Yoneda, memo to Dillon Myer, "Notes and Observation [*sic*]," August 18, 1942, Manzanar, CA, box 10, folder 6, Karl G. Yoneda Papers.

"Jewish Hall" through *"he married a white woman"*: Karl Yoneda, *Camp Diary*, 165, 166–167; Karl G. Yoneda, memo to Roy Nash, "Report on Block Leader's Election in Block 4," August 24, 1942, Manzanar, CA, box 10, folder 6, Karl G. Yoneda Papers.

"You're all Japanese": Karl Yoneda, *Camp Diary*, 165.

"Deputy Leader": Yoneda, 166.

"Our days here": Yoneda, 166.

"staked all around": Elaine Black Yoneda, interview by Hansen, 77.

"felt kind of threatened": John Tateishi, "Interview with Harry Ueno," in *And Justice for All: An Oral History of the Japanese American Detention Camps* (University of Washington Press, 1999), 193.

"Spy!" someone spat out: Karl Yoneda, *Camp Diary*, 167–168.

Someone derided Karl: Karl Yoneda, interview by Larson and Hansen, 39; Karl Yoneda, *Camp Diary*, 167–168

"cowering" in fear: Elaine Black Yoneda, statement to the Commission on Wartime Relocation and Internment of Civilians (CWRIC), 1981, 16, box 3, folder 1 ("Wartime Relocation"), Elaine Black Yoneda Collection.

"still quite shaken up": Ariyoshi, *Kona to Yenan*, 74. Other details from this scene, including documentation of internal thoughts of those involved, can be found in the sources cited previously, as well as in Elaine Black Yoneda, "Manzanar Diary," August 23, 1942; Elaine Black Yoneda, interview with Hansen, 65; and Tamura, *In*

Defense of Justice, 71. For an intriguing and thoughtful perspective on differing, even sometimes conflicting, incarceree accounts of the American concentration camps—and how these can actually enrich our understanding rather than cancel out different accounts—see Alice Yang Murray, "Multiple Histories of Internment," in *Historical Memories*.

"I don't want to remain here": Karl Yoneda, *Camp Diary*, 167–168.

"There are many men": Yoneda, 171; Karl G. Yoneda, to Major General Lewis B. Hershey, National Director, National Selective Service, August 27, 1942, Manzanar, CA, box 10, folder 6, Karl G. Yoneda Papers.

"since been approached by [a] kibei group": Karl Yoneda, *Camp Diary*, 169; Karl G. Yoneda, confidential memo to Roy Nash, August 25, 1942, Manzanar, CA, box 10, folder 6, Karl G. Yoneda Papers.

"Where, how when?": Elaine Black Yoneda, "Manzanar Diary," August 14, 1942.

"You'd better stay with grandma": Elaine Black Yoneda, interview by Hansen, 70.

"regarding Caucasian wives": Temporary leave form, US War Relocation Authority, August 22, 1942, in case file for Rose Elaine Yoneda, 14; Elaine Black Yoneda, "Manzanar Diary," August 21, 1942.

"tearful and despondent": Karl Yoneda, *Camp Diary*, 169.

"Mrs. Karl Yoneda has been granted": "Goes to Daughter," *Manzanar Free Press*, August 24, 1942.

"old lady": Karl Yoneda, *Camp Diary*, 169.

"endured without a word of protest": Yoneda, 170.

"I want to state definitely": Karl G. Yoneda, confidential memo to Nash, August 25, 1942.

"Went looking—no results": Elaine Black Yoneda, "Manzanar Diary," August 26 & 27, 1942.

"August passed without an explosion": Brown, "Story of Joe Kurihara," 29.

7. Fractured: Summer–Fall 1942

"the slightest amount of Japanese blood": Hall to Ennis, November 27, 1942, http://www.javadc.org/java/docs/1942-05-28%20Mixed%20Marriage%20Cases-Ltrs,%20Memos%20dated%201942-05-28%20thru%201943-07-15%20Pgs23_ck.pdf, 10.

"My dear Colonel": Colonel Karl R. Bendetsen, GSC, to Colonel Ralph H. Tate, GSC, July 7, 1942, Japanese American Veterans Association Research Archive, Digitized Documents Project, http://www.javadc.org/java/docs/1942-05-28%20Mixed%20Marriage%20Cases-Ltrs,%20Memos%20dated%201942-05-28%20thru%201943-07-15%20Pgs23_ck.pdf, 6.

"their Americanization" through *"protecting mixed-blood children"*: John L. DeWitt, *Final Report: Japanese Evacuation from the West Coast, 1942* (US Government Printing Office, 1943), 45. Though DeWitt's name appears on the report,

historians generally agree that it was written either by or under the direction of Bendetsen. Brian Niiya, "Final Report, Japanese Evacuation from the West Coast, 1942 (Book)," *Densho Encyclopedia*, accessed October 31 2023, https://encyclopedia.densho.org/Final%20Report,%20Japanese%20Evacuation%20from%20the%20West%20Coast,%201942%20(book).

"infectious Japanese thought": Herman P. Goebel Jr., memo to W. H. Cheney, "Release of Mixed Marriage Families," July 12, 1942, General Correspondence File, reel 54, Turlock Center Manager, Procurement of Supplies thru Release of Mixed Marriage, National Archives, San Bruno, CA; Wilkie C. Courier, memo to Major Ray Ashworth, "Emancipation of Japanese Children, Issue of Mixed Marriages," November 13, 1942, Mixed Marriage File, National Archives, College Park, MD, cited in Paul R. Spickard, "Injustice Compounded: Amerasians and Non-Japanese Americans in World War II Concentration Camps," *Journal of American Ethnic History* 5, no. 2 (Spring 1986): 10.

"unemancipated" through *"or any incident bearing upon"*: Tracy Slater, "Mixed-Marriage Policy/Mixed-Blood Policy," *Densho Encyclopedia*, accessed September 29, 2023, https://encyclopedia.densho.org/Mixed-Marriage%20Policy/Mixed-Blood%20Policy.

"The heretofore impenetrable gates": "Four Depart as Families Are United," *Manzanar Free Press*, August 5, 1942. Though three other incarcerees are also mentioned by the *Free Press* in this article ("four residents of Manzanar who are leaving to join families outside," they wrote), clear records only exist in WRA files for Raymond, who in any case was only one allowed to return home to the West Coast. According to the *Free Press*, the others left to join family in Louisiana, Colorado, and Missouri.

"official release": "Eleven Newcomers Arrive from Other Assembly Centers," *Manzanar Free Press*, July 27, 1942; Togo Tanaka, "Caucasian Wife of Evacuee Leaves Manzanar with Children," July 24, 1942, in Manzanar documentary reports 21–33, US War Relocation Authority, 194, via Online Archive of California, https://oac.cdlib.org/ark:/28722/bk0013c985v/.

"sired": Attachment to report from Frank E. Davis to Emil Sandquist, July 16, 1942, Mixed Marriage Policy Files, record group 499, box 28, folder 291.1, National Archives, College Park, MD; Karl R. Bendetsen to William P. Scobey, November 21, 1942, Japanese American Veterans Association Research Archive, Digitized Documents Project, http://www.javadc.org/java/docs/1942-05-28%20Mixed%20Marriage%20Cases-Ltrs,%20Memos%20dated%201942-05-28%20thru%201943-07-15%20Pgs23_ck.pdf, 8.

"whose non-Japanese blood": Margaret Watkins, memo to Elizabeth B. MacLatchie, "Memo on Mixed Marriages," Department of Social Welfare, War Services Bureau,

October 9, 1942, California State Archives, https://exhibits.sos.ca.gov/s/exhibits /media/52858.

"The Spandrio family asked": "WCCA Policy Relating to Exemptions by Virtue of Mixed Marriage," US War Relocation Authority, 1942, Japanese American Veterans Association Research Archive, Digitized Documents Project, http://www.javadc.org /java/docs/1942-11-27%20Ltrs,%20Memos,%20Rules,%20Regs%20re%20contraband, %20travel,%20curfews%20in%20WDC%20dated%201942-11-27%20thru %201942-12-08%20Pgs30_ck.pdf, 3. The *Manzanar Free Press* later documented that Honda was finally allowed to return to his family two years later, in 1944. They wrote, "Richard Honda, local resident, returned to the home of his foster parents, Mr. and Mrs. Serafino Spandrio of Port Huenene, Calif., the Manza-knoll reported this week. Richard is eight years old and has been residing at the local Children's Village for the past two years." "Local Resident Leaves for Port Huenene," *Manzanar Free Press*, August 16, 1944.

"Japanese pure and simple": John Hall, telephone call to Karl Bendetsen, May 24, 1943, transcript cited in Raymond Okamura, "A Japanese Pure and Simple," *Newsletter of the National Council for Japanese American Redress* 3, no. 3 (May 1985): 3.

"not appear to be Japanese": Attachment to letter from Nils Aanonson to R. L Nicholson, June 10, 1942, "IN RE: Mrs. Mitsuko Komuro Ramos, USES #28745," General Correspondence File, reel 149, Tulare Center Manager, Mixed Marriages/Evacuee, National Archives, San Bruno, CA.

"Neither of them had any contact": "Mrs. Bettine Y. Lawson," in Richard S. Nishimoto, "Survey of Mixed Marriages," 1942, 39, via Online Archive of California, https:// oac.cdlib.org/ark:/28722/bk0013c5x9z/.

"This office declines": Cited in Spickard, "Injustice Compounded," 13. Documentation of Ethel Taylor's place of incarceration can be found in case file for Ethel H. Taylor, evacuee case files, 1942–1946, Records of the War Relocation Authority, National Archives, College Park, MD.

"for a definite determination": N. L. Bican to E. Sandquist, "Mixed Blood Individuals and Mixed-Marriage Families," August 14, 1942, General Correspondence File, reel 238, Portland Center Manager, Correspondence and Teletypes Regarding, Evac- uee—Mixed Marriages—Correspondence, Instructions and Teletypes, National Archives, San Bruno, CA.

"Today was Elaine's birthday": Karl Yoneda, *Camp Diary*, 175.

"He's having difficulty" through *"Elaine, where ARE you?"*: Yoneda, 177.

"It's unreasonable for nine people": Yoneda, 174. Aileen Hitomi Lane, Chotaro Nishimu- ra's great-granddaughter, explains that only eight members of the Nishimura family ended up living together: "According to my father [Donald Nishumura], George

and Chotaro lived with the Yonedas until the wall separating their rooms were moved to enlarge their space. Then George moved into the Nishimura family section and Chotaro moved to a room in the adjacent building." Email interview with the author, November 16, 2023.

"simple": "Ariyoshi-Ito Marriage Performed," *Manzanar Free Press*, September 14, 1942.

"who swear allegiance to the United States": Karl Yoneda, *Camp Diary*, 176.

"anti-Roosevelt": Yoneda, 176; Karl G. Yoneda, letter to the editor, *Manzanar Free Press*, September 7, 1942.

CAUCASIAN DOCTOR ADVOCATES through *"Tommy is ecstatic"*: "Fewer," *San Francisco Chronicle*, September 7, 1942, cited in Karl Yoneda, *Camp Diary*, 336n1; Yoneda, 178.

"Saw Joyce": Elaine Black Yoneda, "Manzanar Diary," August 31, 1942.

"She sounds extremely happy": Karl Yoneda, *Camp Diary*, 173.

"Saw Joyce," she wrote again: Elaine Black Yoneda, "Manzanar Diary," September 5, 1942.

"the indigent sick" and An old photograph: "Mount Zion History," UCSF Medical Center at Mt Zion, September 11, 2020, https://mountzion.ucsfmedicalcenter.org/history/.

"Saw Joyce for the last time": Elaine Black Yoneda, "Manzanar Diary," September 10, 1942. Other details from this section about Elaine, Joyce, and Molly in San Francisco can be found throughout entries in Elaine Black Yoneda, "Manzanar Diary," August 28–September 19, 1942; Karl Yoneda, *Camp Diary*, 172, 173; and Elaine Black Yoneda, statement to the CWRIC, 16.

"finish the war in a hurry" through "You preferred certain inconveniences": Elaine Black Yoneda, interview by Hansen, 70–71.

"Letter from mama" and "Nothing new re: J": Elaine Black Yoneda, "Manzanar Diary," September 19 & 21, 1942.

"calculation": Kurihara, "Autobiography," 46–47; J. Kurihara, letter to the editor, *Manzanar Free Press*, September 19, 1942. Historian Elaine Tamura, citing a report by Togo Tanaka, writes that Kurihara had also hoped to publicly debate the MCF members about the question, "Should the Nisei affirm 'their allegiance to the United States' under the existing circumstances, or should they highlight the hypocrisy of America, reject the United States, and affirm their Japanese identity?" Tamura, *In Defense of Justice*, 65.

"marked individuals" through "death list": Tanaka, "Report on the Manzanar Riot," 32.

EVACUEES ADVISED: Cited in Togo Tanaka, Manzanar documentary report 61, September 15, 1942, in Manzanar documentary reports 60–91, US War Relocation Authority, 294, via Online Archive of California, https://oac.cdlib.org/ark:/28722/bk0013c987z/.

"It is the policy": Colonel Karl R. Bendetsen, GSG, Assistant Chief of Staff, Civil Affairs Division, WCCA, memo to regional director, War Relocation Authority, "Travel

Permits to Be Issued Japanese on Leaving War Relocation Projects," September 18, 1942, Japanese American Veterans Association Research Archive, Digitized Documents Project, http://www.javadc.org/java/docs/1942-11-27%20Ltrs, %20Memos,%20Rules,%20Regs%20re%20contraband,%20travel,%20curfews %20in%20WDC%20dated%201942-11-27%20thru%201942-12-08%20Pgs30 _ck.pdf, 30.

"Extensive investigation": "Issei and Kibei Now Eligible for Permanent Relocation," *Manzanar Free Press*, October 24, 1942.

"Even if America wins": Togo Tanaka, Manzanar documentary report 33, July 24, 1942, in Manzanar documentary reports 21–33, US War Relocation Authority, 195–196, via Online Archive of California, https://oac.cdlib.org/ark:/28722/bk0013c985v/. For a general explanation of this topic and more primary sources on repatriation from the camps in general, see description and links at "Expatriation/Repatriation/ Deportation," Densho Digital Repository, accessed November 7, 2024, https://ddr .densho.org/browse/topics/107/.

"from 'Col B' about repatriation!!": Elaine Black Yoneda, "Manzanar Diary," October 17, 1942.

"Certain Japanese persons": Karl R. Bendetsen, "Form Letter to Persons Under Repatriation Consideration," in "Selection of Important Record and Registration Forms Utilized by the Civil Affairs Division Western Defense Command," US War Relocation Authority, 58–59, via Online Archive of California, https://oac.cdlib .org/ark:/13030/k6kk9k6p/.

"I've strengthened my determination": Karl Yoneda, *Camp Diary*, 180, 181.

"WE HAVE EXHAUSTED EVERY MEANS": North Montana Beet Growers Association, telegram to Senator B. K. Wheeler, May 6, 1942, FDR Library, cited in Weglyn, *Years of Infamy*, 98.

"Japs live like rats": "Would Send Japs Back to Orient," *Spokesman-Review* (Spokane, WA), May 23, 1942; Karl Yoneda, *Camp Diary*, 145.

"To date I have received": Karl G Yoneda to Major General Lewis B Hershey, National Director, Washington Selective Service, October 6, 1942, box 10, folder 6, Karl G. Yoneda Papers.

a *"proposition" for Karl*: Elaine Black Yoneda, "Manzanar Diary," October 7, 1942.

"an authority on minority problems": "Open Forum" *Manzanar Free Press*, October 8, 1942.

"Some of the questions": Elaine Black Yoneda, "Manzanar Diary," October 10, 1942.

uncommonly eager to share: Togo Tanaka to Dorothy Swaine Thomas, July 4, 1943, in "Tanaka, Togo," Japanese American Evacuation and Resettlement Study, 109, via Online Archive of California, https://oac.cdlib.org/ark:/28722/bk001307t57.

Satterlee had argued in the 1930s: Helen Nace Satterlee, "We Should Not Furnish Aid to Any European Embroglio," *New York Times*, March 17, 1933.

"the Japanese problem" and *"feted guests"*: "Fete Guests with Chicken Spread," *Manzanar Free Press*, October 15, 1942.

"pleasantly holed up": Tanaka to Thomas, 109.

"Mrs. Satterlee??": Elaine Black Yoneda, "Manzanar Diary," October 10, 1942.

"Will he bring back a football?": Yoneda, October 22, 1942.

"Mother in SF" through *"Nothing new"*: Yoneda, November 7–22, 1942.

"Blood Brothers Who Worry" through *"beware of punishment"*: "Literal Translation of a Letter Received by Tom Imai; Friday, Nov. 6, 1942, Mailed from Manzanar, November 5, 1942" and "Case #242: Letter Received by Mr. Fred Ogura, Block 1 Leader (Manager), Friday, November 6, 1942, Literal Translation by Akira Itami, Information Office," US War Relocation Authority, box 16, folder 8, file "Law and Order—Incident—Events Leading Up to and Including Incident—August 1944—December 21, 1942," Manzanar War Relocation Center Records.

"Blood Brothers Corps": Opler, "History of Internal Government," 49–51; Ralph P. Merritt, Project Director, memo to E. R. Fryer, Regional Director, "Project Report No. 74 [*sic*]: Preliminary Findings; Surveys on 'Underground' Groups," US War Relocation Authority, December 1, 1942, in "The Manzanar Riot," US War Relocation Authority, https://oac.cdlib.org/ark:/28722/bk0013c9780/. Despite the WRA's use of "74" in the memo's subject line, the actual document this memo's information was drawn from was Togo Tanaka's Manzanar documentary report 84, not 74, from November 18, 1942.

"know of nothing": Elaine Black Yoneda, interview by Hansen, 77; Karl Yoneda, *Camp Diary*, 207; translator's notation, Yoneda, 342n7.

"attack Karl Yoneda": Harry Y. Ueno to Dr. Arthur A. Hansen, September 8, 1994, cited in Hansen, "Riot of Voices," 128.

8. Pursued: Fall 1942

"They guarded us like cattle": Cited in Togo Tanaka, Manzanar documentary report 85, November 19, 1942, in Manzanar documentary reports 60–91, US War Relocation Authority, 376, via Online Archive of California, https://oac.cdlib.org/ark:/28722/bk0013c987z/.

refused meals at restaurants: Tanaka, 376.

"The furlough workers": "Beet Furlough," *Manzanar Free Press*, November 9, 1942.

"Dear Editor": Karl Yoneda, letter to the editor, *Manzanar Free Press*, November 2, 1942.

"Let's get those Japs!": Karl Yoneda, *Ganbatte*, 144; Karl Yoneda, *Camp Diary*, 209.

"No matter how often": Yoneda, 210.

"only relationship": Cited in Richard Drinnon, *Keeper of Concentration Camps: Dillon S. Myer and American Racism* (University of California Press, 1987), 48.

"on [a] volcano": Brown, "Story of Joe Kurihara," 31.

"Look out the window": Cited in Unrau, *Evacuation and Relocation*, https://www.nps.gov/parkhistory/online_books/manz/hrs11e.htm.

"even the nomad tribes": "Substitute for Charter Is Discussed," *Manzanar Free Press*, December 5, 1942.

"anti-American, disruptive elements": Karl Yoneda, *Camp Diary*, 212–213.

"defiant group of pro-Axis Japanese": "Another Setback," *Manzanar Free Press*, November 26, 1942.

"Manzanar Kokuryukai": Entry for November 25, 1942, Fukuwa, "Manzanar Diary," 1942–1943, via CSU Dominguez Hills Collection, https://ddr.densho.org/ddr-csujad-34-2/.

"fanatic tendencies": Merritt, memo to Fryer, "Project Report No. 74 [*sic*]," https://oac.cdlib.org/ark:/28722/bk0013c9780/.

"The authorities are doing nothing": Karl Yoneda, *Camp Diary*, 213.

"I have a feeling" and *"Things popping"*: Elaine Black Yoneda, "Manzanar Diary," November 24–27, 1942.

"the beginnings of the Nazis' campaign": Karl Yoneda, *Camp Diary*, 158.

"infants, the elderly, and the infirm": "Nazis Wiping Out Jews in Cold Blood" and "Half of Jews in Europe Dead," *Los Angeles Times*, November 25, 1942; "Million Polish Jews Perish: Mass Executions and Gas Wiping Out All but Able-Bodied," *Los Angeles Times*, November 26, 1942. News had also broken that week in the Jewish press in Palestine of "concrete gas-chamber buildings in eastern Europe and a report that trains were carrying Jewish adults and children 'to great crematoriums at Oswiecim [Auschwitz], near Cracow.'" It remains unclear whether the news had yet been reported, however, in the Yiddish dailies and English-language leftist papers the Buchmans may have had access to in L.A. It had certainly not yet been reported in any major American media. David S. Wyman, *The Abandonment of the Jews: America and the Holocaust, 1941–1945* (New Press, 2007), 52.

"There is such a widespread feeling": Mari Okazaki to Miss Watson, November 26, 1942, 6–7, in "Okazaki, Mari, Diary Excerpts, Notes and Correspondence (2 of 2)," US War Relocation Authority, 1942, via Online Archive of California, https://oac.cdlib.org/ark:/28722/bk0013c983r/; Patricia Wakida, "Mari Okazaki," *Densho Encyclopedia*, accessed January 16, 2024, https://encyclopedia.densho.org/Mari%20Okazaki.

"Tried to call" through *"I married someone"*: Elaine Black Yoneda, "Manzanar Diary," November 24–28, 1942. Given the difficulty of reading Elaine's handwriting, especially in entries where she seemed particularly upset or unsettled, it's possible that

Joyce's husband's middle initial was "S." rather than "G." Documentation exists for a Joyce E. Barnett in San Francisco who had married an Ernest Barnett, but his middle initial does not appear on this document. Legal Notices, *San Francisco Examiner*, March 6, 1943. Tommy Yoneda, just a year before his death, recalled the story of young Joyce running away and having "shacked up with a sailor," but did not offer the name of Joyce's first husband. Tom Yoneda, interview by Rachel Schreiber, February 23, 2019, Santa Rosa, CA, in Schreiber, *Elaine Black Yoneda*, 145.

"At last, the long awaited": Karl Yoneda, *Camp Diary*, 214.

"exception": Watkins, memo to MacLatchie, https://exhibits.sos.ca.gov/s/exhibits /item/52857; Bendetsen to Scobey, November 21, 1942, http://www.javadc.org/java /docs/1942-05-28%20Mixed%20Marriage%20Cases-Ltrs,%20Memos%20dated %201942-05-28%20thru%201943-07-15%20Pgs23_ck.pdf, 8.

"potential dangerous enemy!": Elaine Black Yoneda, "Manzanar Diary," November 30, 1942.

"Why don't you go": Elaine Black Yoneda, interview by Hansen, 80.

"My plans do not include": Yoneda, 80.

"Ever since we enlisted": Karl Yoneda, *Camp Diary*, 215.

"Again, gang around": Elaine Black Yoneda, "Manzanar Diary," December 1, 1942.

"requesting induction of all Nisei": Kurihara, "Autobiography," 47.

"committing the lives of thousands": Kurihara, "Murder in Camp Manzanar," 25.

"to ask the War Department": Art Hansen, "The 'Invented Fiction' of the Model Minority and the Controversy Behind the JA Creed," *Nichi Bei Weekly*, January 1, 2015, https://www.nichibei.org/2015/01/the-invented-fiction-of-the-model-minority -and-the-controversy-behind-the-ja-creed/.

"the temper of the people": Kurihara, "Autobiography," 47.

"everywhere in the center" through *"We are going to kill"*: Tanaka, "Report on the Manzanar Riot," 64–65.

"pro-Japan element": Kiyoshi Higashi, Resident Chief of Internal Security at Manzanar, with support from Chief Commissioner Willard Schmidt, report for the National Emergency Conference of the Japanese American Citizens League at Salt Lake City, UT, November 17–24, 1942, reprinted in Tanaka, "Report on the Manzanar Riot," addenda.

"segregation of known troublemakers": Higashi, addenda. Unlike others who submitted reports to Manzanar administrators and the WRA in general, Higashi was able to submit this report without fear of reprisal because he was closely backed by his former brethren from Terminal Island, another group considered "toughs." "Those Blood Brothers don't dare attack or lay hands on me," Higashi reportedly

told Togo Tanaka. "They know that the whole Terminal Island gang stands behind me and will back me to the limit." Tanaka, "Report on the Manzanar Riot," 59.

"simmering and boiling": George T. Fukasawa, interview by Arthur Hansen, August 12, 1974, Fullerton, CA, transcript in oral history 1336, 51, Japanese American Oral History Project.

SHRIEKING ORDERS: Karl Yoneda, *Camp Diary*, 216–217.

"demand and re-demand protection": Elaine Black Yoneda, interview by Hansen, 87.

"This was not a time for fanfare": Ariyoshi, *Kona to Yenan*, 79.

"deny us a final embrace": Karl Yoneda, *Camp Diary*, 217.

"desert city of exiles": Ariyoshi, *Kona to Yenan*, 79.

Will we ever be together: Karl and Elaine Yoneda, "Manzanar: Another View."

"Karl walked out": Elaine Black Yoneda, "Manzanar Diary," December 4, 1942.

"You could show the issei": Morton Grodzins, US War Relocation Authority, "The Manzanar Shooting," January 10, 1943, 11–12, via Online Archive of California, https://oac.cdlib.org/ark:/28722/bk0013c981n/.

"stooges, dogs, flagwavers": Opler, "History of Internal Government," 76.

"a cross-section" through *"terribly sorry"*: Togo Tanaka, Manzanar documentary report 89, December 3, 1943, in Manzanar documentary reports 60–91, US War Relocation Authority, 395–400, via Online Archive of California, https://oac.cdlib.org/ark:/28722/bk0013c987z/.

DECORATED: "Officer Who Evacuated West Coast Japs Honored," *San Francisco Examiner*, December 5, 1942.

"Possible results [include]": "Aliens: Medal for Moving," *Time*, November 30, 1942.

9. Caught: December 5–7, 1942

"Too bad": Cited in Tanaka, "Report on the Manzanar Riot," 25.

small blue spiral notebook: Tanaka, 25; Tateishi, "Interview with Harry Ueno," 198; Susan Kunitomi Embrey, Arthur Hansen, and Betty Kulberg Mitson, *Manzanar Martyr: An Interview with Harry Y. Ueno* (Oral History Program, California State University, 1986), 54.

Another of the anti-American: Karl's transcription from Elaine's diary, in Karl Yoneda, *Camp Diary*, 222. In the section of Karl's diary corresponding to the time after he left Manzanar for MIS training, Karl interspersed his own entries with snippets from Elaine's diary to explain what was happening in camp while we was gone, indicated subsequently by notations of "Karl's transcription." Frequently, his transcriptions differ slightly from the handwritten version of Elaine's "Manzanar Diary"—in word choice and order of information divulged, and occasionally in details provided. However, nothing Karl transcribes in his diary contradicts what

Elaine wrote in hers or what she said later about her experiences in Manzanar. Thus, I attribute these differences to 1) changes of word choice resulting from multiple translations into Japanese and then back into English (since *Camp Diary* is a translation into English of his original diary in Japanese, where he transcribed translations from English into Japanese of Elaine's handwritten diary); and 2) the process of preparing *Camp Diary* for publication, when he filled in details he learned later from conversation with Elaine or others.

"Why permit that sneak": Kurihara recalled saying these words to the crowd before they reached the administration building, when they were still gathered near Block 22, though others remember him making similar threats in front of the administration area. Either way, no one, including Kurihara himself, disputes that he urged the crowd to kill Tayama and the others on his "death list." Kurihara, "Murder in Camp Manzanar"; Janet Goldberg, "The Manzanar 'Incident,' December 5, to December 19, 1942," US War Relocation Authority, 6–7, box 16, folder 8, file "Law and Order—Incident—Events Leading Up to and Including Incident—August 1944—December 21, 1942," Manzanar War Relocation Center Records.

"He says that it's too bad": Elaine Black Yoneda, statement to the CWRIC, 22; Elaine Black Yoneda, "Manzanar Diary," December 6, 1942; Karl G. Yoneda, interview by Satoru Kamikawa, August 27, 1972, Los Angeles, CA, box 11, folder 7, Karl G. Yoneda Papers; Elaine Yoneda, letter to the editor, *Hokubei Mainichi*, May 10, 1983, box 11, folder 7, Karl G. Yoneda Papers.

"Get home, quickly!": Karl's transcription from Elaine's diary, in Karl Yoneda, *Camp Diary*, 222.

"continue[d] to keep company": Karl's transcription from Elaine's diary, in Yoneda, 222; Elaine Black Yoneda, "Manzanar Diary," December 6, 1942.

If only Karl: Karl's transcription from Elaine's diary, in Karl Yoneda, *Camp Diary*, 223.

Something terrible is about to happen: Citation from Elaine's December 1942 letter to Karl, recalling the events of the Manzanar uprising and those in the immediate aftermath. Elaine Black Yoneda to Karl Yoneda, December 12, 1942, transcribed in Karl Yoneda, *Camp Diary*, 234–235.

That's where the Yonedas live: Karl's transcription of Elaine's diary, in Karl Yoneda, *Camp Diary*, 223.

"he didn't care": Robert B. Throckmorton, Project Attorney, memo to Ralph P. Merritt, Project Director, "Report on Evacuees Who Have Been Jailed as a Result of the Incident of December 6, 1942," US War Relocation Authority, December 15, 1942, box 16, folder 8, file "Law and Order—Incident—Events Leading Up to and Including Incident—August 1944—December 21, 1942," Manzanar War Relocation Center Records.

"a fanatical tirade" through *"Members of the crowd"*: Cited in Unrau, *Evacuation and Relocation*, https://www.nps.gov/parkhistory/online_books/manz/hrs11.htm.

"Turn that inu over": Cited in Tanaka, "Report on the Manzanar Riot," 109.

"suffering from anxiety neurosis": Dr. Little, statement, reprinted in Goldberg, "The Manzanar 'Incident.'"

"Stones, sand, and lighted cigarettes": Cited in Unrau, *Evacuation and Relocation*, https:// www.nps.gov/parkhistory/online_books/manz/hrs11.htm.

"The cause of death": Morse Little, MD, Project Medical Officer, memo to Ralph P. Merritt, Project Director, "Concerning James Ito," US War Relocation Authority, December 18, 1942, box 16, folder 8, file "Law and Order—Incident—Events Leading Up to and Including Incident—August 1944—December 21, 1942," Manzanar War Relocation Center Records.

"Mess hall bells tolled": Cited in Unrau, *Evacuation and Relocation*, https://www.nps .gov/parkhistory/online_books/manz/hrs11.htm.

"A group of men": Sue Kunitomi Embrey, "Manzanar National Historic Site," National Park Service, accessed January 18, 2024, https://www.nps.gov/articles/000/sue -kunitomi-embrey.htm; Sue Kunitomi Embrey, interview by John Allen, November 6, 2002, Manzanar National Historic Site Collection, https://ddr.densho.org /interviews/ddr-manz-1-2-10/.

"Mob rule became the law": Togo Tanaka, Manzanar documentary report 90, December 6, 1942, in Manzanar documentary reports 60–91, US War Relocation Authority, 405, via Online Archive of California, https://oac.cdlib.org/ark:/28722 /bk0013c987z/.

"I was in the mob": Tanaka, "Report on the Manzanar Riot," 71.

"If he's not in" through *"The wife and baby"*: Tanaka, "Report on the Manzanar Riot," 73.

"frozen horror": Girdner and Loftis, *Great Betrayal*, 265.

"Things have calmed down": Karl's transcription from Elaine's diary, in Karl Yoneda, *Camp Diary*, 223.

her T's crossed: Elaine Black Yoneda, "Manzanar Diary," December 6, 1942.

"I can't even sleep": Karl's transcription from Elaine's diary, in Karl Yoneda, *Camp Diary*, 223.

I'm just going through *with their fascist behavior*: Elaine Black Yoneda to Karl Yoneda, December 12, 1942, 235–236.

Demolish Jap Forces: Cited in Karl Yoneda, *Camp Diary*, 223.

"outbreak of pro-Axis violence": "Martial Law Quells Riots at California Jap Colony," *Minneapolis Star*, December 7, 1942.

"On the eve of the first anniversary": Press statement, US War Relocation Authority, December 6, 1942, Manzanar, CA, record group 499, entry 137, box 56, folder 4,

pt. 2, National Archives and Records Administration (NARA) Records, via 442nd Regimental Combat Team, http://www.the442.org/archivedocuments.html.

"the terrorists responsible": Karl Yoneda, *Camp Diary*, 226; Private Karl G. Yoneda, MILS, Camp Savage, Minnesota, to Dillon Myer, National Director, War Relocation Authority, Washington, DC, December 7, 1942, in case file for Rose Elaine Yoneda.

"The American government": Karl Yoneda, *Camp Diary*, 226.

"What are you doing here?" through *"My daddy's a soldier"*: Elaine Black Yoneda, interview by Hansen, 84–85.

"Oh": Elaine Black Yoneda, statement to the CWRIC, 24.

Deep down inside: Elaine Black Yoneda to Karl Yoneda, December 12, 1942, 236.

"the building surrounded": Elaine Black Yoneda, "Manzanar Diary," December 7, 1942.

10. Finished: December 7–17, 1942

"God, I thought they were coming" through *"And no one was shot"*: Tanaka, "Report on the Manzanar Riot," 53–54.

"Guys still looking": Elaine Black Yoneda, "Manzanar Diary," December 8, 1942.

"People must have been stunned": Tad Uyeno, "Point of No Return: A True Story by Tad Uyeno," pt. 12, *Rafu Shimpo*, August 22–October 20, 1973, box 11, folder 7, Karl G. Yoneda Papers.

Where is she?: Elaine Black Yoneda, interview by Hansen, 85.

We can scarcely move: Karl's transcription from Elaine's diary, in Karl Yoneda, *Camp Diary*, 227.

"Hurry!": Elaine Black Yoneda, interview by Hansen, 87.

"like a camp of the dead": Ariyoshi, *Kona to Yenan*, 102.

"since we knew the Yonedas": Alys Ukita, interview by Richard Potashin, 2010, transcript in oral history 1295, 25, 27, Manzanar Oral History Project, Manzanar National Historic Site, National Park Service.

"certain persons of Japanese ancestry": Karl Bendetsen, memo to acting regional director, December 10, 1942, in "JERS Copies of Correspondence," US War Relocation Authority, 1942–1943, via Online Archive of California, https://oac.cdlib.org/ark:/13030/k6542vqv/.

"a definite show of weakness": "Transcript of Telephone Conversation Between General DeWitt and Mr. McCloy, Assistant Secretary of War, Washington D.C.," December 10, 1942, record group 499, entry 137, box 56, folder 4, pt. 1, National Archives and Records Administration (NARA) Records, via 442nd Regimental Combat Team, http://www.the442.org/archivedocuments.html.

"exiles": Uyeno, "Point of No Return," pt. 14; Karl's transcription from Elaine's diary, in Karl Yoneda, *Camp Diary*, 230.

"this was the last time": Tad Uyeno, "Point of No Return," pt. 14.

"unfit for shelter": Karl's transcription from Elaine's diary, in Karl Yoneda, *Camp Diary*, 230. Somewhat bafflingly, Tad Uyeno described the buildings as "in good condition," a claim all other sources refute. In Karl and Elaine's copy of Uyeno's article where he made this claim, one can still see underlining and a question mark to indicate their surprise in this section at his description of Cow Creek camp upon arrival. The same sort of markings appear in the section where Uyeno characterized Ned Campbell as a "good, open-minded administrator . . . the most democratically inclined . . ." (Uyeno, "Point of No Return," pt. 23), another claim refuted by almost all other sources.

"refugees" through *"soldiers fraternalizing"*: Uyeno, "Point of No Return," pt. 25.

even marked "emergency": Elaine Black Yoneda, "Manzanar Diary," December 10, 1942; Karl Yoneda, *Camp Diary*, 231, 237. The dates for this scene are noted variously in Karl's and Elaine's diaries, resulting in a contradiction. Elaine mentions seeing the photo on December 10, but since they arrived at Cow Creek late in the evening of December 10, one can assume she meant to mark this event on the page for December 11. Moreover, Karl's diary, reprinting some of Elaine's diary entries (after they were first translated by Karl into Japanese, then back into English for the translated edition of Karl's diary), mentions Elaine asking Campbell about the permit twice, on two different days, one being December 11, the other December 12. At no time did Elaine seem to trust his response.

"as if we had come to a ghost town": Uyeno, "Point of No Return," pt. 17.

"dog food": Tanaka, "Report on the Manzanar Riot," 97; Uyeno, "Point of No Return," pt. 24.

"WIFE AND CHILD SAFE": Ralph P. Merritt, Project Director, telegram to Karl Yoneda, US War Relocation Authority, December 11, 1942, box 16, folder 7, file "Law and Order—Incident—Death Valley Group," Manzanar War Relocation Center Records.

"We've gone through so much": Elaine Black Yoneda to Karl Yoneda, December 12, 1942, 232.

the dunes looked beautiful to her: Elaine Black Yoneda, "Manzanar Diary," December 14, 1942.

name that fit: Elaine Black Yoneda to Karl Yoneda, December 12, 1942, 237.

"Pearl Harbor! Banzai!": Elaine Black Yoneda to Karl Yoneda, December 12, 1942, 232–237. No other documentation seems to exist about taunts specifically to Jewish MPs, although every eyewitness to the event remembered clearly that the MPs in general were goaded with apparently pro-Axis heckling (the Japanese National Anthem, military marching songs and hymns) and physical taunts, including

traditional Japanese dances, "thumbing their noses at the soldiers" and "turn[ing] around [to] point at their own rear ends in derisive fashion." Tanaka, "Report on the Manzanar Riot," 83; Tanaka, documentary report 90, 405. It also remains unclear how Elaine knew that one of the MPs was Jewish. They could have met in passing and discussed it, though this remains unprovable, and no other mention of a specific meeting or conversation with or about a Jewish MP exists in either of the Yonedas' archives that I could locate. There is, however, documentation of at least one Jewish MP there during the uprising: a Lieutenant Stanley N. Zwaik, who was charged with helping to clear the crowd, among other duties. Goldberg, "The Manzanar 'Incident,'" 12. Stanley N. Zwaik eventually became national commander of the Jewish War Veterans of the United States. A brief history of his life, including a cursory mention of his time at Manzanar, appears in his obituary in *Newsletter of the Worldwide Congregation Charlap/Yahya* 12, no. 3 (October 2001): 6, 8, https://www.avotaynuonline.com/wp-content/uploads/2015/04/Charlap-12_3 .pdf. Most relevant to this history, beyond what's provable in various archives, is the undisputed fact that Elaine aligned the experience of the seemingly pro-Axis jeering with the intimate danger of unchecked antisemitism, and that in her terrified state, she found reflections of one in the other, a dynamic that repeated itself throughout the Yonedas' time in Manzanar and that remains difficult to trace in other testimonies from the camps, since Elaine and Tommy remain the only Jewish incarcerees on record from any of the Japanese American concentration camps.

"special camps": "Nazis Wiping Out Jews in Cold Blood" and "Half of Jews in Europe Dead," *Los Angeles Times*; "Million Polish Jews Perish," *Los Angeles Times*.

"Your loving wife, Elaine": Elaine Black Yoneda to Karl Yoneda, December 12, 1942, 237.

"pro-Japan": Elaine Black Yoneda to Karl Yoneda, 236.

"Absolutely nobody has been speaking": Karl's transcription from Elaine's diary, in Karl Yoneda, *Camp Diary*, 238.

"with no stockade": Karl's transcription from Elaine's diary, in Yoneda, 241.

dilapidated wheelbarrows: "Death Valley, Cow Creek Camp. Infirmary" (photo), Ralph P. Merritt Collection, Ralph P. Merritt Collection, via Densho Digital Repository, https://ddr.densho.org/ddr-densho-343-20/.

"in a half-dead condition": Karl's transcription from Elaine's diary, in Karl Yoneda, *Camp Diary*, 242.

"brought into the hospital cold": "Notes on Discussion with Dr. Morse Little, Surgeon in Charge of Center Hospital—12/8/42," December 10, 1942, record group 499, entry 137, box 56, folder 4, pt. 1, National Archives and Records Administration (NARA) Records, via 442nd Regimental Combat Team, http://www.the442.org /archivedocuments.html.

"*crowd started to break up*": David J. McFadden, Major, Infantry, memo to Colonel William A. Boekel, January 11, 1943, Wartime Civil Control Administration, San Francisco, CA, record group 499, entry 137, box 56, folder 4, pt. 1, National Archives and Records Administration (NARA) Records, via 442nd Regimental Combat Team, http://www.the442.org/archivedocuments.html.

"*that virtually every wound inflicted*": Grodzins, "Manzanar Shooting," 35.

"*A white doctor took his place*": "'A Place Like This,'" *Berkeley Remix*, https://update.lib .berkeley.edu/2023/11/13/the-berkeley-remix-season-8-episode-2a-place-like-this -the-memory-of-incarceration/; Ellen Endo, "Unsolved Murder in Manzanar," *Rafu Shimpo*, July 22, 2013, https://rafu.com/2013/07/unsolved-murder-in-manzanar/.

"*an accident*": Nancy Ukai Russell, "James Hatsuaki Wakasa," *Densho Encyclopedia*, accessed January 31, 2024, https://encyclopedia.densho.org/James%20Hatsuaki %20Wakasa.

"*leaders of the Manzanar Incident*" through "*no warrants*": Tamura, *In Defense of Justice*, 81, 92.

"*It occurred to me*": Cited in John Tateishi, *And Justice for All*, 26.

TO ALL PERSONS CONCERNED: Photocopy of leave clearance permit for Thomas Yoneda, Headquarters Western Defense Command and Fourth Army, November 17, 1942, Yoneda family personal papers, sent by Yvonne Yoneda Donaldson to the author, March 26, 2021.

"*Immediately upon your arrival*": Ralph P. Merritt, Project Director, Manzanar Relocation Project, to Mrs. Elaine Yoneda, Cow Creek Camp, Death Valley, December 16, 1942, in case file for Rose Elaine Yoneda.

"*or another Caucasian escort*" through "*subpoena him*": Elaine Black Yoneda, interview by Hansen, 90.

"*What's the matter, Mommy?*" through "*and into 'free' America*": Karl's transcription from Elaine's diary, in Karl Yoneda, *Camp Diary*, 245–246.

11. Burned: January 1943–1945

"*I would like to make it clear*": Eleanor Roosevelt, My Day, *Hollywood (CA) Citizen-News*, July 29, 1943.

"*certain Japanese Americans in mixed marriage*": Warren Magnuson, telegram to Colonel Moffitt, December 3, 1943, Mixed Marriage Policy Files, record group 499, box 28, folder 291.1, National Archives, College Park, MD, cited in Eunhye Kwon, "Interracial Marriages Among Asian Americans in the U.S. West, 1880–1954" (PhD diss., University of Florida, 2011), 160.

"*belt line*" and "*That's how it should be*": Elaine Black Yoneda to Karl Yoneda, February 3, 1942, cited in Raineri, *Red Angel*, 230–231.

"keep me warm": Elaine Black Yoneda to Karl Yoneda, May 5, 1943, cited in Raineri, 232.

"Be well dearest": Elaine Black Yoneda to Karl Yoneda, August 1, 1945, box 3, folder 8, Elaine Black Yoneda Collection.

"Taken a short haircut": Elaine Black Yoneda to Karl Yoneda, August 1, 1945, box 3, folder 8, Elaine Black Yoneda Collection.

"because he was considered": Elaine Black Yoneda to Karl Yoneda, August 2, 1945, Elaine Black Yoneda Collection.

"I will always love you": Elaine Black Yoneda to Karl Yoneda, December 12, 1943, cited in Raineri, *Red Angel*, 238.

"raise our darling son": Elaine Black Yoneda to Karl Yoneda, May 5, 1943, cited in Raineri, 232.

"He used to tell me": Elaine Black Yoneda to Karl Yoneda, February 13 1943, cited in Raineri, 231.

as if in a "spell": Elaine Black Yoneda to Karl Yoneda, June 22, 1944, cited in Raineri, 239.

"the mean ones": Raineri, 239.

"fear of having to destroy": Elaine Black Yoneda to Karl Yoneda, January 30, 1943, cited in Raineri, 230.

"in the regions controlled by Hitler": "Plight of Jews Under Hitler Truly Terrible," *Los Angeles Times*, December 3, 1942.

"2,000,000 European Jews": "Revelations of Atrocities Against Jews Shock FDR," *Los Angeles Evening Citizen News*, December 8, 1942. FDR's shock, however, seemed not quite enough to move him to support any attempt to rescue Europe's Jews. On the slow creep of news from Europe about the Nazi Holocaust and the even slower response of Allied governments to it, see David S. Wyman's thorough exploration in *The Abandonment of the Jews*. On FDR's near total inaction in particular, as well as the passivity of his entire government on the topic of trying to rescue Europe's Jews from total annihilation as soon as possible, rather than waiting for the end of the war, see Wyman, *Abandonment of the Jews*, 311–330.

"There are the extermination centers": Varian Fry, "The Massacre of the Jews," *New Republic*, December 21, 1942, 816–19, via Oxford Learning Link, https://learning link.oup.com/access/content/schaller-3e-dashboard-resources/document-varian -fry-the-massacre-of-the-jews-new-republic-december-21-1942.

"almost stunned into silence": Edward R. Murrow, *In Search of Light: The Broadcasts of Edward R. Murrow, 1938–1961*, ed. Edward Bliss Jr. (Alfred A. Knopf, 1967), 56–57.

"were sure there would be ovens": Karl and Elaine Yoneda, "Manzanar: Another View."

"violated our Constitutional": Karl Yoneda, *Ganbatte*, 123.

"good 'oven-tenders'": Karl and Elaine Yoneda, "Manzanar: Another View."

"trouble makers and leaders": H. S. Covington, District Intelligence Officer, Twelfth Naval District, memo to director of Naval Intelligence, "Manzanar Relocation Project, Conditions at," February 16, 1943, San Francisco, CA, box 11, folder 7, Karl G. Yoneda Papers.

"dangerous, pro-Japanese leaders": "Manzanar Relocation Center, Summary of Information" (memo), War Department, Headquarters Ninth Service Command, Office of the Director, Intelligence Division, Fort Douglas, UT, January 16, 1943, Salt Lake City, UT, 5–6, box 11, folder 7, Karl G. Yoneda Papers.

"learned the names": "Manzanar Relocation Center, Summary," 5–6.

"Last Monday we buried": Ralph P. Merritt to Aunt Luella, December 25, 1942, appendix 2 in *Final Report: Manzanar Relocation Center*, 1:A-75, entry 4b, box 71, file "Manzanar Final Reports," Records of the War Relocation Authority, National Archives, College Park, MD, cited in Unrau, *Evacuation and Relocation*, https://www.nps.gov/parkhistory/online_books/manz/hrs11a.htm.

incarcerees were being "coddled": Greg Robinson, "War Relocation Authority," *Densho Encyclopedia*, accessed December 13, 2024, https://encyclopedia.densho.org/War%20Relocation%20Authority.

"commit 'almost any act'": Ralph R. Merritt to Dillion Myer, March 4, 1943, Manzanar Records, 1942–1946, University Research Library, UCLA, cited in Weglyn, *Years of Infamy*, 153. See also Brian Niiya, "Chandler Committee," *Densho Encyclopedia*, accessed February, 18 2024, https://encyclopedia.densho.org/Chandler%20Committee.

"would swear unqualified allegiance": Cited in Cherstin Lyon, "Loyalty Questionnaire," *Densho Encyclopedia*, accessed February 15, 2024, https://encyclopedia.densho.org/Loyalty%20questionnaire.

"man-proof": Barbara Takei, "Tule Lake," *Densho Encyclopedia*, accessed February 19, 2024, https://encyclopedia.densho.org/Tule%20Lake.

"During three years": Commission on Wartime Relocation, *Personal Justice Denied*, 252.

"Debates continue to rage": Eileen Tamura, "Joe Kurihara," *Densho Encyclopedia*, accessed February 15, 2024, https://encyclopedia.densho.org/Joe%20Kurihara; Tamura, *In Defense of Justice*, 166. For an intimate and in-depth look at the impact of the loyalty questionnaire on three incarceree families in particular, see Frank Abe and Tamiko Nimura, *We Hereby Refuse: Japanese American Resistance to Wartime Incarceration* (Chin Music Press, 2021), as well as Frank Abe's ongoing online project, RESISTERS.COM: Japanese American Resistance to Wartime Incarceration, at https://resisters.com.

"As a race, the Japanese": "Stupid and Dangerous" (editorial), *Los Angeles Times*, April 22,1943, cited in Commission on Wartime Relocation, "Ending the Exclusion," chap. 8 of *Personal Justice Denied*, 224–225.

"a holy war": Walter B. Clausen, *Blood for the Emperor: A Narrative History of the Human Side of the War in the Pacific* (D. Appleton-Century, 1943), cited in Michael L. Krenn, ed., *The Impact of Race on US Foreign Policy: A Reader* (Routledge, 1999), 161.

"Fighting Japs is not like": *New York Times*, January 9, 1943, cited in Dower, *War Without Mercy*, 71. Dower's book provides a fascinating, thorough, and deeply disturbing look at the utter racism underlying many aspects of WWII beyond the commonly accepted example of the Holocaust in Europe.

"Oriental Races Against Occidental" and *"a family affair"*: *"Los Angeles Examiner*, March 23, 1943, cited in Raineri, *Red Angel*, 228–229; *San Francisco Examiner*, January 25, 1943, cited in Raineri, 228–229. Japan's military shared a similar view vis-à-vis the battle between "Oriental races" and "Occidental aggression," as they termed it in the summer of 1943, in a report written by their Greater East Asia War Inquiry Commission, although it remains interesting to note that the Japanese imperialists termed the struggle as one of Asian repression from Caucasian colonialism, not Caucasians in general. Dower, *War Without Mercy*, 58. Dower also describes the Japanese obsession with race among Asians and the view of imperialists that the "Yamamoto [Japanese] race" was the purest among other so-called Oriental races (Dower, 7).

"In Europe we felt": Cited in Dower, 77.

No Japs Allowed: Cited in Commission on Wartime Relocation, "Ending the Exclusion," chap. 8 of *Personal Justice Denied*, 242.

Japs Keep Out: "Hero's Reward," *San Francisco Chronicle*, November 12, 1944.

"This is a white man's country": "West Coast Terror," *Washington Post*, May 7, 1945, reprinted in *Topaz (UT) Times*, May 18, 1945, via Densho Digital Repository, https://ddr.densho.org/ddr-densho-142-408/.

"Of course [the difficulty]": Karl R. Bendetsen and John M. Hall, telephone conversation, January 19, 1943, cited in Commission on Wartime Relocation, "Ending the Exclusion," chap. 8 of *Personal Justice Denied*, 216.

"Maybe our ideas on the Oriental": Bendetsen and Braun, telephone conversation, January 22, 1943, cited in Commission on Wartime Relocation, "Ending the Exclusion," chap. 8 of *Personal Justice Denied*, 217.

"I'm scared to death": Bendetsen and Hall, telephone conversation, 216.

"persons of Japanese ancestry" through *"predominantly American"*: DeWitt, *Final Report*, 145–147. Though *Final Report* does not explicitly state that the released mixed-race children were under the age of eighteen, the Mixed-Marriage/Mixed-Blood Policy defined children in mixed families eligible for release as only those who could be proven "unemancipated," meaning from birth through the age of eighteen.

"livid" at two claims through *"regardless of the improved military"*: Commission on Wartime Relocation, "Ending the Exclusion," chap. 8 of *Personal Justice Denied*, 222.

"the constitutionality": John L. DeWitt to John McCloy, April 15, 1943, Coram Nobis Litigation Collection, via Densho Digital Repository, https://ddr.densho.org/ddr-densho-405-5/.

"I certify that this date": Theodore E. Smith, witness statement, June 29, 1943, Coram Nobis Litigation Collection, via Densho Digital Repository, https://ddr.densho.org/ddr-densho-405-13/.

"Albert M. Bendetsen": Karl R Bendetsen's World War II Jewish serviceman card, November 30, 1943, American Jewish Historical Society, Center for Jewish History, via Ancestry.com, https://www.ancestry.com/discoveryui-content/view/12007:2125.

"The programs were a breath": Karl Yoneda, *Ganbatte*, 157–160.

"should be returned for cancellation": Chas A. Middleton, Major, AUS, Acting Assistant Adjutant General, to Elaine Yoneda, October 31, 1944, box 3, folder 1, Elaine Black Yoneda Collection.

"Tommy was proud as a peacock": Elaine Black Yoneda to Karl Yoneda, November 27, 1944, cited in Raineri, *Red Angel*, 245.

"promoted soon": Elaine Black Yoneda to Karl Yoneda, June 4, 1942, box 3, folder 8, Elaine Black Yoneda Collection.

"Not responsible for any debts": Classified ad, *San Francisco Examiner*, March 6, 1943.

"Says she's going to stay": Elaine Black Yoneda to Karl Yoneda, April 27, 1945, box 3, folder 8, Elaine Black Yoneda Collection.

"good [yet] rather fat": Elaine Black Yoneda to Karl Yoneda, June 21 and July 21, 1945, box 3, folder 8, Elaine Black Yoneda Collection; Elaine Black Yoneda to Karl Yoneda, September 13, 1945, cited in Raineri, *Red Angel*, 252.

"Dear Soldier Dad Karle": Elaine Black Yoneda to Karl Yoneda, June 21, 1945, box 3, folder 8, Elaine Black Yoneda Collection.

"bedlam" through *"because every move"*: Elaine Black Yoneda to Karl Yoneda, August 19, 1945, box 3, folder 8, Elaine Black Yoneda Collection; Elaine Black Yoneda to Karl Yoneda, August 27, 1945, cited in Raineri, *Red Angel*, 251.

"two most shining stars": Karl Yoneda, *Ganbatte*, 165.

"devastated": Tamura, *In Defense of Justice*, 133; Eileen Tamura, "Joe Kurihara," *Densho Encyclopedia*, accessed February 15 2024, https://encyclopedia.densho.org/Joe%20Kurihara.

12. Returned: 1945–1985

"coalition of the Social Mass": "A Loyal American: The Story of a Nisei Soldier, and What He Thinks of Japan's Future," *San Francisco Chronicle*, November 11, 1945; Karl Yoneda, *Ganbatte*, 180.

"a strong light" through *"It was hell"*: Yoneda, 180

"Wanted: two-bedroom house": Yoneda, 170

"warmth and sincere regret": Yoneda, 169; Raineri, *Red Angel*, 252.

"From an intelligence point of view": "Japanese-American Soldiers Get Praise; Racial Prejudice Rapped," *Honolulu Star-Bulletin*, January 22, 1946; "Army Nisei Praised by M'Arthur Officer," *Wilmington Daily Press Journal*, January 21, 1946.

"knew from nothing": Cited in Raineri, *Red Angel*, 256.

"deemed ineligible": Evacuation claim no. 146-35-13678, Department of Justice, April 11, 1952, box 3, folder 1, Elaine Black Yoneda Collection.

"as if a person of Japanese": Slater, "Mixed-Marriage Policy," https://encyclopedia.densho.org/Mixed-Marriage%20Policy/Mixed-Blood%20Policy; Nakamura, "Request and Waiver of Non-excluded Person," https://cdm16855.contentdm.oclc.org/digital/collection/p16855coll4/id/12429.

"When a great democracy is destroyed": Joseph McCarthy, speech, February 1950, Wheeling, WV, Patterns of World History, Oxford Learning Link, https://learninglink.oup.com/access/content/von-sivers-3e-dashboard-resources/document-joseph-mccarthy-speech-in-wheeling-west-virginia-1950.

"Will I have to go": "Elaine Yoneda's Remarks," *Hokubei Mainichi* (San Francisco, CA), May 12, 1981, photocopy in Yoneda family personal papers, sent by Yvonne Yoneda Donaldson to the author, March 26, 2021.

"If you want to know why": Cited in Schreiber, *Elaine Black Yoneda*, 164–167.

"bounced around between affairs": Donaldson, interview by the author, February 27, 2021.

"To this day": Elaine Black Yoneda, oral history by Lucille Kendall, 1976–1977, Women in California Collection, California Historical Society, pt. 19, 10:38–10:51, via Internet Archive, https://archive.org/details/chi_000015/.

"Tommy still loved his sister": Donaldson, interview by the author, February 27, 2021.

"walked off with just about": "The Yonedas in Japan," *Petaluma (CA) Argus-Courier*, September 14, 1960, in Yoneda family personal papers, sent by Yvonne Yoneda Donaldson to the author, March 26, 2021; "Penngrove News Notes," *Petaluma Argus-Courier*, June 12, 1947.

"I am Keiko": Karl Yoneda, wartime diary, 1944, trans. Ian Forsyth, translation in process emailed to author, February 9, 2024; "Karl Yoneda and Elaine Black—Star-Crossed Lovers in a Class War," *People's World*, November 19, 2020, https://www.peoples

world.org/article/karl-yoneda-and-elaine-black-star-crossed-lovers-in-a-class-war/; Rainieri, *Red Angel*, 292.

"a 'renegade' group": Cited in Ranieiri, 280. Elaine, in her 1981 statement to the Commission on Wartime Relocation and Internment of Civilians, noted that she and Karl had actually joined the Sonoma chapter of the JACL in 1957, before moving to back to San Francisco and joining the local chapter there. Elaine Black Yoneda, statement to the CWRIC, 31.

"There wasn't a petition": Raineri, *Red Angel*, 268, 270.

"hurry off in her high heels": Tommy Yoneda, "A Eulogy: Grandmother, Mother Has Joined You," cited in Ranieri, 295.

"the life of the party": FBI informant's statement, box 5, folder 1, Elaine Black Yoneda Collection; Raineri, *Red Angel*, 263–264.

FORMER PETALUMAN HELPS: "Former Petaluman Helps Project," *Petaluma Argus-Courier*, July 27, 1965.

"famous Asian actor": Cited in Ranieri, *Red Angel*, 278–279.

"Soul Consoling Tower": Dexter Waugh, "A Painful Visit to a WWII Relocation Center," *San Francisco Examiner*, January 1, 1970; Gann Matsuda, "Video: The First Manzanar Pilgrimage—1969," Manzanar Committee, February 25, 2017, https:// manzanarcommittee.org/2017/02/25/video-1st-pilgrimage/.

"it must never happen again": Karl Yoneda, *Ganbatte*, 200; Stanley O. Williford, "Japanese Detention Camp: Old Law Now New Target," *Los Angeles Times*, January 2, 1970.

"When people ask me": "Remember 1942?," *Girda* 2, no. 1 (January 1970): 2.

"fierce": Williford, "Japanese Detention Camp."

"Manzanar is everywhere": Manzanar Committee, "Karl and Elaine Yoneda—Bay Area Members of Manzanar Committee," in *The Manzanar Pilgrimage: A Time for Sharing* (Manzanar Committee, 1981), 16.

"I am appalled": Elaine Black Yoneda, interview by Hansen, 93. For an important perspective on how some Japanese American descendants of the camps interpret use of the term *concentration camp*, see "'A Place Like This,'" *Berkeley Remix*, https://update.lib.berkeley.edu/2023/11/13/the-berkeley-remix-season-8-episode -2a-place-like-this-the-memory-of-incarceration/. For the full wording of the Manzanar plaque, along with more about the ongoing controversy over language, see Gann Matsuda, "Manzanar Committee Calls on JACL Board to Honor Intent of Power of Words Handbook," Manzanar Committee, February 21, 2013, https:// manzanarcommittee.org/2013/02/21/manzanar-committee-calls-on-jacl-board-to -honor-intent-of-power-of-words-handbook/.

"racial prejudice, war hysteria": On August 10, 1988, President Ronald Reagan signed the Civil Liberties Act of 1988, ordering payment of reparations and an official

apology. On November 21, 1989, President George Bush signed into law an entitlement bill, providing $20,000 to each of the 60,000 surviving incarcerees. Elaine was not alive to see either.

"Karl was [incensed] to the end": Donaldson, interview by the author, February 27, 2021.

"war chest" through *"cannot and must not"*: Karl G. Yoneda, letter to the editor, *Pacific Citizen* (Los Angeles), January 16, 1970, box 11, folder 7, Karl G. Yoneda Papers.

"hero for the '70s": Cited in Tamura, *In Defense of Justice*, 149.

"We were wrong": William Hohri, address to the National Council for Japanese American Redress National Coalition for Redress/Reparations Conference, November 15–16, 1980, Los Angeles, CA, reprinted in "Democracy and Redress," *Rafu Shimpo*, December 4, 1980, box 11, folder 7, Karl G. Yoneda Papers.

terming the event a "revolt": Arthur A. Hansen and David A. Hacker, "The Manzanar 'Riot': An Ethnic Perspective," in *Voices Long Silent: An Oral Inquiry into the Japanese American Evacuation, Japanese American Project*, ed. Arthur A. Hansen and Betty E. Mitson (Fullerton Oral History Program, 1974), 53.

"distortion of history": Karl G Yoneda, letter to the editor, *New York Nichibei*, October 9, 1980, box 11, folder 7, Karl G. Yoneda Papers. See this entire folder (Manzanar Riot) in the Karl Yoneda archive for the many clippings and responses by the Yonedas, as well as box 3, folder 3 (Reparations), Elaine Black Yoneda Collection.

"misinformed" and "a great disservice": Karl G. Yoneda, letter to the editor, *Pacific Citizen*, February 13, 1970, box 11, folder 7, Karl G. Yoneda Papers, and as cited in Tamura, *In Defense of Justice*, 149. For another rebuttal to the representation of Kurihara as hero, this same edition of *Pacific Citizen* carried the words of John Hamada, who was sixteen at the time of the uprising: "Now what about those [Kurihara] tried to have murdered?" Others "ate the same bad food, slept in the same tar paper barracks, suffered the same barbed wire enclosure. But who instead of turning sour and preaching defeat said: 'Lets get out of here.'" The people "whose names appeared on Kuriharas death list preached a gospel of hope. It took far more courage to do what they did . . . than it did to assemble hoodlum would-be assassins who manipulated the anxiety of people in confinement." John Hamada, letter to the editor, *Pacific Citizen*, March 13, 1970, as cited in Tamura, *In Defense of Justice*, 149. For more of the Yonedas' rebuttals to the ongoing issue of Kurihara as hero throughout the 1970s and 1980s, see Karl G. Yoneda, letter to the editor, *Rafu Shimpo*, October 22, 1981, box 11, folder 7, Karl G. Yoneda Papers; and Elaine Black Yoneda, letter to the editor, *Hokubei Mainichi*, May 10, 1983, box 3, folder 3, Elaine Black Yoneda Collection.

"To me, he never was either": Elaine Black Yoneda, letter to the editor, May 10, 1983.

"Were they then truly 'genuine protesters'": Karl and Elaine Yoneda, "Manzanar: Another View."

"the nightmares of the ensuing riot": Elaine Black Yoneda, letter to the editor, May 10, 1983.

"Certainly, the Manzanar riot": Karl and Elaine Yoneda, "Manzanar: Another View."

"since they were denied": Karl G. Yoneda to Arthur A Hansen, October 7, 1974, box 3, folder 2, Elaine Black Yoneda Collection. The Yonedas' sympathy for the Issei also seemed to dim by the end of this letter, mentioning once again their disappointment that no known leaders of the Japanese or Japanese American community ever "spoke out against Japan's treacherous rape of Nanking nor joined any action against the war and rising fascism that were held throughout the U.S." during the prewar period. A final point that Karl in particular argued against was the historians' characterization of Karl and other leftists as "superpatriots" who chose to support the government and WRA during wartime because they could see no wrong in their own country. Karl pointed out that "this characterization as a blind patriot hardly jibes with my activities in Japan as a youth and the United States since 1926 to date. My life has been an open struggle against imperialism, exploitation, fascism, racism and for decent working conditions."

had all "denounced" the leaders: Peter Suzuki, letter to the editor, *Pacific Citizen*, September 19, 1986, box 11, folder 7, Karl G. Yoneda Papers.

"I, too, advocated" through *"What if Hitler's hordes"*: Karl G. Yoneda, letter to the editor, *Rafu Shimpo*, July 27, 1981, box 11, folder 7, Karl G. Yoneda Papers.

"stock phrases, terms, labels": Suzuki, letter to the editor, September 19, 1986.

"We personally made many mistakes": Elaine and Karl Yoneda to Mrs. Ellen Endo, English Editor, *Rafu Shimpo*, November 24, 1973, in box 11, folder 7, Karl G. Yoneda Papers.

"our acquiescence": Elaine Black Yoneda, interview by Hansen, 93.

"The fact that I finally acquiesced" and *"In fact, I really thought"*: Elaine Black Yoneda, oral history by Kendall, pt. 25, 18:20–18:50, https://archive.org/details/chi_000015/.

"did not speak out loudly": Karl G. Yoneda, Manzanar pilgrimage speech, March 25, 1972, box 3, folder 3, Elaine Black Yoneda Collection.

"Those who resisted": Karl Yoneda, interview by Larson and Hansen, 38.

"utilize the manpower": "Petition to Honorable Franklin D. Roosevelt," August 5, 1942.

"the citizen manpower": "Petition to Honorable Franklin D. Roosevelt," July 23, 1942.

"What was wrong with the petition": Karl G. Yoneda, letter to the editor, *Rafu Shimpo*, October 22, 1981, no. 23,503, Karl G. Yoneda Papers.

"request that you accept": Karl Yoneda, *Camp Diary*, 148–149.

"Manzanar Concentration Camp Diary": "A Note Concerning the Title," "Original Title Page," and reproduction of handwritten letter from Karl Yoneda to Ian Forsyth, all in Karl Yoneda, *Camp Diary*, 6, 8, 9. Tom Yoneda, a grandfather himself by 1997, also strenuously agreed with this change, according to Forsyth.

"we feel we followed a path": Elaine and Karl Yoneda to Endo, November 24, 1973.

"My strongest desire": Karl G. Yoneda, Manzanar pilgrimage speech.

"Although we were guilty": Karl and Elaine Yoneda, "Manzanar: Another View."

"The story of Evacuation": Karl and Elaine Yoneda, "Manzanar: Another View."

"I literally forced my way": "Elaine Yoneda's Remarks," *Hokubei Mainichi*.

"That was another part of the family": Donaldson, interviews by the author, February 27, 2021, and April 21, 2023.

"The trauma really fractured": Donaldson, interview by the author, February 27, 2021.

"so absent from the record": Schreiber, *Elaine Black Yoneda*, 179.

"You work so hard": Yvonne Yoneda, "For Father's Day," *Hokubei Mainichi*, April 11, 1986, Yoneda family personal papers, sent by Yvonne Yoneda Donaldson to the author, March 26, 2021. In a private email correspondence on March 4, 2024, with the author, Yvonne indicated that she wrote this poem in 1985, though it was published after proud grandfather Karl submitted it, without her knowing, to the *Hokubei Mainichi* newspaper.

"Jewish and Buddhist": Schreiber, *Elaine Black Yoneda*, 178.

"We hold these dramatic moments": Schreiber, 179.

"almost levitating": Donaldson, interview by the author, April 21, 2023.

"My skin grows hot": Yvonne Yoneda, "Manzanar," *Hokubei Mainichi*, April 11, 1986, Yoneda family personal papers, sent by Yvonne Yoneda Donaldson to the author, March 26, 2021.

13. Settled: 1945–2021

"Despite having renounced": Tamura, *In Defense of Justice*, 140.

"Among the personal possessions": Tamura, 145.

"Assistant Chief of Staff" through *"No assignment"*: De Nevers, *The Colonel*, 252.

"no mention of his successful efforts": Ken Ringle, "Architect of Relocation Prefers Case Stay Shut," *Washington Post* December 7, 1982.

"any resident of a relocation center": Ringle, "Architect of Relocation."

"Great Japanese 'rip off'": John McCloy to Karl Bendetsen, May 2, 1982, cited in De Nevers, *The Colonel*, 286.

"certainly didn't want this task": Ringle, "Architect of Relocation."

"Bendetsen, Karl Robin": *National Cyclopaedia of American Biography*, vol. L (James T. White, 1972): 481–483, cited in De Nevers, *The Colonel*, 286.

"*Danish ancestor came over*": De Nevers, 286.

a birth certificate without: Brookes McIntosh Bendetsen was born May 2, 1943, and christened in summer 1943 at the Presidio Chapel. Though Karl and Billie's Washington marriage certificate from 1938 listed the new couple as the Bendetsons, their son's California birth certificate listed the family name as Bendetsen. Billie and Karl R. Bendetson's marriage certificate, March 10, 1938, Washington State Archives, via Ancestry.com, https://www.ancestry.com/search/collections/2378/records/48138; "Brookes Mcintosh Bendetsen," May 2, 1943, San Francisco, California Birth Index, Center for Health Statistics, State of California Department of Health Services, via Ancestry.com, https://www.ancestry.com/search/collections/5247/records/2895098. For information about Karl filing paperwork with the army to change his name, see De Nevers, *The Colonel*, 349n72. On the Bendetsens' son's christening, see De Nevers, 193.

"*I don't think he had*": De Nevers, 306.

"*an intention to deceive*": Cited in Murray, *Historical Memories*, 350.

"*Karl R. Bendetsen, 81*": Eric Charles May, "Karl Bendetsen Dies: Internment Planner in 1942," *Washington Post*, June 30, 1989.

Karl's eternal "muse": Donaldson, interview by the author, February 27, 2021.

"*always had to be moving*": Donaldson, interview by the author, February 27, 2021.

"*It is so reassuring*": Wendy Yoshimura to Elaine Black Yoneda, box 6, folder 7, Elaine Black Yoneda Collection; Ann Loftis, "Memories of the Life and Times of Elaine Black Yoneda," box 4, folder 10, Elaine Black Yoneda Collection; Dorothy Ray Healey, tribute to Elaine Black Yoneda, box 6, folder 7, Elaine Black Yoneda Collection.

"*or even a heaven if there was one*": Karl G. Yoneda, "The Last Days of Elaine" (unpublished manuscript), May 31, 1988, Yoneda family personal papers, sent by Yvonne Yoneda Donaldson to the author, March 26, 2021.

"*Grandma liked to play*": Donaldson, interview by the author, February 27, 2021.

"*She's gone*": Donaldson, interview by the author, February 27, 2021.

"*I didn't know death*": Karl G. Yoneda, "Last Days of Elaine."

ran her obituary: "Elaine Black Yoneda, 81, Radical Labor Activist, Katherine Bishop," *New York Times*, May 30, 1988.

"*Elaine is unionizing Heaven*": Cited in Raineri, *Red Angel*, 287.

"*Oh, my beloved comrade*": Karl Goso Yoneda, "Spring Flows On," *People's World Daily*, June 8, 1988, Yoneda family personal papers, sent by Yvonne Yoneda Donaldson to the author, March 26, 2021.

"*My name is Thomas*": Lily Rothman, "Why Were Activists 45 Years Ago Protesting 'Against Death?,'" *Time*, November 13, 2014, https://time.com/3579109/march-against-death/; Karl Yoneda, *Ganbatte*, 193.

INDEX